HANDBOOK OF ECONOMIC STAGNATION

HANDBOOK OF ECONOMIC STAGNATION

Edited by

L. RANDALL WRAY

Professor of Economics, Levy Economics Institute and Bard College, Annandale-on-Hudson, NY, United States

FLAVIA DANTAS

Associate Professor, Economics Department, State University of New York, Cortland, NY, United States

ELSEVIER

ACADEMIC PRESS

An imprint of Elsevier

Academic Press is an imprint of Elsevier
125 London Wall, London EC2Y 5AS, United Kingdom
525 B Street, Suite 1650, San Diego, CA 92101, United States
50 Hampshire Street, 5th Floor, Cambridge, MA 02139, United States
The Boulevard, Langford Lane, Kidlington, Oxford OX5 1GB, United Kingdom

ISBN: 978-0-12-815898-2

For information on all Academic Press publications visit our website at https://www.elsevier.com/books-and-journals

Publisher: Joseph P. Hayton
Editorial Project Manager: Susan Ikeda
Production Project Manager: Niranjan Bhaskaran
Cover Designer: Mark Rogers

Typeset by TNQ Technologies

Contents

Contributors

Yılmaz Akyüz
Former Director, UNCTAD and Former Chief Economist, South Centre, Geneva, Switzerland

Eliane Cristina Araújo
State University of Maringã, Maringá, PR, Brazil

Robert A. Blecker
Department of Economics, American University, Washington, DC, United States

Luiz Carlos Bresser-Pereira
Getúlio Vargas Foundation, São Paulo, SP, Brazil

Flavia Dantas
Economics Department, State University of New York, Cortland, NY, United States

Steven M. Fazzari
Departments of Economics and Sociology, Washington University, St. Louis, MO, United States

Carmem Feijó
Fluminense Federal University, Niterói, RJ, Brazil

Fernando Ferrari Filho
Department of Economics, Federal University of Rio Grande do Sul, Porto Alegre, Brazil; National Council of Scientific and Technological Development, Brasília, Brazil

Eckhard Hein
Institute for International Political Economy (IPE), Berlin School of Economics and Law, Berlin, Germany

Arturo Huerta G.
Facultad de Economía, UNAM, Mexico City, Mexico

David M. Kotz
Department of Economics, University of Massachusetts Amherst, United States

Olivia Bullio Mattos
St. Francis College, Brooklyn, NY, United States

Yeva Nersisyan
Franklin and Marshall College, Lancaster, PA, United States

Michalis Nikiforos
Department of History, Economics and Society, University of Geneva, Geneva, Switzerland

Leon Podkaminer
The Vienna Institute for International Economic Studies, Vienna, Austria

Peter Skott
University of Massacusetts Amherst, Amherst, MA, United States; Aalborg University, Aalborg, Denmark

Servaas Storm
Delft University of Technology, Delft, Netherlands

Eric Tymoigne
Department of Economics, Lewis & Clark College, Portland, OR, United States

L. Randall Wray
Economics, Levy Economics Institute of Bard College, Annandale-on-Hudson, NY, United States; Economics, Levy Economics Institute and Bard College, Annandale-on-Hudson, NY, United States

Introduction: Handbook on economic stagnation

A common theme arises in most of the contributions to this volume: aggregate demand drives growth in the short run, the medium term, and the long run. This position stands in contrast to orthodoxy, even of the Keynesian variety. Typically, orthodox economists argue that long run growth depends on growth of the supply of resources, as well as growth of productivity—which in turn depends largely on innovations that enhance productivity of the two main factors of production, labor, and capital. In the short run, demand might play a role, too, as deviations from full capacity utilization can induce or hinder investment in a cyclical manner. Supply side variables dominate in the long run.

Robert Gordon's fascinating book, *The Rise and Fall of American Growth* offers[1] a twist on conceived wisdom, focusing on the role played by significant innovations that boosted growth of total factor productivity (TFP) in the USA over the half century following 1920 and that led to unprecedented economic growth. To put his thesis as simply as possible, innovations developed since 1870 came to fruition by 1920 that allowed for significant increases in the ability to move quickly, both vertically (think elevators enabled by electricity) and horizontally (the internal combustion engine in automobiles and trucks). That in turn led to developments on both the supply side and the demand side of the economy that generated rapid growth in living standards.

The productivity improvements on the supply side are obvious, as they completely transformed the USA, but Gordon's novelty is his recognition of the importance played by growth of demand that provided the stimulus needed to take advantage of growing productivity. Much of this came from the private sector—as automobiles increased mobility, and as development of suburban shopping malls and drive-through hamburger joints boosted growth in a self reinforcing matter. And, of course, Gordon includes the role of the government—Federal government spending for the New Deal, WWII, and the cold war, and state and local government spending

[1] Robert J. Gordon The Rise And Fall Of American Growth: The U.S. Standard of Living Since the Civil War, 762 pp. Princeton University Press.

to provide for the baby boom and the move to the suburbs. Thus, the demand side was also important for fueling the growth of TFP over the half century—at a pace triple that of the half centuries both before and after the 1920–70 period. Without that demand, the innovations would not have been put to use to boost production. This was the golden half of the "special century" that ran from the end of the civil war to the relative stagnation that began in the early 1970s.

What this means is that the special period relied on the happy coincidence of major improvements of TFP and as well growing demand over a sustained period—demand was not just important for the short period but was needed to maintain high trend growth. Since 1970, however, both demand and supply enhancing innovations that would boost TFP have faltered. In sector after sector of the economy, the demand was satiated, and this reinforced the downward pressure on prices that came from increased competition from global markets (that also held wages in check) as well as from productivity growth.

Most of the improvements to living standards that were first enjoyed by urbanites had spread to rural areas by 1970. Also, by 1970, the race to build larger houses had slowed, the interstate highway system was largely completed, and air conditioning had already penetrated businesses and homes. The baby boom was over, followed by a baby bust. Later, the aging of the population, stagnant wages, and rising inequality would add to the headwinds. At the same time, productivity-enhancing innovations became increasingly rare. While it is not difficult to point fingers at clever innovations—the *iPhone*, of course—as has been repeated endlessly, one can see technological advances everywhere one looks except in the productivity numbers. They just do not amount to the revolutionary changes brought on by electricity and internal combustion.

The case for secular stagnation that one can make from the evidence presented by Gordon relies on the TFP numbers—whose growth has fallen to a crawl. He admits that the slow-down of growth of aggregate demand plays a role, and he discusses several reasons why the measure of TFP might be biased downward (e.g., prices of output could be falling while the quality of consumer goods is rising—so real production is undercounted). Still, he concludes that the real story can be found in the TFP estimates. Of course, TFP is largely a residual, or as Abramovitz[2] put it, "measure of our

2 Abramovitz, M., May, 1956. Resource and output trends in the United States since 1870. American Economic Review 46 (2), 5–23.

ignorance." Using an orthodox production function, one can calculate the contributions of labor and capital deepening to output growth, but together these account for only about a third of productivity growth over the period from 1920 to 70. The other two-thirds is the Solow residual, presumed to represent the contribution of innovations, with emphasis on the word "presumed".

Ultimately, then, the orthodox presumption presented in Gordon's book is that today's apparent secular stagnation can be blamed on problems of the supply side. The solution is, largely, to encourage innovations that would raise TFP. Gordon is pessimistic, seeing nothing on the horizon. Perhaps secular stagnation is the new normal.

Gordon's work renewed interest in a topic raised earlier by Alvin Hansen at the end of WWII. With the worry that downsizing after the war might put the nation back into the Great Depression (the fall of GDP in 1947 was larger than both the downturns in the 1930s), economic growth temporarily became a topic of debate that continued through the mid-1960s. It set off the Cambridge Controversies—a war waged between the followers of Keynes at Cambridge, UK, and the bastard[3] version of Keynesian economics taught at Harvard (Cambridge, US). The debate was finally settled in favor of the UK Keynesians, but the war was won by the bastard Keynesians. In spite of the demonstrated logical flaws of Neoclassical growth theory (based on its incoherent production function), that approach is still the basis of mainstream macroeconomic theory—and the basis of Gordon's approach. Amusingly, today's textbook writers have no knowledge of the two-Cambridges debate and its consequences. For example, the top textbook writer, Greg Mankiw, claims in his text[4] that the "proof" of the neoclassical theory is the fit of the macroproduction function to the data. Anwar Shaikh[5] had famously proven nearly a half century ago that any production function—even one that graphs HUMBUG—will fit the data because the specification estimates an identity!

3 This is a reference to the well-known put-down of the Samuelson-Hicks "neoclassical synthesis" version of Keynes: we know who the mother was (neoclassical theory), but we do not know who the father was.

4 Mankiw NG. Macroeconomics, seventh Edition. Worth Publishers; 2010.

5 Shaikh, A., February 1974. Laws of production and laws of Algebra: the Humbug Production Function. The Review of Economics and Statistics 56 (1), 115–120.

Gordon's book revived interest in growth (or, lack thereof), but it was really the work of Larry Summers and Paul Krugman that shaped much of the discussion of the past few years.[6] According to Summers, declining population growth, higher capital intensity of industry, reduced rate of technological progress, and lower capital prices all generated lower investment spending. On the other hand, rising concentration of income and wealth among those with a low propensity to consume increased the supply of saving. This created a lower equilibrium real rate of interest, the rate at which saving equals investment at full employment. As it dropped below zero, and as nominal interest rates are normally bounded from below at zero, we cannot get the real rate low enough unless we can get inflation ramped up. Unfortunately, even with the most expansionary monetary policy the world has ever seen, inflation remained stuck just above zero. While it is true that some countries have achieved negative rates on their own sovereign debt, they did not reduce market rates enough to stimulate demand.

Hence, Summers argued that the cause of secular stagnation can be attributed to a reversal of Say's Law, where "Lack of demand creates its own lack of supply." This is based on the application of a Wicksellian version of the loanable funds approach. The equilibrium rate that matches saving and investment at full employment is a real rate determined by loanable funds. However, the policy rate is a nominal rate determined by the central bank. The actual real rate is determined through the Fisher Effect as a nominal rate minus expected inflation. But if expected inflation is near zero, and if the lower bound of the nominal rate is also near zero, it is not possible to push the actual real rate to the negative equilibrium real rate determined by saving and investment in a world with too much global saving.

Krugman and Summers are willing to support expansionary fiscal policy to resolve the problem. Given the special circumstances of negative real equilibrium rates, monetary policy becomes ineffective (Krugman has long argued that we are in a liquidity trap that neuters monetary policy). Fiscal policy could work. Further, given extremely low interest rates (and with some $25 trillion worth of sovereign debt issued internationally paying negative nominal rates), Krugman and Summers proposed that it was time

6 A link to the argument made by Summers is here: https://equitablegrowth.org/this-mornings-must-watch-larry-summers-on-thedanger-of-a-japan-like-generation-of-secular-stagnation-here-in-the-north-atlantic/. And here is a speech he gave: https://www.youtube.com/watch?v=KYpVzBbQIX0. Accessed 8–22-2019. A link to Krugman's argument is here: https://krugman.blogs.nytimes.com/2013/11/16/secular-stagnation-coalmines-bubbles-and-larry-summers/?_r=0. Accessed 8–22-2019.

for governments to run deficits without worrying about sustainability of interest payments on its debt.[7]

On the eve of the Global Covid Pandemic, ignoring the incoherent theoretical framework adopted by Summers and Krugman, one could not help but agree that "more fiscal policy" would help. In Congressional Testimony in fall of 2019, Blanchard joined Wray in making a similar argument[8]—for the foreseeable future, it would not be dangerous to increase government spending even if that were to increase the deficit. Once the pandemic hit, policymakers in the rich countries abandoned the usual fears of deficit spending and mounted an unprecedented fiscal response. The new administration of President Biden added proposed spending of trillions more—topping out at $9 trillion since the pandemic began. As this volume goes into publication, some (including Larry Summers) are beginning to worry again about affordability and possible inflation. Biden's proposals include massive investments in restructuring the supply side of the economy. It is possible that these could provide the boost to innovation that Gordon wants to see.

On the other hand, as argued[9] in the concluding section of this volume, there is a danger that the initial burst of spending to implement the Green New Deal will not be followed by the sustained boost to aggregate demand that we saw in the postwar period. In that case, the dangers of secular stagnation will return. As Vatter and Walker[10] argued, government spending needs to operate like a "ratchet," expanding in times of crisis to prop up demand, but also growing during expansions to keep demand high enough to absorb growing capacity. This was accomplished during the "special half century" due to special factors identified by Gordon—the baby boom, growth of the suburbs, and the cold war. We need a plan to sustain growth of demand once the Green New Deal's transformation of the economy and society is successfully completed.

7 Krugman persistently argued that the US was in a "liquidity trap", where monetary policy is impotent, thus, we needed fiscal policy. See https://krugman.blogs.nytimes.com/2011/10/09/is-lmentary/?_r=0; accessed 8—22-2019.

8 Hearing link: https://budget.house.gov/legislation/hearings/reexamining-economic-costs-debt; Wray testimony: http://www.levyinstitute.org/pubs/tst_11-20-19.pdf.

9 Especially in the chapters by Nersisyan and Wray, Wray, and Dantas and Wray.

10 See Wray http://www.levyinstitute.org/pubs/wp_488.pdf.

Overview of the contributions to this volume

The authors of this volume take different routes to the same conclusions: we face secular stagnation largely because of problems on the demand side, and fiscal policy is part of the solution. However, they do not adopt the orthodox framework and do not rely on aggregate production functions, loanable funds theory and excessive saving supply, Wicksellian natural rates, or lack of innovations to reach these conclusions. Instead they use a variety of heterodox approaches, some of which were developed by Keynes's followers in the 1950 and 1960s during the first round of speculation on the dangers of secular stagnation. They also use models developed by Kalecki, Kaldor and Verdoorn, Steindl, and Baran and Sweezy, as well as later approaches of Minsky and Godley. They identify stagnationary pressures coming from the rise of inequality, fiscal austerity, stagnant wages, and international competition (also included by Gordon in his analysis). While not completely inconsistent with Gordon's analysis, they place much more emphasis on the endogeneity of innovations and productivity-enhancing investments: high demand with rising wages stimulates entrepreneurial effort to raise labor productivity.

Importantly, low growth of TFP is a symptom of the problem, not the cause: if demand were growing faster, there would be more innovation and more investment. The authors here can point to the brief surge of TFP growth (as measured by the Solow residual) during the Clinton years. Gordon uses that episode as a cautionary tale to make his case that we do not have the important innovations required to restore growth to its pace achieved during the "special century," but an alternative argument is that the higher growth was based on unsustainable private sector deficits and a debt bubble. Higher sustained growth is possible, but it must be placed on sounder footing. The sectoral balance approach developed by Wynne Godley helps us to understand why we do not have the conditions required for sustained high growth. Hyman Minsky had argued back in 1963 that growth led by private sector investment is likely to increase financial instability and hence may not be sustainable. This is probably even more true if growth is led by household spending fueled by consumer debt—which was the case in the lead-up to the Global Financial Crisis.

The key conclusion is that demand drives growth in the short, medium and long run. This is as true for advanced economies, as it is for emerging economies. This is not to deny the importance of the supply side. Resource availability does matter, but constraints can be relieved through substitution, imports, and greater efficiency. In modern economies, the service sector accounts for most of GDP and it is generally labor-intensive. Truly full employment is rarely reached—so quantity of labor is not normally a constraint. Quality of labor—real or imagined—can be a constraint, but is always potentially resolvable, particularly over the medium and long run. Even in the short term, migration can relieve quality and quantity constraints. But the most important point is that there is an interaction between the demand and supply side: growth of demand is required to encourage increases of the quality and quantity of resources. This is obvious in the data presented by Gordon, but he fully recognizes the relationship only for the period 1920–1970—when aggregate demand grew fast enough to require rapid improvement in the quality of resources (especially labor) and to deepen and enhance the quality of capital.

Let us turn to a quick summary of each of the contributions to the volume.

Part A: Secular stagnation: theory, causes, and evidence

Hein: Stagnation policy: a Steindlian perspective

Hein begins by outlining two mainstream approaches to secular stagnation—both of which are based on Neoclassical growth theory and macroeconomic production functions: (a) the supply side determinants of productivity growth become exhausted so that potential growth falls; or (b) with excessive saving, the natural interest rate falls below zero so that it becomes impossible to get the market rates sufficiently negative to induce growth. Stagnation, then, results from problems with resources, technology, or preferences. Post Keynesians have raised three objections to such arguments. First, the Cambridge Controversies showed that there is no monotonic relation between interest rates and investment demand, so reject the notion of an aggregate production function that is based on supposed links between factor productivities and payments. Second, following Keynes's argument in the *General Theory,* loanable funds theory is rejected as an explanation of the determination of interest rates. Further, saving is not a source of finance in either the short run or the long run. Third, following the work of Post Keynesians after WWII, growth is demand led, and potential growth is not independent of actual growth.

Hence, secular stagnation from a Post Keynesian view could be caused by a variety of factors, including depressed animal spirits, misguided monetary policy, the shift of distribution to the capitalist and rentier classes, a change in the type of technological change, and austere fiscal policy.

Kalecki had warned in his famous article, "Political aspects of full employment" that capitalists fight rising wages by adopting austerity. This generates a political business cycle. Steindl adapted this idea, arguing that it influences trend growth—as capitalists reacted against the longer-term shift of distribution over the postwar period toward labor. Hein uses a model based on the work of Steindl, Kalecki, and Post Keynesians concerning the relationship of distribution and growth. Unlike earlier models, Hein makes technical progress endogenous, as rising wages encourage labor-augmenting technical progress to protect the profit share.

Hein concludes that stagnation can be caused by an autonomous decline of the growth of government spending, or by replacing demand-management policy with structural reform (austerity); a decline of productivity-enhancing public investment in research and development; weakening worker and union bargaining power (that reduces wage growth); rising inequality; and rising real interest rates that shift income to rentiers, or increased use of outside finance that increases the debt burden on firms. He suggests several policies to reverse trend stagnation: stable and rising public spending with anti-cyclical fiscal policy; rising public investment; a combination of full employment policy, lower interest rates, and reregulation of financial institutions; and income redistribution.

Skott: Growth and stagnation in mature and dual economies

Skott discusses interrelations between the demand and supply sides along the lines discussed above. While he supports the Post Keynesian insistence on the importance of demand, he argues that we must be careful in applying theory developed for "mature" economies to "dual" economies that are characterized by the existence of a modern sector alongside an informal, low-productivity sector. He uses a simple model for the mature economy to find the condition for steady growth with full employment. In such an economy, labor is the main constraint on growth. Following Lerner, he argues that a government following functional finance should pursue both full employment and maintenance of a desirable share of investment in output. Fiscal policy based on functional finance has many benefits: it can stabilize the private debt-income ratio (with government deficits putting safe sovereign debt in private portfolios); avoiding tax hikes on low- and middle-income workers to "pay for" government spending allows growth without increasing inequality that would lead to higher debt to finance household consumption; maintenance of full employment and moderate growth also lead to low government debt ratios in the long run. By contrast,

Neoliberal pursuit of austerity ("fiscal consolidation") promotes slow growth, high unemployment, rising private debt and inequality, and—paradoxically—more government debt.

The situation faced by dual economies is quite different, however. These typically do not face structural aggregate demand problems, so existence of high unemployment does not necessarily indicate that demand should be increased because capital can be the binding constraint. While rapid accumulation of capital in the modern sector is desirable (and would alleviate supply side constraints), this is possible only if labor can be moved from the low productivity sector. Further, it might require a tradeoff of more investment and less consumption output. Inflation as well as balance of payments problems could interfere. Skott suggests that Lerner's functional finance must be redefined for dual economies, to target not full employment but rather the right balance between investment and consumption to promote a stable macroeconomic environment. Furthermore, the balance between luxury consumption and consumption by low-income households must be addressed—policy should favor provision of education, healthcare, and food over luxury goods in both the domestic sector as well as with respect to imports.

Skott contrasts the successful rapid development strategy of Japan (1945–1970) with the recent high growth period in Brazil (2003–2011) to illustrate the problems that can be encountered in a dual economy. During the 1960s in Japan, there was a dual economy with a large proportion of hidden unemployment. Rapid growth (with 8.2% annual growth from 1945 to 70) pulled those workers into the modern sector and by 1970 Japan faced labor constraints. Growth slowed to 3.6% from 1970 to 1990. By 1990 Japan was a mature economy with a high saving rate and a slow growth rate (just 0.8% annually after 1990). Slow growth was now due to structural aggregate demand problems, relieved temporarily by bubbles. Growth was largely constrained by domestic politics (serial experiments in austerity) and by the limits to Japan's ability to export.

In the case of Brazil, rapid growth was fueled by a commodities boom (and accompanying increase of exports) as well as by domestic consumption. Over this period, the minimum wage and transfer payments were increased while consumer debt rose. Currency appreciation kept inflation in check until 2007, after which inflation began to rise while the current account turned to deficit. In 2014 commodities prices fell and the country slipped into recession. What went wrong? According to Skott, during the boom Brazil did not grow the modern sector and consumption rose too much relative to investment. While policy did raise living standards at the bottom, it did not move to reign in luxury consumption. Thus, Brazil was not able to replicate Japan's "miracle" that led to the development of a mature economy.

Storm: The secular stagnation of productivity growth

As Storm notes, orthodoxy generally blames slow growth of the economy and of productivity on supply side problems. Much earlier, Alvin Hansen had warned of stagnation in 1939, attributing it to a combination of slow population growth (thanks to the Great Depression), lack of a sufficient number of investment opportunities, and a dearth of important innovations. However, WWII, more equality, the baby boom, the rise of the middle class and suburbs, and the cold war together generated strong growth. The stagnation thesis returned in 2008, but with a pre-Keynesian twist: an influx of foreign saving lowered the natural interest rate, reducing potential growth. It is the decline of potential growth that has caused actual growth to drop. In addition to the low natural rate, other supply side factors have compounded the problem, including aging.

Storm argues that what we actually face is a demand management crisis, with underconsumption driven by low wages, rising inequality, job insecurity, and polarization. He uses a growth accounting framework to analyze the slowdown of labor productivity growth and real wage growth. While the mainstream uses production functions and claim that the unobserved TFP accounts for the slowdown (attributed to weak innovations, as well as institutional rigidities and regulations that prevent firms from taking advantage of innovations), Storm defines TFP as the weighted average of labor and capital productivity growth. He finds that labor productivity growth accounts for 85% of TFP growth. He also notes, following Shaikh, that the Solow residual is just the weighted average of growth rates of the wage and profit rates. This means the measured decline of TFP's rate of growth is due to a secular decline in the rate of growth of real wages and profits.

While neoclassical economists interpret the constraint on real wage (or profit) growth as growth of labor (or capital) productivity, Storm's alternative interpretation is that stagnant real wages are the main contributing factor to declining TFP growth. Low real wage growth, in turn reduces the incentive to invest, which reduces growth of the capital stock, hinders capital deepening, and generates low productivity growth. Low wage growth, in turn, is partly caused by macropolicy: pursuit of low inflation creates a bias against wage growth and promotes attacks on social protection and unions. Storm argues that the decline of unionization rates alone "explains" about two-thirds of the decline of the rate of growth of real wages. Weak labor bargaining positions generates "alternative work arrangements" that in turn reinforces pressure on wages.

Ironically, depressed demand lowers potential growth and in a sense lowers the economy's "speed limit," the actual growth rate beyond which inflation could be stoked. In conclusion, policy should promote higher aggregate demand to stimulate demand and investment; increased capacity will not only increase productivity (if demand remains high) but also will remove bottlenecks by raising the speed limit. Policy makers should abandon needless austerity and work to raise wages and shift distribution back to workers so that their income is recycled back through consumption, validating the investments.

Kotz: Stagnation and social structures of accumulation

Kotz focuses on the effects of the evolving institutional structure of the economy on accumulation, adopting the Social Structures of Accumulation (SSA) approach to growth elaborated by David Gordon and others. Each SSA promotes accumulation by initially creating conditions of stability and predictability, raising the profit rate, and promoting an increase of the rate of growth of aggregate demand. This promotes investment. Eventually, however the SSA becomes an impediment to growth, which leads to a period of stagnation—for example, Kotz points to the 1870–1890s, the 1930s, the 1970s, and today since 2008. To resolve the current long-term crisis, we must have a major restructuring of capitalism through the creation of a new SSA.

The 1930s crisis saw the emergence of regulated capitalism, with the state and unions playing a big role; this lasted until the 1970s when a new SSA took its place with neoliberal capitalism and a relatively free market. The neoliberal SSA of the 1980s promoted increasing income inequality, a financial sector driven by speculation, and large asset bubbles. Together these promoted accumulation. However, the neoliberal SSA also generated unsustainable trends, including a rising household debt ratio, increased financial sector debt ratio, and spreading of toxic assets. This could continue only so long as asset prices rose, and when that stopped the system collapsed into crisis.

Kotz warns there is no auto-corrective mechanism to end this stagnation; even a large fiscal stimulus would only temporarily raise growth rates.

Nor can we find a solution in innovations. What we need is a new SSA. He notes (with some optimism?) that (1) stagnation cannot last forever because it fuels movements on both the right and the left that are seen as threatening by elites and (2) SSAs tend to cycle between regulation and neoliberal forms. So perhaps we are on the verge of creating a new SSA structured around a Green New Deal.

Hein: Financialization and stagnation—a macroeconomic regime perspective

In Hein's second piece, he pursues a "regime perspective" that is similar to the SSA approach of Kotz. Our economy has become financialized, defined as a finance-dominated capitalist regime. It is characterized by deregulation of banking, the rise of shadow banks, growing indebtedness of the private sector, shareholder dominance, rising share of income going to gross profits (and a falling wage share), liberalization of capital markets and national accounts, and financialization of everyday life. This regime collapsed into the Global Financial Crisis and remained mired in stagnation a decade later (before collapsing into the COVID crisis).

Hein looks at six countries—France, Germany, Spain, Sweden, the UK, and the US—and the core Eurozone (the EA-12), identifying the main elements of three regimes of finance-dominated capitalism. The first is a regime that relies on a debt-led private demand boom; the second is an export-led mercantilist regime; and the third is a domestic demand-led regime. Before the crisis, the UK, the US, and Spain exhibited the characteristics of regime 1, with growing private debt; Germany and Sweden were in regime 2, relying on export demand; and France and the EA-12 fell somewhere between, with small current account surpluses and domestic demand but without growing debt.

After the crisis, those in regime one had to deleverage, with falling consumption and rising government deficits—except Spain, which because it was within the Euro zone, had to adopt austerity, allowing it to move to a current account surplus. Income inequality worsened in all of them, as the wage share fell. The mercantilists in regime two fared better, relaxing budget constraints, allowing growth of consumption by stabilizing the wage share, but mostly relying on exports for recovery. France used a government deficit to stabilize output, and the wage share rose. The rest of the Eurozone turned to exports as they adopted "budget consolidations."

The reaction to the GFC in the face of relative global stagnation has opened global imbalances, with the US, the UK, France, Argentina,

Australia, Brazil, Canada, India, and South Africa running current account deficits (and many also running budget deficits), which has generated political and market reactions. As much of the world has redistributed income away from wages, depressing domestic consumption, the prospects for capital accumulation, productivity growth, and potential output growth are all bleak. This stagnation is neither due to natural forces nor is it inevitable. It results from distributional and economic policies—what Steindl called "stagnation policies."

Fazzari: Hyman Minsky meets secular stagnation

Unlike the previously discussed contributions, that focus on approaches derived from or similar to those adopted by Steindl, Kalecki, Baran and Sweezy, and David Gordon, Fazzari adopts another Post Keynesian approach to economic crisis, the financial instability hypothesis developed by Minsky. This focuses more directly on the evolution of balance sheets, at both the individual level and at the level of the economy as a whole, from relatively robust (hedge, in Minsky's terminology) through increasing fragility (speculative) and finally to unsustainable positions (Ponzi). Minsky's FIH is well known, but Fazzari's application deviates in two ways from the typical exposition. First, he applies it to longer-term transformations than the usual business cycle, and second, he applies it to the household sector and specifically to consumption rather than to investment by firms.

Like the other contributions, Fazzari emphasizes demand constraints. He argues that Minsky was both Keynesian (expectations and demand drive income) and Kaleckian (investment drives profits). Supply constraints are rare (we could add Skott's caveat that Minsky's analysis applies to mature economies, and in practice Minsky only really analyzed the US). Minsky grounded his theory in two basic concepts, validation and fragility. Debt is incurred based on expectations about the future and needs to be validated by income flows to service the debt. If the validation occurs, this can raise expectations and fuel more borrowing—which increases fragility as the debt ratio rises, as increased use of more dangerous short-term finance occurs, as more borrowing is based on collateral rather than income flows, and as financial institutions circumvent regulations to keep the credit flowing. When fragility overcomes validation, the "Minsky moment" (financial crisis) arrives.

While Minsky (like Keynes) pointed to investment as the driving variable (and Minsky added a "financial theory of investment" to Keynes's "investment theory of the cycle"), Fazzari argues that household finances grew in importance from the 1970s onward, and that Minsky's framework is useful for the analysis of the rise of the "consumer age"—when consumption rose from 60% to 68% of GDP between the 1970s and 2007. A dramatic drop of household spending after 2007 is what drove the US and the global economy into a deep and long-lasting recession.

Fazzari shows that this long-wave consumer boom fueled the so-called great moderation as consumption grew rapidly and stably. It was fueled by aging of baby boomers, who reached their peak earning years (and in contradiction to the life cycle consumption smoothing hypothesis, reduced personal saving), by deregulation of finance that increased lending to households, by the 1986 tax reform that boosted home equity lending, and by falling interest rates after the Volcker monetarist experiment that goosed mortgage refinancing. The debt ratio increased considerably over the period, to a breaking point. When households retrenched and stopped borrowing, the economy collapsed. Even a decade later, output remained nearly 10% below its precrisis trend. The gains from the recovery have gone almost entirely to the top of the income distribution (as Tcherneva's work has shown[11]) so that it captures so much of the growth of income that only another debt-fueled consumer boom can bring relief from secular stagnation.

Nikiforos: Demand, distribution, productivity, structural change, and (secular?) stagnation

Like several other contributions, Nikiforos criticizes the neoclassically inspired focus of Gordon's book for excessive reliance on supply side factors such as population growth and the rate of technological change for explaining economic growth. According to Gordon, growth has slowed because over the past half century innovations have been limited to the information and telecommunications sectors. Nikiforos faults Gordon for ignoring the role played by effective demand, the endogenous nature of technological change and the fact that the slow-down of productivity growth is less than the slow-down of output growth. Nikiforos, like others, invokes the Kaldor-Verdoorn Law and the theory of induced technical change as the main explanations of the recent productivity-growth slowdown. Technological change is endogenous and requires a larger market to encourage investment that would raise the capital-labor ratio; higher wages are an incentive for firms to introduce labor-saving technical change. While Gordon seems to sometimes recognize

11 http://www.levyinstitute.org/pubs/pn_17_1.pdf.

this (in Chapter 16 of his book when discussing the "great leap forward" made from the 1930s to the 1950s) he abandons the endogeneity of adoption of innovations in production processes when he turns to the poor performance of productivity over the past half century.

Nikiforos also employs Godley's sectoral balance approach in his analysis of the US economy since 1990. Over that period, the US current account balance deficit increased from about zero to 6% of GDP just before the crisis. Why? Because the US embraced free trade while adopting austerity to bust organized labor, reducing the wage share of income, depressing aggregate demand, and shifting income to the top. As Fazzari also emphasizes, households could only keep spending by borrowing as the household debt to disposable income ratio rose to 1.6. Since the GFC, the government has maintained a restrictive fiscal stance (until the COVID pandemic!), and while the current account deficit has not returned to precrisis levels (thanks to fracking that reduced oil imports), the recovery was the slowest on record over the post-war period.

In sum, the alternative story told by Nikiforos is that secular stagnation is due to a decline of US exports, fiscal conservatism, and rising income inequality. In addition, the rise of monopoly power has shifted income to those who save, so that lower- and middle-income households have been saddled with debt. Financialization of the economy has also shifted profits toward finance and away from nonfinancial corporations that invest in real plant and equipment, who have taken on a lot of debt. Like Hein, Nikiforos insists that secular stagnation is not inevitable; indeed, it is engendering a political economy response that may bring on a new progressive era.

Podkaminer: Economic stagnation in the Euro area

Podkaminer examines secular stagnation in the Euro area, which he argues began with the end of the Bretton Woods system, with the rate of growth of productivity falling since the early 1970s. The deceleration was produced by a combination of liberalization of capital flows, increased labor market flexibility, downsizing of the welfare state, adoption of a one size fits all monetary policy, and growing cross-country trade imbalances.

Most of these forces were already in place before adoption of the euro; however, the problems were compounded by integration. Adoption of the single currency eliminated the possibility of exchange rate adjustment so that internal devaluation was the only way to protect exports. Germany pursued an export-led growth strategy based on keeping real wage growth below the rate of growth of productivity that made it a low-cost producer and kept its consumer demand in check. Integration did increase trade among members (as promised), but trend decline of labor shares contributed to rising inequality both within and between member nations. Fiscal rules and the common currency contributed to growth suppression—the growth of GDP per capita has fallen from an average of 3–5% for the Euro area before the end of Bretton Woods to just over 1 percent afterward.

Paradoxically, the Euro area enjoys high profitability with low investment, thanks to repressed wages that weaken consumption and thus investment. Germany can already produce far in excess of its domestic demand so must export its surplus. Despite Gordon's view that productivity drives growth, Podkaminer points out that German productivity growth has been lower than that of several other members. Germany's advantage remains its low wage growth. Germany also benefits from what is for it an undervalued currency and very low interest rates.

To increase growth of output and productivity, demand must be raised. But the Growth and Stability Pact requires reduction of debt ratios, which in the context of slow economic growth means budget surpluses. Government thus would suck demand out of economies, eliminating private sector surpluses for any countries that cannot run export surpluses. One might only add that the Euro zone as a whole is too large and too rich to rely on the rest of the world to fuel its growth. And continuing to rely on internal markets means there are winners and losers, leading to more competition for internal devaluation. The only way out is to end fiscal austerity as well as the low wage strategy imposed by Germany.

Part B: Secular stagnation in the Global South

Akyüz: Inequality, stagnation, financialization, and the Global South

Akyüz analyzes the spillover of economic stagnation in advanced economies to emerging market economies (EMEs). Like others in this volume, Akyüz attributes economic stagnation in advanced economies to a structural aggregate demand gap due mainly to growing inequality and financialization. He rejects the mainstream thesis that stagnation was caused by vanishing investment opportunities and excessive savings. Instead, over the past 40 years, liberal reforms and globalization have reduced the bargaining power of labor relative to capital, which contributed to the declining wage share of income. Financialization—the increased size, scope, and influence of finance—has increased the concentration of wealth and asset income at the top, aggravating the inequality problem. Underconsumption and falling wages reduced the profitability of capacity-creating investment.

Further, monetary policy and financial deregulation in advanced economies encouraged growth via unsustainable debt accumulation and excessive credit expansion. Stagnant wages reduced inflationary pressures, which allowed for low interest rate environments in advanced economies that fueled unsustainable debt accumulation and search for yield. Sustained ultra-easy monetary policy and further deregulation were seen as the primary tools to fight secular stagnation. In reality, they created boom-bust cycles, and aggravated the problems of growing inequality and insufficient demand. In each round, a bigger asset bubble and indebtedness was fueled to fight economic contraction resulting from the burst of the previous bubble.

Sluggish growth, declining interest rates, and rising indebtedness in advanced economies spilled over to EMEs mainly in the form of an international search-for-yields that increased external vulnerability and financial fragility. Capital inflows to emerging countries surged in the early 2000s, declined sharply in the aftermath of the global financial crisis, but quickly resumed following the monetary policy response to the crisis in advance economies. Financial liberalization in EMEs exacerbated the external vulnerability problem.

Akyüz identifies several ways in which increased capital inflows in the new millennium changed the pattern of external vulnerability in EMEs. First, there was an important shift from the traditional cross-border lending and borrowing channels dominated by international banks to equity and debt finance from nonbank financial institutions' capital inflows into local bond and equity markets. This allowed for, among other things, a large build-up of corporate debt denominated in dollars, larger swings in stock prices in EMEs according to international investors' risk perceptions, and significant exposure of EMEs to interest rate movements and equity and debt market fluctuations in advanced economies. Greater importance of subsidiaries of international banks lending in the domestic currency has also allowed for greater transmission of credit crunches from international markets to domestic markets, while the shift from bank credit to bond finance increases the vulnerability of EMEs to US and advanced economies interest rate policy movements. On top of these vulnerabilities, the deepened integration of EMEs into global finance has also resulted in significant net resource transfers from EMEs to advanced economies via negative net investment income positions and cross-border wealth transfer due to changes in the valuation of gross external assets and liabilities.

Bresser-Pereira, Feijó, and Araújo: Does the liberal policy regime condemn Latin America to quasi-stagnation?

This chapter discusses the main reasons behind the quasi-stagnation in Latin American countries—represented by Brazil, Mexico, Chile, and Uruguay—since the 1980s. The authors identify the establishment of the liberal policy regime as an important factor behind the slowdown in long-term growth in Latin America. Liberalism is defined as a policy regime in which state intervention in the economy is kept to a minimum, and tight alignment with the Washington consensus doctrine of deregulation, privatization, financial and trade liberalization, and fiscal austerity. This doctrine is in stark contrast to the more moderate interventionist developmental policy regime and import substitution strategies that had prevailed in the region from the 1930s to the early 1980s.

Latin American countries liberalized their economies before the consolidation of the industrialization process that would have allowed these countries to reorient their domestic markets, eliminate the Dutch disease problem, and compete on more equal grounds with the rest of the world. The adoption of liberalism subjected economic growth in Latin America to constant interruptions imposed by external constraints and the narrowing of the space for countercyclical fiscal and monetary policy. Economic policy became ultimately subordinated to views and perception of international financial markets. Liberalism interrupted long-term development strategies, including tariffs on imports and export subsidies, to support the completion of the industrialization process of the noncommodity export industrial, which would have allowed these countries to overcome the Dutch disease problem and compete on more equal grounds in international markets. Public investment was reduced and public companies privatized, reducing the domestic infrastructure and incentives for private investment.

The authors discuss several additional compelling reasons for why liberalism led to deindustrialization and quasi-stagnation of Latin American countries including the effects of trade and capital account liberalization on the capital accumulation and technological development process of the competitive, noncommodity exporting domestic industrial sector. The interruption of the domestic industrialization process subjected Latin American countries to balance of payment imbalances and the long-term overvaluation of the exchange rate, which further hindered domestic investment and promoted the consumption of imported goods. These problems were made worse by the attempt to speed up growth (and domestic investment) by attracting foreign savings along with the use of the exchange-rate anchor to stabilize domestic prices, both of which required high interest rates to attract capital inflows and the accumulation of external reserves, which in turn worsened the secular trend of long-term exchange rate overvaluation and external imbalances.

Blecker: Mexico: unequal integration and "stabilizing stagnation"

The Mexican economy went from the frequent crises of the 1980–1999 period to a period of secular stagnation characterized by relative macroeconomic stability but persistent low and unequal growth. Over the 2000–2018 period, the Mexican economy averaged an annual rate of GDP growth of 2.2 percent and per capita GDP growth of 0.8 percent, which is in line with its North American neighbors and significantly below the rates of growth experienced by other middle income emerging countries.

In this chapter, Blecker examines secular stagnation in Mexico in the 21st century. Like other authors in this volume, he argues against the conventional wisdom that secular stagnation and low average productivity growth are the result of supply side constraints such as human capital deficiencies, or the dualism allegedly caused by labor regulations, tax burdens, and social safety nets which discourages employment in the highly productive, technologically advanced "formal" sector, thereby pushing a significant portion of the labor force into the low productivity, technologically obsolete "informal" sector. While Blecker admits that some structural problems such as a highly concentrated financial system, low rates of bank credit to the private sector, corruption and crime do hinder economic growth in Mexico, they do not constitute the main obstacles to economic growth. The overexpansion of the informal sector is a symptom, not a cause, of the slow growth of formal productive activities.

Secular stagnation in Mexico is primarily caused by demand-side constraints. Contractionary macroeconomic stabilization policies, overvaluation of the peso, and trade liberalization have put downward pressure on domestic and foreign aggregate demand. On the fiscal policy side, the commitment to balanced budgets made government spending procyclical and significantly reduces government spending in key areas such infrastructure, health, and sanitation. The adoption of a strict inflation targeting regime left little room for monetary policy to pursue other goals such as employment, growth, or the maintenance of a competitive exchange rate. The (over) appreciation of the peso, particularly in the early 2000s, dramatically reduced Mexico's export growth and had lingering effects on capital accumulation in the manufacturing sector and tradable goods industries. Further, trade liberalization subjects the Mexican economy to a high degree of dependency on foreign market conditions, primarily in the US.

Blecker concludes that Mexico needs to reorient its economic policy to put greater emphasis on domestic demand-led growth instead of export-led growth. Economic policies need to focus on increasing consumption by workers and the middle class, increasing government spending on infrastructure and other basic social needs, and tax reforms. Monetary policy needs to focus on a pro-investment stance and on preventing the overvaluation of the peso to minimize the external constraints to economic growth. While other reforms may be important, none of them will promote long-run growth in the absence of a strong domestic demand.

Huerta: The stagnation of the Mexican economy is here to stay

Similarly, Huerta attributes secular stagnation in Mexico to growing inequality, free-trade agreements, and contractionary macroeconomic stabilization policies. The government actively pursues economic policy to stabilize nominal exchange-rates, which, in essence reduces the domestic fiscal and monetary space for expansionary demand policies. The result is contraction in domestic demand and a decrease in domestic public and private investment, which in turn affects domestic productivity and technological development and leads to further deindustrialization. Domestically produced goods cannot compete with imported goods, which tends to increase imports relative to exports, further deteriorating the countries' external position. The central bank reacts to contain pressures on exchange rates by increasing interest rates, which depresses domestic growth even further. All these trigger subsequent rounds of economic austerity to maintain the confidence of international investors and to continue to attract capital inflows to supposedly promote short and long-term economic prosperity. The economy is trapped in selfimposed secular stagnation.

The domestic scenario is complicated by selfimposed fiscal targets, which can never be met if the economy is contracting—tax revenue declines and mandatory spending increases—and by the paralyzing fear that budget deficits will increase the debt, cause inflation, and further deteriorate Mexico's trade position. On the other hand, the concern with the devaluation of the exchange rate during contractions causes monetary policy to also behave procyclicality—fear of capital flight leads the central bank to maintain its high interest-rate policy. Another round of austerity measures is introduced as the solution to rising deficits. Reduced public spending in a scenario of economic stagnation is especially harmful. The economy contracts further, idle productive capacity increases, private sector income and profitability are depressed, and private investment is discouraged. Procyclical economic policy accentuates the vicious cycle of stagnation.

To escape the economic stagnation trap, policymakers need to abandon the commitment to primary fiscal surpluses, high interest-rates, and most importantly, its exchange-rate policy. Truly flexible exchange-rates will create the sovereign fiscal and monetary space for the government to pursue policies to increase domestic demand, employment, incomes, and the competitiveness of the domestic sector. In fact, without expansionary fiscal policy, the public deficit and debt cannot be reduced, and the trade deficit will continue to worsen, regardless of exchange rate policy. Government spending needs to be targeted to create demand for domestically produced goods and services, which would increase incomes and profitability, and attract the kind of private investment that increases productivity and competitiveness. Additionally, free-trade agreements would need to be revised, and capital controls added to restrict highly speculative capital movements. Without these measures, the Mexican economy will be trapped in economic stagnation for years to come.

Ferrari-Filho: The Brazilian stagnation and an economic agenda to ensure macroeconomic stability and social development

Ferrari-Filho examines the causes of the recent economic stagnation in Brazil and proposes a way forward. Over the 2010–2014 period, it seemed like the Brazilian economic had finally found its way to sustained prosperity: millions were raised out poverty, the unemployment rate achieved low levels, and economic growth reduced the gap between the rich and the poor. Starting in 2015, the path to prosperity was sharply reversed, and the Brazilian economy entered a deep recession followed by a period of stubborn stagnation. Ferrari-Filho explains that beyond the deteriorating political scenario, the worker's party candidate Dilma Rousseff's second administration marked the shift from demand-led growth to a return of the neoliberal agenda that had been in place in Brazil until 2002.

The mild slowdown that had started in late 2014 was deepened by a series of contractionary fiscal and monetary policies to combat accelerating inflation and the deteriorating budget position. Over the period 2015–2018, the primacy of monetary policy as the tool for economic growth was reestablished while a series of neoliberal reforms were passed through congress. Solidifying supply side as the [only] "way forward" was the passage of a constitutional amendment in 2016 that freezes public spending for 20 years.

The chapter returns to the contributions of Keynes and American Institutionalists to suggest an agenda for prosperity and macroeconomic stability. Ferrari-Filho argues that Brazilian monetary policy needs to be reformed to explicitly target employment stability while monetary authorities need to emphasize macroprudential regulation for financial stability. Fiscal policy must prioritize public investment, especially infrastructure, and social spending. Exchange-rate policy should be formulated to contain speculative capital flows and support the domestic industry while maintaining the purchasing power of domestic wages. Structural reforms need to reincorporate the State as a central engine for economic prosperity. To build capacity and expand potential GDP, structural policy should include a progressive tax reform, an increase in the real minimum wage and social safety nets, policy to mitigate instability in stock markets and excessive private indebtedness, state investment to foment research and innovation, and investment in public education.

Part C: The return of big government and economic prospects after the pandemic

Wray: The role of big government: an introduction

In a series of articles and books, Harold Vatter and John Walker attempted to make the case that the U.S. economy suffers from chronically insufficient demand that leads to growth below capacity. They extended Domar's work on the supply side effects of investment spending and provided a comprehensive analysis of the evolution of the U.S. "mixed" economy. Their analysis of secular growth complements the well-known writings of Hyman Minsky, who also emphasized the role of the "big government" and the "big bank" in stabilizing an unstable economy over the cycle. This chapter summarizes the case for a "big government" to ensure sufficient aggregate demand as a solution to the "Domar problem" to provide support for, and extend the Vatter and Walker approach, concluding with an examination of some of the dangers facing the U.S. economy today.

The somewhat surprising conclusion reached by Vatter and Walker is that not only is government spending needed in the slump, to push up depressed demand, but it is also needed in the recovery. This is because a recovery promotes investment, which boosts the supply side (through capacity effects) more than the demand side (through the spending multiplier)—together, these produce the "Domar Problem," which is insufficient demand to operate at capacity. They argue that government spending should work like a ratchet—always rising—rather than swinging countercyclically. Interestingly, Minsky had reached a similar conclusion, arguing that government-led expansions are naturally more sustainable than are investment-led expansions (which tend to produce both financial and price instability). This is also similar to the extension made by Fazzari in his contribution: consumer-led expansions are also financially unstable.

However, Wray argues against a "pump-priming" and "rising tide lifts all boats" approach to simply raising overall government spending as the solution. Instead, following Minsky, government spending needs to be targeted to ensure sustainability. This is all the more relevant as the past half century of growth has increased inequality—the rewards of growth increasingly go to the top of the income distribution. Finally, it is important to note that Vatter and Walker argue that we have faced secular stagnation tendencies since the early twentieth century—an argument that contrasts sharply with the dating used by Gordon: even the "golden" first half of the 20th century singled out by Gordon was far short of what was possible.

Dantas and Wray: Secular stagnation: as good as it gets?

As discussed throughout this volume, mainstream views of secular stagnation focus on the supply side. Slow growth results from slow productivity growth and slow growth of inputs to production—especially the labor force. It is common to point to the aging of the population and low birth rates as a contributing cause that will worsen over coming decades. In this chapter, Dantas and Wray look closely at US labor markets. But like the other contributions here, they conclude that the main problem is insufficient growth of aggregate demand.

There are several causes of chronic insufficient demand in the US and the rest of the industrialized world, including chronic labor underutilization, wage stagnation, rising inequality, current account deficits, improper policy response, and insufficient government spending. Many of these factors have been analyzed in previous contributions to this volume, so this chapter focuses on the evidence of chronic insufficient of demand in the U.S. through the lenses of labor markets; stagnant worker's incomes, falling participation rates of prime-age men, and relatively slow growth of productivity are all indicative of a problem of insufficient aggregate demand. The fundamental problem is not demographic trends, lack of technological innovations, negative equilibrium real rates of interest, or displacement by robots. The authors argue that the slow "recovery" of labor markets following recessions—especially since 1990, and especially of the employment rate and labor force participation—is due to a combination of insufficient job creation as well as stagnant wages.

Dantas and Wray focus on two slow growth episodes experienced by the US economy (early-mid 1970s to mid-1990s, and then post-GFC—prior to COVID-19) and argue that the US had been suffering from insufficient aggregate demand for several decades before economists like Summers and Krugman took notice. To be sure, stagnation is periodically relieved by short economic bursts—usually brought on by unsustainable asset price bubbles (dot com stocks, commodities, housing prices). But once the bubbles burst, the economy returns to secular stagnation. They believe that, in absence of fundamental changes, the postpandemic US economy will return to the same pattern.

Like the other authors in this volume, Dantas and Wray call for a bigger role for government to play in promoting higher aggregate demand. However, they believe that in addition to the types of policies Biden has called for, spending to promote high employment needs to be well-targeted where it is needed most. Hence, they promote a program of targeted job creation as well as growth of wages at the bottom of the wage ladder. They follow Hyman Minsky's "employer of last resort" proposal developed in the 1960s and revived in recent decades as a "job guarantee" program. This would bring workers back into the labor force without fueling the inflation that would be generated by either the basic income guarantee or the old "Keynesian" reliance on "pump-priming." Further, by setting program wages and benefits at a generous level, with occasional wage hikes, they would be able to push up wages and living standards at the bottom—helping to reduce inequality. This could also reduce the need to rely so heavily on unsustainable consumer debt.

Tymoigne: Secular stagnation and the age of ultra-low interest rates

In his chapter, Tymoigne argues that central bank policy is the main determinant of interest rates, both for short and long maturities. Over the past 20 years (western nations) or 30 years (Japan), central banks have adopted extremely low interest rate targets in an effort to increase growth and raise inflation to target rates. This has been largely unsuccessful but has produced conditions in which raising rates has become very difficult. First, the prospects for robust growth—even in a post pandemic recovery—look improbable. Second, it is unlikely that labor markets would become so tight that central banks would feel impelled to raise rates to fight wage-led inflation. Besides, recoveries since 1990 have been increasingly "jobless," so that it takes many more years to make up for jobs lost in recession. Third, structural changes have increased income inequality, which depresses long-term prospects of growth, as the gains from growth mostly benefit those at the top (with low propensities to spend). Low- and middle-income households have had to rely on debt to sustain consumption—which increases the potential for financial instability and crisis.

All these factors make it less likely that central banks will raise rates at the first signs of perceived inflation pressures—as they had done back in the 1990s. Rapidly raising interest rates would almost certainly bring on a financial crisis as over-indebted firms and households would not be able to adjust to greater costs of servicing debts. Financial corporations, especially, have become accustomed to extremely high leverage ratios that were taken on during the era of very low risk-adjusted returns in an attempt to raise return on equity. As Tymoigne explains, "To counter a low yield, low growth environment, money managers have focused on riskier segments of the credit market and/or have used more leverage in their financial strategies. Both strategies promote the use of leverage in the rest of the economy, increase systemic financial fragility." In such an environment, the central bank's main policy tool—raising rates to demonstrate its commitment to price stability—may be too dangerous to use.

In any case, Tymoigne argues that inflation is largely a problem of the past. What developed nations face is the prospect of continued sluggish growth and excessive unemployment. Fiscal policy must play a bigger role to fight the stagnationary headwinds. More government spending will be required to meet the biggest challenges, including aging of the population, reversing climate change, and building infrastructure for the 21st century. While this could imply bigger budget deficits, that is not foreordained as more rapid growth would increase tax revenue. In any event, growing government debt will put safe assets into private portfolios, and the prospect of low interest rates for the foreseeable future means that interest service on the debt will remain low despite growing government debt ratios.

Mattos: Monetary policy after the crisis—a Post-Keynesian critique

Mattos provides a rich account of monetary policy debates prior to the Global Financial crisis and the failure of the amended postcrisis mainstream framework. Prior to the Great Recession, the consensus among mainstream economists—New Monetary Consensus—was that monetary policy should focus on guaranteeing price stability during normal times and be used as the primary tool for countercyclical policy during downturns. Underlying it was an unabated confidence in selfregulating market mechanisms, and the view that inflation is always a monetary phenomenon. The severity of the Great Recession and the need for extraordinary action from Central Banks to save their domestic (and global) financial systems from catastrophic collapse showed very quickly the limits of conventional monetary theory, especially considering the significant transformations that financial systems had gone through in the 30 years prior to the crisis. Nevertheless, even the extraordinary unconventional actions from Central Banks around the world resulted in sluggish economic recovery with stagnant low demand and persistently low inflation.

With the slow recovery from the GFC, many in the mainstream rediscovered the importance of countercyclical fiscal policy—with some even arguing that active fiscal policy is the only antidote to "secular stagnation"—and the need to revise their macroeconomic policy tool kit to incorporate the central role of finance. However, the central framework for the transmission of monetary policy transmission was left standing after the storm passed, and with it, the reliance on short-term interest rate movements as the primary mechanism to affect aggregate demand.

The alternative framework for macroeconomic policy needs to incorporate Keynes's and Minsky's insights. First, we need to understand the limits of monetary policy. Relying on short-term interest rates to stimulate demand or contain credit booms is a highly ineffective method, to say the least, to achieve full employment and maintain economic stability. Second, Central Banks should focus on their expanded role as lenders of last resort, providing liquidity even beyond traditional banks, to prevent debt deflations, and on oversight and regulation of financial markets so to prevent financial fragility from arising in the first place. Finally, Mattos calls for a stronger coordination between monetary policy and fiscal policy, and for central banks and monetary policy to be understood as an important, but not the primary, mechanism to be used in fighting economic stagnation and achieving and maintaining full employment.

Nersisyan and Wray: Biden's build back better proposal and the future of secular stagnation

As this volume goes to press, President Biden is pushing a proposal to spend approximately $4 trillion over coming years to "build back better." The US had already passed almost $5 trillion of relief (also sometimes called stimulus) to bring the economy out of the economic depths of the

Global Pandemic. The new proposal would focus on greening the economy and improving infrastructure—boosting investments in both physical and human capital. Many have likened his proposal to the revolutionary changes brought on by Roosevelt's New Deal. As we write, it is too early to determine whether that comparison is apt, but it is certainly true that it has been several generations since we have seen such an ambitious proposal coming out of Washington. Unlike Roosevelt, Biden faces much more opposition in Congress, so it is also far from certain that he will get what he wants.

In any event, this chapter focuses on an important question: how do we pay for the ambitious menu of policies? The conventional view—at least since around 1970—has been that tax revenues are needed. While there are differing views of the dangers of deficit spending, most economists and policymakers believe that new large spending programs should be matched by tax hikes. The chapter by Nersisyan and Wray, however, returns to Keynes's 1940 pamphlet on "How to pay for the war." This leads to a different view of the role of taxes, and the proper relationship between government spending and taxing. Taxes can be used to reduce private spending, to release resources for government use. This helps to prevent inflation. They can be also used to reduce inequality; and they can be used for a small set of other purposes (such as incentivizing behavior).

The chapter argues that trying to match expected tax revenues with spending is not necessarily consistent with any of these purposes. Reducing private demand would suggest using taxes that hit those with a high propensity to spend—such as a broad-based payroll tax on wages. Yet, Biden and progressives more generally prefer taxes on high income and high wealth individuals, as well as corporations and financial transactions. These kinds of taxes are particularly ill-suited to the purpose of releasing resources and fighting inflationary pressure. On the other hand, these taxes could be well-targeted to reduce inequality. Still, matching revenues with spending would be inappropriate if the goal is to reduce inequality.

Further, one of Biden's proposals would include 8 years of ramped up spending, but 15 years of higher taxes to "pay for it." Nersisyan and Wray argue that this makes no sense so far as releasing resources—why continue to reduce private spending for seven years after the spending program is wound down? Indeed, if the spending on infrastructure does enhance productivity, we will need to raise aggregate demand as productivity rises. Otherwise, we will be in danger of restoring secular stagnation. The chapter argues that "infrastructure pays for itself" by raising capacity and points to a pre-New Deal example in which Thomas Edison argued that government ought to pay for a major energy project with currency that would be "redeemed" in payment for the electricity produced. In conclusion, it makes more sense to temporarily reduce demand if necessary to prevent inflation, and then to boost it once the infrastructure is in place. In other words, we want to postpone consumption to prevent inflation now, and then release that consumption later to prevent stagnation. This was Keynes's recommendation for war finance and is consistent with the Vatter and Walker arguments.

PART A

Secular stagnation: theory, causes, and evidence

CHAPTER ONE

Stagnation policy: a Steindlian perspective*

Eckhard Hein
Institute for International Political Economy (IPE), Berlin School of Economics and Law, Berlin, Germany

Introduction

The recent economic mainstream debate on "secular stagnation," triggered by the contributions of Summers (2014a,b, 2015), has either focused exclusively on the supply side determinants of productivity growth and has argued that those determinants have turned exhausted and potential growth has slowed down (for example, Gordon, 2012, 2014, 2015). Or the focus has been on a lack of adjustment capacity in the capital market because the equilibrium or natural real rate of interest has turned negative,[1] which means that potential growth cannot be reached anymore, unless governments increase their deficits and debt-financed expenditures (e.g., Rachel and Summers, 2019; Summers, 2014a,b, 2015; von Weizsäcker, 2019; von Weizsäcker and Krämer, 2021). Whereas the former view focuses on technology when it comes to explaining the trend toward falling productivity growth and stagnation, the latter also includes preferences, mainly via the effect of demographical change on the desire to save and to hold net financial wealth.[2]

From a post-Keynesian perspective, this approach can be questioned for three main theoretical reasons: First, this view has to face the challenges of the very existence of a uniquely real interest rate-elastic and downward sloping capital demand curve in a more-than-one-good economy, as put

* This contribution draws on Hein (2016, 2018), summarizing and focusing the arguments presented therein. I am grateful to Ryan Woodgate for helpful comments. Remaining errors are mine, of course.

[1] In the latest contribution by Rachel and Summers (2019), the terminus "natural real rate of interest" is replaced by a "neutral real rate of interest," which, however, is still based on a neoclassical loanable funds concept.

[2] Rachel and Summers (2019) and Summers (2014a,b, 2015) also concede that rising inequality in the distribution of income has contributed to the rise in saving.

Handbook of Economic Stagnation
ISBN: 978-0-12-815898-2
https://doi.org/10.1016/B978-0-12-815898-2.00019-7

forward in the "Cambridge controversies on the theory of capital" (Harcourt, 1969, 1972; Hein, 2014, Chapter 3.6; Lazzarini, 2011). This controversy has shown that in a more-than-one-good economy, the demand for capital is generally not a monotonously downward sloping function of the real rate of interest. Aggregate production functions with these properties are thus not convincing from a theoretical perspective. The same holds true for the choice of technique: We cannot be sure that, as the real rate of interest decreases methods of production turn more "capital intensive" or more "roundabout." Second, there is the Keynesian challenge, that in a monetary production economy, saving adjusts to investment, where the latter is financed independently of aggregate saving through a developed financial sector, which generates money and credit out of nothing. This is not only true for the short run, but also for long-run growth, as Joan Robinson (1962, pp. 82–83) has famously claimed. These long-run macroeconomic adjustments of saving to investment occur via changes in output growth and capacity utilisation—the Kalecki/Steindl mechanism—and/or through changes in functional income distribution—the Kaldor/Pasinetti/Robinson mechanism (Hein, 2014). Third, in a demand-led growth approach it can be argued that potential growth is not independent of actual growth, but turns endogenous toward the latter, as suggested by Kaldor's (1957, 1961) technical progress function or Kaldor's (1966) Verdoorn's law, for example.

Therefore, taking a post-Keynesian perspective, a careful analysis of the determinants of both saving and investment has to be provided in order to identify the causes of stagnation tendencies. These include the evolvement of "animal spirits" affecting entrepreneurs'/managers' investment decisions, as well as monetary variables (interest rates, credit availability), distributional variables (profits vs. wages, retained earnings vs. interest and dividends, but also wage dispersion and personal income distribution), the type of technological change, and, most importantly, the stance of economic policies, each of them affecting both aggregate saving and investment in the short and in the long run.

Josef Steindl (1952) has provided such an analysis focusing on the interwar US economy, and he has updated his view in Steindl (1976, 1979), where he analyses the shift from the post-war Golden Age period of modern capitalism with high growth and low unemployment to the neo-liberal period with low growth and high unemployment since the mid-1970s. In particular, Steindl (1979) has highlighted the switch toward "stagnation policy," which he already referred to 3 years earlier: "thus we witness stagnation not as an incomprehensible fate, as in the 1930s, but stagnation as policy" (Steindl, 1976, p. xvii). Obviously, this terminology is related to Kalecki's (1943) "Political aspects of full employment," in which Kalecki argued that, although governments might know how to maintain full employment in a capitalist economy, they will not do so, because of capitalists' opposition. Whereas in Kalecki (1943), this gives rise to a "political business cycle," Steindl (1979) argues that this will generate a "political trend" causing or contributing to stagnation. In the following sections, we will present Steindl's approach to "stagnation policy" as an alternative to the mainstream views put forward in the debate on "secular stagnation," and we will derive the broad economic policy conclusions needed in order to avoid stagnation.

A Steindlian model of distribution and growth

In order to identify the main channels of "stagnation policy" in Steindl's work, we go back to the distribution and growth model, which Steindl (1952, Chapter XIII) had suggested. We present here a simplified version based on Dutt's (2005) interpretation. As is well known, Steindl's work, together with Kalecki's, has provided the foundations of modern neo- or post-Kaleckian distribution and growth theory. Therefore, the model outlined here bears close similarities with these modern Kaleckian/Steindlian distribution and growth models.[3]

The basic model

We assume a closed economy in which just one type of commodity is produced, which can be used for consumption and investment purposes. For a given technology the relationship between the employed volume of labor (L) and real output (Y) is fixed so that we get a constant labor-output ratio (a), that is, there is no overhead-labor. The capital-potential output ratio (v), the relation between the real capital stock (K) and potential real output (Y^p), is also constant for a given technology, and the capital stock is assumed not to depreciate. In Section Equilibrium growth with endogenous technological progress, we will introduce technological progress for which Harrod neutrality will be assumed, that is a fall in the labor-output ratio but a

3 See, for example, the overviews in Blecker (2002), Blecker and Setterfield (2019, Chapter 4), Dutt (1990), Hein (2014, Chapters 6—11) and Lavoie (2014, Chapter 6).

constancy of the capital-potential output ratio. Capital intensity and labor productivity for a given rate of capacity utilization will hence grow at the same rate. The rate of capacity utilization (u) is given by the relation between actual real output and potential real output and is an endogenous variable in the model.

The goods market is dominated by oligopolies, which set prices (p) according to a mark-up (m) on unit labor costs, which are constant up to full capacity output:

$$p = [1 + m(\rho, \gamma)]wa, \quad m > 0, \frac{\partial m}{\partial \rho} \geq 0, \frac{\partial m}{\partial \gamma} \geq 0. \tag{1.1}$$

The mark-up is determined by the degree of price competition in the goods market, by overhead costs and by the bargaining power of workers and trade unions. The profit share (h), that is, the proportion of profits (Π) in nominal output (pY), is therefore determined by the mark-up:

$$h = \frac{\Pi}{pY} = 1 - \frac{1}{1 + m(\rho, \gamma)}, \quad \frac{\partial h}{\partial \rho} \geq 0, \frac{\partial h}{\partial \gamma} \geq 0. \tag{1.2}$$

The mark-up and the profit share may become elastic with respect to overhead costs, and thus to the rentiers' rate of return on equity and bonds (ρ), which is a composite of the interest rate and the dividend rate, as will be explained further below. Alternatively, a change in the outside finance-capital ratio (γ) with a constant rentiers' rate of return may have the same effect. The profit rate (r) relates the flow of profits to the nominal capital stock and can be decomposed into the rate of capacity utilization, the profit share, and the inverse of the capital-potential output ratio:

$$r = \frac{\Pi}{pK} = \frac{\Pi}{pY} \frac{Y}{Y^p} \frac{Y^p}{K} = hu\frac{1}{v}. \tag{1.3}$$

The pace of accumulation and growth is determined by firms' decisions to invest, independently of prior saving. Long-term finance of the capital stock consists of firms' accumulated retained earnings (E_F), long-term credit granted by banks and rentiers (B), and equity issued by firms and held by rentiers (E_R):

$$pK = B + E_R + E_F. \tag{1.4}$$

The rentiers' share in the capital stock, the outside finance-capital ratio, is given by γ:

$$\gamma = \frac{B + E_R}{pK}, \tag{1.5}$$

while ϕ denotes the accumulated retained earnings-capital ratio or the inside finance-capital ratio:

$$\phi = \frac{E_F}{pK}. \tag{1.6}$$

Total profits (Π) are split between firms' retained profits (Π_F) and dividends plus interest paid to rentiers (R):

$$\Pi = \Pi_F + R. \tag{1.7}$$

Interest payments to rentiers are given by the rate of interest and the stock of debt, whereas dividend payments are determined by the dividend rate and the stock of equity held by rentiers. Following Steindl (1952, p. 217) and Dutt (2005), we assume that the interest rate and dividend rate are equal, such that the rentiers' rate of return (ρ), which determines rentiers' income, represents these two rates[4]:

$$R = \rho(E_R + B). \tag{1.8}$$

Discussing consumption and saving decisions, Steindl's (1952) model distinguishes between firms retaining profits which are saved by definition, and households receiving incomes (wages, dividends, and interests), which are partly consumed and partly saved. However, in his later work, Steindl (1979, 1985, 1989) follows Kalecki's worker-capitalist class distinction rather than the institutional firm-household classification. Here, we follow this work and distinguish between firms, workers' and capitalists'/rentiers' households. We assume a classical saving hypothesis, that is, workers do not save. Retained profits are completely saved by definition. Profits distributed to rentiers' households, the interest and dividend payments, are used by those households according to their propensity to save (s_R). Hence, we get

[4] Alternatively, we can also assume that the interest rate and dividend rate differ and the rentiers' rate of return is then the weighted average of these two rates, with the weights given by rentiers' portfolio choice.

the saving-capital rate (σ) that relates total saving to the nominal capital stock:

$$\sigma = \frac{S}{pK} = \frac{\Pi - R + s_R R}{pK} = h\frac{u}{v} - (1 - s_R)\rho\gamma, \quad 0 < s_R \leq 1. \tag{1.9}$$

The investment function in the model includes several of Steindl's (1952) arguments. Two major determinants are (expected) demand and internal means of finance. For the former, Steindl takes the deviation of the realized rate of capacity utilization from the planned rate of utilization ($u - u_0$) as an indicator. The latter determinant is given by retained profits (as a difference between total profits and profits distributed to rentiers as interest and dividends) normalized by the capital stock, and hence by the rate of profit, the rentiers rate of return and the outside finance-capital ratio. An increase in the rentiers' rate of return, that is, of the interest rate and/or the dividend rate, or the rise in the outside finance-capital ratio each have a negative effect on capital accumulation. We have included a constant (α) in the investment function, which may be taken to capture autonomous investment expenditures, as well as "animal spirits" of firms or management driving investment decisions. Finally, we have included the effects of technological progress and innovations on capital accumulation, which Steindl (1952) had ignored in his model but conceded in his later work, and highlighted in Steindl (1981), in particular. Therefore, we have added a positive effect of innovation and (potential) labor productivity growth ($\widehat{y}$), because technological progress is (at least partially) capital-embodied. Let us also assume that technological progress is Harrod-neutral and that the capital-potential output ratio hence remains constant. From all these considerations, the following investment function (g), relating net investment (I) to the capital stock, emanates:

$$g = \frac{pI}{pK} = \alpha + \omega\widehat{y} + \beta(u - u_0) + \theta\left(h\frac{u}{v} - \rho\gamma\right), \quad \beta, \theta, \omega > 0, \quad \theta < 1. \tag{1.10}$$

The goods market equilibrium is given by the equality of saving and investment decisions:

$$g = \sigma. \tag{1.11}$$

The usual Keynesian/Kaleckian stability condition requires the saving rate to respond more to a change in the rate of capacity utilization than the rate of capital accumulation:

$$\frac{\partial \sigma}{\partial u} - \frac{\partial g}{\partial u} > 0 \Rightarrow (1 - \theta)\frac{h}{v} - \beta > 0. \tag{1.12}$$

Equilibrium growth with exogenous technological progress

For the analysis of the demand regime, we assume technological progress to be exogenous for the moment. The goods market equilibrium rates of capacity utilization, capital accumulation, and profit are hence as follows:

$$u^* = \frac{\alpha + \omega\widehat{y} - \beta u_0 + \rho\gamma(1 - s_R - \theta)}{(1-\theta)\frac{h}{v} - \beta}, \tag{1.13}$$

$$g^* = \frac{(\alpha + \omega\widehat{y} - \beta u_0)\frac{h}{v} + \rho\gamma\left[\beta(1 - s_R) - \theta s_R\frac{h}{v}\right]}{(1-\theta)\frac{h}{v} - \beta}, \tag{1.14}$$

$$r^* = \frac{[\alpha + \omega\widehat{y} - \beta u_0 + \rho\gamma(1 - s_R - \theta)]\frac{h}{v}}{(1-\theta)\frac{h}{v} - \beta}. \tag{1.15}$$

Here, we will not discuss the endogenous dynamics of the outside finance-capital ratio and its stability properties, the potential for "paradoxes of debt" or "paradoxes of outside finance," and so on.[5] We will also not deal with the question of whether an equilibrium rate of utilization (u^*) deviating from firms' target rate of utilization (u_0) should be considered as an equilibrium beyond the short run. Steindl (1952, p. 12, emphasis in the original) is quite explicit on that issue, when he argues that "(t)he degree of utilization actually obtaining in the long run, we must conclude, is no safe indication of the *planned* level of utilization."[6]

From Eqs. (1.13) to (1.15), the effects of changes in α, $\omega\widehat{y}$, s_R and u_0 on the goods market equilibrium rates of capacity utilization, capital accumulation, and profit are clear. A fall in animal spirits or in the growth of autonomous investment, also in the growth of autonomous consumption, government deficit spending or exports in more elaborated models, have negative effects on economic activity, growth, and the rate of profit. A lower rate of technological progress and innovations, that is, lower (potential) labor

[5] See the discussions based on similar models in Dutt (1995), Hein (2007, 2010, 2013, 2014, Chapter 9—10), Lavoie (1995), Sasaki and Fujita (2012), and Franke (2016), for example.

[6] See also Hein (2021). For surveys of the Marxian and Harrodian critique and a presentation of Kaleckian/Steindlian responses, see Hein et al. (2011, 2012), Hein (2014, Chapter 11) and Lavoie (2014, Chapter 6.5), for example.

productivity growth, or a lower responsiveness of investment toward technological progress have contractive effects on all equilibrium values as well. The same is true for a higher propensity to save out of rentiers' income. The paradox of thrift is thus valid for Steindl's approach. Additionally, a higher target rate of utilization of firms has depressive effects on capacity utilization, capital accumulation, and the profit rate. For the effects of changes in the profit share, and hence in functional income distribution, we get the following results:

$$\frac{\partial u^*}{\partial h} = \frac{-(1-\theta)\frac{u}{v}}{(1-\theta)\frac{h}{v} - \beta} < 0, \tag{1.13a}$$

$$\frac{\partial g^*}{\partial h} = \frac{-\beta\frac{u}{v}}{(1-\theta)\frac{h}{v} - \beta} < 0, \tag{1.14a}$$

$$\frac{\partial r^*}{\partial h} = \frac{-\beta\frac{u}{v}}{(1-\theta)\frac{h}{v} - \beta} < 0. \tag{1.15a}$$

Demand and growth in the Steindlian model are hence wage-led, and for the rate of profit we have the "paradox of costs," that is, a higher wage share and thus higher real unit labor costs trigger a higher profit rate. The effects of changes in our financial variables, the rentiers' rate of return and the outside finance-capital ratio, are as follows:

$$\frac{\partial u^*}{\partial \rho} = \frac{\gamma(1 - s_R - \theta) - (1-\theta)\frac{u}{v}\frac{\partial h}{\partial \rho}}{(1-\theta)\frac{h}{v} - \beta}, \tag{1.13b}$$

$$\frac{\partial u^*}{\partial \gamma} = \frac{\rho(1 - s_R - \theta) - (1-\theta)\frac{u}{v}\frac{\partial h}{\partial \gamma}}{(1-\theta)\frac{h}{v} - \beta}, \tag{1.13c}$$

$$\frac{\partial g^*}{\partial \rho} = \frac{\gamma\left[\beta(1 - s_R) - \theta s_R\frac{h}{v}\right] - \beta\frac{u}{v}\frac{\partial h}{\partial \rho}}{(1-\theta)\frac{h}{v} - \beta}, \tag{1.14b}$$

$$\frac{\partial g^*}{\partial \gamma} = \frac{\rho\left[\beta(1 - s_R) - \theta s_R \frac{h}{v}\right] - \beta \frac{u}{v}\frac{\partial h}{\partial \gamma}}{(1 - \theta)\frac{h}{v} - \beta}, \tag{1.14c}$$

$$\frac{\partial r^*}{\partial \rho} = \frac{\gamma(1 - s_R - \theta)\frac{h}{v} - \beta \frac{u}{v}\frac{\partial h}{\partial \rho}}{(1 - \theta)\frac{h}{v} - \beta}, \tag{1.15b}$$

$$\frac{\partial r^*}{\partial \gamma} = \frac{\rho(1 - s_R - \theta)\frac{h}{v} - \beta \frac{u}{v}\frac{\partial h}{\partial \gamma}}{(1 - \theta)\frac{h}{v} - \beta}. \tag{1.15c}$$

With interest- and dividend-inelastic mark-ups and profit shares ($\partial h/\partial \rho = \partial h/\partial \gamma = 0$), a rise in the rentiers' rate of return or an increase in the outside finance-capital ratio will redistribute income from firms, which do not consume, to rentiers, who consume at least a part of the income. This will boost consumption demand and, through the accelerator in the investment function, also investment demand and hence capital accumulation. However, the drain of firms' internal means of finance will have a partially negative effect on capital accumulation. The overall or equilibrium effect will thus depend on the relative strength of each of these partial effects. Three potential cases or regimes can be distinguished[7]: the "normal case" (Lavoie, 1995) and a "debt-burdened" economy (Taylor, 2008, p. 275), in which an increase in the rentiers' rate of return or in the outside finance-capital ratio depresses the economy; the "intermediate case," in which the effects on the rates of capacity utilization and profit are expansionary, but the effects on the rate of capital accumulation and growth are depressing; and finally a "puzzling case" (Lavoie, 1995) and a "debt-led" economy (Taylor, 2008, p. 275), in which we have overall expansionary effects of a rising rentiers' rate of return or outside finance-capital ratio. If we allow for effects on functional income distribution ($\partial h/\partial \rho > 0$, $\partial h/\partial \gamma > 0$), too, expansionary effects of a rising rentiers' rate of return or the outside finance-capital ratio will become less likely, but not impossible, because our economy is wage led.

[7] See Hein (2014, Chapters 9 and 10) for derivations.

Looking at the late Steindl's work, it seems that he has endorsed the "normal case," "debt-burdened" regime as the one that dominates, because he relates stagnation tendencies and stagnation policy to an increasing dominance of the financial sector in modern capitalist economies. In Bhaduri and Steindl (1985), stagnation policy is associated with "the rise of monetarism as a social doctrine," because monetarism is inherently linked to restrictive fiscal and monetary policies, which are supported by banks and the financial sector (or the rentiers). The application of monetarist policies thus indicates a shift of powers from the nonfinancial sector of the economy to the financial sector. In Steindl (1989), it is stressed that, starting in the 1980s, the tendencies toward weak investment and stagnation have then been amplified by a shift of the interest of corporations and their managers from production toward finance and an increasing role of financial investment in comparison to real investment, an idea which in the 2000s has reemerged in the literature on financialization and investment (Hein, 2012).[8]

Equilibrium growth with endogenous technological progress

In the next step, we can endogenize technological progress, or the productivity regime, which is absent in Steindl's work, and which Steindl himself considered to be lacking in his own theory (Steindl, 1976, 1979, 1989). Starting with Rowthorn (1981), Dutt (1990, Chapter 5), Taylor (1991, Chapter 10), and Lavoie (2014, Chapter 6.9), post-Keynesian authors have introduced endogenous technological change and labor productivity growth into Steindlian/Kaleckian distribution and growth models, as reviewed and elaborated in Hein (2014, Chapter 8). Relying on Kaldor's (1957, 1961) technical progress function and/or on Kaldor's (1966) Verdoorn's Law, labor productivity growth is assumed to be positively affected by capital stock growth, due to capital-embodied technological change, and/or by demand growth and hence the rate of capacity utilization, due to dynamic returns to scale. Following Marx (1867) and Hicks (1932), several authors have also integrated a wage-push variable into the productivity growth function of the model, arguing that higher real wages or a higher wage share induce capitalists to speed up the implementation of labor-augmenting technological progress in order to protect the profit share.

[8] However, Steindl has not seen the short-run potential of an increasing dominance of finance to stimulate the economy, through debt-financed consumption in particular.

If we add a summary variable (η) representing the effect of "learning by doing," on the one hand, and basic or autonomous innovations, on the other hand, we get the following function for labor productivity growth:

$$\hat{y} = \eta + \varepsilon g - \psi h, \quad \eta, \varepsilon, \psi > 0. \tag{1.16}$$

Plugging Eq. (1.16) into Eq. (1.14), we can derive the long-run equilibrium rate of capital accumulation and growth:

$$g^{**} = \frac{\alpha - \beta u_0 + \omega(\eta - \psi h) + \rho\gamma\left[\beta(1 - s_R) - \theta s_R \frac{h}{v}\right]}{(1-\theta)\frac{h}{v} - \beta - \omega\varepsilon}. \tag{1.17}$$

Using Eqs. (1.16) and (1.17), we finally arrive at the long-run equilibrium rate of productivity growth:

$$\hat{y}^{**} = \frac{(\eta - \psi h)\left[(1-\theta)\frac{h}{v} - \beta\right] + \varepsilon\left\{\alpha - \beta u_0 + \rho\gamma\left[\beta(1 - s_R) - \theta s_R \frac{h}{v}\right]\right\}}{(1-\theta)\frac{h}{v} - \beta - \omega\varepsilon}. \tag{1.18}$$

Graphically, the equilibrium values in Eqs. (1.17) and (1.18) can be obtained as in Fig. 1.1, which is making use of Eq. (1.14) for capital stock growth as determined by the demand regime and Eq. (1.16) for the productivity regime.

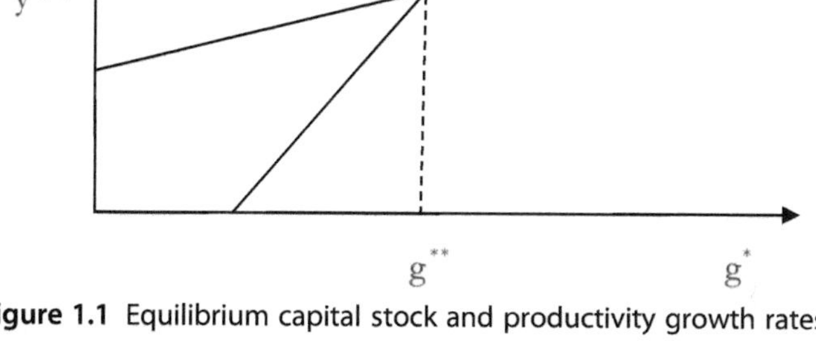

Figure 1.1 Equilibrium capital stock and productivity growth rates.

Table 1.1 summarizes the effects of changes in exogenous variables and parameters on the long-run equilibrium rates of capital accumulation and productivity growth derived from our Steindlian demand-driven endogenous growth model.

In Fig. 1.2, any fall in the goods market equilibrium rate of capital accumulation, that is, a leftwards shift in the g^*-function, triggered by a fall in α, a rise in u_0, s_R or h, as well as a rise in ρ or γ in the "normal," "debt-burdened" case, will also cause a lower long-run equilibrium rate of productivity growth and hence of potential growth through the Kaldor technical progress- or Verdoorn-effect. The economy will move from the equilibrium in

Table 1.1 Responses of the long-run equilibrium rates of capital accumulation and productivity growth toward changes in exogenous variables and parameters.

	g^{**}	$\hat{y}^{**}$
α	+	+
u_0	−	−
s_R	−	−
h	−	−
ρ	− (Normal, debt-burdened) + (puzzling, debt-led)	− (Normal, debt-burdened) + (puzzling, debt-led)
γ	− (Normal, debt-burdened) + (Puzzling, debt-led)	− (Normal, debt-burdened) + (Puzzling, debt-led)
η	+	+

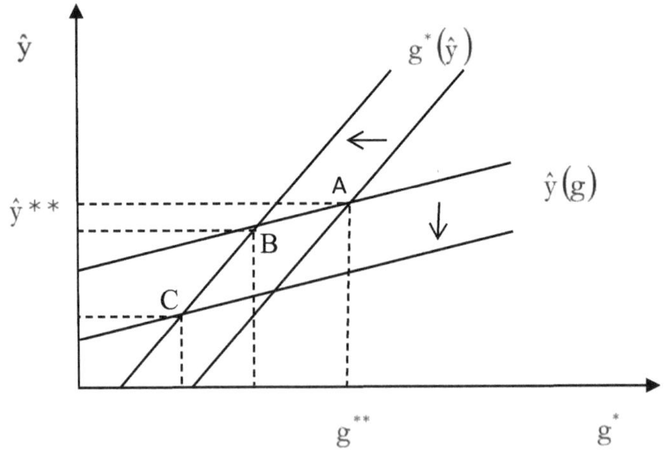

Figure 1.2 Stagnation with endogenous productivity growth.

A to the one in B. And if the fall in capital accumulation is caused by a higher profit share, the directly negative impact on productivity growth has to be included as well, and the economy will move to the long-run equilibrium in *C* with even lower capital stock, output, and productivity growth.

The channels of stagnation policy and implications for its reversal

From the demand-led endogenous growth model presented in the previous section the following major channels of stagnation policy emerge:

- Decreasing autonomous government expenditure growth, as well as replacing aggregate demand management policies by policies of structural reforms weakening overall private expectations and hence animal spirits, will lead to a decrease in the autonomous component α in the investment function.
- Lowering productivity enhancing public investments in R&D will cause a fall in η, the autonomous component in the productivity growth function.
- Weakening workers' and trade unions' bargaining power through policies of (labor) market deregulation, abandoning aggregate demand management, and accepting high rates of unemployment, as well as higher interest and divided rates and hence higher overhead costs, will each raise the total profit share h.
- Generating or accepting rising inequality and a higher profit share in the distribution of incomes through various channels, as well as generating higher uncertainty and thereby precautionary saving, will lead to a rise in the average propensity to save $(s = h-(1-s_R)R/pY)$.
- Raising real rates of interest through tight monetary policies, and rising dividend rates through structural reforms in favor of shareholders will each cause the rentiers' rate of return ρ and the outside-finance capital ratios of firms γ to rise with depressing effects in the "normal case" and "debt-burdened" regimes, which Steindl assumed to dominate.

In order to avoid stagnation, stagnation policy would have to be reversed. From a Steindlian perspective, this should include the following areas[9]

[9] See, for example, Guger et al. (2006), Hein (2018), and Hein and Martschin (2020) for applications to the European Union or the Eurozone.

- Stabilizing and raising public autonomous expenditure growth, as well as discretionary anticyclical fiscal policies, will stabilize effective demand growth, prevent deflation with its negative effects on private demand, and improve the general climate for private sector investment and consumption.
- Raising growth-enhancing public investment, focusing on infrastructure, technology, R&D, and education expenditures, will also stimulate private investment and R&D outlays.
- Full employment policies improving workers' bargaining power, low interest rate policies reducing overhead costs, and the reregulation of the financial sector reducing the power and income claims of rentiers and shareholders will each contribute to stabilizing and raising the wage share.
- Redistributing income, both pretax via higher wage shares and a more compressed wage structure and after-tax by progressive taxation and social transfers, as well as removing the uncertainty that triggers precautionary saving, will each lower private households' average propensity to save.

Going beyond our simple closed economy model, in order to avoid severe current account imbalances, "beggar thy neighbor" strategies, on the one hand, and rising indebtedness in foreign currencies, on the other hand, international economic and monetary policy coordination would have to be improved.

Conclusions

In this contribution, we have presented a Steindlian demand determined endogenous growth model in order to explain the sources for stagnation and the role of stagnation policy. This approach provides an alternative to the recent mainstream theories of "secular stagnation" with their supply side focus on technology and preferences. The Steindlian approach does not view stagnation as an inescapable trend, but it allows for the identification of the various channels through which economic policies have an impact on distribution, on demand in the short run, and on capital accumulation and growth in the long run. Therefore, it has also allowed us to derive the economic policy implications for overcoming stagnation tendencies.

References

Bhaduri, A., Steindl, J., 1985. The rise of monetarism as a social doctrine. In: Arestis, P., Skouras, T. (Eds.), Post-Keynesian Economic Theory. Wheatsheaf, Sussex.

Blecker, R.A., 2002. Distribution, demand and growth in neo-Kaleckian macro-models. In: Setterfield, M. (Ed.), The Economics of Demand-Led Growth. Edward Elgar, Cheltenham.

Blecker, R.A., Setterfield, M., 2019. Heterodox Macroeconomics: Models of Demand, Distribution and Growth. Edward Elgar, Cheltenham.

Dutt, A.K., 1990. Growth, Distribution and Uneven Development. Cambridge University Press, Cambridge, UK.

Dutt, A.K., 1995. Internal finance and monopoly power in capitalist economies: a reformulation of Steindl's growth model. Metroeconomica 46, 16–34.

Dutt, A.K., 2005. Steindl's theory of maturity and stagnation and its relevance today. In: Mott, T., Shapiro, N. (Eds.), Rethinking Capitalism. Essays on the Economics of Josef Steindl. Routledge, London, New York.

Franke, R., 2016. A supplementary note on Professor Hein's (2013) version of a Kaleckian debt accumulation. Metroeconomica 67 (3), 529–550.

Gordon, R., 2012. Is US Economic Growth over? Faltering Innovation Confronts the Six Headwinds. NBER Working Paper No. 18315.

Gordon, R., 2014. The turtle's progress: secular stagnation meets the headwinds. In: Teulings, C., Baldwin, R. (Eds.), Secular Stagnation: Facts, Causes and Cures. Centre for Economic Policy Research (CEPR), London. A VoxEU.Org eBook.

Gordon, R., 2015. Secular stagnation: a supply side view. American Economic Review: Papers and Proceedings 105 (5), 54–59.

Guger, A., Marterbauer, M., Walterskirchen, E., 2006. Growth policy in the spirit of Steindl and Kalecki. Metroeconomica 57, 428–442.

Harcourt, G.C., 1969. Some Cambridge controversies in the theory of capital. Journal of Economic Literature 7, 369–405.

Harcourt, G.C., 1972. Some Cambridge Controversies in the Theory of Capital. Cambridge University Press, Cambridge, UK.

Hein, E., 2007. Interest rate, debt, distribution and capital accumulation in a post-Kaleckian model. Metroeconomica 58 (2), 310–339.

Hein, E., 2010. Shareholder value orientation, distribution and growth – short- and medium-run effects in a Kaleckian model. Metroeconomica 61 (2), 302–332.

Hein, E., 2012. The Macroeconomics of Finance-Dominated Capitalism – and its Crisis. Edward Elgar, Cheltenham.

Hein, E., 2013. On the importance of the retention ratio in a Kaleckian distribution and growth model with debt accumulation – a comment on Sasaki and Fujita (2012). Metroeconomica 64, 186–196.

Hein, E., 2014. Distribution and Growth after Keynes: A Post-Keynesian Guide. Edward Elgar, Cheltenham.

Hein, E., 2016. Secular stagnation or stagnation policy? Steindl after Summers. PSL Quarterly Review 69 (276), 3–47.

Hein, E., 2018. Stagnation policy in the Eurozone and economic policy alternatives: a Steindlian/neo-Kaleckian perspective. Wirtschaft und Gesellschaft 44 (3), 315–348.

Hein, E., 2021. Harrodian instability in Kaleckian models and Steindlian solutions: an elementary discussion. In: Basu, D., Das, D. (Eds.), Conflict, Demand and Economic Development: Essays in Honour of Amit Bhaduri. Routledge, London (India).

Hein, E., Lavoie, M., van Treeck, T., 2011. Some instability puzzles in Kaleckian models of growth and distribution: a critical survey. Cambridge Journal of Economics 35, 587–612.

Hein, E., Lavoie, M., van Treeck, T., 2012. Harrodian instability and the 'normal rate' of capacity utilisation in Kaleckian models of distribution and growth – a survey. Metroeconomica 63, 139–169.

Hein, E., Martschin, J., 2020. The Eurozone in crisis – a Kaleckian macroeconomic regime and policy perspective. Review of Political Economy 32 (4), 563–588.

Hicks, J., 1932. The Theory of Wages. Macmillan, London.

Kaldor, N., 1957. A model of economic growth. The Economic Journal 67, 591–624.

Kaldor, N., 1961. Capital accumulation and economic growth. In: Lutz, F.A., Hague, D.C. (Eds.), The Theory of Capital. Macmillan, London.

Kaldor, N., 1966. Causes of the Slow Rate of Economic Growth in the United Kingdom. Cambridge University Press, Cambridge, UK.

Kalecki, M., 1943. Political aspects of full employment. Political Quarterly 14 (4), 322–331.

Lavoie, M., 1995. Interest rates in post-Keynesian models of growth and distribution. Metroeconomica 46, 146–177.

Lavoie, M., 2014. Post-keynesian Economics: New Foundations. Edward Elgar, Cheltenham.

Lazzarini, A., 2011. Revisiting the Cambridge Capital Controversies: A Historical and Analytical Study. Pavia University Press, Pavia.

Marx, K., 1867. Das Kapital. In: Engels, F. (Ed.), Kritik der politischen Ökonomie, Erster Band: Der Produktionsprozeß des Kapitals, fourth ed. reprinted as Marx-Engels-Werke, Volume 23, Berlin: Dietz Verlag 1962, Englisch translation: Capital: A Critique of Political Economy, Volume 1: The Process of Capitalist Production, New York: International Publisher, 1967, 1890.

Rachel, L., Summers, L.A., 2019. On Falling Neutral Rates, Fiscal Policy, and the Risk of Secular Stagnation, Brooking Papers on Economic Activity, March, 1–66.

Robinson, J., 1962. Essays in the Theory of Economic Growth. Macmillan, London.

Rowthorn, R.E., 1981. Demand, Real Wages and Economic Growth, Thames Papers in Political Economy. Autumn, pp. 1–39.

Sasaki, H., Fujita, S., 2012. The importance of the retention ratio in a Kaleckian model with debt accumulation. Metroeconomica 63, 417–428.

Steindl, J., 1952. Maturity and Stagnation in American Capitalism, Oxford: Blackwell, second ed. Monthly Review Press, New York, London. 1976.

Steindl, J., 1976. Introduction. In: Steindl, J. (Ed.), Maturity and Stagnation in American Capitalism, second ed. Monthly Review Press, New York, London.

Steindl, J., 1979. Stagnation theory and stagnation policy. Cambridge Journal of Economics 3, 1–14.

Steindl, J., 1981. Ideas and concepts of long run growth. Banca Nazionale del Lavoro Quarterly Review 34 (136), 35–48.

Steindl, J., 1985. Distribution and growth, political economy. Studies in the Surplus Approach 1, 53–68.

Steindl, J., 1989. From stagnation in the 30s to slow growth in the 70s. In: Berg, M. (Ed.), Political Economy in the Twentieth Century, Oxford: Philip Allan, Reprinted in: J. Steindl, Economic Papers, 1941–88. Macmillan, Basingstoke, 1990.

Summers, L.A., 2014a. U.S. economic prospects: secular stagnation, hysteresis, and the zero lower bound. Business Economics 49 (2), 65–73.

Summers, L.A., 2014b. Reflections on the 'new secular stagnation hypothesis'. In: Teulings, C., Baldwin, R. (Eds.), Secular Stagnation: Facts, Causes and Cures. Centre for Economic Policy Research (CEPR), London. A VoxEU.Org eBook.

Summers, L.A., 2015. Demand side secular stagnation. American Economic Review: Papers and Proceedings 105 (5), 60–65.
Taylor, L., 1991. Income Distribution, Inflation, and Growth: Lectures on Structuralist Macroeconomic Theory. MIT Press, Cambridge, MA, London.
Taylor, L., 2008. Reconstructing Macroeconomics: Structuralist Proposals and Critiques of the Mainstream. Viva Books, New Delhi.
von Weizsäcker, C.C., 2019. Capital abundance and its consequences for trade policy. Intereconomics: Review of European Economic Policies 54 (5), 275–279.
von Weizsäcker, C.C., Krämer, H., 2021. Saving and Investment in the 21st Century: The Great Divergence. Springer, Cham/Switzerland.

CHAPTER TWO

Growth and stagnation in mature and dual economies

Peter Skott[1,2]
[1]University of Massacusetts Amherst, Amherst, MA, United States
[2]Aalborg University, Aalborg, Denmark

Introduction

Some economies grow rapidly, others stagnate. The variation can be explained partly by differences in the initial levels of income and in the potential for technological catch-up. Not all poor countries grow rapidly, however. Senegal saw declining per capita income between 1960 and 1994 and did not return to its 1960 level until 2014. Individual countries also go through periods of rapid and slow growth. In Brazil, an average growth rate of GDP per capita above 6% between 1968 and 1980 was followed by 20 years of stagnating per capita incomes.

Economic stagnation can occur for a variety of reasons. This paper addresses explanations that see an important role for aggregate demand and its interactions with the supply side. The emphasis on interactions between the demand and supply sides is in contrast to explanations that focus exclusively on either the supply side or the demand side. Most of the endogenous-growth literature falls into the first category. The second category is represented by some of the post-Keynesian literature. Prominent neo-Kaleckian contributions suggest that neither capital nor labor represents a constraint on long-run growth, contending that economic growth is determined by the growth rate of aggregate demand.

The post-Keynesian insistence on the importance of aggregate demand is well-founded. But the supply side is important too, and the conduct of aggregate demand policy must take into account the supply side constraints. The constraints vary across economies and, as a first approximation, a distinction must be made between "mature" and "dual" economies.

Handbook of Economic Stagnation
ISBN: 978-0-12-815898-2
https://doi.org/10.1016/B978-0-12-815898-2.00016-1

Labor is the binding supply side constraint on long-run growth in mature economies. An economy need not have "full employment" in order to be mature.[1] Labor becomes a relevant constraint on the medium- and long-run growth rate if attempts to raise the growth rate significantly through aggressive aggregate demand policies would generate labor shortages and inflation within a relatively short period. By this criterion the Japanese, German and US economies are labor constrained: official unemployment rates may be misleading but even taking into account discouraged workers, Chinese-style annual growth rates of 10 percent could not be maintained for more than a couple of years. In principle, immigration could alleviate impending labor shortages, but this route is blocked by political constraints.

Dual economies are different. Official rates of unemployment can be low in these economies. According to the ILO, the Indian unemployment rate is below 4%, but large amounts of hidden unemployment and underemployment make the figure almost meaningless. India may experience shortages of some types of skilled workers but underemployment, learning by doing, and the potential for technological catch-up imply that growth rates of 10 percent a year could be maintained for many years without a general labor shortage.

The modern sector in dual economies is constrained by a combination of low stocks of private fixed capital, inadequate public infrastructure, and shortages of human capital. The precise form of the capital constraint differs across countries, and the details are crucial in the formulation of concrete development policies. For the purposes of this paper, however, the point is simply that current resources must be invested in order to expand the modern sector.

The supply side interacts with the demand side. Mature economies, I shall argue, may suffer from a structural aggregate demand problem ("secular stagnation"). If this happens, sustained fiscal stimulus—fiscal deficits and/or a high public debt ratio—will be needed to maintain full-employment growth. Dual economies, by contrast, face a structural transformation problem, and a sensible fiscal policy will typically avoid sustained deficits and high debt: high saving rates represent an opportunity to increase investment and the growth rate of the modern sector. It is not sufficient, however, to provide the space for investment. The private sector must have an incentive

[1] The very concept of full employment is poorly defined in economies with employment hysteresis. Employment hysteresis does not, however, eliminate constraints on the long-run growth rate of employment.

to invest, and macroeconomic stabilization policies that ensure sufficient demand for the modern sector will be needed; in open economies this requirement includes ensuring the international competitiveness of the domestic modern sector. Dual and mature economies both require short-run stabilization policies. The differences concern the role of aggregate demand policies in the long run.

The next section considers the aggregate demand problem in mature economies. This is followed by a section on structural transformation problems in dual economies. To illustrate the argument, the last section offers a brief discussion of growth and stagnation in Japan and Brazil.

Mature economies, functional finance, and secular stagnation

The nature of the long-run demand issue in mature economies can be illustrated by a few, simple equations. The first equation is the equilibrium condition for the goods market in a closed economy,

$$\frac{Y}{K}=\frac{C}{K}+\frac{I}{K}+\frac{G}{K} \tag{2.1}$$

As a convenient normalization, the familiar $Y = C + I + G$ equation has been divided through by the capital stock.

The ratio of government consumption to the capital stock is taken to be exogenous,

$$\frac{G}{K}=\gamma \tag{2.2}$$

The appropriate size of government is contentious. How much should we spend on prisons, public education, or public health care, for instance? These are important questions, but the answers should not be decided based on the exigencies of demand management, and debates on the appropriate size of the public sector are largely irrelevant for present purposes. The need for aggregate demand policy in the long run can be addressed independently of the precise level of the government consumption ratio.

The third equation represents straightforward accounting. In order to maintain full-employment growth and a constant output-capital ratio, the ratio of gross investment to the capital stock must be equal to the sum of the growth rate of the labor supply in efficiency units (n) and the rate of depreciation (δ) :

$$\frac{I}{K} = n + \delta \tag{2.3}$$

Using Roy Harrod's terminology, I shall refer to n as the natural rate of growth.

By definition, the output capital ratio is constant in steady growth, but its steady-growth value may be endogenous. With capital and labor as the only inputs, the cost of finance, and the wage rate determine the choice of technique. Under perfect competition, the zero profit condition pins down the real wage for any given cost of finance, while under imperfect competition the real wage is determined by the markup and the cost of finance. Thus, if we take the degree of competition as given, the output-capital ratio (σ) can be written as

$$\sigma = \frac{Y}{K} = f(r) \tag{2.4}$$

where the real interest rate r is used as a proxy for the cost of finance.

Combining Eqs. (2.1)–(2.4), the condition for steady growth with full employment can be written as

$$f(r) - \frac{C}{K} = \gamma + n + \delta \tag{2.5}$$

The variables on the right-hand side of Eq. (2.5) are exogenous, and any adjustment has to come through the output-capital ratio (the real rate of interest) or the consumption-capital ratio. The question is, will these adjustments happen automatically or is there a need for active policy?

Models that have Ramsey optimization at their core suggest that there will be no need for policy. Full employment growth is maintained through a combination of endogenous adjustments in the saving rate and changes in the capital intensity. Moreover, the capital intensity will be socially optimal if the representative agent's utility function is used as the welfare criterion. The Ramsey case is extreme and highly special, however. Other models, including neoclassical overlapping generations models, traditional Keynesian models and stock-flow consistent models with a more developed financial sector give different answers. Strikingly, moreover, the answers are qualitatively similar across these different models.

Disregarding the extreme Ramsey case, the rate of interest could be chosen to influence the choice of technique and the output capital ratio σ. This route is the one taken by the Solow model and retained as an important element in the DSGE models that dominate contemporary macroeconomic theory. The Cambridge capital controversy cast doubt on the existence of a well-defined and known set of production techniques and showed that, if such a set exists, reswitching and capital reversing cannot be ruled out; a rise in the interest rate may lead to an increase in the capital intensity.[2] High levels of capital intensity, moreover, may be unambiguously suboptimal: if the intensity exceeds the level associated with the golden rule, per capita consumption could be raised at every moment by allowing a reduction in the capital output ratio.

Lerner (1943) outlined a better approach. Policy makers, he argued, should adjust fiscal and monetary instruments so as to achieve both full employment and a desirable share of investment in output.[3] In a growth context, the second target translates into a "desirable output capital ratio": we have $I/Y = (I/K)(K/Y) = (n+\delta)(K/Y)$, and choosing the investment-output ratio corresponds to choosing an output capital ratio σ^*. Thus, Lerner's investment argument in combination with Eq. (2.4) implies that

$$r = f^{-1}(\sigma^*)$$

This requirement pins down the steady-growth value of the real interest rate, and policy makers must turn to fiscal policy to adjust aggregate demand and maintain full employment.[4]

I have taken government consumption as exogenous (Eq. 2.2), but taxes and transfers can be used to influence consumption and maintain aggregate demand at a level that ensures full employment growth. Private saving rates that are excessive in relation to the natural growth rate can be countered by

2 Thus, if the f -function in Eq. (2.4) is differentiable, we may have $f' < 0$, rather than $f' > 0$; a Leontief production function without any choice of technique corresponds to the special case with $f' \equiv 0$. The general expression in Eq. (2.4) is consistent with all three cases, and for present purposes there is no need to impose any restrictions of the range and functional form of $f(r)$. The analysis neither requires nor excludes a neoclassical production function with smooth, well-behaved substitution and $f' > 0$.

3 A large Keynesian literature takes positions that are similar to functional finance (even if not always directly inspired by Lerner); examples include Godley and Lavoie (2007), Arestis and Sawyer (2010), Wray (2012).

4 In the Leontief case without a choice of technique, the interest rate has no effect on the right hand side of Eq. (2.4), and it can be set to satisfy some other objective (to affect the share of income going to rentiers, for instance). The underlying determinants of σ^* and r^* are irrelevant for the subsequent analysis of the fiscal policy requirements.

a reduction in taxes and an increase in the government deficit; analogously, private saving rates that are too low call for contractionary policies.

Continuous adjustments of tax rates to satisfy the full-employment condition generate dynamic trajectories for government debt and private wealth. The change in government debt is given by $\dot{B} = rB + G - T$, and the rate of change of the debt-capital ratio, accordingly, can be written

$$\dot{b} = b\left(\widehat{B} - \widehat{K}\right) = \frac{\dot{B}}{K} - nb = \frac{rB + G - T}{K} - nb = (r - n)b + \left(\gamma - \frac{T}{K}\right) \tag{2.6}$$

where B, r, T, b denote the public debt, the interest rate, taxes and the debt ratio B/K; dots and hats are used to indicate rates of change and growth rates, respectively; that is, $\dot{x} = dx/dt$ and $\widehat{x} = \dot{x}/x$. For any given specifications of the consumption function and the structure of taxation, the required ratio of taxes to capital is determined by the full-employment condition and the current value of the debt ratio b. Substituting this solution for T/K into Eq. (2.6) produces a one-dimensional differential equation to determine the dynamics of the debt ratio b.

The precise implications for public debt depend on the specification of consumption behavior and the structure of taxation. The qualitative properties are quite robust, however.[5]

A fiscal policy based on functional finance produces strong stabilizing effects on the debt-income ratio. An increase in public debt raises private wealth and stimulates consumption, and policy makers need to raise taxes in order to prevent overheating and inflation. This stabilizing effect is combined with the automatic erosion of the debt ratio B/K as the capital stock increases. The stabilizing forces could in principle be offset by the positive feedback effect from higher debt to increased interest payments. For plausible specifications of the consumption function, however, the debt ratio converges to a steady growth value, $b \rightarrow b^*$.

The analysis stands in contrast to policy experiments in which the ratio of the primary deficit to income is kept constant and in which the stability conditions are more stringent. Policy experiments with constant primary deficits make little sense. Why would a government want to pursue policies

[5] Ryoo and Skott (2013) consider a stock-flow consistent Keynesian model; Skott and Ryoo (2014) analyze a standard OLG model, and Skott and Ryoo (2017) a modified "Keynesian OLG model." An earlier paper by Schlicht (2006) derived some of the results using a traditional Keynesian model.

of this kind? The economic analysis of monetary policy typically looks for "optimal" policies (or policy rules), given some welfare function and a model of how the economy operates. The functional-finance approach introduces Keynesian elements that are absent in contemporary DSGE-based analysis of monetary policy, but the search for appropriate policies is in a similar spirit: fiscal policy is adjusted to meet welfare targets, in this case maintaining full-employment growth.

Having established convergence, one may examine the determinants of the steady-growth debt ratio. An increase in the growth rate n, first, reduces the long-run value of the debt ratio b^*. This result, which is robust across models, has clear implications for the interpretation of negative correlations between debt ratios and the rate of growth. The influential study by Reinhart and Rogoff (2010) contained elementary spreadsheet errors, but a (milder) negative correlation remains after correction of these errors. Correlation, however, is not causation, and the above analysis shows that we should expect a causal effect from low growth to high debt: the natural growth rate was taken as exogenous, and the high debt unambiguously represents an effect, not a cause of low growth.[6] Expansionary fiscal policies are required precisely because the slow growth of full-employment output reduces the investment and aggregate demand.

The long-run debt ratio, second, depends on the structure of taxation. Taxing low-income households with a high marginal consumption rate produces a high debt ratio; taxing high income households with a low marginal consumption rate produces a low debt ratio. Tax reforms in many OECD countries have shifted the relative tax burden from the corporate sector and the rich toward low- and middle-income households. These shifts will tend to increase the long-run debt ratio if full employment is to be maintained.

Increases in inequality, third, tend to raise the private saving rate. To maintain full employment, the increase in equality must be countered by expansionary fiscal policy, and the long-run debt ratio will rise.

Paradoxically, fourth, high levels of government consumption produce low debt ratios in the long run. Austerity policies which aim to reduce

[6] Empirical studies show that slow growth tends to precede the rise in debt (e.g., Ash et al., 2017). It is difficult, however, to establish causal links between long-run growth rates and debt ratios from purely empirical methods.

public debt by cutting government consumption can have—and have had—devastating short- and medium-run economic and social consequences. The analysis shows that the policies will also fail on their own terms in economies with a structural demand problem: a return to full employment will require an increase in the debt ratio if the share of government consumption in income has been reduced.

Fiscal policy does not always follow a pure functional finance prescription—European austerity policy after the financial crisis is an obvious example. But real-world policies often amount to a kind of "impure functional finance." It is no coincidence that Japanese public debt rose rapidly from the early 1990s or that the US implemented a fiscal stimulus package in 2009. The analysis of functional finance therefore has real-world relevance. It is of descriptive interest because of automatic fiscal stabilizers and because policy makers facing high unemployment will be pulled toward expansionary discretionary policies. It is of prescriptive interest because it shows that fears of "debt unsustainability" are unfounded, but that the long-run debt implications depend, inter alia, on the structure of taxation and the size of the public sector.

There are complications and caveats. Economies, first, that do not issue debt in their own currency cannot control the interest rate on public debt and may be forced to default, a possibility that severely limits their policy space. Even if debt is being issued in a sovereign currency, second, the conduct of fiscal policy in open economies must consider the balance of payments and the real exchange rate as well as unemployment and inflation. High debt levels, finally, can have negative side effects with respect to the effectiveness of monetary policy and the intragenerational distribution of income. The complications must be considered carefully in concrete applications. But they invalidate neither the possibility of structural aggregate demand problems in a mature economy nor the general principle of functional finance. Fiscal deficits and public debt should be judged on their implications for economic outcomes that we care about; intrinsically, they are neither good nor bad.

Dual economies and structural transformation

It is the low natural rate of growth that puts a damper on investment and generates a structural aggregate demand problem in mature economies. This problem does not arise in dual economies: rapid accumulation in the modern sector is desirable—the higher the accumulation rate the better—and high accumulation rates are associated with high shares of investment in income.

The one-sector analysis of functional finance in mature economies Mature economies, functional finance, and secular stagnation can be used to analyze a dual economy if it is assumed that the modern sector can draw on an infinitely elastic labor supply from an informal, low-productivity sector but that otherwise each of the two sectors is entirely self-contained.[7] With these assumptions, the equilibrium condition (5) still holds for the modern sector. Unlike the mature economy, however, the modern sector in a dual economy is not constrained by the growth rate of the labor force in efficiency units, and Eq. (2.5) describes a tradeoff between accumulation and current consumption. If g denotes the accumulation rate, the equation can be rewritten

$$g+\frac{C}{K}=\sigma-\gamma-\delta$$

High current accumulation comes at the expense of low current consumption but improves future incomes and employment in the modern sector, and one can debate how to balance these concerns. In a dual economy, however, there are no structural aggregate demand problems: the expansion of current consumption is not the only way to maintain high demand. On the contrary, contractionary policies may be desirable as a way to squeeze consumption and create space for high accumulation. This association of rapid growth with fiscal surpluses and low public debt comes with a caveat. Public investment in infrastructure, education, and health is crucial for successful development, complementing and crowding in private investment.[8] To the extent that rapid growth of the modern sector is associated with a large share of government investment in total investment, the implications for government deficits become ambiguous.

Demand policy has short-run dimensions, and stabilization policies can be vital for successful development. Shocks to modern sector demand are amplified by both multiplier and accelerator effects, and Harrodian

[7] A more satisfactory analysis needs to consider the interaction between the modern and informal sectors; for example, Razmi et al. (2012) and Skott (2021).

[8] Not all modern-sector activities are equally conducive to long-term economic growth, and industrial policy can also play a decisive role in promoting structural transformation.

instability is likely in the absence of stabilizing intervention.[9] Upward instability and overheating of the modern sector will be curbed eventually by capacity ceilings, but can cause serious damage in the form of inflation and/or balance of payments crises if the instability remains unchecked until these limits kick in. Downward instability meets no similar capacity floors, and stabilization policy may be necessary to prevent crises and long-term stagnation. Macroeconomic volatility, more generally, deters long-term private investment, and aggregate demand policy in a dual economy should aim to secure a stable macroeconomic environment with appropriate levels and growth rates of demand for the output of the modern sector. Recessions should be countered by expansionary measures but, equally important, overheating of the economy should be avoided.

Monetary policy in the form of inflation targeting has been the favored instrument of stabilization. This policy approach, however, poses significant dangers. To the extent that the use of interest rates to control inflation is successful, it may owe its success in large part to its effects on the real exchange rate. Exchange rate appreciation may bring down inflation, but overvalued exchange rates can do great damage: they hurt the international competitiveness of the modern (and overwhelmingly tradable) sector, put downward pressure on profitability and accumulation, and thereby sacrifice sectoral transformation and long-run growth. Large fluctuations in real exchange rates, more generally, impede the expansion of a modern sector, especially if the fluctuations turn into intermittent currency and balance of payments crises.[10]

Returning to the principle of functional finance, Lerner's original analysis considered the policy problems in mature economies with a well-defined position of full employment, and in these economies his two targets make sense. Many additional policy targets could be added, but aggregate demand policy arguably should focus primarily on employment and the balance between consumption and investment. Other policy instruments will be called upon for interventions that aim to address environmental problems, for instance, or reduce economic inequality.

[9] Ryoo and Skott (2017) analyze fiscal and monetary policy rules in an economy with Harrodian instability.

[10] Martins and Skott (2021) analyze the effects of inflation targeting in developing economies. The argument in this section has affinities with development theory, both new and old; for example, Ros (2013), Bresser-Pereira et al. (2015), Damill et al. (2016).

Lerner's targets need to be modified in a dual economy. Observing large amounts of hidden un- and underemployment, it may be tempting to recommend an expansion of aggregate demand. But underemployment in a dual economy is not primarily the result of insufficient aggregate demand. If capital represents a binding constraint, the expansion of aggregate demand and current consumption can generate a toxic blend of inflation and economic stagnation. Fiscal policies should not be guided by a full-employment target but by a target for the balance between capital accumulation and current consumption (Skott, 2021).

Importantly, the tradeoff between current consumption and the rate of growth in dual economies need not imply a reduction in the living standards of the poor. The resources for investment can come from policies that curb luxury consumption. It should be noted also that large parts of "consumption" are mis-labeled and should be considered investment. Education is an obvious example but health care, food, and housing for low-income families also contain significant elements of investment: healthier and better educated children can raise future labor productivity and profitability in the modern sector and improve the prospects for future growth. Needless to say, the political and economic power of the elites can present formidable obstacles to egalitarian policies. It is a dangerous illusion, however, to believe that egalitarian priorities and rapid growth can be achieved simultaneously without having to shift resources away from Mercedes cars, designer kitchens, and Guzzi handbags.

The analysis of dual economies in this section is at odds with many post-Keynesian growth models. The absence of labor constraints in these models is justified in applications to dual economies, but neo-Kaleckian versions of the models also ignore capital constraints and assume that a permanent increase in the share of consumption in income will raise the accumulation rate. This combination of long-run increases in the accumulation rate I/K and reductions in the saving rate S/Y is made possible by an increase in the utilization rate of capital. The output capital ratio is an endogenous variable in these models, and it is assumed that the long-run accumulation rate is very insensitive to persistent changes in the utilization rate of capital. This insensitivity is hard to square with goal-oriented behavior (Skott, 2012).[11] The models assume that, blinded by uncertainty and conventions, private firms

[11] The analysis in this paper has gone to the other extreme: it was assumed that the utilization rate must be at a uniquely defined desired rate in steady growth. This simplifying assumption can be relaxed, however, without affecting the qualitative results.

willingly keep investing at a constant rate, even if they have large amounts of excess capacity. As the flip side of this assumption, a positive shock to demand—a reduction in saving rates, for instance—generates a large demand-induced increase in the steady growth value of the utilization rate and allows long-run increases in both the accumulation rate and the share of consumption in income. These neo-Kaleckian predictions, however, are behaviorally implausible and at odds the empirical evidence: countries with low shares of saving and investment in output do not tend to have high rates of economic growth (e.g., Girardi and Pariboni, 2020).

Two cases: Japan and Brazil

The distinction between mature and dual economies and its policy implications can be illustrated by the experiences of Japan and Brazil.

Japan experienced 25 years of miracle growth as GDP per capita grew at an average annual rate of 8.2% between 1945 and 1970. The growth rate dropped to 3.6% between 1970 and 1990, and with average per capita growth of less than 1% between 1990 and 2019, Japan has become the poster case for secular stagnation. Interest rates have hit the zero lower bound, and public debt has climbed to more than 200% of GDP.

The Japanese economy was characterized by large amounts of hidden unemployment and underemployment until the late 1960s; Japan was a dual economy. Throughout this period, the labor supply to the modern sector was highly elastic, and there was a large potential for technological catch-up. As the experience of many developing economies demonstrates, these conditions do not ensure rapid growth. In the absence of state intervention—improvements in infrastructure and education along with successful industrial strategies—the Japanese economy could have followed a very different, slow-growth trajectory. But the elastic labor supply and the catch-up potential were important by permitting rapid growth. High growth rates, in turn, were associated with high investment demand which allowed the goods market to be in equilibrium, despite high saving rates.

Labor constraints began to appear around 1970, and by 1990 Japan was a world leader in many industries. Japan had become a mature economy. The growth rates of the previous period exceeded the post-1990 natural rate of growth, and a decline in the rate of growth was inevitable. But a combination of high saving rates and slow growth produced a structural aggregate problem (Nakatani and Skott, 2007).

With high saving rates, a low natural rate of growth and a reduced accumulation potential, Japan needed other sources of aggregate demand. The financial and real estate bubbles of the 1980s alleviated the incipient demand problems for a while, but when the bubbles burst, the public, and foreign sectors would have had to pick up the slack to maintain full employment. International political constraints excluded large and sustained trade surpluses, and domestic political constraints restrained fiscal expansion. The result was limping growth with persistent underperformance, weak labor markets, and deflationary tendencies.

The structural demand problems have been loosened, partly as a result of the rise in debt that has been allowed to take place. The fiscal expansion may have been weaker than it should have been, had the authorities followed a pure functional finance approach, but fiscal deficits and a large debt (corresponding to an increase in private wealth) have contributed to a decline in the saving rate; the household saving rate out of net disposable income has fallen from around 20% in the mid-1970s to about 2% after 2010.[12]

This broad story of Japanese growth and stagnation draws on both demand- and supply side elements. The fundamental change on the supply side was the transition from a dual to a mature economy. This transition and the associated decline in the share of investment in output led to structural demand-side problems. Looking ahead, China (and other fast-growing developing economies) will face a similar transition at some point.

The supply side appears in most accounts of Japanese stagnation, but typically in a very different way. The OECD Economic Surveys persistently push for "bold structural reforms" of the supply side while on the fiscal side the "top fiscal priority is reducing government debt" (OECD, 2015, p. 5). The fiscal priorities reappear in OECD (2019) which emphasizes how "fiscal sustainability requires a detailed consolidation plan" A plan of this kind becomes especially important, it is argued, because the government will miss its previous target of a primary surplus by 2020. The failure to reach this target "strengthens the case for an independent fiscal institution" (p. 22). There appears to be little or no recognition that weak aggregate demand may lie behind the failure to meet the earlier target and that economic performance would have suffered had the original plans for fiscal

[12] Rising debt is only one element behind this fall. Demographic changes and an aging population have also played an important role.

consolidation been carried out. The potential adverse demand effects of structural reforms that reduce age-related spending or increase inequality also go unnoticed.[13]

Like Japan, Brazil has experienced periods of rapid growth and periods of stagnation, most recently a deep and prolonged recession starting in 2014.

The Brazilian economy benefitted from the commodities boom which saw broad indices of commodity prices treble between 2002 and 2008 and then—following a blip immediately after the financial crisis—return to and fluctuate around the 2008 level until 2014.

The commodities boom relaxed the balance of payments constraint, and Brazilian GDP grew relatively fast at about 4% between 2003 and 2011. The growth was driven in large part by consumption which increased at an average rate of about 5%. Private consumption was boosted by an impressive reduction in inequality; the Gini coefficient fell from about 58% in 2002% to 52% in 2014. The real minimum wage increased by more than 5% a year between 2000 and 2014, and social transfers expanded significantly, partly as a result of the indexation of many programs to the minimum wage (Summa and Serrano, 2018). Policy intervention also contributed to a relaxation of credit constraints. Household debt increased from 10% of GDP in 2003 to more than about 25% by 2012; car sales more than trebled between 2002 and 2012; GDP from construction almost doubled between 2002 and 2012; and the ratio of employment in nontradables over tradables sector rose from about 1.15 in 2002 to more than 1.6 in 2015 (Garber et al., 2018).

Inflation was kept in check by an appreciation of the Real. Inflation, which had peaked at over 17% in 2003, declined rapidly between 2003 and 2007, as the exchange rate moved from 3.8 Reais to one US dollar in 2003 to 1.6 Reais to the dollar in 2008. From 2007, however, inflation started increasing again, rising from about 3% in 2007 to about 10% in 2014. The current account had moved into surplus in 2003—partly reflecting the rise in commodity prices and the benefits of a real depreciation of

[13] Demand-side explanations of Japanese economic stagnation have focused on inadequate fiscal and monetary policies in combination with the slowdown of investment following the bubble period in the late 1980s (Krugman, 1998). As far as they go, these explanations are in line with the argument in this paper. But until recently at least, there has been a tendency to view the aggregate demand problems as largely transitory implications of the bursting of the bubble, not as reflections of a structural, long run demand issue. This may be changing with the rediscovery of secular stagnation by Summers and others.

the Real between 2000 and 2003—but the surplus was short-lived. The current account returned to deficit in 2007, and the deficit widened in the following years.

By 2014 Brazil was already heading toward a recession when commodity prices dropped precipitously. A deep recession followed, ascendant right-wing movements are busily working to reverse the gains in income distribution, and as of 2019 output is still below its level in 2013.

This rough outline raises several questions. The large reductions of inequality were real achievements. But the distributional change would have become more sustainable and the economy would have been in a better state when commodity prices collapsed if the windfall gains from the commodity boom had been used to expand the formal sector. The relaxation of the balance of payments constraint could have allowed higher rates of accumulation as well as some increase in consumption, without running up deficits on the current account. This did not happen. The share of investment in GDP increased modestly from a trough of about 18.5% of GDP in 2002–05 to about 21% 2006–08, but residential investment made up an increasing proportion of total investment, and the overall investment share stayed below its levels in the mid-1990s and far below the levels in the 1970s. The profit share started to fall from 2004 (Martins and Rugitsky, 2018).

The sources of Brazil's stagnation are quite different from those that led to Japanese stagnation after 1990. The commodities boom gave Brazilian policy makers extra degrees of freedom, but in order to achieve ambitious and sustainable gains for the poor as well as an increase in accumulation, it would have been necessary to confront entrenched interests and cut luxury consumption. The failure to do this meant that accumulation and real progress in the structural transformation of the Brazilian economy were sacrificed in favor of short-term gains.

In short, fiscal and monetary policies should be judged on their implications for outcomes that we care about. But aggregate demand policies that work well in one economy may be disastrous in economies with a different supply side. In mature economies with structural aggregate demand problems, fiscal deficits and high public debt ratios are needed in order for consumption to fill the gap between full-employment output and the sum of investment and government consumption. The challenge in dual economies is quite different: structural transformation requires resources for the expansion of the modern sector as well as incentives for the expansion to take place.

References

Arestis, P., Sawyer, M., 2010. The return of fiscal policy. Journal of Post Keynesian Economics 32 (3), 327–346.

Ash, M., Basu, D., Dube, A., 2017. Public Debt and Growth: An Assessment of Key Findings on Causality and Thresholds. UMass Department of Economics WP 2017-10.

Bresser-Pereira, L.C., Oreiro, J.L., Marconi, N., 2015. Developmental Macroeconomics. Routledge, Abingdon.

Damill, M., Rapetti, M., Rozenwurcell, G. (Eds.), 2016. Macroeconomics and Development. Roberto Frenkel and the Economics of Latin America. Columbia University Press, New York.

Garber, G., Mian, A., Ponticelli, J., Sufi, A., 2018. Household Debt and Recession in Brazil. NBER WP 25170.

Girardi, D., Pariboni, R., 2020. Autonomous demand and the investment share. Review of Keynesian Economics 8 (3), 428–453.

Godley, W., Lavoie, M., 2007. Fiscal policy in a stock-flow consistent (SFC) model. Journal of Post Keynesian Economics 30 (1), 79–100.

Krugman, P., 1998. It's baaack: Japan's slump and the return of the liquidity trap. Brookings Papers on Economic Activity 29 (2), 137–206.

Lerner, A.P., 1943. Functional finance and the federal debt. Social Research 10 (1), 38–51.

Martins, G.K., Rugitsky, F., 2018. The Commodities Boom and the Profit Squeeze: Output and Profit Cycles in Brazil (1996–2016). FEA-USP Working Paper 2018–9.

Martins, G.K., Skott, P., 2021. Sources of inflation and the effects of balanced budgets and inflation targeting in developing economies Umass Amherst working paper 2020-08. Industrial and Corporate Change 30 (2), 409–444.

Nakatani, T., Skott, P., 2007. Japanese growth and stagnation: a Keynesian perspective. Structural Change and Economic Dynamics 18 (3), 306–332.

OECD, 2015. Economic Surveys – Japan April 2015. OECD.

OECD, 2019. Economic Surveys – Japan April 2019. OECD.

Razmi, A., Rapetti, M., Skott, P., 2012. The real exchange rate and economic development. Structural Change and Economic Dynamics 23, 151–169.

Reinhart, C.M., Rogoff, K.S., May 2010. Growth in a Time of Debt. American Economic Review Papers and Proceedings, 100, pp. 573–578.

Ros, J., 2013. Rethinking Economic Development, Growth and Institutions. Oxford University Press, Oxford.

Ryoo, S., Skott, P., 2013. Public debt and full employment in a stock-flow consistent model of a corporate economy. Journal of Post Keynesian Economics 35 (4), 511–527.

Ryoo, S., Skott, P., 2017. Fiscal and monetary policy rules in an unstable economy. Metroeconomica 68 (3), 500–548.

Schlicht, E., 2006. Public debt as private wealth: some equilibrium considerations. Metroeconomica 57 (4), 494–520.

Skott, P., 2012. Theoretical and empirical shortcomings of the Kaleckian investment function. Metroeconomica 63, 109–138.

Skott, P., 2021. Fiscal policy and structural transformation in developing economies. Structural Change and Economic Dynamics 56, 129–140.

Skott, P., Ryoo, S., 2014. Public debt in an OLG model with imperfect competition: long-run effects of austerity programs and changes in the growth rate. BE Press Journal of Macroeconomics 14 (1), 533–552.

Skott, P., Ryoo, S., 2017. Functional finance and intergenerational distribution in a Keynesian OLG model. Review of Keynesian Economics 5 (1), 112–134.

Summa, R., Serrano, F., 2018. Distribution and conflict inflation in Brazil under inflation targeting, 1999–2014. Review of Radical Political Economics 50 (2), 349–369.

Wray, R., 2012. Modern Money Theory: A Primer on Macroeconomics for Sovereign Monetary Systems. Palgrave, New York.

CHAPTER THREE

The secular stagnation of productivity growth

Servaas Storm
Delft University of Technology, Delft, Netherlands

The 'slow-moving turtle'

The anemic economic recovery after the Great Financial Crisis of 2008–09 has revived interest in the hypothesis of secular stagnation, which was first proposed in December 1938 by Alvin E. Hansen in a foreboding Presidential Address to the *American Economic Association*. Hansen's original idea was that the feeble recovery from the Great Depression could become a permanent state for the U.S. economy, because, as he argued, "sick recoveries [....] die in their infancy and depressions [....] feed on themselves and leave a hard and seemingly immovable core of unemployment" (Hansen, 1939, p. 4). While the U.S. economy was facing a crisis of woefully inadequate aggregate demand, Hansen's (1939, p. 11) main concern was the lack of sufficiently profitable investment outlets: "It is my growing conviction that the combined effect of the decline in population growth, together with the failure of any really important innovations of a magnitude sufficient to absorb large capital outlays, weighs very heavily as an explanation for the failure of the recent recovery to reach full employment." Hansen warned that without a more rapid advance of technology than in the past, the U.S. economy would be unable to find private investment opportunities adequate to maintain full employment. However, Hansen's worries soon became obsolete as the post-World War II economic order formed itself—and a much more equal income distribution, an expanding middle class and suburbanization, and Cold-War-era "military Keynesianism" turned his under-consumptionist fears irrelevant. The U.S., and other OECD countries, returned to strong economic growth, as (public and private) investment in research and development rose sharply, also as part of Cold War military spending, spurring decades of technological progress and ending the dearth of profitable investment outlets. Hansen's secular stagnation thesis failed to take hold.

Handbook of Economic Stagnation
ISBN: 978-0-12-815898-2
https://doi.org/10.1016/B978-0-12-815898-2.00013-6

But now the wheel of history has turned: Hansen's thesis has made a come-back in (global) macroeconomic policy discourse, chiefly because the "Great Recession," which followed the Great Financial Crisis of 2008, looked so uncomfortably familiar and similar to what happened during the 1930s. Lawrence Summers (2013, 2015) revived Hansen's original idea for the U.S. economy, but Summers did this with a distinctly pre-Keynesian twist. In Summers analysis, an aging population, heightened income inequality and a large inflow of foreign finance raised savings and created an excess supply in the market for loanable funds, due to which the equilibrium ("natural") rate of interest was pushed down to its zero-lower bound. The outcome is, according to Summers, a structural demand deficiency—and stagnation. However, unlike in Hansen's time, when *actual* output was much lower than *potential* output, this time around the output gap is surprisingly narrow. Indeed, virtually all empirical studies of both *actual* and *potential* growth in the OECD countries show a remarkable slowdown, which started well before the Great Financial Crisis of 2008–09 (Fernald, 2014; Ollivaud and Turner, 2014; Storm, 2017; Kiefer et al., 2020; Fontanari et al., 2020). For the majority of observers, it must have been declining *potential* growth which forced down the rate of *actual* (demand-determined) growth, reflecting deep-rooted theoretical beliefs that while demand does affect *actual* growth, it does not and cannot influence *potential* growth, which is completely determined by "demography" (labor force growth) and "technology" (productivity growth).

Hence, in its modern incarnation, secular stagnation is not so much a matter of a deficiency of demand (as was Hansen's view), but a symptom of deep structural problems on the supply side of the economy (Fernald, 2014, 2016; Furman, 2015; Gordon, 2014, 2015). An aging labor force and demographic stagnation constitute a first supply side problem (Aaronson et al., 2014). But the real problem is the alarming steady decline in total-factor-productivity (TFP) growth, the main component of potential output growth. Diminishing TFP growth is taken to reflect a deep-rooted technological torpor, which lowers the returns on investment and hence pushes desired investment spending down too far. This, in turn, is argued to have lowered the growth rates of both potential and actual GDP (Fernald, 2016; Gordon, 2015). Importantly, the stagnation of potential output growth cannot be attributed to a mismeasurement of productivity growth (Syverson, 2016). Thus, the conclusion must be that the U.S. is "riding on a slow-moving turtle," and "there is little politicians can do about it," as Robert Gordon (2015, p. 191) expressed it.

This chapter, which focuses on the secular stagnation of productivity growth, wishes to cast doubt on the view that the secular stagnation of U.S. growth must be attributed to supply side factors.[1] The chapter argues instead that the slowdown in productivity growth reflects a demand (management) crisis, with the "under-consumption" driven by stagnating real wages, rising inequality, and greater job insecurity and polarization. After defining "potential growth" in Section Potential output growth and productivity growth, we scrutinize its main component (total-factor-productivity or TFP growth) using growth accounting schemes. We show that the secular decline in TFP growth in the U.S. is driven almost completely by the long-term slowdown of labor productivity growth and/or the secular decline in real wage growth. In the supply side narrative, fading labor productivity is supposed to have forced down real wage growth. We present alternative, demand-driven, explanations of the productivity growth slowdown, and argue, based on empirical evidence, that the secular stagnation of productivity growth in the U.S. is almost completely caused by demand-side factors, including the secular decrease in real wage growth. The recognition that demand drives productivity growth and potential growth finally forces us to deeply rethink concepts of "steady-inflation potential growth" and "output gaps," which are commonly used as anchors for monetary and fiscal policy-making (see Fontanari et al., 2020; Taylor et al., 2019).

Potential output growth and productivity growth

We start by defining the growth of "potential output" x_P in terms of TFP growth. To do so, let ℓ_P be potential labor supply (defined in terms of hours of work) and let $\lambda_P = x_P/\ell_P$ denote the level of potential labor productivity per hour of work. By definition, we have:

$$x_P = \lambda_P \times \ell_P \tag{3.1}$$

If we logarithmically differentiate Eq. (3.1) and write in difference-form, we get the following expression in growth rates:

$$\widehat{x}_P = \widehat{\lambda}_P + \widehat{\ell}_P \tag{3.2}$$

[1] This paper is based in part on Storm (2017) and presents a structurally revised, updated, and shortened formulation of the main arguments made therein.

where a circumflex indicates an instantaneous growth rate (or a difference in natural logarithms). Potential output growth depends on potential labor productivity growth ("technology") and the growth of potential labor supply ("demography"). Empirical estimates of U.S. labor force growth during 1948–2015 appear in Table 3.1. However, let us concentrate on productivity growth and assume that $\widehat{\ell}_P = 0$. Next, to explain $\widehat{\lambda}_P$ and following standard growth-accounting practice, we consider this (constant-returns-to-scale) Cobb–Douglas production function:

$$x = A\ell^{\phi}K^{1-\phi} \tag{3.3}$$

where x is output (or real value added at factor cost); ℓ is the *actual* number of hours worked; K is the value of the capital stock (expressed in constant dollars); and A is a scale factor. Exponent ϕ is typically assumed to correspond to the observed labor share in income. If one divides both sides of Eq. (3.3) by x^{ϕ} and then solves for (x/ℓ), or productivity per hour of work, one obtains (see Jones, 2016):

$$\lambda = A^{1/\phi}\kappa^{-(1-\phi)/\phi} \tag{3.4}$$

where $\lambda = x/\ell$ is actual labor productivity per hour of work and $\kappa = x/K$ is capital productivity. Writing Eq. (3.4) in growth rates gives this expression for labor productivity growth:

$$\widehat{\lambda} = \left(\frac{1}{\phi}\right)\widehat{A} - \left(\frac{1-\phi}{\phi}\right)\widehat{\kappa} \tag{3.5}$$

where $\widehat{A}$ stands for TFP growth. In the steady state of a neoclassical growth model, the capital-output ratio must be constant, which means capital productivity is constant ($\widehat{\kappa} = 0$). Eq. (3.5) then becomes:

$$\widehat{\lambda}_P = \left(\frac{1}{\phi}\right) \times \widehat{A} \tag{3.5$'$}$$

Potential labor productivity growth depends completely on TFP growth, which is here assumed to be exogenous. When we next substitute Eq. (3.5′) into Eq. (3.2), we obtain:

$$\widehat{x}_p = \left(\frac{1}{\phi}\right) \times \widehat{A} \tag{3.2$'$}$$

Table 3.1 Alternative measures of aggregate TFP growth in the U.S., 1948–2015 (average annual growth rate in per cent).

	"Solow residual" Eq. (3.6′)	Weighted factor productivity growth Eq. (3.7)	Total factor payment growth Eq. (3.10)	Potential output growth Eq. (3.2′)	Labor force growth	Potential output growth (*d*) + (*e*)
	(*a*)	(*b*)	(*c*)	(*d*)	(*e*)	(*f*)
1948–1972	1.60	1.57 (88%)	1.57	2.68	1.17	3.85
1972–1995	1.06	1.04 (80%)	1.04	1.75	1.35	3.10
1995–2008	1.35	1.34 (85%)	1.34	2.28	0.77	3.05
2008–2015	0.73	0.72 (73%)	0.73	1.26	0.21	1.47
1948–2015	1.27	1.25 (84%)	1.26	2.14	1.15	3.29

Notes: The numbers in parentheses in column (*b*) give the percentages of weighted factor-productivity growth explained by labor productivity growth as per Eq. (3.7).
Source: Reproduced from Storm (2017); estimates in columns (*a*) to (*d*) are based on *Bureau of Economic Analysis* data. Estimates of labor force growth are derived as the difference between column (*f*) and (*d*). Estimates of potential output growth in column (*f*) are based on data on Real Potential Gross Domestic Product by the U.S. Congressional Budget Office (Available at: https://alfred.stlouisfed.org).

This way, potential output growth can be shown to depends on exogenous TFP growth—which is today's "decided opinion" (Fernald, 2014, 2016; Furman, 2015; Gordon, 2015).

Estimates of potential output growth for the U.S. economy (1948–2015), exclusively based on TFP growth as in Eq. (3.2′), appear in column (*d*) of Table 3.1. Estimates of potential growth by the U.S. Congressional Budget Office, which include TFP growth and labor force growth, appear in column (*e*). It can be seen that potential growth of the U.S. economy was 3.85% per year during the period 1948–72, which then slowed down to 3.1% per year during 1972%–95%, and to 3.05% per year during the years of the Great Moderation (1995–2008). After 2008, potential growth dropped by 1% point to 1.5% per year. Two-thirds of the decline in potential growth between 1948–72 and 2008–15 must be attributed to the decline in TFP growth — in line with Eq. (3.2′). What then is this thing called "TFP growth"? And is it a purely supply side factor?

Total-factor-productivity (TFP) growth: solow variations

Ever since Robert Solow (1957) began cranking the numbers more than 6 decades ago, TFP growth has been treated as a nonobservable variable that can only be quantified as an "unexplained residual" in a growth-accounting scheme (Jones, 2016; Furman, 2015). Specifically, if we express production function Eq. (3.3) in growth rates, we get:

$$\widehat{x} = \widehat{A} + \phi\widehat{\ell} + (1-\phi)\widehat{K}, \tag{3.6}$$

from which TFP growth $\left(\widehat{A}\right)$ can be determined as a *residual*:

$$\widehat{A} = \widehat{x} - \phi\widehat{\ell} - (1-\phi)\widehat{K}. \tag{3.6′}$$

Eq. (3.6′) defines TFP growth as the unexplained "Solow residual." Estimates of the "Solow residual" for the U.S. economy (1948–2015) appear in column (*a*) of Table 3.1. Aggregate TFP growth in the U.S. economy declined—from 1.6% per year during the 1950 and 1960s to 0.73% per annum during 2008–15. And future TFP growth in the U.S. looks set to get worse: Fernald's (2016) modal forecast for U.S. TFP growth during 2016–2023/26 is in the range of 0.41%–0.55% per year.

Textbook convention interprets TFP growth $(\widehat{A})$ as an indicator of Hicks-neutral disembodied technological progress. TFP growth is a key diagnostic for policy-making, because it "tells us how efficiently and intensely inputs are used" and "this is easily mapped to innovation of the technological and managerial sorts" (Furman, 2015, p. 2). To Furman (2015) TFP growth measures "pure innovation." Waning TFP growth must therefore mean that the cumulative growth effects of the latest innovations (in microprocessors & computer chips, artificial intelligence (AI), robotics, materials, and biotechnology) is weaker than those of past technologies (Gordon, 2015; Fernald, 2014; IMF, 2015; Jones, 2016). This is surprising, perhaps, and it reminds one of Robert Solow's well-known aphorism that "you can see the computer age everywhere but in the productivity statistics." Most observers agree that waning TFP growth must be therefore be due to the fact that institutional rigidities in and regulation of labor and product markets limit the ability of firms and markets to restructure and reorganize to benefit from ICT, robotics and AI (Fernald, 2016). If so, remedying this situation will require a supply side policy agenda—which should include, following Furman (2015), further labor market deregulation, business tax reforms and more public investment in infrastructure, education, and RD&D (Gordon, 2015; Fernald, 2016). However, even if we accept textbook convention and treat TFP growth as an indicator of Hicks-neutral disembodied technological progress, Eq. (3.6′) lacks any deeper analytical insight into the structural determinants of such technological progress. Moses Abramovitz (1956) called the Solow residual a "measure of our ignorance," and while the search for dependable and robust determinants of TFP growth has consumed the research efforts of at least two generations of (growth-accounting) economists, Abramovitz's conclusion still rings true: "a rigorous conceptual understanding of that [*residual*] continues to elude economists even today," is Furman's (2015, p. 2) anamnesis. This is problematic, because TFP growth is supposed to be the main determinant of potential output growth. Fortunately, TFP growth is less of a mystery than Furman and others think, because it can be measured directly in two different ways—using real observable data.

The first approach to direct measurement of TFP growth is as follows. Using definitions $\widehat{\lambda} = \widehat{x} - \widehat{\ell}$ and $\widehat{\kappa} = \widehat{x} - \widehat{K}$, TFP growth in Eq. (3.6′) can be rewritten as:

$$\widehat{A} = \phi\widehat{\lambda} + (1 - \phi)\widehat{\kappa} \tag{3.7}$$

Eq. (3.7) is rather unsurprising, as it defines $\widehat{A}$ as the weighted average of the growth rates of labor and capital productivities. Estimates of TFP growth for the U.S. (1948–2015), based on Eq. (3.7), appear in column (*b*) of Table 3.1. It is noteworthy that labor productivity growth "explains" around 85% of TFP growth and is a quantitatively far more important determinant of TFP growth than capital productivity growth. This finding is consistent with one of Nicholas Kaldor's (1961) stylized facts on growth, namely that the capital-output ratio does not exhibit a systematic trend in the long run—which means $\widehat{\kappa} = 0$. If Kaldor's stylized fact holds true, Eq. (3.7) simplifies to: $\widehat{A} = \phi\widehat{\lambda}$. Note that TFP growth is now no longer exogenous (unlike in the "Solow residual" approach), as it is causally determined by labor productivity growth. Crucially, the direction of causality in Eq. (3.7) is the opposite of that in Eq. (3.5′). Indeed, if labor productivity growth is the only structural determinant of TFP growth in the long run, it follows not just that $\widehat{x}_P = \widehat{\lambda}_P = \left(\frac{1}{\phi}\right) \times \widehat{A} = \widehat{\lambda}$, but also that TFP growth adds no additional analytical insight and can be dropped from the economist's growth-accounting toolkit without consequence.

The second approach is the so-called dual approach (Simon and Levy, 1963; Jorgenson and Griliches, 1967; Shaikh, 1974; Barro, 1999; Rada and Taylor, 2006; Felipe and McCombie, 2012). It starts off from the National Income and Product Accounts (NIPA) accounting identity that real GDP at factor cost is the sum of wage income and capital income:

$$x = w\ell + rK \tag{3.8}$$

where w is the real wage rate per hour of work and r is the real profit rate on the capital stock. This condition must hold if all the GDP is attributed to one of the factors. Dividing Eq. (3.8) by x, we get: $1 = \left(\frac{w\ell}{x}\right) + \left(\frac{rK}{x}\right) = \phi + (1-\phi)$, where ϕ is the observed labor share in income at any time and $(1-\phi)$ is the observed capital share. Eq. (3.8) can be written in terms of growth rates as follows:

$$\widehat{x} = [\phi\widehat{w} + (1-\phi)\widehat{r}] + \phi\widehat{\ell} + (1-\phi)\widehat{K}\frac{1}{2} \tag{3.9}$$

Eq. (3.9) remains an accounting identity, because its derivation uses only the NIPA condition $x = wL + rK$. We must note that Eq. (3.9) holds true even if the aggregate production function does not exist (Felipe and McCombie, 2012). Eq. (3.9) is functionally equivalent to Eq. (3.6)—but the latter must be read as a wrongly specified representation of the former

(Felipe and McCombie, 2012). This isomorphism between production function Eq. (3.6) and NIPA value-added accounting identity Eq. (3.9) does not permit us to make any direct inference about "aggregate technological progress." "Solow's measure of technical change," as Shaikh (1974, p. 118) already noted, "is merely a weighted average of the growth rates of the wage *w* and rate of profit *r*." Hence, the aggregate production function, as Shaikh concludes, is based on "a law of algebra, not a law of production." Given this isomorphism, statistically estimating Eq. (3.3) means that one is estimating an identity. This explains why the empirical fit (measured by $\overline{R}^2$) is generally exceptionally good for production functions (Felipe and McCombie, 2012).

Empirically, the only valid interpretation of TFP growth is, therefore, in terms of "total-factor-payment growth":

$$\widehat{A} = \phi\widehat{w} + (1-\phi)\widehat{r} \tag{3.10}$$

Estimates of TFP growth for the U.S. (1948–2015), based on Eq. (3.10), appear in column (*c*) of Table 3.1. Measured TFP growth is declining over time, and based on Eq. (3.10) this reflects a secular decline in the growth rates of real wages and real profits—as is shown in Table 3.2. Average annual real wage growth in the U.S. declined from 2.68% during 1948%–72% to 0.58% during 2008–15 and this lowered annual TFP growth by 1.3 percentage points (using the values for ϕ given in Table 3.2). The secular decline in real wage growth is, in other words, another key factor playing a role in the fading of TFP growth and potential output growth. This inference is confirmed by the econometric analysis by Kiefer et al. (2020),

Table 3.2 Distributional shifts associated with aggregate U.S. TFP growth, 1948–2015.

	ϕ	$\widehat{w}$	$\widehat{\lambda}$	$\phi(\widehat{w}-\widehat{\lambda})$	$1-\phi$	$\widehat{r}$	$\widehat{\kappa}$	$(1-\phi)(\widehat{r}-\widehat{\kappa})$
	(1)	(2)	(3)	(4)	(5)	(6)	(7)	(8)
1948–1972	0.60	2.68	2.32	0.21	0.40	−0.06	0.46	−0.21
1972–1995	0.60	1.15	1.38	−0.14	0.40	0.88	0.52	0.14
1995–2008	0.59	1.92	1.92	0.00	0.41	0.49	0.49	0.00
2008–2015	0.57	0.58	0.91	−0.20	0.43	0.93	0.46	0.20
1948–2015	0.60	1.80	1.78	0.01	0.40	0.46	0.49	−0.01

Notes: ϕ = the period-average labor income share; $\widehat{w}$ = average annual real wage growth (per hour); $\widehat{\lambda}$ = average annual hourly labor productivity growth; $\widehat{r}$ = average annual real profit rate growth; $\widehat{\kappa}$ = average annual capital productivity growth; $(\widehat{w}-\widehat{\lambda})$ = average annual (real) wage share growth; and $(\widehat{r}-\widehat{\kappa})$ = average annual (real) profit share growth.
Source: Reproduced from Storm (2017).

who find that the secular stagnation of *potential* growth of the U.S. economy during 1948–2016 is closely associated with the long-term decline in the wage share.

However, as a matter of accounting, the "primal" estimate of TFP growth in Eq. (3.7) must equal the "dual" estimate based on the share-weighted growth of factor prices in Eq. (3.10)—and it must also equal the "Solow residual" of Eq. (3.6′). Indeed, the estimated TFP growth rates are the same across definitions (see Table 3.1)—and in all cases, the evidence points to a secular stagnation of productivity growth and hence of *potential* growth. The neoclassical *intuition* for the dual of Eq. (3.10) is, as Barro (1999) explains, that rising factor prices can be sustained only if factor productivities in Eq. (3.7) are increasing in tandem. In the neoclassical steady state, and assuming "perfect competition" in product and factor markets, real wage (profit) growth *must* converge to labor (capital) productivity growth, or $\widehat{w} = \widehat{\lambda}$ and $\widehat{r} = \widehat{\kappa}$. In the hypothetical case of a "perfectly competitive" economy, the primal and dual estimates must fully coincide. However, there is nothing in the NIPA accounting to ensure that these conditions $\left(\widehat{w} = \widehat{\lambda} \text{ and } \widehat{r} = \widehat{\kappa}\right)$ do hold—empirically, we find that $\widehat{w} \neq \widehat{\lambda}$ and $\widehat{r} \neq \widehat{\kappa}$ (see the historical evidence for the U.S. in Table 3.2), and hence Eqs. (3.7) and (3.10) do not coincide (Storm, 2017). The most we can infer from the above is this. Subtracting Eq. (3.7) from Eq. (3.10), we get:

$$\phi\left(\widehat{w} - \widehat{\lambda}\right) + (1 - \phi)(\widehat{r} - \widehat{\kappa}) = 0 \tag{3.11}$$

which is, as is pointed out by Rada and Taylor (2006, p. 488), "a cost-side restriction on observed growth rates of average productivities and factor payments." Eq. (10.11) states that, for any given rate of TFP growth, the weighted sum of wage share growth $\left(\widehat{w} - \widehat{\lambda}\right)$ and profit share growth $(\widehat{r} - \widehat{\kappa})$ must be zero—which underscores the zero-sum distributive conflict between workers and profit-recipients underlying TFP growth.

Let me summarize the discussion so far. Using simple growth accounting schemes, we have identified three separate accounts of the secular stagnation of potential output growth:

- a first narrative in which the declining "Solow residual" signals a lack of innovation and general technological *malaise* on the supply side of the economy;
- a second explanation centered on the slowdown of (especially) labor productivity growth;

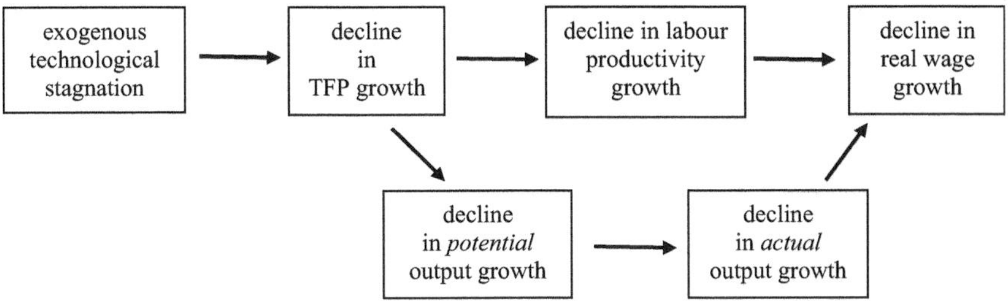

Figure 3.1 The economics of secular stagnation: the supply side view. *Source: Constructed by the author.*

- and a third account centered on stagnating real wage growth as a factor playing the most prominent role in declining TFP growth.

How can these three explanations be aligned into one single, consistent explanation? The dominant view, illustrated in Fig. 3.1, is that the technological torpor captured by the exogenous decline in TFP growth $(\widehat{A})$ leads to lower labor productivity growth $(\widehat{\lambda})$, as in Eq. (3.5′), which in turn forces down real wage growth. That is, in line with the marginal productivity theory of income distribution, neoclassical "intuition" holds that real wage growth "follows" exogenous productivity growth, because profit-maximizing firms will hire workers up until the point at which the marginal productivity of the final worker hired is equal to the real wage rate (Barro, 1999; Jones, 2016). There is, in this view, nothing surprising about the cooccurrence of a shrinking "Solow residual," declining labor productivity growth and decreasing real wage growth, as the technological stagnation forces profit-maximizing firms to lower their real wage growth offer. In this view, the secular stagnation of productivity growth exclusively has supply side origins. This is the decided opinion today. But, as John Stuart Mill observed long ago, "the fatal tendency of mankind to leave off thinking about a thing when it is no longer doubtful, is the cause of half their errors" and Mill appositely warned about the "deep slumber of a decided opinion."

Bringing demand in from the cold

The "supply-side intuition" does not allow for any influence of demand factors on the secular decline in productivity growth and blames the decline in potential growth on the slowdown of exogenous technological progress. However, the problem with this simple "intuition" is that it is wrong. There are sound theoretical reasons, and there is robust empirical evidence, to blame (a substantial part of) the long-run decline in productivity growth on stalling demand growth (Storm, 2017; Girardi et al., 2020; Fontanari et al., 2020). This goes against a deep-rooted theoretical belief system which maintains that long-run trend growth, which is argued to be determined by the supply side factors "technology" and "demography," can be completely separated from short-run fluctuations of actual growth around this trend, which are held to be due to changes in demand. It is this belief system—that "Keynes" holds only for the short run, whereas the inexorable supply side factors "demography" and "technology" govern the long-run, and on which macroeconomics has built its notions of "potential output" and "output gaps," which are widely employed to anchor macroeconomic, and especially monetary, policy (Fatás, 2019)—which has to be radically rethought (Girardi et al., 2020; Fontanari et al., 2020).

A first theoretical channel through which a shortage of demand affects labor productivity growth is through a slower accumulation of capital. To see this, consider Eq. (3.3). If we divide both sides of the equation by total hours worked (ℓ), rearrange and express in growth rates, we obtain this expression for $\widehat{\lambda}$:

$$\widehat{\lambda} = \widehat{A} + (1 - \phi)\left(\widehat{K} - \widehat{\ell}\right) \tag{3.12}$$

A decline in capital-intensity growth $\left(\widehat{K} - \widehat{\ell}\right)$ reduces labor productivity growth. Capital intensity growth in the U.S. decreased from 1.86% per annum during the 1950 and 1960s to 0.86% per year during 1972–95 and further to 0.45% during 2008–15 (Table 3.3). Using Eq. (3.12), we find that 60 percent of the drop in U.S. labor productivity growth from 2.32% per year during 1948%—–72% to 0.91% per year during 2008–15 must be attributed to the drop in U.S. capital intensity growth.

Capital stock growth $\widehat{K}$ depends on business investment—and in the New Keynesian account of Summers (2015), business investment depends on the rate of interest or the cost of capital. With higher savings (due to aging and a supposed global savings glut), the interest rate came down in the market for loanable funds, which in turn should have raised investment. But once the interest rate got stuck at the zero-lower bound, excess savings could no longer be channeled into higher investment—and stagnation was the outcome. The problems with Summers' argument are that (i) U.S. business investment is not very sensitive to changes in the cost of capital, but overwhelmingly depends on (expected) demand; and (ii) the market for loanable funds does not exist, as money-creating commercial banks can and do originate credit to finance investment irrespective of whether they have the savings deposits beforehand.

Table 3.3 TFP growth, capital deepening, and utilization, 1948–2015 (average annual growth rates in percent).

Contribution of	1948–72	1972–95	1995–2008	2008–15	1948–2015
Capital deepening	1.10	0.52	0.84	0.25	0.77
Capacity utilization	0.48	0.53	0.50	0.47	0.50
TFP growth	1.58	1.05	1.34	0.72	1.26
Memo items					
- Solow residual	1.60	1.06	1.35	0.73	1.27
- Capital-intensity growth	1.86	0.86	1.43	0.45	1.29

Note: Table 3.3 is based on Eq. (3.14). In Eq. (3.15), TFP growth is a function of the ratio of gross domestic investment to GDP. The OLS regression result for 1948–2015 is.
TFP growth = −3.42 + 0.20 (Investment/GDP) + 1.88 D2010. $\overline{R}^2 = 0.09$; $n = 68$.
(2.50)** (3.32)*** (8.02)***.
Source: Reproduced from Storm (2017).

In reality, business investment is overwhelmingly dependent on (expected) aggregate demand and (expected) profitability (Cynamon and Fazzari, 2017). Recent econometric findings on U.S. business investment (during 1983Q4 and 2016Q4) by IMF economists Kopp et al. (2019, p. 4) confirm this conclusion. The authors write that there "appears to be little unexplained component of business investment beyond the expected demand effect. Other factors, such as reductions in the cost of capital, thus appear to have played a relatively minor role." Accordingly, a structural decline in demand growth depresses labor productivity growth—through dithering business investment and a decline in capital deepening, a relationship known in the literature as the Kaldor-Verdoorn relation (Storm and Naastepad, 2012). As a result, TFP growth must decline as well (via Eq. 3.7), and potential output growth is forced down—an empirically plausible story, but one which is fundamentally at odds with "decided opinion."

We can uncover the same theoretical channel, through which a demand shortage contributed to the secular stagnation of *potential* growth, in one more way. Let us assume that $\chi = 1/\kappa$ is the constant capital-to-potential-output ratio. We define *potential* output as $x^* = K/\chi$ and capacity utilization as $u = x/x^*$. It then follows that *actual* output $x = uK/\chi$. Writing in (instantaneous) growth rates we get:

$$\widehat{x} = \widehat{u} + \widehat{K} \tag{3.13}$$

Actual output growth in Eq. (3.13) depends on the growth of the capital stock (which reflects potential growth) and the growth of capacity utilization which mirrors cyclical demand factors which may cause actual growth to deviate from potential growth. Combining Eqs. (3.13) and (3.6) and rearranging, TFP growth becomes:

$$\widehat{A} = \widehat{u} + \phi(\widehat{K} - \widehat{\ell}) \tag{3.14}$$

The key diagnostic "TFP growth" now directly depends on capital deepening and the growth of utilization. Eq. (3.14) could be read as a variant of the AK-model of endogenous growth, since TFP growth rises with capital stock growth, but, unlike in new growth theory, here we do not need to invoke microeconomic (knowledge) externalities to justify it, but only have to assume that χ is constant. Table 3.3 presents evidence on Eq. (3.14) for the U.S. economy (1948–2015). The contribution to TFP growth of capital deepening declined from 1.1% per year during 1948%–72% to 0.84%% per year during 1995–2008—a decline of 0.26 percentage points which fully explains the fall in TFP growth from 1.6% per year in the first period to 1.35% per annum during the second period. Likewise, the decline in TFP growth by 0.62 percentage points between 1995–2008 and 2008–15 is almost completely due to declining capital-intensity growth, which in turn is caused by a sharp, crisis-induced, drop in the investment-GDP ratio (see the note to Table 3.3; Ollivaud et al., 2016; Storm, 2017; Kopp et al., 2019).

If we next define $i = \Delta K/x$ as the investment-GDP ratio, then it follows that.

$i = \frac{\Delta K}{K} \times \frac{K}{x^*} \times \frac{x^*}{x} = \widehat{K}\, \chi\, u^{-1}$. This gives us the following expression for $\widehat{K}$:

$$\widehat{K} = \frac{u \times i}{\chi} \tag{3.15}$$

A higher investment-to-GDP ratio leads to faster capital stock growth—at constant capacity utilization. Since empirically investment is usually completely dominated by "accelerator effects" operating through aggregate demand (Kopp et al., 2019), it follows from Eqs. (3.14) and (3.15) that a structural decline in demand growth depresses TFP growth—through stagnating business investment, a decline in capital deepening and/or declining capacity utilization. As a result, the growth rate of potential output must be low—this causal chain is illustrated in Fig. 3.2. Crucially, once the demand deficiency has lowered potential output growth, this means a low "speed

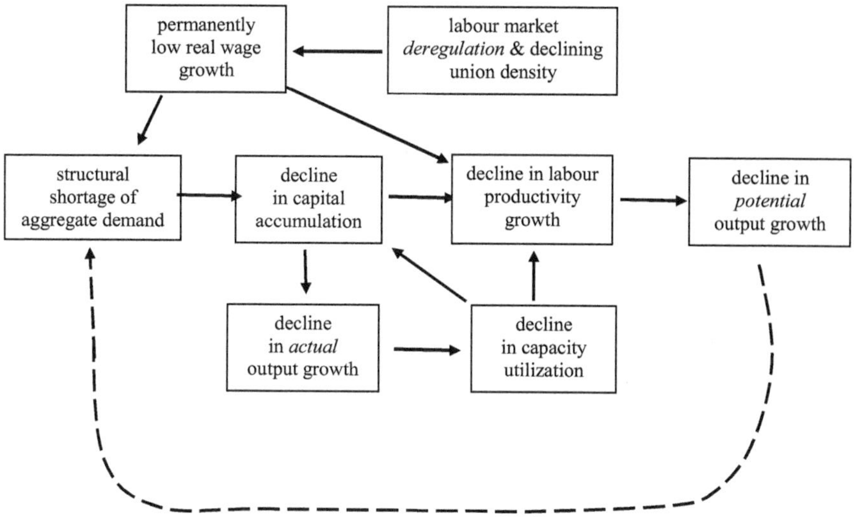

Figure 3.2 The economics of secular stagnation: the demand-side view. *Source: Constructed by the author.*

limit" for *actual* growth, as inflation-adverse monetary policymakers, convinced that low TFP growth is due to a technological *malaise*, will keep actual growth close to sluggish potential growth. This is illustrated in Fig. 3.2 by the dashed arrow from "potential output growth" to a "structural shortage of aggregate demand": because the "observed" output gap is small (which makes the risk of inflation look relatively large), monetary policy authorities will be inclined to step on the brakes and raise interest rates in response to a revival of actual growth—nipping the recovery in the bud and creating a "sick recovery" which "dies in its infancy." Stagnation, while being avoidable because *potential* growth can be raised by higher investment and demand, becomes a selffulfilling process (Storm, 2017; Fontanari et al., 2020).

D2010 is a dummy for the year 2010. The decline in the U.S. investment-GDP ratio from 23.9% on average per year during 1995%—2008% to 20.7% per year during 2008—15 "explains" more than 80% of the post-2008 decline in TFP growth in the U.S. (Ollivaud et al. (2016) present similar findings for the OECD). The same holds true in the long run. The slowdown of capital accumulation from 24.4% of GDP on average per year during 1948%—72% to 22.8% of GDP on average per year during 1995—2015 is found to "explain" more than 60% of the long-run decline in U.S. TFP growth.

Wage growth as a determinant of productivity growth

In the supply side explanation of secular stagnation (of Fig. 3.1), productivity growth is treated as an exogenous variable, and if and when it declines, real wage growth is forced down—because profit-maximizing firms will not allow unit labor costs to increase. What is neglected in this narrative, however, is that causality may run in the opposite direction as well: indeed, real wage growth is found to be a major *determinant* of productivity growth (Gordon, 1987, 2015; Foley and Michl, 1999; Marquetti, 2004; Basu, 2010; Storm and Naastepad, 2012). Theoretically, the influence of real wage growth on labor productivity growth has been variously explained in terms of "induced technical change" (Hicks, 1932; Funk, 2002; Brugger and Gehrke, 2017), "Marx-biased technical change" (Foley and Michl, 1999; Basu, 2010), or "directed technical change" (Acemoglu, 2002)—but the key mechanism is this: rising real wages, as in the U.S. economy during the period 1948–72 (Table 3.2), provide an incentive for firms to invest in *labor-saving* machinery and productivity growth surges as a result; but when wage growth is low, as in the U.S. during 1972–2015 (Table 3.2), businesses have little incentive to invest in the modernization of their capital stock and productivity growth falters.

Seen this way, labor productivity growth is *endogenous* and (at least partly) determined by real wage growth. If so, then the secular stagnation of productivity growth in the U.S. economy must be attributed at least partly to the long-term decline in the growth rate of U.S. hourly real wages. This is illustrated in the mnemonic of Fig. 3.2 by the arrow from "permanently low real wage growth" to "decline in labor productivity growth." The decline in real wage growth in turn is strongly associated with the post-1980 reorientation in macroeconomic policy, away from full employment and toward low and stable inflation, which paved the way for labor market deregulation, a scaling down of social protection, a lowering of the reservation wage of workers, and a general weakening of the wage bargaining power of unions (Storm and Naastepad, 2012). The recent rise in persons "working in alternative work arrangements" in the U.S. (Katz and Krueger, 2019) is merely the culmination of this earlier trend. To empirically illustrate this point, Fig. 3.3 shows that there is a statistically significant (at 1%) positive long-run relation between the degree of unionization and real wage growth in the U.S. (1948–2015). The association is remarkably strong: all by itself, the secular decline in unionization "explains" about two-thirds of the

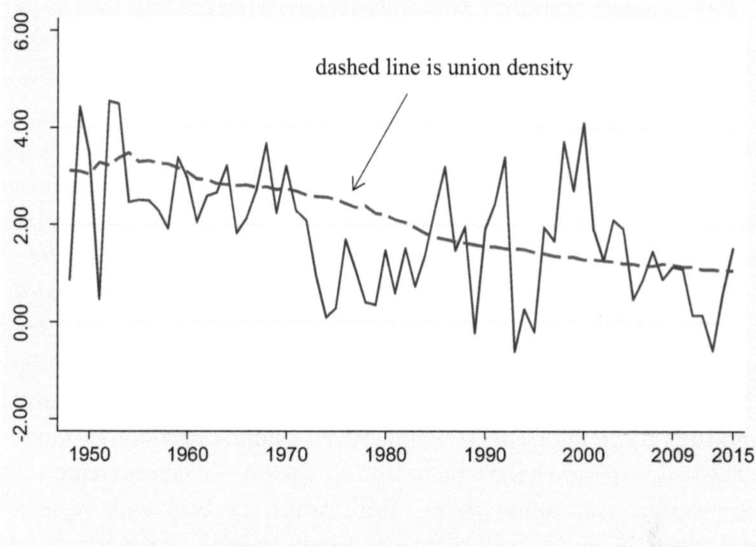

Figure 3.3 Stagnating hourly real wage growth and declining union density: U.S. economy, 1948–2015. Notes: The *dashed line* represents national union density (defined in terms of 10 percentage points), which declines from 3 (or about 30%) in the early 1950s to 1.1 (or 11%) in 2015. Hourly real wage growth and union density are very strongly correlated (see Storm, 2017). *Source: Reproduced from Storm (2017).*

long-term fall in real wage growth—which minimally suggests that domestic regulatory changes leading to greater job and income insecurity have contributed to real wage restraint.

However, real wage stagnation generates additional damage to potential output growth, as is illustrated in Fig. 3.2. Stagnant real wage growth adds to the aggregate demand shortage, which lowers capacity utilization and capital stock growth in Eq. (3.15), or alternatively, it reduces utilization and TFP growth in Eq. (3.14). Either way, potential growth gets hurt—and economic growth slows down. The recognition that real wage growth is a major driver of productivity growth holds an important insight for macroeconomic policy, as Robert Gordon (1987, pp. 154–155) explains:

> *... a stimulus to aggregate demand provides not only the direct benefit of raising output and employment, but also the indirect benefit of raising the real wage and creating substitution away from labor that boosts productivity [....] With this dual benefit obtainable from demand expansion, the case against demand stimulation must rest on convincing evidence that such policies would create an unacceptable acceleration of inflation.*

Higher wage growth may raise inflation considerably less than expected, in other words, because the rate of *potential* growth goes up in response to the increases in productivity, demand and *actual* output induced by the extra wage growth (see Fig. 3.2; Storm and Naastepad, 2012; Storm, 2017; Girardi et al., 2020; Fontanari et al., 2020). If so, the reverse holds true as well: sluggish business investment in the U.S. has been a key factor behind the stagnation of TFP growth and has also been responsible for propagating hysteresis-like adverse consequences for TFP and potential output after 2008 (see Hall, 2014; Ollivaud et al., 2016; Fazzari et al., 2018; Cynamon and Fazzari, 2017; Girardi et al., 2020). This conclusion only becomes stronger once we acknowledge the "cumulative causation" at work: sluggish investment weakens aggregate demand and this, in turn, weakens accumulation through the "accelerator effect"—which was Nicholas Kaldor's argument—as well as real wage growth, which reduces the rate of labor-saving technological progress (as argued here). Both ways, cyclical and/or structural demand shortfalls, must carry over into lower growth of potential output.

Conclusion: weak demand growth pulls down potential output growth

The theoretical arguments and empirical evidence presented in this chapter make the case for demand-led secular stagnation in the U.S. economy since the early 1980s. Obviously, no single chart or empirical test "proves" the case. Rather the case rests on a historical analysis of multiple pieces of evidence, which al point in the same direction. The present theoretical analysis and the evidence, when taken together, do lead to an unmistakeable conclusion: demand is leading supply, in the short as well as in the long run—which is an insight that runs counter to today's "decided opinion." The important dynamic macro channels through which demand growth influences potential output growth, listed in Fig. 3.2, deserve more attention in research.[2] After all, it is through these channels that stagnant business investment leads to a slower adoption of new technologies, a more limited space for learning by doing and exploiting economies of scale, and—as Hansen rightly argued—a discouragement to (demand-pull) initiatives to uncover further possibilities for innovation.

[2] Key studies on these channels include Storm and Naastepad (2012), DeLong and Summers (2012), Hall (2014), Fazzari et al. (2018), Storm (2017), Girardi et al. (2020), Taylor et al. (2019) and Fontanari et al. (2020).

Recognizing the importance of demand growth to long-run growth has profound and radically upsetting consequences for macro policy-making. Indeed, the all-too-neat separation between a "Keynesian" short run and "supply determined" potential growth in the long run breaks down—and so do standard notions and measurements of "potential" output growth and "output gaps" (Fontanari et al., 2020). What must be recognized is that structurally weak demand growth forces down potential growth, whereas faster demand growth, supported by more expansionary, full-employment oriented fiscal and monetary policies, raises productivity growth and potential output. Conventional (supply side) measures of potential output which ignore the dynamic demand-side channels, systematically overemphasize the "inflation barrier"and methodically underestimate the margins for expansion of actual output (Fontanari et al., 2020) and thereby legitimate a structural deflationary bias in macro policy (Storm and Naastepad, 2012; Girardi et al., 2020; Storm, 2017). What is not recognized is that higher demand may gradually remove the scarcities and bottlenecks which in the short run might create inflation pressures. To illustrate this important point: as shown by a model analysis of Fazzari et al. (2018), it is entirely plausible for changes in demand growth from something like 1% –3% to be accommodated by endogenous adjustments of supply, without generating additional inflation. Hence, we need new, more realistic and less biased measures of potential output growth, which take the dynamic impacts of demand on potential growth into account and remove all the unwarranted deflationary policy biases of existing approaches.

The unwarranted deflationary bias shows up in constant needless fiscal austerity, the abandonment of demand management in order to maintain full employment, overly restrictive monetary policy, and real wage stagnation (and rising income inequality), which jointly explain most, if not all, of the secular stagnation (as has been argued here). Real wage restraint directly reduces labor-saving technological progress and productivity growth. Moreover, when the top income-earners ("the 1%") are allowed to capture most of the growth, the economy's central function to recycle income back into demand is deeply compromised. As real incomes stagnate for the large majority of households, weak aggregate demand in turn feeds into sluggish business investment and a decline in capital deepening and ultimately into a slowing down of productivity growth and potential growth (Fig. 3.2). Stagnation is a sad instance of iatrogenesis, as it is a pathology caused by the exact economists whose task it is to improve the economy's health. To do better, we must look more deeply at shifting social norms that affect wage setting and allow higher inequality, and think creatively about how income growth can be restored across the distribution. Understanding these issues is difficult; designing effective macro policies to keep up demand growth in line with full employment and with potential growth may be even harder. But one thing is clear: unless we discard "decided opinion" that secular stagnation is an exclusively supply side phenomenon and recognize that demand drives growth "all the way" (see Taylor et al., 2019), macropolicy will retain its deflationary biases and secular stagnation remains the "normal." Hansen had it right after all.

Acknowledgments

The author is grateful to the *Institute for New Economic Thinking* for financial support (under individual grant #INO 1800015).

References

Aaronson, S., Cajner, T., Fallick, B., Galbis-Reig, F., Smith, C., Wascher, W., 2014. Labor Force Participation: Recent Developments and Future Prospects. Brookings Papers on Economic Activity. Brookings Institution Press, pp. 197−255.

Abramovitz, M., 1956. Resource and Output Trends in the United States since 1870. NBER Occasional Paper 52.

Acemoglu, D., 2002. Directed technical change. The Review of Economic Studies 69 (4), 781−809.

Barro, R.J., 1999. Notes on growth accounting. Journal of Economic Growth 4 (1), 119−137.

Basu, D., 2010. Marx-biased technical change and the neoclassical view of income distribution. Metroeconomica 61 (4), 593−620.

Brugger, F., Gehrke, C., 2017. The neoclassical approach to induced technical change: from Hicks to Acemoglu. Metroeconomica 68 (4), 730−776.

Cynamon, B.Z., Fazzari, S.M., 2017. Secular demand stagnation in the 21st century U.S. economy. In: Paper Presented at the INET Secular Stagnation Conference. Available at: https://www.ineteconomics.org/uploads/papers/Cynamon-Fazzari-Secular-Demand-Stagnation-in-the-21st-Century-U.S.-Economy.pdf.

DeLong, J.B., Summers, L.H., 2012. Fiscal policy in a depressed economy. In: Brookings Papers on Economic Activity. Brookings Institution Press, pp. 233−274.

Fatás, A., 2019. Fiscal policy, potential output and the shifting goalposts. IMF Economic Review 67, 684−702.

Fazzari, S.M., Ferri, P.E., Variato, A., 2018. Demand-led growth and accommodating supply. Cambridge Journal of Economics 44 (3), 583−605.

Felipe, J., McCombie, J.S.L., 2012. Aggregate Production Functions and the Accounting Identity Critique: Further Reflections on Temple's Criticisms and Misunderstandings. Working Paper No. 718. Levy Economics Institute of Bard College.

Fernald, J.G., 2014. Productivity and potential output before, during, and after the Great recession. NBER Macroeconomics Annual 29, 1−51.

Fernald, J.G., 2016. Reassessing Longer-Run U.S. Growth: How Low? Federal Reserve Bank of San Francisco Working Paper 2016−18.

Foley, D.K., Michl, T.R., 1999. Growth and Distribution. Harvard University Press, Cambridge, Mass.

Fontanari, C., Palumbo, A., Salvatori, C., 2020. Potential output in theory and practice: a revision and update of Okun's original method. Structural Change and Economic Dynamics 54, 247–266.

Funk, P., 2002. Induced innovation revisited. Economica 69 (273), 155–171.

Furman, J., July 9 2015. Productivity Growth in the Advanced Economies: The Past, the Present, and Lessons for the Future. Remarks at Peterson Institute for International Economics.

Girardi, D., Paternesi Meloni, W., Stirati, A., 2020. Reverse hysteresis? Persistent effects of autonomous demand expansions. Cambridge Journal of Economics 44 (4), 835–869.

Gordon, R.J., 1987. Productivity, wages, and prices inside and outside of manufacturing in the U.S., Japan, and Europe. European Economic Review 31 (3), 685–733.

Gordon, R.J., 2014. U.S. economic growth is over: the short run meets the long run. In: Dervis, K., Kharas, H. (Eds.), Growth, Convergence and Income Distribution: The Road from the Brisbane G-20 Summit. Brookings Institution Press, Washington, D.C., pp. 173–180

Gordon, R.J., 2015. Secular stagnation: a supply-side view. American Economic Review 105 (5), 54–59. https://www.aeaweb.org/articles.php?doi=10.1257/aer.p20151102.

Hall, R.E., 2014. Quantifying the lasting harm to the U.S. economy from the financial crisis. NBER Macroeconomics Annual 29, 71–128.

Hansen, A., 1939. Economic progress and declining population growth. American Economic Review 29 (1), 1–15.

Hicks, J.R., 1932. The Theory of Wages. MacMillan, London.

IMF, 2015. The New Normal: A Sector-Level Perspective on Productivity Trends in Advanced Economies. IMF Staff Discussion Notes No. 15/3.

Jones, C.I., 2016. The facts of economic growth. Chapter 1. In: Taylor, J.B., Uhlig, H. (Eds.), Handbook of Macroeconomics, vol. 2. Elsevier, Amsterdam.

Jorgenson, D.W., Griliches, Z., 1967. The explanation of productivity change. Review of Economic Studies 34 (99), 249–283.

Kaldor, N., 1961. Capital accumulation and economic growth. In: Lutz, F.A., Hague, D.C. (Eds.), The Theory of Capital. St. Martin's Press, New York, pp. 177–222.

Katz, L.F., Krueger, A.B., 2019. The rise and nature of alternative work arrangements in the United States, 1995–2015. International Labour Review 72 (2), 382–416.

Kopp, E., Leigh, D., Mursula, S., Tambunlertchai, S., 2019. U.S. Investment since the Tax Cuts and Jobs Act of 2017. IMF Working Paper No. WP/19/120. IMF, Washington, DC.

Kiefer, D., Mendieta-Muñoz, I., Rada, C., von Arnim, R., 2020. Secular stagnation and income distribution dynamics. Review of Radical Political Economics 52 (2), 189–207.

Marquetti, A., 2004. Do rising real wages increase the rate of labor-saving technical change? Some econometric evidence. Metroeconomica 55 (4), 432–441.

Ollivaud, P., Turner, D., 2014. The effect of the global financial crisis on OECD potential output. OECD Journal: Economic Studies 2014, 41–60.

Ollivaud, P., Guillemette, Y., Turner, D., 2016. Links between Weak Investment and the Slowdown in Productivity and Potential Output Growth across the OECD. OECD Economics Department Working Papers No. 1304. OECD, Paris.

Rada, C., Taylor, L., 2006. Empty sources of growth accounting, and empirical replacements à la Kaldor and Goodwin with some beef. Structural Change and Economic Dynamics 17, 486–500.

Shaikh, A., 1974. Laws of production and laws of algebra: the HUMBUG production function. The Review of Economics and Statistics 56 (1), 115–120.

Simon, H.A., Levy, F.K., 1963. A note on the Cobb-Douglas function. The Review of Economic Studies 30 (2), 93–94.

Solow, R.M., 1957. Technical change and the aggregate production function. The Review of Economics and Statistics 39 (3), 312–320.
Storm, S., Naastepad, C.W.M., 2012. Macroeconomics beyond the NAIRU. Harvard University Press, Cambridge, Mass.
Storm, S., 2017. The new normal: demand, secular stagnation, and the vanishing middle class. International Journal of Political Economy 46 (4), 169–210.
Summers, L.H., 2013. Speech at the IMF economic forum. In: 14th Annual IMF Research Conference: Crises Yesterday and Today, November 8.
Summers, L.H., 2015. Demand side secular stagnation. American Economic Review: Papers & Proceedings 105 (5), 60–65.
Syverson, C., 2016. Challenges to Mismeasurement Explanations for the U.S. Productivity Slowdown. NBER Working Paper Series WP 21974. National Bureau of Economic Research, Cambridge, MA.
Taylor, L., Foley, D.K., Rezai, A., 2019. Demand drives growth all the way: goodwin, Kaldor, Pasinetti and the steady state. Cambridge Journal of Economics 43 (5), 1333–1352.

CHAPTER FOUR

Stagnation and social structures of accumulation

David M. Kotz
Department of Economics, University of Massachusetts Amherst, United States

Introduction[1]

The recovery from the financial crisis and Great Recession of 2008–09 has been sluggish in the United States and more so in a number of other developed countries. This has given rise to a literature about possible secular stagnation (Gordon, 2012, 2014, 2016; Krugman, 2014; Summers, 2014; Ball et al., 2014). This paper proposes an approach to explaining the current stagnation that differs from that found in the above literature. We will argue that the current stagnation stems from the effect of the evolving institutional structure of the economy on long-run macroeconomic performance. This explanation for the current stagnation is based on the social structure of accumulation (SSA) theory (Gordon et al., 1982, Chapter 2; Kotz et al., 1994; McDonough et al., 2010), which is explained below.

Fig. 4.1 shows the U.S. GDP growth rate for all recoveries from quarterly recession troughs since 1949 through the next quarterly cyclical peak. Before 2000 the only recovery that fell below a 4% growth rate is 1991–2000, which was somewhat sluggish through 1995 but then accelerated substantially after 1995.[2] However, the last two recoveries had growth rates well below that of the previous ones. The recovery from 2009 to date stands out, with a growth rate of only 2.29% per year. This is consistent with the claim that a long-run stagnation emerged after 2008.

[1] This chapter is a revised and updated version of Kotz and Basu (2019). Baris Guven provided research assistance for this chapter.

[2] The GDP growth rate from 1991 to 1995 was 3.33% per year, rising to 4.30% per year in 1995–2000. The stock market bubble of the second half of that decade accelerated GDP growth after 1995 (Kotz, 2003).

Handbook of Economic Stagnation
ISBN: 978-0-12-815898-2
https://doi.org/10.1016/B978-0-12-815898-2.00014-8

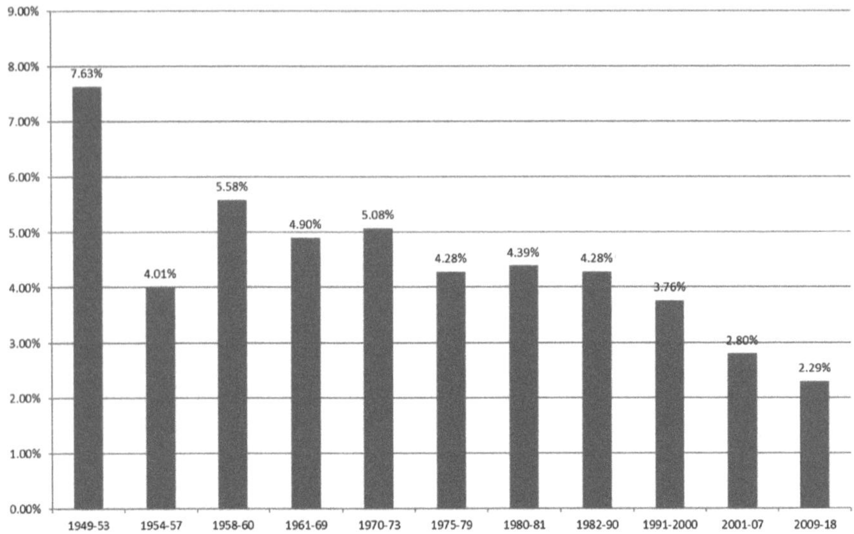

Figure 4.1 Annual growth rate of GDP from trough quarter to following peak quarter or most recent quarter, 1949–2018. Note: Compounded annual growth rate from trough quarter to next peak quarter, or most recent quarter for 2009–18. *Source: U.S. Bureau of Economic Analysis (2019), NIPA Table 1.1.6.*

Output growth in a capitalist economy is promoted by the capital accumulation drive of enterprises that results from pursuit of profit combined with competition. The capital accumulation drive, particularly if interpreted broadly as including the introduction of new technologies that accompanies enlargement of the value of capital, is a key distinguishing feature of capitalism. It is the underlying cause of capitalism's remarkable record of promoting economic progress, although a rising education and skill level of the workforce also contribute to economic advance. The GDP growth rate can be considered a rough indicator of the strength of the accumulation drive, and we regard a substantial drop in the long-run GDP growth rate to a level well below the norm as evidence of "stagnation." The rate of capital accumulation will also be examined in this chapter.

This chapter proceeds as follows. The Section Social structure of accumulation theory and stagnation explains the SSA theory and draws some implications from SSA theory about the cause of long-run stagnations. The Section History of SSAs in the United States presents historical data about SSAs in US history and economic performance. The Section The neoliberal SSA and stagnation in the U.S. presents an argument that the institutional form of capitalism that emerged in the U.S. around 1980, referred to as free-market, or neoliberal, capitalism, can explain the stagnation since 2009. We will show that the character of the last several decades of relatively stable economic expansion prior to 2008 as well as the outbreak of the financial crisis and Great Recession—and the stagnation that has followed—all derive from the working, and the evolution over time, of the neoliberal form of capitalism. The Section Data analysis presents empirical evidence for the claim that institutional factors underlie the current stagnation by focusing on the relations among an SSA, the rate of capital accumulation, and the rate of profit.

Social structure of accumulation theory and stagnation

SSA theory claims that periods of "normal" economic expansion occur when a set of economic and political institutions emerges that is favorable for capital accumulation. Such a set of mutually reinforcing, expansion-promoting institutions is called an SSA. While an SSA can promote normal economic expansion for one or several decades, eventually it turns from a promoter of expansion into an obstacle to further normal expansion, which ushers in a period of stagnation and/or macroeconomic instability, referred to as a long-run economic crisis. Such a crisis can be resolved within capitalism only by the construction of a new SSA. According to this theory, such long-term crises have occurred in the 1870s–1890s, 1930s, 1970s, and again today since 2008.

SSA theory argues that, while capitalism gives rise to a strong accumulation drive, it also presents obstacles to accumulation. Capitalism generates uncertainties and periods of declining profit, which arise from the conflicts and coordination problems that characterize that system. An SSA promotes accumulation by regulating the key relationships of a capitalist system so as to create a condition of relative stability and predictability, to promote a rising rate of profit in the economy as a whole, and to foster growing aggregate demand over time that is essential for sustained accumulation.[3] In the absence of an effective SSA, the economy suffers from stagnation and/or instability.

[3] A detailed explanation of how an SSA promotes accumulation and expansion, and why normal expansion is not expected to occur in the absence of an effective SSA, is found in Gordon et al. (1982, Chapter 2) and Kotz (1987).

Each past long-run crisis was resolved only after a major restructuring of capitalism, involving transformation of economic and political institutions, leading to the emergence of a new SSA that again promoted normal expansion. The restructuring following the late nineteenth century crisis included the rise of giant corporations and banks and a new state regulation of some sectors of the economy. The crisis of the 1930s was resolved shortly after World War II with the emergence of "regulated capitalism" in which the state and trade unions played an active role in regulating economic activity. The crisis of the 1970s was resolved by the emergence of a relatively free-market and trade union-free form of capitalism, today often called neoliberal capitalism.[4]

Thus, SSA theory attributes long periods of relatively vigorous economic growth to institutional factors, rather than pointing to major new technological advances cited in the widely discussed book by Gordon (2016). SSA theory asserts that, whatever the time pattern of discovery of new technologies, the time pattern of their introduction, imitation, and further development will be mainly determined by economic conditions that may or may not promote long-run capital accumulation. Hence, long periods of strong macroeconomic performance will be associated with new technologies, but the latter are not regarded as the explanation for the timing of such periods. For example, during the 1930s and the first half of the 1940s, new technologies continued to appear, but conditions were not favorable for their application, except in weapons production in the later part of that period. After the emergence of an effective SSA following the end of World War II had created favorable conditions for long-run capital accumulation, capitalists were able to draw on the backlog of innovations from the preceding period.

Wolfson and Kotz (2010) offered a critique and reinterpretation of SSA theory. The analysis here is based on their modified version of SSA theory. Following are some of the modifications they proposed:

(1) Gordon et al. (1982) had argued that each SSA gives rise to a long period of accumulation and economic growth that is rapid by historical comparison. Wolfson and Kotz (2010) argued that both theoretical considerations and historical evidence suggest that not every SSA necessarily brings economic expansion that is rapid. Instead, they proposed that

[4] Each new SSA also involves a shift in the dominant economic ideas. Keynesian ideas achieved dominance during the period regulated capitalism, while free-market, or neoliberal, economic thought displaced Keynesian ideas in the period of neoliberal capitalism. The shift in economic ideas plays an important role in the rise of a new SSA.

an SSA should be understood to promote stable accumulation and high profits.

(2) SSAs come in two varieties, liberal (free-market) and regulated. In the former type of SSA, the institutions reinforce the role of market relations and market forces in the regulation of economic activity while nonmarket institutions such as states and trade unions play a limited role. In the latter type of SSA, nonmarket institutions play an active role in regulating economic activity with market relations and market forces playing a lesser role. Furthermore, they argue that a regulated SSA is based on capital-labor compromise while a liberal SSA reinforces the domination of capital over labor. The post-World War II SSA is viewed as a regulated SSA while the current SSA is a liberal type.

(3) Regulated SSAs bring faster economic expansion than liberal SSAs. To the above three claims by Wolfson and Kotz (2010) one more is added here, which is the central argument of this paper:

(4) The crisis of a liberal SSA gives rise to long-run stagnation (although this claim is not made for the crisis of a regulated SSA).

To understand the rationale for claim #4, consider that an SSA promotes accumulation through three channels: (1) providing stability and predictability; (2) promoting a high rate of profit; (3) promoting rising demand over the long run. When a liberal SSA enters its crisis phase, it no longer provides stability and predictability and it no longer promotes rising demand. If capital remains strongly dominant over labor, the profit rate is likely to recover after the initial phase of the crisis has passed, but the erosion of the first and third channels for promoting accumulation has the effect of weakening or even breaking the usual link in a capitalist system between profitability and accumulation.

The intuition for this change in responsiveness is the following. As long as the SSA works well, the capitalists are motivated to accumulate. A higher profit rate would increase accumulation through an incentive effect. However, in the crisis phase of a liberal SSA, the SSA no longer creates stability or assures growing markets. Hence, capitalists have no confidence that they can predict the future profit from an investment, so an increase in the current/past profit rate does not necessarily indicate an expectation of a higher profit rate in the future when the investment would bear fruit. Secondly, if the SSA no longer assures growing markets, then a rising profit rate in the recent past would not call for expanding productive capacity through net investment since it is irrational to expand productive capacity if no increase in demand is expected. Hence, we argue that the responsiveness of accumulation to profitability should weaken significantly in the crisis phase of the neoliberal SSA. As a result, even if the profit rate recovers after the initial phase of the crisis of a liberal SSA, accumulation would not return to a normal rate as capitalists sit on their cash instead of investing it.[5]

History of SSAs in the United States

U.S. history provides preliminary evidence for the claims we are making. Here we will briefly review the historical evidence starting in 1929. This requires specifying the timing of the emergence of each SSA and the time when it stopped being effective. We will refer to the first period of an SSA during which the SSA effectively promotes accumulation as "phase 1" and the period in which the SSA is an obstacle—the crisis phase—as "phase 2." The year of emergence of an SSA should be determined based on the timing of institutional transformation, which is not an exact matter. The boundary year marking the transition from phase 1 to phase 2 of an SSA should be decided based on the start of the deterioration of macroeconomic performance.[6] The dating of both phases should take account of the business cycle to avoid distortion of the long-run GDP growth rate and other data series by cyclical factors. One way to do this is to select business cycle peak years for the boundaries between SSA phases.

Based on the above considerations, we will use the following SSA phase timing for the U.S. since 1929, which is the first year for which reliable data on the U.S. macroeconomy are available:

(1) 1929–37 phase 2 of the post-World War I SSA[7]
(2) 1948–73 phase 1 of the postwar regulated SSA
(3) 1973–79 phase 2 of the postwar regulated SSA

[5] In the crisis of a regulated SSA, the SSA is likely to continue to promote growing markets for output, since state spending is likely to increase and, with workers empowered by the regulated SSA, wages are likely to continue to rise. That removes one of the grounds for expecting a weakening of the effect of a rising profit rate on accumulation.

[6] Selecting the date of transition from phase 1 to phase 2, when an SSA shifts from promoting good macroeconomic performance to deterring it, by noting the date when macroeconomic performance worsens of course does not excuse the analyst from showing that the worsened performance resulted from institutional factors. In the Section Data analysis below we will present an argument linking the evolution of the neoliberal SSA in the U.S. to the 2008 phase shift after which that SSA has no longer promoted good performance.

[7] The early SSA literature viewed the SSA that emerged around 1900 as lasting through the Great Depression. Kotz (2015) argues that a new SSA emerged shortly after World War I. This will be discussed further below.

(4) 1979–2007 phase 1 of the neoliberal SSA
(5) 2007–2018 phase 2 of the neoliberal SSA

The above selection of phase boundaries requires some comment.[8] All of the above years were business cycle peak years, except for 2018 which is the most recent year for which data are available. The gap between 1937 and 1948 was a special period in the U.S. economy. After 2 years of normal recovery from the 1937–38 recession, in 1941 government expenditure leaped up by 43% as war preparations began. The following year, the federal government took control of the economy, instituting a regime of central planning. Real GDP grew at the rate of 15.3% per year in 1940–44, a rate in excess of China's remarkably rapid growth after 1978. In 1944, the economy hit full capacity utilization, as the unemployment rate fell to 1.2% with the government share of GDP reaching 81.6%. During 1945–47 the economy underwent a painful structural adjustment back to a market economy and civilian production, which was completed by the end of 1947. Thus, we eliminated the period 1937–48 from our analysis.

The year 1948 marked the establishment of the main institutions of the post-World War II SSA in the U.S., which also happens to be a business cycle peak year. However, the end of phase 1 of that SSA has some ambiguity. After 1966 one important indicator, the average rate of profit, began a long downturn that lasted through 1982 (Fig. 4.2). However, several other important variables (inflation rate, unemployment rate, severity of the business cycle) indicate that the final year of the effective phase of the postwar SSA was 1973.

Based on institutional considerations, the neoliberal SSA appears to have been established during the late 1970s to early 1980s. The business cycle peak year 1979 was selected as the final year of the regulated SSA, which was a year in which the trend in many economic series shifted.[9]

We regard 2007 as the last year of phase 1 of the neoliberal SSA, with the financial crisis and Great Recession marking the transition to phase 2. The final year of data for the current phase 2 of the neoliberal SSA is 2018, and while that is not a business cycle peak year, it is the ninth year of expansion following the trough in the spring quarter of 2009, an expansion that lowered the unemployment rate below 4% in 2018.

[8] The dating of the SSA phases above is based on the analysis of institutional change and economic performance in Kotz (2015).

[9] Kotz and Basu (2019) present a data analysis that supports the claim that a new neoliberal SSA arose in the U.S. around 1979.

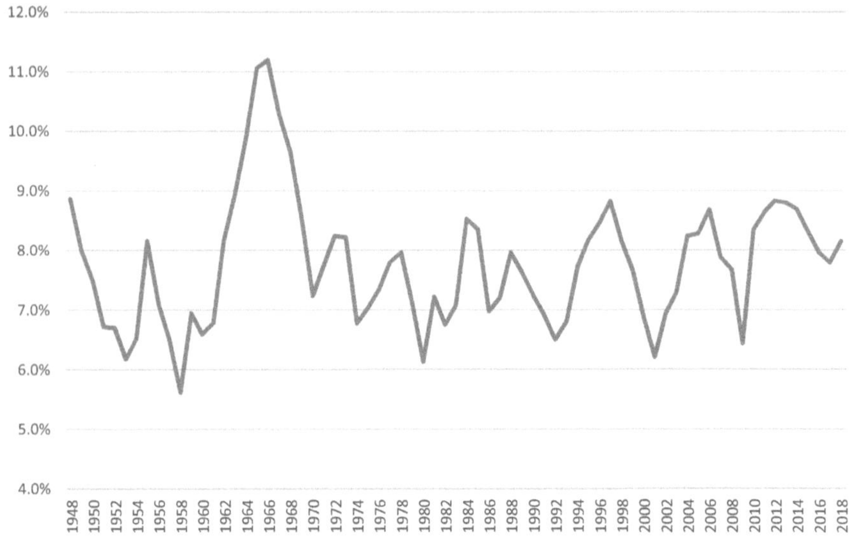

Figure 4.2 After-tax Rate of Profit of the Nonfinancial Corporate Business Sector. Note: Profit after tax plus net interest paid divided by beginning-of-year value of net fixed assets. *Source: U.S. Bureau of Economic Analysis (2019), Table 1.14 and Fixed Assets Table 4.1.*

Fig. 4.3 shows the GDP growth rates in the five periods under consideration.[10] As Fig. 4.3 shows, GDP growth was a robust 4.03% from 1948 to 73, compared to the severe stagnation of 1929–37 indicated by a GDP growth rate of 0.67%. Indeed, the decades following World War II have been dubbed the "Golden Age of Capitalism" based on the strong macroeconomic performance throughout the developed capitalist world in that period.

The growth rate of the US economy during the crisis phase of regulated capitalism does not suggest stagnation. As Fig. 4.3 shows, while the GDP growth rate was one percentage point lower in 1973–79 than it had been in the preceding period, a peak-to-peak growth rate of about 3% cannot be called stagnation for the U.S. economy. If the period 1973–79 is to be considered a long-run crisis, the designation must rest on other variables than the GDP growth rate. As Fig. 4.2 showed, that period saw a sharply

[10] We regard a long-run GDP growth rate (undistorted by cyclical effects) of 2% or below for the U.S. economy as indicating stagnation, a rate of 3% or above as "normal" growth or nonstagnation, while the range of 2%–3% is ambiguous. The GDP growth rates shown in Fig. 4.1 are for trough-to-peak business cycle recoveries, not long-run peak-to-peak measures.

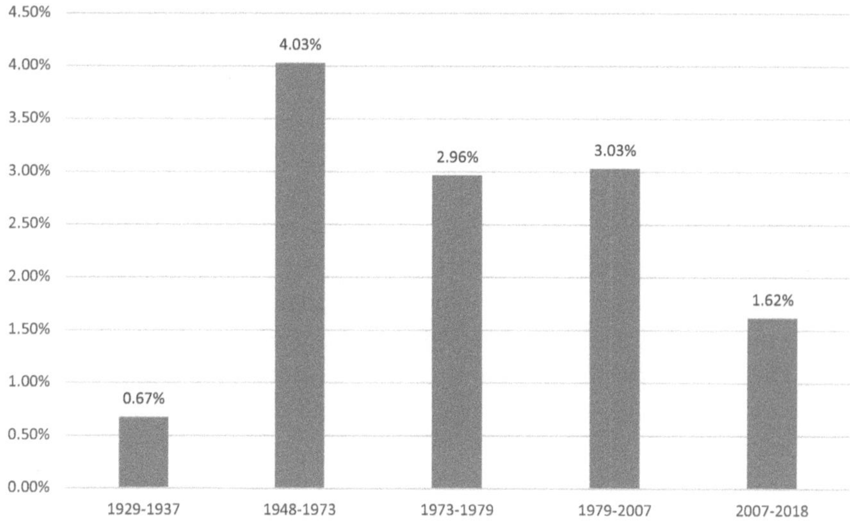

Figure 4.3 Annual GDP Growth Rates for Selected Periods. Note: Compounded annual growth rate from initial year to final year using annual GDP data. *Source: U.S. Bureau of Economic Analysis (2019), NIPA Table 1.1.6.*

declining trend in the average rate of profit, one that began in 1967 and lasted through 1982. The 1973–79 period began with a severe recession in 1974–75 that drove GDP down by 3.2% and the unemployment rate up by 4.2 percentage points, a recession that ranks as the most severe since 1950 by both measures (until 2008–09). However, as Fig. 4.1 shows, the recovery from the 1974–75 recession was relatively robust. The economy experienced a rising trend in unemployment and inflation in the 1970s, with inflation seemingly surging out of control. The international monetary and financial system became very unstable after 1973. This SSA crisis phase was marked by a declining trend in the rate of profit, a high degree of macroeconomic instability, and some slowdown in the rate of GDP growth although not to a rate that could be regarded as stagnation.[11]

The establishment of the neoliberal SSA did not bring a significant acceleration of the GDP growth rate in the U.S., which was 3.03% in 1979–2007 compared to 2.96% in the crisis phase of the preceding SSA during 1973–79. An increase of 0.07 percentage points in the GDP growth rate cannot be considered significant given the degree of accuracy of GDP

[11] The rate of labor productivity growth also slowed sharply in the 1970s.

growth series. However, at the end of the depressed years 1980——82 the long decline in the rate of profit was arrested, and there followed 25 years of long economic expansions punctuated by relatively mild and brief recessions along with little price inflation. The term "Great Moderation" arose to describe this period. The GDP growth rate for phase 2 of the neoliberal SSA, from 2007–2018, was only 1.62%, which qualifies as a condition of stagnation.

The above review of the historical evidence from 1929 to today is consistent with the view that every SSA-induced long-run crisis involves a long-term worsening of macroeconomic performance—but not always stagnation. The crisis of the 1930s gave rise to long-lasting stagnation as has the current crisis, but that of the 1970s did not, instead taking the form of intense macroeconomic instability.

Kotz (2015, Chapter 6) argues that the Great Depression of the 1930s emerged from a decade-long liberal SSA in the U.S. that arose after World War I, replacing the modestly regulated form of capitalism of 1900–18.[12] If that interpretation of the interwar period is adopted, then the historical evidence supports the claim that a crisis of a liberal SSA takes the form of stagnation (the 1930s and today) while the crisis of a regulated form of capitalism takes the form of instability (the 1970s), although of course the number of data points supporting this conclusion is small.

The neoliberal SSA and stagnation in the U.S.

If the crisis of a liberal SSA gives rise to stagnation, this offers a possible explanation for the current stagnation. The next step is to explain the process through which the neoliberal SSA that emerged by the early 1980s eventually shifted from promoting capital accumulation to obstructing it in a way to give rise to stagnation.[13] Table 4.1 lists the main institutions of the neoliberal SSA in the U.S.

The neoliberal SSA gave rise to three economic developments that, taken together, promoted a long period of stable accumulation and economic expansion: (1) rising income inequality between capital and labor and among households; (2) a financial sector increasingly devoted to

[12] Kotz (2015, Chapter 6) presents a case that the regulated SSA that emerged in the US around 1900 was replaced by a liberal SSA around 1920 as a result of forces that arose during World War I and its aftermath, which ended the post-1900 regulated SSA before a long-run crisis had emerged.

[13] The analysis in this section is based on Kotz (2015, Chapters 4 and 5).

Table 4.1 Ideas and institutions of neoliberal capitalism in the U.S.

1. Dominance of economic ideas and theories that view an unregulated market system as optimal and view state intervention as a threat to economic efficiency and individual liberty.
2. The Global Economy: Relatively free movement of goods, services, and capital across national boundaries.
3. The Role of Government in the Economy
   - **(a)** Macropolicy aimed solely at inflation control through monetary policy
   - **(b)** Deregulation of infrastructure sectors (transportation, communication, electric power)
   - **(c)** Deregulation of the financial sector
   - **(d)** Reduced regulation of consumer product safety, job safety, and the environment
   - **(e)** Privatization and contracting out of public goods and services
   - **(f)** Cutbacks in or elimination of social welfare programs
   - **(g)** Tax cuts for business and the rich
4. The Labor Market
   - **(a)** Determination of wages and working conditions by employers instead of based on compromise with labor
   - **(b)** Job tenure determined by employers rather than bureaucratic rules and seniority
5. The Corporate Sector
   - **(a)** Unrestrained competition
   - **(b)** Corporate CEOs hired from outside the corporation in a market for CEOs

Adapted from Kotz (2015, Table 2.1, p. 42).

speculative, risky activities; and (3) a series of large asset bubbles. Those three developments are well known and need no documentation here (a detailed account is available in Kotz, 2015, Chapter 4). Those three developments are not inherent in capitalism. In the preceding period in the U.S., the degree of income inequality declined somewhat, financial institutions were confined to offering traditional financial services, and there were no large asset bubbles.

Rising inequality meant rising profit which encouraged economic expansion, but at the same time rising inequality limited demand growth from households. That, along with the slow growth of government spending in the neoliberal period, threatened to block continuing expansion. However, that potential obstacle was overcome by the other two developments cited above. The large asset bubbles (particularly the 1990s stock market bubble and the 2000s real estate bubble) enabled, and promoted, consumer demand rising faster than disposable income, which occurred in both decades.[14] In the 2000s, the speculatively oriented financial institutions, whose practices were a major cause of the series of big asset bubbles, found ways to lend to even low-income households that were suffering from wage stagnation or decline but owned a home. This enabled a broad section of the population to increase its consumer spending. Several features of the neoliberal SSA promoted price stability, including very limited bargaining power of workers, the more intense competition of neoliberal capitalism, and a tendency for total demand growth to lag behind growing productive capacity despite the promotion of consumer spending via asset bubbles.

However, this growth mechanism, which no one planned, gave rise to three trends that were unsustainable in the long-run. First, it led to a rising household debt ratio. Household debt relative to disposable income doubled from 1980 to 2007. Second, it led to a rising financial sector debt ratio, as financial institutions could not resist rapidly raising their leverage ratios given the very high profits from their new activities. Third, it led to the spread of toxic financial assets throughout the financial system, whose market values depended on the inflating real estate bubble.

This growth mechanism was dependent on trends that were sustainable only as long as a big asset bubble kept expanding. The 1990s stock market bubble collapsed in 2000, but a real estate bubble quickly arose and began to stimulate economic expansion, reversing a rather sharp decline in business fixed investment that had followed the stock market crash of 2000.[15] Each asset bubble of the neoliberal period was larger than its predecessor, from the bubble in Southwestern commercial real estate in the 1980s to the stock market bubble of the 1990s and the real estate bubble of the 2000s.

However, every asset bubble must eventually deflate. The huge real estate bubble stopped inflating in 2006, and in 2007 it began to collapse. Households could no longer easily borrow against their homes and instead began paying down their debt, leading to a decline in consumer spending in the first quarter of 2008 which initiated the Great Recession. The real estate

[14] During 1991—2000, personal consumption expenditures rose from 88.3% to 91.8% of disposable income. During the expansion of 2001—07 personal consumption expenditures as a share of disposable income rose further, from 91.6% to 92.8% of disposable income (U.S. Bureau of Economic Analysis, 2015, NIPA Table 2.1). By contrast, in all but one of the economic recoveries in the regulated capitalist era the ratio of consumer spending to disposable income declined during the expansion.

[15] Nonresidential fixed investment declined at an accelerating pace in 2001 and 2002 and increased by only 1.9% in 2003 before starting to grow rapidly in 2004 through 2006.

bubble collapse also caused the toxic financial assets to plummet in value, driving the highly leveraged big financial institutions toward insolvency and causing a financial panic. Declining consumer spending along with plummeting asset values caused investor expectations to turn suddenly negative, and business fixed investment collapsed. The crisis had begun.

The key question here is why this process led, not just to a severe financial crisis and real sector recession, but to a continuing stagnation after the financial panic had subsided and the Great Recession had ended. Our analysis suggests that, once the real estate bubble had burst, the toxic financial assets had collapsed in value, and the speculators who had been driving the series of asset bubbles were humbled, there was no possibility of another big asset bubble arising that could assist in promoting accumulation. The neoliberal SSA has continued to promote rising inequality and continues to allow financial institutions to engage in risky, speculative activities despite the increased oversight under the Dodd-Frank bill. However, this does not amount to an effective growth promoting mechanism. The neoliberal SSA is continuing to suppress demand growth, leaving profit-rich companies with little incentive to expand production. Also, in the aftermath of the big financial crisis and steep recession the neoliberal SSA no longer provides the stability and predictability necessary to promote the long-run investments that bring normal economic expansion.

Data analysis

This section examines the rate of accumulation in the U.S. economy since 1948 to investigate two claims about the causes of stagnation:

(1) Stagnation arises in phase II of a liberal SSA but not necessarily in phase II of a regulated SSA.

(2) The positive effect of the rate of profit on the rate of accumulation is weakened or eliminated in phase II of a liberal SSA although not in phase II of a regulated SSA.

The large volume of cash held by both banks and nonfinancial corporations suggests something is deterring firms from investing despite the rapid recovery of the rate of profit after 2009, as is shown in Fig. 4.2. Fig. 4.4 shows the annual rate of capital accumulation for the nonfinancial corporate business sector from 1948 to 2018. However, it is difficult to draw a firm inference about the relation between the rate of profit and the rate of accumulation from a visual inspection of those two graphs.

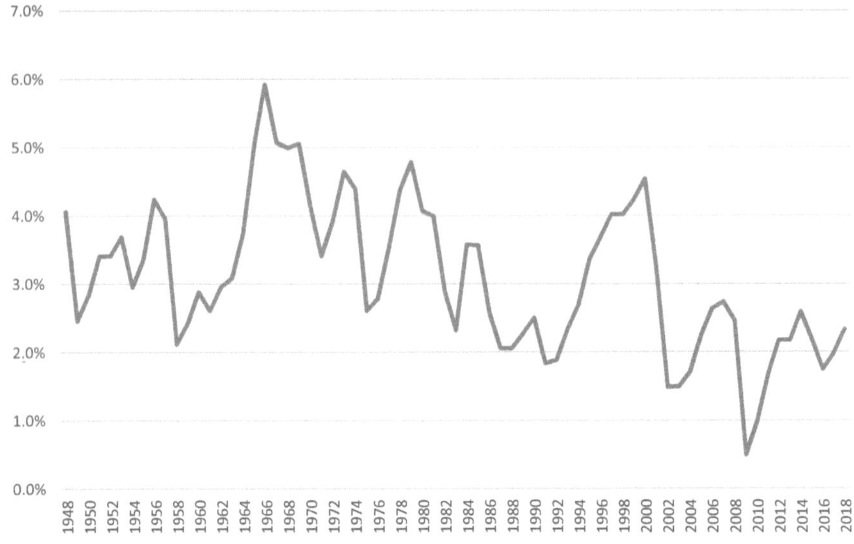

Figure 4.4 Annual Rate of Capital Accumulation for the Nonfinancial Corporate Business Sector. Note: Net investment divided by beginning-of-year net stock of fixed assets. *Source: U.S. Bureau of Economic Analysis (2019), Fixed Assets Tables 4.1, 4.4, 4.7.*

The changing relationship between profitability and capital accumulation for the postwar U.S. economy was investigated using a regression of the rate of accumulation on the rate of profit and a constant. The analysis is for the nonfinancial corporate business sector of the US economy during the period 1948–2018. The rate of accumulation is measured as the ratio of the flow of net investment (gross investment less depreciation) to the replacement cost value of nonresidential fixed assets (structures, equipment, and intellectual property products) at the beginning of the period. The rate of profit is measured as the ratio of the flow of after-tax profit (profit after tax plus interest paid) to the replacement cost value of fixed assets at the beginning of the period.[16] An explanation of the methodology and data sources for this analysis is presented in Kotz and Basu (2019). In that article, the data ran only through 2014. Here only the results of the updated data analysis are presented.

Table 4.2 provides summary statistics for the rate of accumulation and the rate of profit for four periods: phase 1 and 2 of both regulated and

[16] Since total fixed assets are in the denominator of the profit rate, which includes assets acquired with borrowed funds, the numerator of this profit rate measure should include interest paid.

Table 4.2 Summary statistics.

	Regulated SSA		Neoliberal SSA	
	Phase 1	Phase 2	Phase 1	Phase 2
	(Mean/SD)	(Mean/SD)	(Mean/SD)	(Mean/SD)
Rate of accumulation (%)	3.70	3.74	2.86	1.89
	0.98	0.91	0.91	0.64
Rate of profit (%)	7.98	7.34	7.52	8.15
	1.50	0.46	0.76	0.69
Observations	26	6	28	11

Notes. Regulated SSA: 1948–79 (Phase 1: 1948–73; Phase 2: 1974–79). Neoliberal SSA: 1980–2018 (Phase 1: 1980–2007; Phase 2: 2008–18).

neoliberal capitalism. The average rate accumulation in phase 1 and 2 of regulated capitalism was 3.70 and 3.74% per year, respectively. By contrast, the average rate accumulation in phase 1 and 2 of neoliberal capitalism was 2.86% and 1.89% per year, respectively. This is consistent with the recent version of SSA theory although not with the original version. Note that the average rate of accumulation in both phases of regulated capitalism was higher than the averages in the corresponding phases of neoliberal capitalism. In fact, the average rate of accumulation in phase 2 (crisis phase) of regulated capitalism was higher than the average in phase 1 of neoliberal capitalism. Also, the difference in the average rate of accumulation between the two phases is significant in neoliberal capitalism but not in regulated capitalism. These data are in line with the claim that phase 2 of a liberal SSA witnesses stagnation (in output and capital accumulation) but stagnation does not necessarily arise in the corresponding phase of a regulated SSA.

Turning to the rate of profit, we see that the average in phases 1 and 2 of regulated capitalism was 7.98 and 7.34% per year, respectively. The average of the rate of profit in the corresponding phases of neoliberal capitalism was 7.52 and 8.15% per year. The most striking aspect of these numbers is that the average of the rate of profit is highest in phase 2 of neoliberal capitalism. When we juxtapose this to the fact that this regime also saw the weakest capital accumulation, we see an interesting phenomenon: the weakening of the link of profitability and capital accumulation. This is preliminary evidence in support of the hypothesis about the changing relationship between capital accumulation and profitability over SSAs and across different phases within each SSA. We now turn to results from the econometric analysis to see if this preliminary evidence has further support in the data.

Table 4.3 Responsiveness of the rate of accumulation to the rate of profit.

Regulated capitalism: Phase 1	
Estimate	0.551
P-value	0.000
Regulated capitalism: Phase 2	
Estimate	0.596
P-value	0.000
Neoliberal capitalism: Phase 1	
Estimate	0.492
P-value	0.011
Neoliberal capitalism: Phase 2	
Estimate	0.338
P-value	0.058

Table 4.3 shows that the responsiveness of capital accumulation to the rate of profit in phase 1 of regulated capitalism is 0.551 (this is statistically significant). This means that a 1 percentage point increase in the rate of profit was associated with a 0.551 percentage point increase in the rate of accumulation during phase 1 of postwar regulated capitalism, which is a sizable effect in relation to the average rate of capital accumulation over that period. The corresponding responsiveness in phase 2 of postwar regulated capitalism was 0.596 (this is also statistically significantly different from zero). Although this is numerically larger than the responsiveness in phase 1, the difference is not statistically significant. This supports the conclusion that phases 1 and 2 of the postwar regulated SSA display similar responsiveness of capital accumulation to profitability.

Turning to neoliberal capitalism, we see a very different picture. From Table 4.3 we see that responsiveness of the rate of accumulation to the rate of profit in phase 1 of the neoliberal SSA was 0.492 and statistically significant. The corresponding effect during phase 2 fell to 0.338 and was not statistically significant (*P*-value = .058). Moreover, the difference between these two effects was itself statistically significant.

Thus, bringing together the results in Tables 4.2 and 4.3, we have the following. First, capital accumulation did indeed slow down significantly in phase 2 of the neoliberal SSA but not in phase 2 of the regulated SSA. Second, for neoliberal capitalism the responsiveness of the rate of accumulation to the rate of profit declines and is not statistically significant in phase 2, an effect that was not observed in phase 2 of regulated capitalism. This is consistent with our claim that phase 2 of a liberal SSA indirectly leads to stagnation by weakening or eliminating the impact of a rising profit rate on accumulation.

Concluding comments

In our view, the current stagnation in the U.S. economy ultimately results from the persistence of an SSA that can no longer promote normal accumulation and instead obstructs it. This kind of condition of the U.S. economy has arisen before, in the Great Depression of the 1930s, although the features of the current stagnation differ in important ways from those of the 1930s mainly due to the greatly increased size of the state relative to the economy along with a readiness to undertake state intervention as soon as a severe crisis develops. But both the stagnation of the 1930s and that of today derive from a transition in a liberal SSA from the phase that promotes accumulation to the phase that is a barrier to it.

SSA theory claims that no automatic corrective mechanism in a capitalist economy will end the stagnation and/or instability that emerges in phase 2 of an SSA. Another round of expansionary fiscal policy at this time might increase the GDP growth rate of the U.S. for a few years, but according to this analysis it would not overcome the powerful stagnation tendency in the private sector of the economy. Only the construction of a new SSA can end the stagnation and give rise to normal capital accumulation and economic expansion.

Both history and SSA theory suggest that there is a tendency for regulated and liberal SSAs to alternate, with each type of SSA resolving the obstacles to normal capital accumulation that arose in phase two of the preceding SSA.[17] The construction of a new regulated SSA takes some time to complete, given the complexities of achieving a capital-labor compromise and establishing an active state role in the economy that is acceptable to big business. For those reasons, SSA theory suggests that the current stagnation will be a long-lasting one. The previous regulated SSA

[17] Wolfson and Kotz (2010) provide a justification for expecting an alternation of regulated and liberal SSAs.

took almost 20 years to construct following the start of the Great Depression in 1929.

However, SSA theory does suggest that the current stagnation, while likely to last for a long period, will not be permanent. Although the construction of a new SSA during the crisis phase of the preceding one is not guaranteed, there are powerful forces that push in the direction of constructing a new SSA. As long as the neoliberal SSA lasts, stagnation will continue, and stagnation is a dangerous condition for U.S. capitalism. A persistent stagnation, with a continuing increase in inequality, tends to generate rising antiestablishment sentiment on both the left and the right. Both represent threats to the stability of U.S. capitalism. We saw this in the U.S. presidential campaign in 2016, as the Republican nomination and the presidency were won by a candidate well to the right of what has been the U.S. political mainstream, while a self-identified democratic socialist was a serious contender for the Democratic Presidential nomination for the first time in U.S. history.

It is likely that powerful groups will begin to propose significant institutional change in the U.S. to address the obstacles to normal economic expansion, leading eventually to a new regulated SSA that would again promote normal economic expansion (Kotz, 2015, Chapter 7). If that does emerge in the next five to 10 years, the current stagnation will have been a long-term one but not a permanent condition of the U.S. economy.

References

Ball, L., DeLong, B., Summers, L., April 2, 2014. Fiscal Policy and Full Employment. Center on Budget and Policy Priorities, Washington, D.C. Available at: http://www.pathtofullemployment.org/wp-content/uploads/2014/04/delong_summers_ball.pdf..

Gordon, D.M., Edward, R., Reich, M., 1982. Segmented Work, Divided Workers. Cambridge University Press, Cambridge.

Gordon, R.J., August 2012. Is U.S. Economic Growth over? Faltering Innovation Confronts the Six Headwinds. Working Paper 18315. National Bureau of Economic Research. Available at: http://www.nber.org/papers/w18315.

Gordon, R.J., January 20, 2014. The Demise of U. S. Economic Growth: Restatement, Rebuttal, and Reflections. Available at: http://www.scribd.com/doc/208017699/The-Demise-of-U-S-Economic-Growth-Restatement-Rebuttal-and-Reflections.

Gordon, R.J., 2016. The Rise and Fall of American Growth. Princeton University Press, Princeton.

Kotz, D.M., 1987. Long waves and social structures of accumulation: a critique and reinterpretation. Review of Radical Political Economics 19 (4), 16–38.

Kotz, D.M., 2003. Neoliberalism and the U.S. Economic expansion of the 1990s. Monthly Review 54 (11), 15–33.

Kotz, D.M., 2015. The Rise and Fall of Neoliberal Capitalism. Harvard University Press, Cambridge, MA.

Kotz, D.M., Basu, D., 2019. Stagnation and institutional structures. Review of Radical Political Economics 51 (1), 5–30.
Kotz, D.M., McDonough, T., Reich, M. (Eds.), 1994. Social Structures of Accumulation: The Political Economy of Growth and Crisis. Cambridge University Press, Cambridge.
Krugman, P., 2014. Four observations on secular stagnation. In: Teulings, C., Baldwin, R. (Eds.), Secular Stagnation: Facts, Causes and Cures. Center for Economic Policy Research, London, pp. 61–68.
McDonough, T., Reich, M., Kotz, D.M. (Eds.), 2010. Contemporary Capitalism and its Crises: Social Structure of Accumulation Theory for the Twenty First Century. Cambridge University Press, Cambridge.
Summers, L.H., 2014. U.S. Economic prospects: secular stagnation, hysteresis, and the zero lower bound. Business Economics 49 (2), 65–73.
U.S. Bureau of Economic Analysis, various years. U.S. Economic Accounts available at http://www.bea.gov.
Wolfson, M., Kotz, D.M., 2010. A Re conceptualization of social structure of accumulation theory. In: McDonough, T., Reich, M., Kotz, D.M. (Eds.), Contemporary Capitalism and its Crises: Social Structure of Accumulation Theory for the Twenty First Century. Cambridge University Press, Cambridge, pp. 72–90.

Further reading

Hansen, A.H., 1939. Economic progress and declining population growth. American Economic Review 29 (1), 1–15.

CHAPTER FIVE

Financialization and stagnation—a macroeconomic regime perspective*

Eckhard Hein
Institute for International Political Economy (IPE), Berlin School of Economics and Law, Berlin, Germany

Introduction

Financialization or finance-dominated capitalism—the terminology is used interchangeably in this contribution—as a dominating trend in developed capitalist economies since the 1980s has been analyzed from several perspectives: the deregulation of the financial sector and the rise of shadow banking, rising gross indebtedness of the private sector, the ascendance of shareholder dominance at the firm level, the financialization of everyday life, and the emergence of several macroeconomic regimes under the dominance of finance, among others. This has been reviewed in papers by Sawyer (2013/2014) or van der Zwan (2014), and shown in books by Guttmann (2016), Hein (2012) and Palley (2013), among others. In this contribution, we will analyze how financialization, which has led to the worldwide financial crisis and the Great Recession 2007–09, has contributed to stagnation tendencies since then. From the post-Keynesian perspective applied here, the analysis of stagnation tendencies requires to focus on income distribution, macroeconomic demand regimes, and on the stance of macroeconomic policies (Blecker, 2016a; Cynamon and Fazzari, 2015, 2016; Hein, 2016, 2018b; Palley, 2016; van Treeck, 2015). Therefore, in this contribution, the focus will be on the macroeconomic demand and growth regimes under the dominance of finance, before and after the crisis, and the instability and stagnation tendencies included in the latter, in particular.

* This contribution draws on Hein (2018a, 2019) and provides a focused update of the analysis provided there. For research assistance and help with the editing I would like to thank Ryan Woodgate. Remaining errors are mine, of course.

Handbook of Economic Stagnation
ISBN: 978-0-12-815898-2
https://doi.org/10.1016/B978-0-12-815898-2.00001-X

The effects of financialization on income distribution before and after the crisis have been analyzed for a set of six developed OECD countries in detail in Hein et al. (2017a,b, 2018): France, Germany, Spain, Sweden, the UK, and the US. The focus in this contribution will be on the macroeconomic demand and growth regimes for these six countries,[1] and furthermore for the core Eurozone, the EA-12, because the transformation of its macroeconomic regime in the course of the Eurozone crisis seems to be a major contributor to current stagnation tendencies and it contains a major threat to global development and stability (Hein, 2018a). In what follows, we will first introduce the concept of macroeconomic regimes under financialization. Then we will provide the analysis of the respective regimes—both before and after the crisis. Finally, we will relate the changes in regimes to the emanating tendencies toward instability and stagnation.

The concept of macroeconomic regimes under financialization

From a macroeconomic perspective, finance-dominated capitalism or financialization can be described by four characteristics, as elaborated in detail in Hein (2012, 2014, Chapter 10), for example.

1. With regard to distribution, financialization has been conducive to a rising gross profit share, including retained profits, dividends, and interest payments, and thus a falling labor income share, on the one hand, and to increasing inequality of wages and top management salaries and thus of personal or household incomes, on the other hand (Hein, 2015). It can be argued that finance-dominated capitalism has contributed to the falling labor income share since the early 1980s and to rising inequality through several channels: the falling bargaining power of workers and trade unions, rising profit claims imposed in particular by increasingly powerful rentiers (both creditors and shareholders), a change in the sectoral composition of the economy in favor of the financial corporate sector at the expense of the nonfinancial corporate sector or the public sector with higher labor income shares (Hein, 2015; Hein et al., 2017a,b, 2018; Köhler et al., 2019).
2. Regarding investment in the capital stock, financialization has meant increasing shareholder power vis-à-vis firms and workers, the demand

[1] Detailed studies on financialization and the financial and economic crisis in the countries of our study can be found in the contributions to Hein et al. (2016).

for an increasing rate of return on equity held by rentiers, and an alignment of management with shareholder interests through short-run performance related pay schemes, such as bonuses, stock option programs, and so on. On the one hand, this has imposed short-termism on management and has caused a decrease in management's animal spirits with respect to real investment in the capital stock and to long-run growth of the firm and increasing preference for financial investment, generating high profits in the short run. On the other hand, it has drained internal means of finance available for real investment purposes from nonfinancial corporations, through increasing dividend payments and share buybacks in order to boost stock prices and thus shareholder value. These "preference" and "internal means of finance" each have had partially negative effects on firms' real investment in capital stock, as several econometric studies for different countries have shown (Stockhammer, 2004; van Treeck, 2008; Orhangazi, 2008; Onaran et al., 2011; Davis, 2016, 2017, 2018; Tori and Onaran, 2017, 2018).

3. Regarding consumption, financialization has generated an increasing potential for wealth-based and debt-financed consumption in some countries, thus creating the potential to compensate for the depressing demand effects of financialization, which have been imposed on the economy via redistribution of income and via the depressing impact of shareholder value orientation on real investment. Stock market and housing price booms have each increased notional wealth against which households were willing to borrow. Changing financial norms, new financial instruments (credit card debt, home equity lending), deterioration of creditworthiness standards, triggered by securitization of mortgage debt and "originate and distribute" strategies of commercial banks, made credit increasingly available to low income, low wealth households, in particular. This potentially allowed for consumption to rise faster than median income and thus to stabilize aggregate demand. But it also generated increasing debt-income ratios of private households. Barba and Pivetti (2009), Cynamon and Fazzari (2008, 2013), Guttmann and Plihon (2010), van Treeck and Sturn (2012), and van Treeck (2014) have presented extensive case studies on wealth-based and debt-financed consumption, with a focus on the USA. As Kim (2013, 2016) has pointed out, although new credit to households will boost aggregate demand and output in the short run, the effects of household debt

variables on output and growth turn negative in the long run. This indicates contradictory effects of the flow of new credit and the stock of debt on consumption.

4. The liberalization of international capital markets and capital accounts has allowed for rising and persistent current account imbalances at the global, but also at the regional levels, in particular within the Eurozone, as has been analyzed by several authors, including Hein (2012, Chapter 6), Hein (2014, Chapter 10), Hein and Mundt (2012), Horn et al. (2009), Stockhammer (2010, 2012, 2015), UNCTAD (2009) and van Treeck and Sturn (2012).

The country-specific stances of the four macroeconomic features of financialization can give rise to different macroeconomic demand and growth regimes. The idea of demand and growth regimes used here is built on the demand-driven post-Kaleckian distribution and growth models proposed by Bhaduri and Marglin (1990) and Kurz (1990) which may generate wage- or profit-led regimes. Extended econometric research for several developed capitalist economies and a few emerging market economies has found wage-led medium to long-run regimes for most of the advanced capitalist economies, except for some small very open economies.[2] This is in particular true for the countries in the data set of the current contribution (Onaran and Galanis, 2014; Onaran and Obst, 2016). Based on these results, the redistribution effects of financialization should have had a depressive impact on aggregate demand and growth in these economies, further reinforced by the constraining effects of financialization on real investment. However, through debt-financed private consumption, and partially real estate investment, in some countries, or through rising net exports and current account surpluses in other countries, with the related current account deficits in the counterpart economies, these depressive effects on aggregate demand and growth have been partly compensated or even overcompensated. This has been shown by Hein (2018a) in a stylized Kaleckian model and by Belabed et al. (2018) and Detzer (2018) in simulated stock-flow consistent models.

From this literature it follows that under the conditions of the dominance of finance, income redistribution at the expense of labor and low income

[2] For a presentation of the post-Kaleckian distribution and growth model in the tradition of Bhaduri and Marglin (1990) and Kurz (1990) and a summary of the econometric estimation results for the model see Hein (2014, Chapters 6–7). For a discussion of the debate around the theoretical model and the empirical findings clarifying several misunderstandings, see recently Blecker (2016b) and Stockhammer (2017).

households, and weak investment in the capital stock, different demand and growth regimes may emerge. Considering the growth contributions of the main demand aggregates (private consumption, public consumption, investment, net exports) and the sectoral financial balances of the main macroeconomic sectors (private household sector, financial and nonfinancial corporate sectors, government sector, external sector), in this contribution three broad types of regimes can be distinguished: (a) a debt-led private demand boom regime, (b) an export-led mercantilist regime, and (c) a domestic demand-led regime.

The debt-led private demand boom regime is characterized by negative or close to zero financial balances of the private household sectors, which means that major parts of the private household sector have negative saving rates out of current income, are hence running current deficits, financed by increasing their stock of debt and/or reducing their stock of assets. These private household deficits are reinforced by corporate deficits and thus we have deficits of the private domestic sectors as a whole. The external sector has positive financial balances, which means that debt-led private demand boom countries are usually running current account deficits. There are high growth contributions of private domestic demand, financed by credit to a considerable extent, and negative growth contributions of the balance of goods and services, driving the current account into deficit in the long run.

The export-led mercantilist regime is characterized by positive financial balances of the domestic sectors as a whole, and hence negative financial balances of the external sector, and thus, current account surpluses. The growth contributions of domestic demand are rather small or even negative in certain years, and growth is mainly driven by positive contributions of the balance of goods and services and hence rising net exports.

The domestic demand-led regime is characterized by positive financial balances of the private household sector. Here it is usually the government and, to a certain degree, the corporate sector, running deficits. The external sector is roughly balanced, with only slight deficits or surpluses. We have positive growth contributions of domestic demand without a clear dominance of private consumption, and of credit-financed consumption in particular, and slightly negative or positive growth contributions of the balance of goods and services on average.

The two extreme regimes, the debt-led private demand boom and the export-led mercantilist regimes, have been made possible by the effects of financialization on consumption and private expenditures, on the one hand, and by the effects on the current account, on the other hand. In particular, the deficit financed expenditures in the debt-led private demand boom economies, generating current account deficits in these countries, have provided the conditions for the high and rising current account surpluses in the export-led mercantilist countries.

Assessing the regimes a qualitative analysis based on quantitative data will be applied. Since the core Eurozone as a whole will be included in this analysis, the precrisis time period from 1999 until 2008 will be considered, on the one hand, and the crisis and postcrisis period from 2009 until 2018, on the other. The demand and growth regimes can be distinguished by considering first the financial balances of the main macroeconomic sectors: the private sector, with the private household sector, the financial, and nonfinancial corporate sectors as subsectors; the government sector; and the external sector. Second, the growth contributions of the main demand aggregates are of interest. These are the growth contributions of private consumption, public consumption, as well as private and public investment, which sum up to the growth contribution of domestic demand, and then the growth contribution of the balance of goods and services, that is, of net exports. On the one hand, this provides some information about the main drivers of growth, and, on the other hand, on how demand is financed.

The regimes before the crisis

In the precrisis period from 1999 until 2008, the US, the UK, and Spain were dominated by the debt-led private demand boom regime. In this period, these countries were faced with rising inequality (Table 5.1).

Table 5.1 Distribution trends for selected OECD countries before and after the financial and economic crisis 2007–09.

			US	UK	Spain	Germany	Sweden	France
Distribution trends	Adjusted wage share	Before	–	0	–	–	–	–
		After	–	–	–	0	0	+
	Top income share	Before	+	+	+	+	+	+
		After	+	–	–	?	0	0
	Gini coefficients	Before	+	+	0	+	+	0
		After	+	0	+	+	0	–

Notes: +, tendency to increase; –, tendency to decrease; 0, no tendency; ?, no data. Before: early 1990s until the crisis 2007–09, After: after the crisis 2007–09.
Source: Hein et al. (2017a).

Looking at the financial balances, these countries were characterized by negative financial balances of their domestic private sectors and negative financial balances of the private household sectors in the USA and Spain, in particular (Table 5.2). The public sectors were in deficit, too. The

Table 5.2 Key macroeconomic variables for selected OECD countries and the core Eurozone (EA 12), average annual values for the period 1999–2008.

	USA	UK	Spain	Germany	Sweden	France	EA 12
Financial balances of external sector as a share of nominal GDP, percent	4.1	2.5	5.3	−2.7	−5.1	−0.9	−0.5
Financial balances of public sector as share of nominal GDP, percent	−3.9	−2.0	−0.3	−2.2	1.2	−2.7	−2.0
Financial balance of private sector as a share of nominal GDP, percent	−0.3	−0.6	−5.0	4.9	3.9	3.5	2.5
- Financial balance of private household sector as a share of nominal GDP, percent	−0.2	1.9	−2.5	5.0	1.1	2.6	2.1
- Financial balance of the corporate sector as a share of nominal GDP, percent	0.0	−2.5	−2.5	−0.2	2.8	0.9	0.4
Real GDP growth, percent	2.6	2.6	3.5	1.5	3.0	2.1	2.1
Growth contribution of domestic demand including stocks, percentage points	2.9	2.8	4.1	0.8	2.4	2.3	1.9
- Growth contribution of private consumption, percentage points	2.1	1.9	2.0	0.4	1.3	1.2	1.0

(*Continued*)

Table 5.2 Key macroeconomic variables for selected OECD countries and the core Eurozone (EA 12), average annual values for the period 1999–2008.—cont'd

	USA	UK	Spain	Germany	Sweden	France	EA 12
- Growth contribution of public consumption, percentage points	0.3	0.6	0.8	0.2	0.2	0.4	0.4
- Growth contribution of gross fixed capital formation, percentage points	0.6	0.4	1.4	0.2	1.0	0.7	0.6
Growth contribution of the balance of goods and services, percentage points	−0.2	−0.3	−0.7	0.7	0.6	−0.2	0.1
Net exports of goods and services as a share of nominal GDP, percent	−4.4	−2.1	−3.6	3.9	5.5	0.8	1.7

Source: European Commission (2019), author's calculations.

external sectors were the surplus sectors, and the countries following the debt-led private demand boom regime were thus characterized by current account deficits and negative net exports. We see high growth contributions of private domestic demand and of private consumption demand in particular, financed by household deficits to a considerable degree. Private consumption contributed more than 50% to GDP growth in the case of Spain, and more than 70% in the cases of the USA and the UK. The growth contributions of the balance of goods and services were negative and thus reduced GDP growth, most noticeably in Spain. The debt-led private demand boom regime countries were thus the world demand engines before the crisis, mainly relying on increasing private debt, and household debt in particular.

The export-led mercantilist regime in the precrisis period dominated in Germany and Sweden. Here we also see rising inequality (Table 5.1). We observe positive financial balances of the domestic sectors as a whole, with significantly positive financial balances of the private sector, and a deficit of the public sector in Germany and a surplus in Sweden (Table 5.2). The external sector was in deficit in both countries. These countries were thus running current account surpluses and positive net exports. In both countries, the growth contributions of domestic demand were rather small, and in Germany even negative in certain years. Private consumption only accounted for less than 30% in the case of Germany and slightly above 40% in the case of Sweden for GDP growth on average over the period. Growth was mainly driven by positive contributions of the balance of goods and services and hence rising net exports, which contributed about 50% in the case of Germany and 20% in the case of Sweden to GDP growth. These countries were thus free-riding on dynamic world demand generated by the debt-led private demand boom countries, in particular.

Finally, we have in between the two extremes the domestic demand-led regime, which in the precrisis period can be found in France and also in the core Eurozone taken as a whole, the EA-12. Here we also see rising inequality for France (Table 5.1), and a falling labor income share in the EA-12 (European Commission, 2019). There were positive financial balances of the private household sector and of the private sector as a whole (Table 5.2). The latter was also true for the core Eurozone. Furthermore, we have slightly negative financial balances of the external sectors, and hence, small current account and net export surpluses for both France and the core Eurozone. Growth was almost exclusively driven by domestic demand, with relevant contributions by private consumption, however, without drawing on rising household credit, since private household financial balances remained significantly positive. Growth contributions of the balance of goods and services were slightly negative in the case of France, and weakly positive in the case of the core Eurozone.

The countries following the two extreme regimes before the crisis, the debt-led private demand boom regime and the export-led mercantilist regime, contributed to generating rising current account imbalances in the global economy (Fig. 5.1), but also within the Eurozone (Hein, 2013/14). These global imbalances then led to the severity of the financial crisis and the Great Recession. As is well known, the crisis started in the main debt-led private demand boom country, the USA, and was transmitted to the world economy through the international trade channel and the financial contagion channel. Although the crisis did not turn toward a Great Depression, as in the 1930s, the recovery has been slow in historical comparison (Fig. 5.2), with a "double dip" recession in Spain, Sweden and the Eurozone as whole between 2011 and 2013. This weak recovery has triggered a renewed debate on "secular stagnation" (Summers, 2014, 2015).[3] As will be shown below, the recovery period has been associated with a shift in

[3] For an assessment of this debate from a post-Keynesian perspective see Hein (2016, 2021).

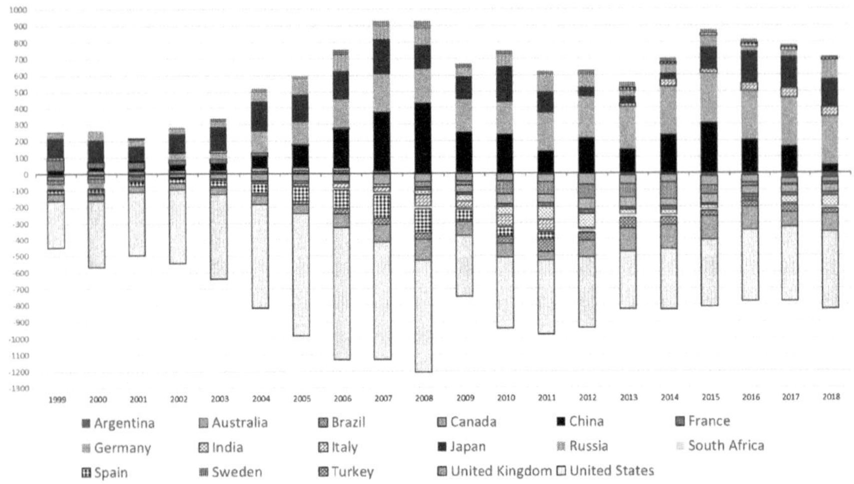

Figure 5.1 Current account balance, major countries, 1999–2018, in billions of US dollars. *Source: IMF (2019), author's presentation.*

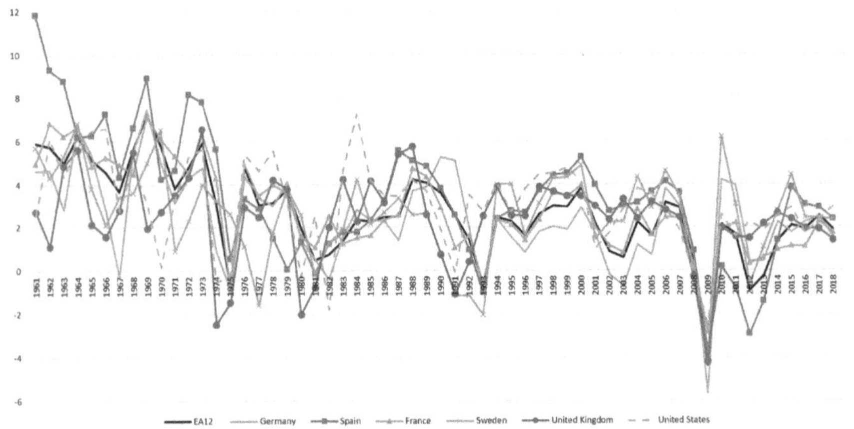

Figure 5.2 Growth rate of real GDP (at 2015 prices), selected countries, 1961–2018, in percent *Source: European Commission (2019), author's calculations.*

the patterns of macroeconomic regimes, which has contributed to stagnation and has created a highly fragile and challenging global economic situation.[4]

[4] For a more in depth analysis of the shift in macroeconomic demand and growth regimes see Hein and Martschin (2021) focusing on the relationship with the macroeconomic policy regimes for four core Eurozone countries and Hein et al., 2020 relating the regime shifts to the different welfare state models for 30 OECD countries. Köhler and Stockhammer (2020) have provided an interesting analysis of underlying growth drivers associated with these regime shifts.

Changes in the regimes in the course of and after the crisis

In the precrisis debt-led private demand boom countries, the USA, the UK, and Spain, the private sectors, that is, the private households and partly the corporations, had to deleverage considerably. On average over the period 2009—18, the financial balances of these sectors thus became positive (with the exception of the corporate sector in the UK) and the growth contributions of private consumption and investment shrank remarkably—in Spain they even became negative. High public deficits stabilized the economy and allowed for low but positive growth in the USA and the UK, which moved from a debt-led private demand boom regime toward a domestic demand-led regime stabilized by public sector deficits. Persistently high external sector surpluses and thus current account deficits in these two countries contributed to the stabilization of global demand in the world economy.

Spain has been a different case. Initially in the crisis, high public sector deficits allowed the private sector to generate financial surpluses and to deleverage. However, with the Eurozone crisis since 2010 and the austerity policies implemented, public deficits have been reduced, public and private domestic demand collapsed and real GDP growth turned negative and has only recovered recently. Positive growth contributions came from the balance of goods and services, through rising exports and falling imports, such that the current account improved and has, on an annual basis, remained positive since 2012. Spain has thus moved from a debt-led private demand boom economy toward an export-led mercantilist economy.

Both in the USA and the UK, as well as in Spain, the regime shifts were associated with a further deterioration of income distribution (Table 5.1): Labor income shares in all three countries have been falling, Gini coefficients for the household distribution of income before and after taxes have been rising in the USA and Spain, and remained constant at very high levels in the UK, and only top income shares have been falling in the UK and Spain, whereas they continued to rise in the USA (Hein et al., 2017a,b, 2018). These developments have prevented a mass income- or wage-driven recovery in these countries, so that the options have been either drawing on government deficits (USA, UK) or on foreign sector deficits (Spain) as stabilizers of demand and growth.

In the export-led mercantilist countries before the crisis, Germany and Sweden, the public sector accepted high financial deficits (Germany) or a strong reduction of surpluses leading to small deficits (Sweden) in the crisis and the years following in order to stabilize the private sector and the macro-economy. However, these deficits could be passively consolidated, because of the economic recovery, initially driven by net exports. The financial balances of the private sectors remained positive, in particular for private households (Table 5.3). On average over the period 2009–18, growth was exclusively driven by domestic demand, with significant contributions of private consumption. This shift has been made possible by stopping the trend toward rising inequality (Table 5.1): Labor income shares stopped

Table 5.3 Key macroeconomic variables for selected OECD countries and the core Eurozone (EA 12), average annual values for the period 2009–18.

	USA	UK	Spain	Germany	Sweden	France	EA 12
Financial balances of external sector as a share of nominal GDP, percent	2.0	4.0	−0.7	−7.1	−4.1	0.8	−2.5
Financial balances of public sector as share of nominal GDP, percent	−7.8	−5.9	−6.9	−0.3	−0.2	−4.5	−3.1
Financial balance of private sector as a share of nominal GDP, percent	5.8	1.9	7.7	7.4	4.3	3.7	5.6
- Financial balance of private household sector as a share of nominal GDP, percent	4.1	3.2	0.9	5.3	5.0	3.2	2.8
- Financial balance of the corporate sector as a share of nominal GDP, percent	1.7	−1.4	6.8	2.1	−0.7	0.4	2.8
Real GDP growth, percent	1.8	1.3	0.5	1.3	2.0	0.9	0.8

Table 5.3 Key macroeconomic variables for selected OECD countries and the core Eurozone (EA 12), average annual values for the period 2009–18.—cont'd

	USA	UK	Spain	Germany	Sweden	France	EA 12
Growth contribution of domestic demand including stocks, percentage points	1.9	1.4	−0.4	1.3	2.1	1.0	0.5
- Growth contribution of private consumption, percentage points	1.4	1.0	0.0	0.7	1.0	0.5	0.3
- Growth contribution of public consumption, percentage points	0.0	0.2	0.1	0.4	0.4	0.3	0.2
- Growth contribution of gross fixed capital formation, percentage points	0.4	0.2	−0.5	0.3	0.5	0.1	0.0
Growth contribution of the balance of goods and services, percentage points	−0.1	−0.2	0.9	0.0	−0.1	0.0	0.3
Net exports of goods and services as a share of nominal GDP, percent	−3.1	−1.4	2.1	6.2	4.0	−1.1	3.3

Source: European Commission (2019), author's calculations.

falling, top income shares were not rising any more, and in Sweden Gini coefficients for pre- and posttax household incomes remained constant, whereas in Germany they continued to rise slightly. However, these countries still show considerable current account and net export surpluses, and thus negative financial balances of the respective external sectors. In Germany, these surpluses have exceeded those before the crisis considerably, whereas in Sweden they are only slightly below what they were before the crisis. Germany and Sweden thus continued to be export-led.

The domestic demand-led regime in France has not changed significantly in the crisis and the following years. Financial surpluses of private households were mopped up by corporations, but even more so by the public sector (Table 5.3). Due to the stabilization requirements, public sector deficits increased relative to the period before the crisis. The balance of the external sector, which had become slightly positive already before the crisis has remained, so that France on average over the second period was running a small current account and a net exports deficit. Public deficits in France have thus been stabilizing global demand for goods and services, too. Growth in France was driven by domestic demand, and mainly by private and public consumption. The former was facilitated by a decline in inequality in the period after the crisis (Table 5.1). France is the only country in the current data set, in which the labor income share has been rising, the Gini coefficients for pre- and posttax incomes of households have been falling and top income shares have at least remained constant in the period after the crisis.

The development in the core Eurozone, which had also been domestic demand-led before the crisis, however, has been different. Although labor income shares for the EA-12 remained roughly constant after the crisis (European Commission, 2019), albeit with wide variations among member countries (Hein, 2018b), the Eurozone has turned toward an export-led mercantilist regime after the crisis (Table 5.3). With considerable private sector financial surpluses due to deleveraging, and shrinking public sector deficits over time due to austerity policies, the foreign sector balances turned negative, and the Eurozone has started to run increasing current account and net export surpluses of more than 3% of GDP. Meagre growth since the crisis has been driven by net exports to a large degree. Of course, the major reason for these developments has been the austerity policies which have been implemented since the start of the Eurozone crisis in 2010, in particular in the crisis countries, Greece, Portugal, Ireland, Portugal, and Spain (Hein, 2013/14, 2018b; Hein and Martschin, 2020). A major economic and currency area in the world economy has thus become a drag on global demand, free riding on world demand generated elsewhere.

Challenges: imbalances, instability, and stagnation

From a global perspective, current account imbalances have been slightly reduced in and after the crisis, if compared to the years before the crises. However, they are still much more pronounced than in the early

2000s (Fig. 5.1). The high current account surpluses by the export-led mercantilist countries—Germany, Spain, the Eurozone as a whole, and Sweden in the current study, but also China, Japan, Italy, and Russia—are matched by current account deficits of domestic demand-led economies with high public sector deficits—in particular the USA, the UK and France in the current study, and furthermore emerging market and commodity producing countries like Argentina, Australia, Brazil, Canada, India, South Africa, and Turkey. The risks of such a global situation are obvious. If ever more economies, like currently the whole Eurozone, move toward an export-led mercantilist regime, the world economy will face an aggregation problem. It will become increasingly difficult to generate the related current account deficits in other regions of the world. Stagnation tendencies are then the inescapable consequences of this failure of demand generation at the global level.

Since global demand stabilization has relied on public sector financial deficits in the mature domestic demand-led economies, as well as on public and private sector deficits in emerging market economies, further risks and dangers have built up. First, high government deficits and debt in mature domestic demand-led economies as stabilizers of national and global demand may be reversed for political reasons (debt ceilings, debt brakes), although there may be no risks of overindebtedness of governments, if debt can be issued in the country's own currency and is backed by the respective central bank. Second, capital inflows into emerging market economies may be unstable and face "sudden stops" because of changes in expectations and/or overindebtedness in foreign currency of these countries. And third, there are the risks of politically induced protection measures in order to reduce current account and net export deficits, which are considered to be too high, as currently observed in the case of the USA.

Apart from these short-to medium-run problems, there arises a long-run stagnation problem associated with weak investment and capital stock growth. Due to the effects of financialization on investment, as outlined in The concept of macroeconomic regimes under financialization section, growth contributions of investment have already been weak before the crisis (Table 5.2) and have turned even lower in the crisis and postcrisis period (Table 5.3). Basically, this is true for all three regimes. In a long-run perspective, capital stock growth has seen a downwards trend, only interrupted by the new economy boom in the second half of the 1990s (and by the

Eurozone boom in Spain in the early 2010s), with particularly low growth rates in the period after the recent crisis (Fig. 5.3). This has led or at least contributed to falling growth rates of labor productivity, which also turned particularly low after the crisis (Fig. 5.4).

Theoretically, the interaction between distribution, capital accumulation, and productivity growth can be shown by extending a basic post-Kaleckian distribution and growth model in the tradition of Bhaduri and Marglin (1990) and Kurz (1990), already referred to above. According to

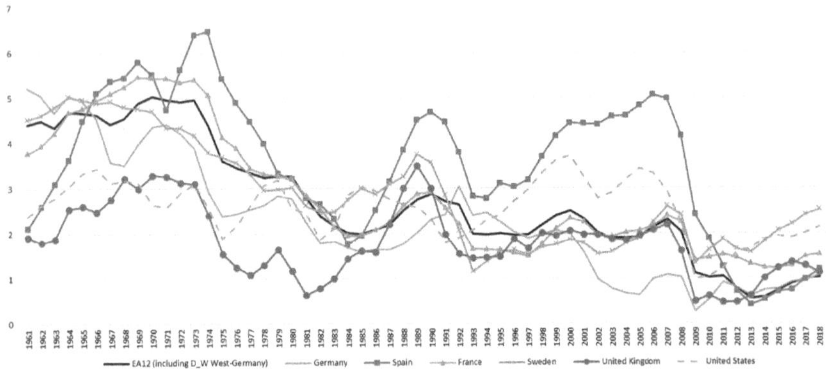

Figure 5.3 Growth rate real net capital stock (at 2015 prices), selected countries, 1961–2018, in percent *Source: European Commission (2019), author's calculations.*

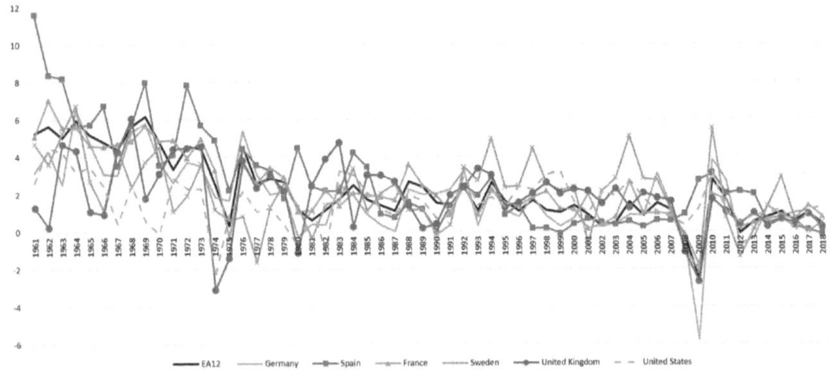

Figure 5.4 Growth rate of real GDP (at 2015 prices) per person employed, selected countries, 1961–2018, in percent *Source: European Commission (2019), author's calculations.*

the open economy version of the post-Kaleckian model, including government deficit spending, the goods market equilibrium rate of capital accumulation and growth—assuming for now that technical progress and hence productivity growth is exogenous—is determined as follows (Hein, 2014, Chapters 7–8):

$$g_{IS} = g_{IS}\left(\alpha, h, s_W, s_\Pi, d, e^r, g^f_{IS}, \widehat{y}\right),$$

$$\frac{\partial g_{IS}}{\partial \alpha} > 0, \frac{\partial g_{IS}}{\partial h} < 0, \frac{\partial g_{IS}}{\partial s_W} < 0, \frac{\partial g_{IS}}{\partial s_\Pi} < 0, \frac{\partial g_{IS}}{\partial d} > 0, \frac{\partial g_{IS}}{\partial e^r} > 0, \frac{\partial g_{IS}}{\partial g^f_{IS}} > 0,$$
$$\frac{\partial g_{IS}}{\partial \widehat{y}} > 0 \tag{5.1}$$

Animal spirits of firms and/or autonomous expenditures (α) have a positive effect on equilibrium accumulation and growth (g_{IS}). The effect of the profit share (h) is theoretically ambiguous, and wage- or profit-led regimes have been derived. However, empirical research has shown that the countries in our data set have been wage-led (Onaran and Galanis, 2014; Onaran and Obst, 2016). Therefore, we have a negative effect of the profit share on equilibrium growth. The propensities to save out of wages (s_W) and out of profits (s_Π) have negative effects, that is, we have the validity of the paradox of thrift. The government deficit expenditure rate (d) has a positive effect. The real exchange rate (e^r) and equilibrium foreign growth (g^f_{IS}) positively affect (net) exports and thus domestic growth. Furthermore, the goods market equilibrium rate of capital accumulation is positively affected by productivity growth ($\widehat{y}$), because of capital embodied technological change, in particular. Firms have to invest in new capital stock in order to benefit from technological inventions.

In order to endogenize productivity growth, we can rely on Kaldor's (1957, 1961) technical progress function and/or on Kaldor's (1966) "Verdoorn's Law." Labor productivity growth can thus be assumed to be positively affected by capital stock growth due to capital-embodied technological change, and/or by demand growth due to dynamic returns to scale. Furthermore, following Marx (1867) we can integrate a wage-push variable into the productivity growth function of the model. Higher real wage rates or a higher wage shares induce capitalists to speed up the implementation of labor augmenting technological progress in order to protect the profit share. Therefore, Eq. (5.2) is obtained for long-run productivity growth:

$$\widehat{y} = \widehat{y}(g_{IS}, h, z_i),$$
$$\frac{\partial \widehat{y}}{\partial g_{IS}} > 0, \frac{\partial \widehat{y}}{\partial h} < 0, \frac{\partial \widehat{y}}{\partial z_i} > 0 \tag{5.2}$$

Productivity growth is thus positively affected by the goods market equilibrium rate of capital accumulation and negatively by the profit share, with z_i representing a set of further institutional factors determining productivity growth, like government technology policies, the education system, etc.

Eqs. (5.1) and (5.2) describe a demand-determined endogenous growth model, and Fig. 5.5 presents the long-run equilibrium values for capital accumulation $\left(g^*_{IS1}\right)$ and productivity growth $\left(\widehat{y}^*_1\right)$, and thus the endogenous potential or "natural" growth grate.[5] Any fall in the goods market equilibrium rate of capital accumulation, as the ones we have seen for both the debt-led private demand boom and the export-led mercantilist regimes, thus causes a leftward shift in the g_{IS}-curve, which lowers the long-run equilibrium rates of capital accumulation and productivity growth, hence weakens potential growth, and stagnation emerges.

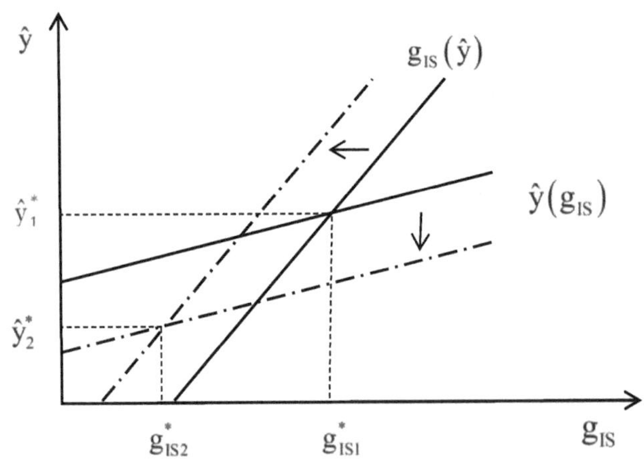

Figure 5.5 A Kalecki-Kaldor-Marx endogenous growth model.

[5] For analytical treatments see Hein (2014, Chapter 8, 2018b).

Finally, Fig. 5.5 also shows the effect of a rise in the profit share on long-run potential growth. In this case, both curves get shifted and the long-run growth equilibrium falls from $g^*_{IS1}, \widehat{y}^*_1$ to $g^*_{IS2}, \widehat{y}^*_2$. Redistribution at the expense of wages is thus detrimental to long-run capital accumulation, productivity growth and thus to potential growth, although there may be short-to medium-run compensatory factors, that is, rising deficit spending of private households, the government or of the foreign sector. These, however, may be difficult to sustain, as we have seen.

Summing up, postcrisis stagnation tendencies can be explained by those factors generating low equilibrium capital stock growth: depressed animal spirits of management of nonfinancial corporations, high propensities to save out of the different types of income, insufficient government deficit rates and expenditures on R&D, in particular in the export-led mercantilist countries, as well as high profit shares and high inequality. High and rising profit shares have an independent depressing effect on innovation activities of firms and on productivity growth; the latter being depressed by low capital accumulation, too. Stagnation is thus no inescapable fate, but it is, to a large degree, the result of distributional and economic policies—of "stagnation policies," as Steindl (1979) has analyzed (Hein, 2016, 2018b).

Conclusions

In this contribution, we have tried to link the recently rediscovered tendencies toward stagnation with the features of financialization, which have started to dominate developed capitalist economies in the early 1980s. We have first reviewed the main macroeconomic channels of transmission of financialization—namely, the effects on distribution, investment in the capital stock, consumption, and on the current and capital accounts. Based on these, we have introduced the concept of macroeconomic regimes under financialization, and we have distinguished three regimes, the debt-led private demand boom, the export-led mercantilist and the domestic demand-led regime. This typology has then been applied to six countries, Germany, France, Spain, Sweden, the UK, and the USA, as well as to the Eurozone, both for the period before (1999–2008) and after (2009–18) the financial and economic crisis. We have shown that the dominance of the debt-led private demand boom regime, on the one hand, and the export-led mercantilist regime, on the other hand, have contributed to global current account imbalances before the financial and economic crisis

2007–09, which has demonstrated that these two regimes were unsustainable. For the period after the crisis we have found a shift toward export-led mercantilist regimes and a move toward domestic demand-led regimes stabilized by government debt with global current account imbalances persisting. Finally, we have elaborated on the challenges of these developments, a highly fragile global constellation with severe problems of aggregate demand generation and a tendency toward stagnation caused by high inequality and weak capital stock growth. We have singled out the underlying causes, from which we concluded that stagnation is no inescapable fate, but that it is, to a large degree, the result of "stagnation policies" (Steindl, 1979).

References

Barba, A., Pivetti, M., 2009. Rising household debt: its causes and macroeconomic implications – a long-period analysis. Cambridge Journal of Economics 33, 113–137.

Belabed, C., Theobald, T., van Treeck, T., 2018. Income distribution and current account imbalances. Cambridge Journal of Economics 42 (1), 47–94.

Bhaduri, A., Marglin, S., 1990. Unemployment and the real wage: the economic basis for contesting political ideologies. Cambridge Journal of Economics 14, 375–393.

Blecker, R.A., 2016a. The US economy since the crisis: slow recovery and secular stagnation. European Journal of Economics and Economic Policies: Intervention 13 (2), 203–214.

Blecker, R.A., 2016b. Wage-led versus profit-led demand regimes: the long and the short of it. Review of Keynesian Economics 4, 373–390.

Cynamon, B., Fazzari, S., 2008. Household debt in the consumer age: source of growth – risk of collapse. Capitalism and Society 3 (2), 1–30.

Cynamon, B., Fazzari, S., 2013. Inequality and Household Finance during the Consumer Age. Working Paper No. 752. Levy Economics Institute of Bard College, Annandale-on-Hudson, NY.

Cynamon, B.Z., Fazzari, S.M., 2015. Rising inequality and stagnation in the US economy. European Journal of Economics and Economic Policies: Intervention 12 (2), 170–172.

Cynamon, B.Z., Fazzari, S.M., 2016. Inequality, the Great recession and slow recovery. Cambridge Journal of Economics 40, 373–399.

Davis, L.E., 2016. Identifying the 'financialization' of the non-financial corporation in the US economy: a decomposition of firm-level balance sheets. Journal of Post Keynesian Economics 39 (1), 115–141.

Davis, L.E., 2017. Financialization and investment: a survey of the empirical literature. Journal of Economic Surveys 31 (5), 1332–1358.

Davis, L.E., 2018. Financialization and the nonfinancial corporation: an investigation of firm level investment behavior in the United States. Metroeconomica 69 (1), 270–301.

Detzer, D., 2018. Inequality, emulation and debt: the occurrence of different growth regimes in the age of financialisation in a stock-flow consistent model. Journal of Post Keynesian Economics 41, 284–315.

European Commission, 2019. AMECO Data Base, Update 7 November 2019. https://ec.europa.eu/info/business-economy-euro/indicators-statistics/economic-databases/macro-economic-database-ameco_en. (Accessed 8 November 2019).

Guttmann, R., 2016. Finance-led Capitalism: Shadow Banking, Re-regulation, and the Future of Global Markets. Palgrave Macmillan, Basingstoke.

Guttmann, R., Plihon, D., 2010. Consumer debt and financial fragility. International Review of Applied Economics 24, 269–283.

Hein, E., 2012. The Macroeconomics of Finance-Dominated Capitalism – and its Crisis. Edward Elgar, Cheltenham.
Hein, E., 2013/14. The crisis of finance-dominated capitalism in the Euro area, deficiencies in the economic policy architecture and deflationary stagnation policies. Journal of Post Keynesian Economics 36 (2), 325–354.
Hein, E., 2014. Distribution and Growth after Keynes: A Post-Keynesian Guide. Edward Elgar, Cheltenham.
Hein, E., 2015. Finance-dominated capitalism and re-distribution of income – a Kaleckian perspective. Cambridge Journal of Economics 39, 907–934.
Hein, E., 2016. Secular stagnation or stagnation policy? Steindl after Summers. PSL Quarterly Review 69 (276), 3–47.
Hein, E., 2018a. Inequality and growth: marxian and post-Keynesian/Kaleckian perspectives on distribution and growth regimes before and after the Great Recession. In: Arestis, P., Sawyer, M. (Eds.), Inequality: Trends, Causes, Consequences, Relevant Policies. International Papers in Political Economy. Palgrave Macmillan, Basingstoke.
Hein, E., 2018b. Stagnation policy in the Eurozone and economic policy alternatives: a Steindlian/neo-Kaleckian perspective. Wirtschaft und Gesellschaft 44 (3), 315–348.
Hein, E., 2019. Financialisation and tendencies towards stagnation: the role of macroeconomic regime changes in the course of and after the financial and economic crisis 2007–9. Cambridge Journal of Economics 43 (4), 975–999.
Hein, E., 2021. Stagnation policy: a Steindlian perspective. In: Dantas, F., Wray, L.R. (Eds.), The Handbook of Stagnation. Elsevier, forthcoming.
Hein, E., Detzer, D., Dodig, N. (Eds.), 2016. Financialisation and the Financial and Economic Crises: Country Studies. Edward Elgar, Cheltenham.
Hein, E., Dünhaupt, P., Alfageme, A., Kulesza, M., 2017a. Financialisation and distribution before and after the crisis: patterns for six OECD countries. In: Arestis, P., Sawyer, M. (Eds.), Economic Policies since the Global Financial Crisis. International Papers in Political Economy. Palgrave Macmillan, Basingstoke.
Hein, E., Dünhaupt, P., Kulesza, M., Alfageme, A., 2017b. Financialisation and distribution from a Kaleckian perspective: the United States, the United Kingdom and Sweden compared – before and after the crisis. International Journal of Political Economy 46 (4), 233–266.
Hein, E., Dünhaupt, P., Alfageme, A., Kulesza, M., 2018. A Kaleckian perspective on financialisation and distribution in three main Eurozone countries before and after the crisis: France, Germany and Spain. Review of Political Economy 30 (1), 41–71.
Hein, E., Martschin, J., 2020. The Eurozone in crisis – a Kaleckian macroeconomic regime and policy perspective. Review of Political Economy 32 (4), 563–588.
Hein, E., Martschin, J., 2021. Demand and growth regimes in finance-dominated capitalism and the role of the macroeconomic policy regime: a post-Keynesian comparative study on France, Germany, Italy and Spain before and after the Great Financial Crisis and the Great Recession. Review of Evolutionary Political Economy 2 (3), 493–527.
Hein, E., Mundt, M., 2012. Financialisation and the Requirements and Potentials for Wage-Led Recovery – a Review Focussing on the G20, Conditions of Work and Employment Series No. 37. ILO, Geneva.
Hein, E., Paternesi Meloni, W., Tridico, P., 2020. Welfare Models and Demand-Led Growth Regimes before and after the Financial and Economic Crisis, Review of International Political Economy. https://doi.org/10.1080/09692290.2020.1744178. Advance access.
Horn, G., Joebges, H., Zwiener, R., December 2009. From the financial crisis to the world economic crisis (II). In: Global Imbalances: Cause of the Crisis and Solution Strategies for Germany, IMK Policy Brief. Macroeconomic Policy Institute (IMK) at Hans-Boeckler Foundation, Duesseldorf.

International Monetary Fund (IMF), April 2019. World Economic Outlook Database. https://www.imf.org/external/pubs/ft/weo/2017/01/weodata/index.aspx. (Accessed 8 November 2019).
Kaldor, N., 1957. A model of economic growth. The Economic Journal 67, 591–624.
Kaldor, N., 1961. Capital accumulation and economic growth. In: Lutz, F.A., Hague, D.C. (Eds.), The Theory of Capital. Macmillan, London.
Kaldor, N., 1966. Causes of the Slow Rate of Economic Growth in the United Kingdom. Cambridge University Press, Cambridge, UK.
Kim, Y.K., 2013. Household debt, financialization, and macroeconomic performance in the United States, 1951–2009. Journal of Post Keynesian Economics 35, 675–694.
Kim, Y.K., 2016. Macroeconomic effects of household debt: an empirical analysis. Review of Keynesian Economics 4, 127–150.
Köhler, K., Guschanski, A., Stockhammer, E., 2019. The impact of financialisation on the wage share: a theoretical clarification and empirical test. Cambridge Journal of Economics 43, 937–974.
Köhler, K., Stockhammer, E., 2020. Growth Models in Advanced Countries before and after the 2008 Crisis: Competitiveness, Financial Cycles and Austerity. Post Keynesian Economics Society. Working Paper 2008.
Kurz, H.D., 1990. Technical change, growth and distribution: a steady-state approach to 'unsteady' growth. In: Kurz, H.D. (Ed.), Capital, Distribution and Effective Demand. Polity Press, Cambridge, UK.
Marx, K., 1867. Das Kapital: Kritik der politischen Ökonomie, Erster band: der Produktionsprozeß des Kapitals, 4th edition 1890. In: Engels, F. (Ed.), English Translation: Capital: A Critique of Political Economy, Volume 1: The Process of Capitalist Production. International Publisher, New York, 1967.
Onaran, Ö., Galanis, G., 2014. Income distribution and growth: a global model. Environment and Planning A 46, 2489–2513.
Onaran, Ö., Obst, T., 2016. Wage-led growth in the EU15 member-states: the effects of income distribution on growth, investment, trade balance and inflation. Cambridge Journal of Economics 40 (6), 1517–1551.
Onaran, Ö., Stockhammer, E., Grafl, L., 2011. Financialisation, income distribution and aggregate demand in the USA. Cambridge Journal of Economics 35, 637–661.
Orhangazi, Ö., 2008. Financialisation and capital accumulation in the non-financial corporate sector: a theoretical and empirical investigation on the US economy: 1973–2003. Cambridge Journal of Economics 32, 863–886.
Palley, T.I., 2013. Financialization: The Economics of Finance Capital Domination. Palgrave Macmillan, Basingtoke.
Palley, T.I., 2016. Inequality, the financial crisis and stagnation: competing stories and why they matter. Real World Economics Review 74, 1–18.
Sawyer, M., 2013/2014. What is financialization? International Journal of Political Economy 42 (4), 5–18.
Steindl, J., 1979. Stagnation theory and stagnation policy. Cambridge Journal of Economics 3, 1–14.
Stockhammer, E., 2004. Financialisation and the slowdown of accumulation. Cambridge Journal of Economics 28 (5), 719–741.
Stockhammer, E., 2010. Income distribution, the finance-dominated accumulation regime, and the present crisis. In: Dullien, S., Hein, E., Truger, A., van Treeck, T. (Eds.), The World Economy in Crisis - the Return of Keynesianism?, Marburg: Metropolis.
Stockhammer, E., 2012. Financialization, income distribution and the crisis. Investigación Económica 71 (279), 39–70.
Stockhammer, E., 2015. Rising inequality as a root cause of the present crisis. Cambridge Journal of Economics 39, 935–958.

Stockhammer, E., 2017. Wage-led versus profit-led demand: what have we learned? A Kaleckian-Minskyan view. Review of Keynesian Economics 5, 25–42.

Summers, L.A., 2014. U.S. economic prospects: secular stagnation, hysteresis, and the zero lower bound. Business Economics 49 (2), 65–73.

Summers, L.A., 2015. Demand side secular stagnation. American Economic Review: Papers and Proceedings 105 (5), 60–65.

Tori, D., Onaran, Ö., 2017. The Effects of Financialisation and Financial Development on Investment: Evidence from Firm-Level Data for Europe, Greenwich Papers in Political Economy 16089. University of Greenwich, Greenwich Political Economy Research Centre.

Tori, D., Onaran, Ö., 2018. The effects of financialisation on investment: evidence from firm-level data for the UK. Cambridge Journal of Economics 42, 1393–1416.

UNCTAD, 2009. The Global Economic Crisis: Systemic Failures and Multilateral Remedies. UNCTAD, New York, Geneva.

Van der Zwan, N., 2014. Making sense of financialization. Socio-Economic Review 12, 99–129.

Van Treeck, T., 2008. Reconsidering the investment-profit nexus in finance-led economies: an ARDL-based approach. Metroeconomica 59, 371–404.

Van Treeck, T., 2014. Did inequality cause the US financial crisis? Journal of Economic Surveys 28, 421–448.

Van Treeck, T., 2015. Inequality, the crisis, and stagnation. European Journal of Economics and Economic Policies: Intervention 12 (2), 158–169.

Van Treeck, T., Sturn, S., 2012. Income inequality as a cause of the great recession?. In: A Survey of Current Debates, Conditions of Work and Employment Series No. 39 ILO, Geneva.

CHAPTER SIX

Hyman Minsky meets secular stagnation*

Steven M. Fazzari
Departments of Economics and Sociology, Washington University, St. Louis, MO, United States

In the aftermath of the 2007–09 Great Recession and global financial crisis, the U.S. recovery has been weak. Indeed, more than a decade after the trough of the recession one might question the extent to which there has been any full "recovery" at all. While real GDP has grown and the labor market has certainly improved, output in 2019 had not returned to anything close to its precrisis trend and there is no indication whatsoever that this gap will be closed in the years to come.[1] This outcome has been labeled "secular stagnation," most prominently by Lawrence Summers (2014). Although Hyman Minsky's contributions to macroeconomics are wide-ranging, he is best known for his theory of financial instability, explaining the cyclical nature of capitalism. This chapter argues that Minsky's insights also help explain recent U.S. secular stagnation when coupled with the dramatic rise of income inequality.

In summary form, the argument is as follows. A major reason for stagnation is high-income households recycle a substantially smaller share of their pretax income back into spending. Therefore, as inequality rises and most of the growth of income goes to the top slivers of the income distribution demand growth stagnates, other things equal. While this basic story might suggest rising inequality is sufficient on its own to explain stagnation, the distribution channel alone must face what seems on the surface as a major empirical inconsistency. Income inequality began its persistent march upward sometime between the mid-1970s and early 1980s, decades *before*

* This chapter has been informed by many years of lectures at the Hyman Minsky summer workshop sponsored by the Levy Economics Institute at Bard College. Comments from the participants at these workshops are gratefully acknowledged.

[1] As of this writing, per capita real GDP in the third quarter of 2019 is 9.4% below the growth trend established between the previous business cycle peaks (that is, the trend from the second quarter of 2000 to the first quarter of 2006). Going back to 1960, real per capita GDP at a cycle peak was never more than 3.5% below its previous peak-to-peak growth trend.

Handbook of Economic Stagnation
ISBN: 978-0-12-815898-2
https://doi.org/10.1016/B978-0-12-815898-2.00007-0

secular stagnation was evident. This is where Minsky enters the story. A massive boom in household borrowing created a classic expansion phase of a long Minsky cycle from the mid-1980s (at the latest) to the eve of the Great Recession. This dynamic helped to keep household demand growth reasonably strong for more than 20 years, masking any potential demand drag from rising inequality. But the collapse of the recession, a classic Minsky crisis, wiped out unsustainably financed household demand. Household demand has not recovered its precrisis trend—the stagnation of higher inequality has come home to roost.

This chapter begins with a summary exposition of Minsky's theoretical perspective. Section The microfoundations of Minsky's theory of investment summarizes Minsky's financial theory of investment at the firm level, explaining the concepts of borrowers' and lenders' risk. In Section From microeconomic investment to macroeconomic instability, I integrate this investment theory into a macroeconomic framework and sketch the basic structure of a Minsky financial cycle emphasizing the interplay of two key concepts in Minsky's financial instability theory: "validation" and "financial fragility." Section Seeds of a Minsky crisis in the household sector shifts the locus of financial instability from business investment to borrowers' and lenders' risk in the household sector. In this section, I interpret household demand and debt data since the early 1980s to argue that Minsky's financial instability theory explains the source of the financial crisis that triggered the Great Recession. Section Weak recovery, rising inequality, and secular stagnation combines Minsky's financial instability theory with the multi-decade trend of rising income inequality to explain the exceptionally stagnant recovery of the US economy in the aftermath of the Great Recession.

Translating Minsky's financial instability theory from the business to the household sector leads to somewhat different outcomes than what he presented in his major published work. However, this chapter concludes that the basic Minsky framework provides an insightful tool for understanding the dramatic macroeconomic dynamics of the U.S. economy over the past several decades.

The microfoundations of Minsky's theory of investment

Macroeconomic theory connects aggregate dynamics with underlying behavior of the agents that comprise the economic system. In recent decades, these behaviors have been labeled the "microfoundations" of macroeconomics. The term has a rather charged meaning in the context of debates between different macroeconomic schools of thought. New classical economists, led by Robert Lucas, equate microfoundations with the goal of building models derived directly from the solution to microeconomic optimization problems grounded in the so-called deep structural parameters of preference and technology. They claim models of this kind provide the basis for counterfactual policy analysis because the model specification and model parameters should be invariant to policy changes, that is, this approach is promoted by those who use it as a solution to the famous Lucas Critique. But many economists find this modeling strategy excessively narrow; it puts the behavioral foundation for macroeconomics in an incredibly constraining box. And given the unrealistic connection of these models to the world in which we live, this approach hardly seems to address the Lucas Critique (What is the benefit of having an unrealistic and likely incorrect model, even if its parameters appear to be invariant to policy?).

But heterodox macroeconomics should not, and does not, abandon the goal of linking macroeconomic results with agent behavior. Indeed, such behavioral links are prominent in many heterodox models.[2] Minsky (1975, 1986) presents extensive behavioral analysis of firms' investment decisions and how they link to finance, as we summarize here.

A simple model of investment

To motivate ideas, consider the simple model of investment presented in Minsky (1975, Chapter 5, also see the exposition in Tymoigne and Wray, 2014, pages 40—44). The profit-seeking firm will invest in projects if the "demand price" of the project (P_K), effectively the present value of expected cash flows (CF) from the investment, exceeds the "supply price" (P_I), what the firm must pay for the project. Minsky followed Keynes in defining P_K as the present value of "quasi rents" generated by new investment projects. The demand price will likely decline as investment increases.[3] This could

[2] For example, consider Keynes's treatment of uncertainty. Other prominent examples include Paul Davidson's analysis of the importance of liquidity for firm and household behavior and Alfred Eichner's treatment of oligopolistic competition by "megacorps."

[3] Minsky (1975, Chapter 5) presents P_K as a constant independent of the level of investment, holding other things equal, such as the state of the business cycle, productivity of capital, etc. The exposition here, however, is enhanced by conceptualizing P_K as a schedule that ranks multiple investment projects according to their expected profitability. This distinction is discussed further below after introducing Minsky's concept of "borrower's risk."

be motivated by the conventional neoclassical assumption of declining marginal productivity of capital. More heterodox microfoundations might arise from Keynes's arguments about the declining marginal efficiency of capital or concerns that the expected utilization rate of capital falls as capacity expands. Uncertainty and Kalecki's "principle of increasing risk" (Mott, 2010) also generate a declining P_K schedule, as shown in Fig. 6.1. Market interest rates affect the P_K schedule because the interest rate determines, in Minsky's words, the "capitalization factors" that transform expected future CFs into a present value demand price.

What determines the supply price? If we assume the firm is a price taker in the market for capital goods, P_I is just a horizontal line determined by the cost of production of capital, and ultimately wages of workers in the industries that produce capital goods. Firm investment, I^*, is set at the intersection of the P_K and P_I schedules in Fig. 6.1. The figure shows the firm's internal funds, or CF, available to finance investment. But the level of CF is irrelevant to the investment decision. If CF fluctuates, the firm simply substitutes internal and external financing as necessary to maintain investment at I^*. The assumption in the analysis so far is that the opportunity cost of internal cash is the same as the market interest rate.[4]

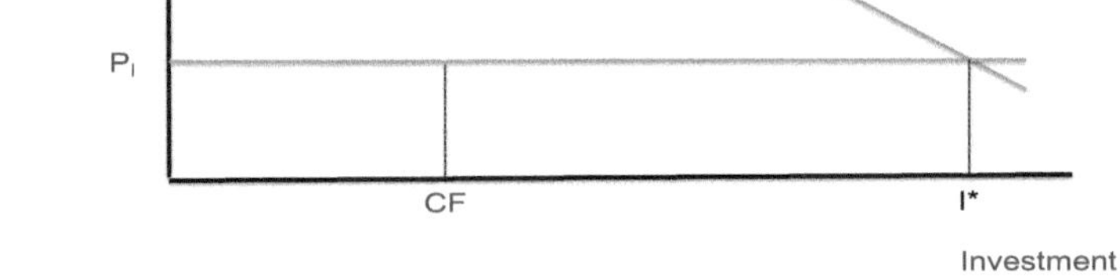

Figure 6.1 A nonfinancial model of firm investment.

[4] It would be reasonable to introduce a small transaction cost that raises the supply price once internal cash flows are exhausted and the firm must obtain external funds. But if this wedge is just a transaction cost, it is likely small and largely irrelevant to the results of the simple model. Larger discrepancies between the cost of internal and external finance are discussed later in this chapter.

One can cast the usual neoclassical model of investment and capital accumulation with the simple relationships depicted in Fig. 6.1. The demand price becomes the marginal product of capital net of depreciation. This approach replaces uncertainty, "animal spirits," and entrepreneurial judgment with just an abstract "technology." Rather than an active, behaviorally motivated agent, the neoclassical firm is largely reduced to a passive repository of a production function, a point discussed in some detail in Minsky (1975, Chapter 5) and also in Fazzari (2009). The horizontal difference between the P_K and P_I schedules is the net present value of the marginal investment project. Investment proceeds up to the point where the net present value is zero, that is, I^* in Fig. 6.1.

In the neoclassical model, the only financial variable that affects investment is the market interest rate used to discount expected future cash flows. Of great importance to understanding how Minsky's investment theory differs from orthodoxy, the source of finance is largely irrelevant in this model because the market interest rate is independent of the firm's financial conditions. This is the "perfect capital market" model of investment that dominated mainstream macroeconomic analysis through much of the postwar period.

Integrating finance: borrowers' and lenders' risk

Minsky strongly criticized the model of investment depicted in Fig. 6.1. He wrote "a decision to invest—to acquire capital assets—is always a decision about a liability structure" and "[i]nvestment is therefore a financial phenomenon" (Minsky, 1986, pages 192 and 209, respectively). The conditions that determine I^* in Fig. 6.1 could be correct only if all investment were financed with internal CF with a constant opportunity cost given by the market interest rate. As soon as investment requires external funds, Minsky argues, following Keynes, that borrowers' risk and lenders' risk affect the investment decision in crucial ways.

Borrowers' risk is subjective; it arises from the threat to the control of a firm its managers and owners perceive from taking on external finance. As investment rises beyond what can be financed internally and external finance increases, the probability that the firm will not be able to meet future cash commitments rises and the probability the firm will lose control of its assets grows. As Minsky (1986, page 214) writes, the rise in "future cash-flow commitments" to creditors "diminishes the margin of safety of management and equity owners."[5] Borrowers' risk represents active behavior by entrepreneurs and managers, that is, business decisions made by *people* who have behaviors that extend beyond narrow maximization of profits with given technologies (Crotty, 1990).

Minsky models borrowers' risk as a discount on the demand price for capital assets that occurs *when investment rises above the level that can be financed by internal cash flow.* Marginal borrowers' risk rises as external financing increases as shown in Fig. 6.2 by the growing gap between the P_K^* schedule (which is independent of the source of finance) and Minsky's effective demand schedule for investment $P_K{}^M$.

Lenders' risk is, in part, symmetric to borrowers' risk. It reflects the risk to lenders (or other providers of external business finance) that arises because of the financial conditions of a particular firm. Minsky models lenders' risk as an increase in the supply price of capital assets representing financial costs imposed on firms by lenders. The most obvious manifestation of lenders' risk is an increase in the interest rate on loans or bond issues relative to the market discount rate used by firms to capitalize their expected returns.

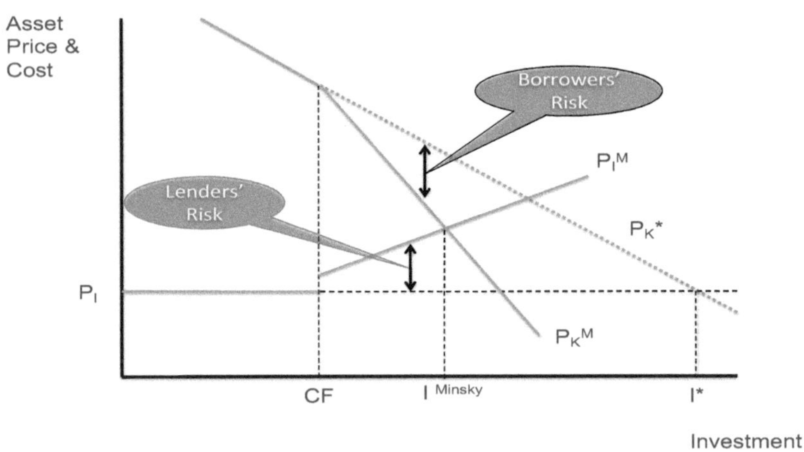

Figure 6.2 Minsky's investment model.

[5] This explanation of borrowers' risk applies most obviously to external debt finance. Minsky (1986, page 214) also recognizes that a related problem arises from new equity finance: "If new issues of common shares are undertaken, the issue price will have to be attractive, which may mean that present stock owners feel their equity interest is being diluted." This argument is similar to the "excessive dilution" phenomenon identified by Myers and Majluf (1984).

The higher present value of these cash commitments raises the cost of acquiring capital assets when the acquisition must be financed externally.

Like borrowers' risk, Minsky asserts that marginal lender's risk rises as investment increases beyond what can be financed with internal CF so that the effective P_I^M schedule in Fig. 6.2 has a positive slope.[6] Different from the subjective character of borrowers' risk, however, Minsky argues that lenders' risk actually shows up in financial contracts (Minsky, 1975, pages 109—110). Higher interest rates for more financially risky borrowing can be observed. In addition, other explicit financial restrictions on firms, such as shorter terms to maturity or loan covenants, reflect lenders' risk.

If borrowers' and lenders' risk are significant empirically, equilibrium investment in Fig. 6.2 (I^{Minsky}) will fall well below what investment that requires external finance would have been in the absence of borrowers' or lenders' risk (I^*).

What determines investment?

In Minsky's model, the drivers of firm investment fall into two broad categories. First, consistent with many other theories of investment, demand for new capital assets depends on expectations or the profits, returns, or "quasi-rents" generated by the new project. In mainstream models, these expectations are tied to technological characteristics of the project (such as the marginal productivity of capital) as well as market competitive structures. Models in the Keynesian tradition add expectations about capacity utilization or other measures of the state of the output market, recognizing the importance of macroeconomic conditions for the profitability of new investment projects. Considerations of confidence, perhaps labeled "animal spirits," also affect the demand for investment, even for projects firms finance with internal funds. Second, and what distinguishes Minsky's investment model from virtually all other treatments of the subject, are the evolving conditions of finance.

Most obviously, fluctuations in firms' internal cash flow will affect the amount of investment that requires external funds, changing marginal borrowers' and lenders' risk. Fig. 6.3 shows the effect of an increase in CF.

6 The positive slope of the P_I^M schedule in Fig. 6.2 is the most important difference between internally and externally financed investment. But Minsky also adds a discontinuity in the schedule when cash flow is exhausted, as shown in Fig. 6.2. This discontinuity does not seem to play a major role in Minsky's analysis although it can be more important for similar "financial hierarchy" models based on asymmetric information discussed later.

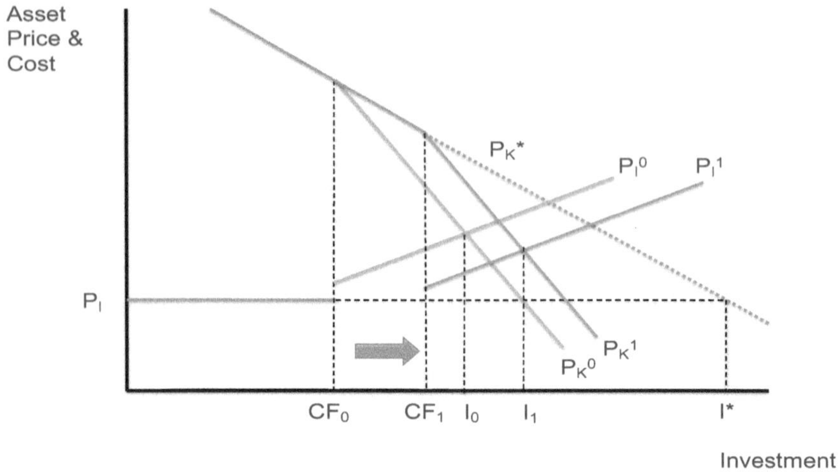

Figure 6.3 Effect of higher cash flow in the Minsky investment model.

Higher CF reduces both borrowers' and lenders' risk at the initial level of investment (I_0) because firms do not need as much external finance. These lower finance premia encourage more investment which rises to I_1. In addition, changes in borrowers' or lenders' risk independent of CF will affect investment. For example, in the boom phase of a Minsky cycle when borrowing and lending lead to higher profits, the perception of financial risks will decline. This change will rotate the P_I schedule in Fig. 6.3 clockwise (lower lenders' risk for external finance) and P_K counterclockwise (lower borrowers' risk so the gap between P_K and the demand price for capital assets without the need for external funds shrinks). Other things equal, these changes, by themselves, lead to higher equilibrium investment. These features of the model illustrate Minsky's view that an investment decision also must be a financing decision.

Minsky understood his financial theory of investment as much different from mainstream investment models. He writes (1986, page 193) "[a]s the standard interpretation of Keynes was assimilated to traditional economics, the emphasis upon finance and debt structures that was evident in the 1920s and 1930s was lost. In today's standard economic theory, an abstract nonfinancial economy is analyzed." This perspective was largely correct for much of Minsky's career. Modigliani and Miller (1958) published a famous paper that presented conditions under which corporate leverage (potentially a key determinant of both borrowers' and lenders' risk) had no effect on a value-maximizing firm's real investment decisions. Jorgenson (1963) developed the influential "neoclassical" model of investment explicitly assuming that the rather strict requirements for finance neutrality from Modigliani and Miller actually held in the real world, relegating finance to a kind of "side show" in firm behavior. This thinking dominated mainstream analysis of investment in macroeconomics well into the 1980s justifying Minsky's skepticism that his focus on finance was missing from almost all of mainstream macroeconomics.

But at approximately the same time Minsky was writing his magnum opus to be published in 1986, things were changing in mainstream investment theory. Prominent mainstream authors began to apply Akerlof's (1970) model of asymmetric information and the market for "lemons" (i.e., the market for poorly performing used cars) to firm investment finance. In a seminal paper, Stiglitz and Weiss (1981) show how asymmetric information between borrowers and lenders could lead to credit rationing so that investment projects that would be undertaken if firms had adequate internal funds might not be financed if they required external borrowing. Myers and Majluf (1984) built a model to explore equity finance for investment projects. They demonstrate that asymmetric information between firm managers, acting in the interest of existing shareholders, and the purchasers of new shares creates a "lemons premium" for external finance. The result is that firms might forego projects that would have a positive net present value when financed internally if the project required new share issues. These models moved part way toward what Minsky had been writing about for decades: finance matters, fundamentally, in the determination of investment. These mainstream models certainly reproduce a positive link between cash flow and investment, a central result in Minsky's analysis.

This new research on the "microfoundations" of asymmetric information and financing constraints led rather quickly to new mainstream models of how finance and monetary policy affect macroeconomic outcomes. Financial intermediation, often viewed as a kind of "technology," could affect macroeconomic outcomes, especially if intermediation reduced information asymmetries. Financial shocks could initiate real fluctuations and the financial system was identified as an institutional structure that could propagate shocks throughout the economic system, a mechanism labeled the "financial accelerator" by Bernanke et al. (1996). Mainstream authors described a "credit channel" for the way monetary policy affects macroeconomic outcomes, a channel separate from the traditional transmission mechanisms through the quantity of money or market interest rates.

This new research marked a significant change in mainstream thinking; recognizing the relevance of credit and finance for macroeconomics moved the mainstream somewhat closer to Minsky's ideas. Some have argued that the asymmetric information concept could help illuminate parts of Minsky's financial theory of investment.[7] But this newer mainstream research still misses important features of Minsky's theory. The asymmetric information microfoundation casts the relevance of finance as an "imperfection" in the market process. If only information were "perfect" (that is, shared symmetrically between all agents), then only "real" considerations would determine investment, relegating finance again to a side show. In contrast, for Minsky, finance is fundamental to capitalism; finance must be incorporated into any useful economic model from the very beginning. Minsky, like Keynes, also emphasizes the importance of fundamental uncertainty, a qualitatively different concept than the "risk" in mainstream models represented by fully known and stationary probability distributions. Nor do mainstream models explain the systematic tendency of financially driven economies toward instability that is the hallmark of Minsky's financial instability (discussed in detail below). Minsky might concur with modern mainstream models that consider financial institutions as technological innovations to overcome information problems. But he also recognizes the tendency for banks and other lenders to magnify instability, especially as they innovate to circumvent prudential financial regulation. Modern mainstream models of asymmetric information and financial constraints constitute a step toward Minsky's perspective, but just one step on a long journey.

Perhaps the most important outcome of the resurrection of finance in the mainstream is that it has spawned extensive empirical research to test the relevance of "financial constraints." These studies are often motivated by rather narrow asymmetric information models, but their results can be more broadly interpreted to explore the overall importance of finance for investment that is central to Minsky's theory. A huge empirical research literature has emerged to test the importance of cash flow for investment. This empirical work must face a basic identification problem. The key implication of the Minsky model (see the discussion of Fig. 6.3 above) is that the financial channels affecting investment imply a positive effect of internal cash flow on investment *holding other factors that determine investment*

[7] Fazzari and Variato (1994) develop some of these ideas, but not without controversy; see, in addition Crotty (1996) and the response in Fazzari and Variato (1996).

constant. If one simply regresses investment on cash flow, which is largely driven by a firm's profits, the cash flow effect from the purely financial aspects of the model will be contaminated by the obvious correlation between a firm's current profits and its expected quasi rents from new projects. One approach to address this problem is to include variables to control for investment demand, such as accelerator effects (Fazzari and Mott, 1987) or Tobin's *q* (Fazzari et al., 1988). This approach is a step in the right direction, but one suspects variation in investment demand not captured by typical control variables will still be correlated with current profits. In Fazzari et al. (1988), we use firm heterogeneity to identify the effect of cash flow on investment due specifically to financial constraints. We divide a large sample of firms into groups that were a priori more and less likely to face financial constraints. We found significantly larger CF effects for the more constrained firms; a result obtained in many further students throughout the years.[8] Studies of the effect of debt leverage on firm-level investment are much less common. Ndikumana (1999) finds results consistent with Minsky's emphasis on the importance of debt for investment. Empirical macroeconomic research also confirms the credit channel/financial accelerator effects proposed by mainstream research but also supporting the empirical implications of Minsky's theory. By the turn of the 21st century the consensus of thinking, even in the mainstream, seemed to be that Minsky was right: finance matters (even if mainstream authors largely ignored Minsky's contributions that predated the 1980s asymmetric information models of financial constraints by decades).

From microeconomic investment to macroeconomic instability

Minsky's theory of firm investment is interesting in its own right at the microeconomic level. But its greatest significance emerges from its macroeconomic implications.

[8] In Fazzari et al. (1988) firms were divided into groups based on dividend payouts because if firms faced a premium on external funds (due to borrowers' and lenders' risk) they would at least retain their internal cash flow. We found cash flow effects about double in size for near-zero-dividend firms compared with firms that paid significant dividends. Other research generated similar findings dividing firms by size, age, the presence of a bond rating, among other characteristics.

Distinguishing firm-level financial constraints from "loanable funds" theory

In transition from the firm level to the economy as a whole, it is important to distinguish between highly relevant microeconomic finance constraints on firm-level investment and misleading views of macroeconomic constraints on the financing of investment attributed to the supply of saving. Confusion could arise from the "loanable funds" theory of aggregate investment which posits that investment depends on the supply of saving coming from the rest of the economy (most obviously, the household sector but also including government and foreign sources of saving that may be positive or negative). This theory seems intuitive, and it is widely accepted in mainstream textbook macroeconomics (especially in the "long run"). But Keynes effectively revealed a fundamental logical flaw in loanable funds theory: it assumes the aggregate supply of saving is independent of the demand for investment. This assumption can be correct only if aggregate income is independent of investment, that is, only if total output and income do not depend on aggregate demand.

Therefore, loanable funds theory and the idea that the supply of saving constraints investment would make sense in an unrealistic world in which output is entirely supply determined, roughly the "classical" macroeconomics that Keynes, and Minsky following Keynes, considered irrelevant in most realistic circumstances. The "neoclassical synthesis" that captured mainstream macroeconomics in the postwar decades asserts the classical supply driven model applies to some kind of "long run" when wages and prices fully adjust to demand shocks. But decades of heterodox research, going back to Keynes himself, criticizes this view.[9] Even some mainstream economists now recognize the importance of aggregate demand "beyond the short run."[10]

Keynesian macroeconomics demonstrates how aggregate saving necessarily accommodates changes in realized investment demand. The channel of causation begins with investment demand raising income and then higher incomes raising saving until the full multiplier process works its way through the economy. Investment *creates aggregate saving,* so the supply of saving cannot constrain aggregate investment.

[9] See Fazzari et al. (1998) and Fazzari (2020) for further discussion.

[10] Stansbury and Summers (2019) show how what for decades have been strictly heterodox views about the relevance of demand dynamics for macroeconomic outcomes beyond the short run have begun to enter mainstream discussion.

Confusion could arise because Minsky tells us investment depends on the availability of finance while Keynes demonstrates that loanable funds will not constrain aggregate investment. Resolution of the confusion comes from recognizing the distinction between Minsky's *microeconomic* analysis of finance constraints and Keynes's *macroeconomic* explanation for how investment creates saving. Financial constraints for Minsky come from decisions by both individual firms and decentralized providers of finance about what financial risks are worth taking. In particular, banks or purchasers of new corporate bonds or equity shares may refuse to finance investment projects (or charge significant premia for funds relative to the opportunity cost of internal cash flow). These microeconomic decisions impose finance constraints on investment. But once an investment project is funded and investment spending takes place, the Keynesian process of income creation assures aggregate saving will match investment financed at the microeconomic level.[11] Financial constraints on investment arise from microeconomic considerations about what projects to finance, not limitations on the aggregate supply of saving.

Dynamics of financial instability: validation and fragility

I have labeled the basic result that the dynamic path of aggregate demand is the engine of macroeconomic activity at indefinite horizons beyond the short run as "intrinsic Keynesian economics."[12] From this perspective, a fundamental question for macroeconomics is to explain the process that generates demand dynamics. Demand is not "automatic," over any horizon; in particular, demand need not converge to some supply-side concept of "potential output" determined independently from the dynamics of demand. Minsky's macroeconomic theory of financial instability provides a salient example of a demand generating process. It puts the static microeconomic investment model into a dynamic macro model by exploring the way borrowers' and lenders' risk evolve systematically through time. It describes an endogenous transition from a relatively safe financial structure that supports economic growth to financial excesses that will eventually lead to

[11] A question might arise about where the funds come from to finance new projects without "prior saving." The answer is endogenous money.

[12] Dictionary.com defines "intrinsic" as "belonging to a thing by its very nature." In our context, the connection between demand and production is the "very nature" of production for market sale in a profit-driven, capitalist economy.

demand collapse and recession or depression. This exposition of Minsky's macro theory grounds the ideas in two basic concepts: validation and fragility.

Minsky's financial instability is inherently cyclical. Descriptions usually begin in a period of conservative finance in the sense of behavioral and institutional conditions in which agents are reluctant to take on financial risk, that is, perceptions of both borrowers' and lenders' risk is high. These conditions could arise after a fairly recent financial crisis that wiped out risky financial positions and the businesses associated with them. Firms and financiers may be somewhat shell-shocked, reluctant to engage in risky financial practices. The economy may have substantial excess capacity and unemployment, leaving plenty of room for expansion if someone is willing to take on a little risk.

And it is the logic of profit-driven capitalism that some firm, some place, is always probing possible new strategies to see if new profits can be made. When someone takes a more aggressive financial position, lending to a new business with uncertain returns, for example, this activity raises aggregate demand and creates new cash flows. In this sense, Minsky is both a Keynesian (greater demand raises incomes) and a Kaleckian (higher investment raises profits). The higher cash flows *validate* the somewhat more aggressive financial positions creating success and profits for the new risk takers. In addition, stronger economic activity raises asset prices and collateral values. Validation lowers the perception of borrowers' and lenders' risk and encourages even greater risk taking, leading to more investment, more income generation, higher profits, and further validation. As Tymoigne and Wray (2014, page 27) write "a central point of Minsky's approach is that lending norms loosen over time and that what was previously considered excessively risky funding methods may become commonly accepted."

Sequential, systematic validation takes place in the context of an intrinsic Keynesian environment in which demand is the proximate constraint on production and employment almost always. Supply constraints, perhaps aside from an occasional microeconomic bottleneck, are rare.[13] So further expansion of spending continues to raise production and boost profits, not just for the several quarters of the mainstream "short run," but possibly for many years. Although Minsky's macro theory usually returns to the

[13] In addition, strong demand raises labor productivity and labor force growth causing demand to pull the supply side along with it along the upward path. See Fazzari et al. (2020) for a model in which demand leads supply.

limelight during financial crises, in many ways his ideas best explain the growth process, predicated on validation, that encourages more aggressive finance and demand growth. The fundamental direction of instability is upward (Tymoigne and Wray, 2014, page 2).

As validation encourages more aggressive, higher risk financial positions, its "evil twin," financial *fragility*, also increases. Minsky identified multiple dimensions of fragility. More lending raises debt ratios.[14] Short-term financing rises as a share of total lending. If short-term loans finance long positions, borrowers will need to roll over financing creating additional risks if financing conditions change (what Minsky called speculative finance). Furthermore, more aggressive lending may rely to a greater degree on collateral rather than established cash flows, creating financial exposure to potentially volatile asset prices and the danger assets could be seized. Institutional changes, perhaps motivated to circumvent financial regulation designed to contain risk, can lead to creation of more risky financial instruments and practices.

The upward phase of the cycle ends when fragility eventually reaches a breaking point, ending the validation process. Paul McCulley has labeled the point at which fragility overcomes validation as the "Minsky Moment." It is the beginning of a financial crisis when lending collapses, demand falls, and the economy faces recession.

The integrated dance of validation and fragility can be described by what I have described in my classes as the "stress test metaphor." Think about how a researcher might measure the strength of a metal rod in the laboratory. The researcher puts some stress on both sides of the rod. If the rod doesn't break, that is, if the strength of the rod is "validated," the researcher adds more stress to each side, increasing the "fragility" of the system. Further validation will induce further fragility until its "Minsky Moment" arrives and the rod breaks. The logic of the test eventually *requires* the rod to break. If it doesn't break, its strength is validated, more stress will be applied, and fragility rises. The financial analogy is that success of more aggressive financial positions will encourage profit seekers to push the risk envelope even harder, until the Minsky Moment. According to the classic Minsky description, "stability" (in the sense of validation of increasingly risky financial practices) is "destabilizing" (in the sense of systematically rising financial fragility).

[14] Although increasing debt-income ratios during expansions are empirically pervasive, Lavoie and Seccareccia (2001) raise theoretical qualifications about generality of this outcome.

Brief digression on uncertainty

This dynamic process that creates the Minsky cycle relies on what post-Keynesians (among others) have labeled fundamental uncertainty, that is, uncertainty about the future that cannot be captured in "ergodic" probability distributions (see Davidson, 1991). This uncertainty answers the criticism sometimes posed to Minsky: "if the dynamic generation of financial crisis is systematic, why don't rational, forward-looking agents learn to recognize the risk and behave more conservatively?" Minsky (1986, page 237) writes "success breeds a disregard of the possibility of failure" implying perceptions of risk and acceptable financial structure evolve over time in a world in which institutions change and outcomes are driven by different specific historical circumstances. Minsky dynamics arise in different specific forms, for example: inflation dynamics and radical monetary policy of the late 1970s and early 1980s, savings and loan instability of the late 1980s, the technology bubble of the late 1990s, and, of course, the massive debt-driven housing bubble leading up to the Great Recession. Agents do not know how and when each expansionary phase will end, but they certainly recognize the profits made by those that ride the rising tide upward, and validation keeps the expansion going.

As Crotty (1994) argues, following Keynes, agents embedded in a world of uncertainty use the recent past as the guide to expectations about future, especially if the recent past reveals big profits from aggressive financial positions. Along the expansion path of the Minsky cycle, validation signals, that new fragility-creating financial positions and practices can be successful. Agents on both sides of financial contracts update their expectations about "what works." And these expectations are formed in a *social environment* in which aggressive behaviors of others validate one's own increase in risk taking. Tymoigne and Wray (2014, page 12) write "[p]sychological factors are complemented by sociological factors because, under uncertainty, individuals tend to look for the approval of others." Indeed, if peers make profits with more aggressive financial positions, one ignores others' validation at the risk of being left behind, possibly driven out of business. It can be costly, perhaps even viewed as foolhardy, not to participate in the boom. As Tymoigne and Wray (2014, page 3) write, capitalism "pushes individuals to anticipate an uncertain future in order to get an edge on competitors." And (page 32), "given the way decisions are made in an uncertain world, a period of good times will lead economic units to change their views about the future and to become more optimistic; not because they are irrational but because current and past results seem to justify an improvement in the state of mind."

This process stands in strong contrast to the so-called "rational" expectations specification that eliminates the psychological nuances of human behavior from expectation formation. Instead, the Keynes-Minsky sense of adaptive behavior under uncertainty recognizes expectation formation as a central microfoundation of economic reality. Expectation formation in the Minsky cycle is not "irrational," rather it is human.

Seeds of a Minsky crisis in the household sector

Minsky developed, described, and applied the theory of financial instability summarized in the previous two sections almost exclusively in the context of business finance and the associated capital investment by firms. This focus is understandable considering the structure of finance in Minsky's formative years of the postwar decades. At that time, the most interesting financial action was in the business sector. Household finance was highly collateralized (home mortgages and auto loans) with large margins of safety. To the extent that consumption mattered for macroeconomic outcomes, it was through the traditional multiplier channel magnifying fluctuations induced by business investment or government spending.[15] Minsky followed Keynes in identifying investment as the engine of the business cycle.

Things changed, however. It is widely accepted that the dynamics of household spending and finance created the conditions that culminated in the Great Recession crisis of 2007–2009. The premise here is that even though Minsky himself said little about household finance, his theory provides a powerful framework for understanding how household finance in the quarter century prior to the Great Recession sowed the seeds of crisis dynamics (also see Dymski, 2010). To support this claim, we shift microfoundations from firms to households and explore how the concepts of validation and financial fragility apply to this fascinating era.

[15] Minsky (1986, pages 34–35) presents an interesting analysis of household financial changes during the 1974–75 recession, particularly in the auto financing market. Minsky clearly realized household finance had become more important in the US economy in the postwar era and household finance could play a nontrivial role in macro fluctuations. Nonetheless, he still identifies the "causal factors in what happens" as business investment and government spending.

Household finance and spending: 1980 through the Great Recession

In earlier work, my coauthor Barry Cynamon and I labeled the decades leading up to the Great Recession as the "Consumer Age" (Cynamon and Fazzari, 2008, 2013). Personal consumption expenditures in the national accounts rose from about 60% of GDP in the first half of the 1970s to just under 68% on the eve of the Great Recession in 2007. Fig. 6.4 presents two measures of household spending relative to disposable income.

The dotted line is the standard measure from the national income and product accounts (NIPA). It shows a clear upward trend during the Consumer Age years and a significant drop in the Great Recession. But NIPA measures of personal consumption and income include significant components that are neither cash spending by households nor cash income to households. For example, NIPA personal consumption includes imputed rent on owner-occupied housing. It also includes government-paid health care costs through the Medicare and Medicaid programs. In Cynamon and Fazzari (2017a), we develop cash flow measures for both household demand and household disposable income. These adjusted measures eliminate noncash imputations as well as spending and income items attributed to households but not actually under the control of households (such as Medicare and Medicaid). Furthermore, adjusted household demand includes

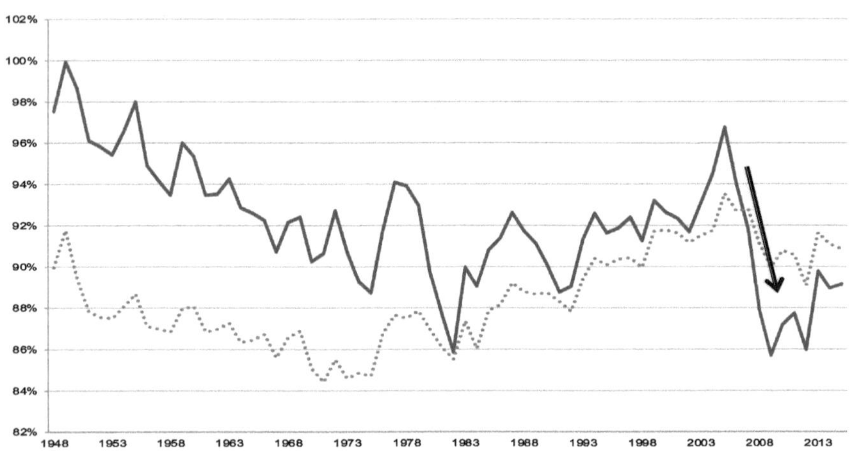

Figure 6.4 Household spending to disposable income. *Dotted line*: NIPA personal consumption expenditure/NIPA disposable income. *Solid line*: adjusted household demand/adjusted disposable income. *From Cynamon and Fazzari (2017a).*

spending on new owner-occupied housing. We argue in Cynamon and Fazzari (2017a) that the adjusted variables provide a better measure of the demand impact of the household sector on output and employment.

The solid line in Fig. 6.4 is more volatile than the NIPA measure of consumption to disposable income, due largely to the way it includes owner-occupied residential construction. The trend in the Consumer Age before the recession is somewhat less evident due to the additional volatility.[16] But clearly the postwar decline in household demand relative to income stopped by the 1980s and the spending rate rose significantly by the early 2000s. As discussed below, strong household demand for the quarter century starting in the early 1980s provides Minsky validation by growing incomes and cash flows. What is most evident in the adjusted data is the dramatic and persistent *collapse* of household demand in the Great Recession years. Following basic Keynesian logic, this collapse is the proximate cause of the worst economic crisis since the 1930s.

There is clear evidence of rising household financial fragility in the Consumer Age years. Fig. 6.5 shows the ratio of household sector debt to

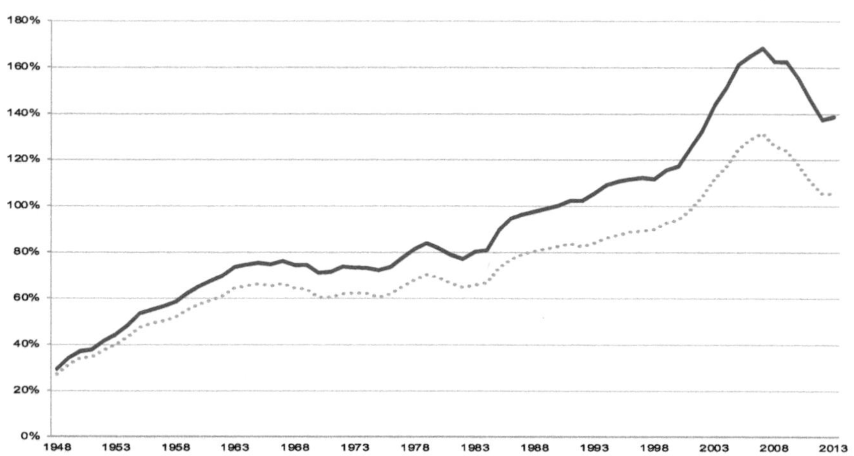

Figure 6.5 Two measures of household debt to disposable income. *Dotted line*: NIPA credit market debt of the household and nonprofit sector/NIPA disposable income. *Solid line*: Household sector debt/Adjusted disposable income. *From Cynamon and Fazzari (2017a).*

[16] Mason and Jayadev (2014) argue that household spending relative to income really did not rise during much of our Consumer Age period. Part of their argument rests on the volatility of the household demand/income ratio graphed in Fig. 6.4.

disposable income. Again, the dotted line is the standard measures from the NIPA accounts. This data series is well known, peaking at just over 130% on the eve of the crisis. The dynamics of the adjusted data are similar, but more dramatic.[17]

Rising household financial fragility as measured in Fig. 6.5 again begins in the Consumer Age starting, at the latest, by the early 1980s. The end of the borrowing boom corresponds to the collapse in household demand shown in Fig. 6.4 that caused the Great Recession. These dynamics are broadly consistent with a Minsky cycle arising from the household sector, as we now discuss in more detail.

Dynamics of validation and fragility in the household sector

The dynamic pattern of household spending is critical to understanding U.S. macroeconomic conditions of the past several decades. The period of reasonably strong household demand growth and the shift in the composition of aggregate demand toward consumption likely was a primary cause of the so-called "Great Moderation." During this period, dated from the middle 1980s up to the Great Recession, the volatility of U.S. real GDP declined and recessions in the early 1990s and early 2000s were comparatively mild. From a Keynesian demand-led perspective, these outcomes depended on strong household demand. For example, in 2000 and 2001, business fixed investment collapsed after the technology stock price bubble burst. But the associated recession was surprisingly mild as consumer spending and residential construction powered through the downturn.[18] Household finance likely played a major role in strong household demand, given the historic rise in household indebtedness during the Great Moderation period as well as the obvious link between the collapse in household borrowing and catastrophic decline in household demand during the Great Recession crisis.

Mainstream consumption theory has little to offer in explaining these dynamics. Again, as Minsky (1986, page 193) writes "in today's standard economic theory, an abstract nonfinancial economy is analyzed." The workhorse life-cycle model of consumption, and the intertemporal "Euler

[17] The primary reason for the additional 36 percentage points in the peak of the adjusted data is that adjusted disposable income excludes government-paid health costs of Medicare and Medicaid. Obviously, government health benefits are not available to service debt!.

[18] Our adjusted measure of annual real household demand never declined from the economy's peak in 2000, in contrast with every other U.S. recession going back, at least, to the mid-1970s.

equation" it implies, ignores finance altogether. This model's primary result, smoothing of consumption spending across a household's life course, also could not account for the rising share of consumption during the Consumer Age decades. The period from the mid-1970s to the mid-2000s corresponds almost exactly with the demographic shift of the large baby-boom generation into their highest earning years. Consumption smoothing, therefore, predicts a *rise* in the aggregate saving rate, which, as Fig. 6.6 obviously shows, is exactly the opposite of what happened. The top dotted line in the figure shows the well-known decline in the NIPA measure of the personal saving rate. The bottom solid line, the "financial saving rate," removes various imputations and measures saving as the accumulation of new financial assets and disposable income as actual household cash flows. The middle "gross saving rate" also eliminates imputations but it includes residential construction of new homes for owner occupancy, in addition to financial assets, as household saving (This measure is "gross" because there is no subtraction for depreciation of the owner-occupied housing stock.)

The different definitions of household saving have significantly different levels. Furthermore, while the severity of the decline during the Consumer Age is somewhat larger with the adjusted measures, all three series strongly contradict the life cycle consumption smoothing story considering the demographics of the baby boom generation during these years.

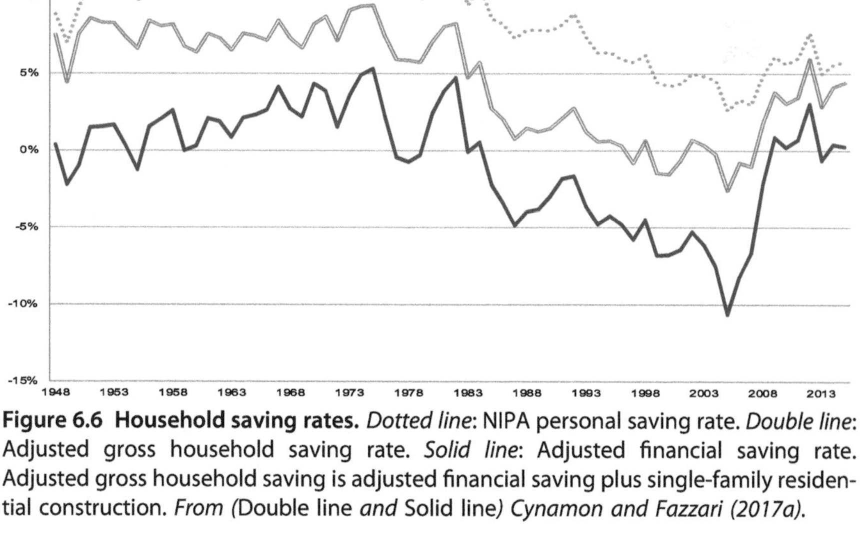

Figure 6.6 Household saving rates. *Dotted line*: NIPA personal saving rate. *Double line*: Adjusted gross household saving rate. *Solid line*: Adjusted financial saving rate. Adjusted gross household saving is adjusted financial saving plus single-family residential construction. *From (*Double line *and* Solid line*) Cynamon and Fazzari (2017a).*

As in the case for investment theory, even though most mainstream consumption studies ignored financial considerations, things have changed to some extent in recent years. A number of prominent mainstream contributions invoke "liquidity constraints" to explore how financial conditions might affect household consumption. The basic story is that asymmetric information between households and lenders prevent households from borrowing against intangible (and therefore illiquid) wealth, most obviously future labor income. Thus, households may not be able to attain the optimal consumption path they would choose in the absence of financial constraints. Institutional and regulatory changes that enhance household credit access might raise consumption, suggesting a possible way to connect rising household indebtedness with declining saving. These developments move some mainstream thinking in the direction of Minsky by introducing a role for finance into the dynamics of consumption and demand.

This approach, however, fails to adequately explain the full household spending/borrowing dynamics of both the strong demand growth through the middle 2000s *and* the collapse of both borrowing and spending that caused the Great Recession. If the "problem" with household spending came from liquidity constraints and such a problem was "fixed" by better financial intermediation, the resulting increase in borrowing and spending would have allowed households to move closer to their optimal *and sustainable* life cycle consumption trajectories. There would be no reason to expect any kind of excessive financial fragility or collapse in lending and spending. I argue here that applying Minsky microfoundations, described in the context of investment earlier, to the household sector leads to much better insights about the dynamics that led to the crisis of 2007–09.

Consider how borrowers' risk evolved during this era. Institutional changes in the personal tax system had an important effect. The goal of the Reagan-era tax reform act of 1986 was to lower personal tax rates but avoid losing tax revenue by expanding the tax base. Prior to this reform, households were able to deduct all interest expenses for tax purposes. The 1986 reform eliminated the interest deduction, *except* for interest paid on a loan secured by the borrower's home. This exception encouraged households who owned their homes to shift borrowing for any purpose to debt secured by the house. Of course, the financial industry responded immediately by creating the home equity line of credit (HELOC). Interest on any draw down of this credit line was tax deductible. These instruments were heavily marketed on very favorable terms (usually there were no "closing costs," unlike conventional first mortgages). It made perfect sense for homeowners to use HELOC borrowing in place of other kinds of debt, such as car loans and credit cards. In addition to the tax benefits, the loans carried lower interest rates because they were secured by reasonably good collateral.

The HELOC, however, led to a more nuanced change in household financial behavior, a change consistent with reduced borrowers' risk. It became much easier to tap home equity for any purpose. Prior to this institutional change, refinancing a mortgage to borrow against home equity required extensive credit checks and expensive transaction costs. But once the HELOC was in place, borrowing against home equity was as simple as writing a check (or, later, making a few clicks in one's online accounts). This change facilitated using home equity as a "piggy bank."

Another important factor affecting borrowers during this the Consumer Age decades was the long downward trend in mortgage interest rates. The 30-year fixed rate mortgage carried a nominal interest rate above 17% for much of 1981 and 1982. Aside from a few small upward bumps in this rate, it mostly followed a downward trend to about 6% on the eve of the Great Recession. Of course, it made perfect sense for households to exploit this trend by refinancing their mortgages, perhaps multiple times, over this period, even with the high transaction costs required to obtain a new mortgage. But these circumstances also opened a new door for further borrowing. Once the fixed costs of a new mortgage are incurred, it was almost costless to raise the principal amount on the new mortgage, and walk away from refinancing with a big check. This activity, along with HELOC borrowing, became common in the run-up to the crisis, with mortgage equity withdrawal adding substantially to aggregate household spending growth.

As we discuss in Cynamon and Fazzari (2008, 2013), these developments changed norms of how households approached borrowing. Refinancing and home equity extraction were rare, if not impossible, in the decades prior to the Consumer Age, if for no other reason than *rising* nominal interest rates made any kind of refinancing very costly. The new conditions of the decades after 1980, however, made borrowing against home equity a normal financial activity that spread among households as friends, neighbors, and family exploited these new activities. It is a good example of how the microfoundations of borrowing choices have a social context.

While changing attitudes toward credit, that is, falling borrowers' risk, encouraged households to take on more debt and spend more in the Consumer Age period, perhaps the bigger change was on the supply side of the household credit market. Deregulation of the financial system, going back to the 1970s, paved the way for more creative, and ultimately unsustainable, lending to the household sector. The emergence of securitization enhanced the ability and profitability of mortgage, credit card, and auto lending (see Kregel, 2013). New information technology also played an important role as credit scoring made household lending more of a commodity with generic characteristics replacing the idiosyncratic personal assessment of household creditworthiness by lending officers.

As strong household spending and the associated rise in household debt led to rather stable growth, mild recessions, and rising home prices, increasingly risky lending practices were *validated*, which then encouraged even greater risk taking, rising financial *fragility*. Again, as Minsky (1986, page 237) writes "[s]uccess breed a disregard for the possibility of failure." For example, Boykin Curry, a managing director of the asset management firm Eagle Capital said:

> *For 20 years, the DNA of nearly every financial institution had morphed dangerously.* Each time someone at the table pressed for more leverage and more risk, the next few years proved them "right" *These people were emboldened, they were promoted and they gained control of ever more capital. Meanwhile, anyone in power who hesitated, who argued for caution, was proved "wrong." The cautious types were increasingly intimidated, passed over for promotion. They lost their hold on capital. This happened every day in almost every financial institution over and over, until we ended up with a very specific kind of person running things.*[19]

This statement perfectly describes the dance between validation ("the next few years proved them 'right'") and rising financial fragility ("more leverage and more risk.") More aggressive finance stimulates demand and, through typical Keynesian channels, more demand raises incomes. Home prices also rise, increasing collateral values, generating wealth effects that raise spending further, and creating expectations of even better conditions ahead. Refinancing occurs in markets with looser credit underwriting. The result is validation coming from consumption spending that is, by far, the dominant sector of the economy. But rising financial fragility ticks along. Debt ratios rise; financing becomes more short term; lending is based on rising collateral values rather than sufficient cash flows to meet debt service obligations. The stress test metaphor discussed in the context of Minsky's

[19] Quoted in "There is a Silver Lining" by Farid Sakaria, *Newsweek*, October 12, 2008, emphasis added.

theory of financial instability earlier applies directly: if the system doesn't break (validation), more stress is put on the system (rising fragility), until it finally breaks.

And break it did. I will not repeat a detailed analysis of what triggered the Great Recession and the historic economic collapse that followed.[20] Fig. 6.4 through 6.6 above show how the upward path of borrowing ended and demand collapsed. Housing prices also plummeted. Financial conditions became desperate. Aggressive monetary, lender-of-last-resort, and fiscal policies managed to put a floor under the collapse, but only after the worst macroeconomic crisis in three generations. The final stage of the Minsky theory of financial instability played out in these dramatic events.

Weak recovery, rising inequality, and secular stagnation

Minsky's financial instability theory provides a deep explanation for the household-demand-led growth of the Consumer Age and how the ticking time bomb of rising financial fragility in the household sector exploded to trigger the Great Recession crisis. Some followers of Minsky "saw it coming" in the years before the crisis; many others recognize the importance of Minsky's insights for understanding these dramatic macroeconomic events after the fact. But there is another major feature of recent US macroeconomic history that is not fully addressed by the Minsky cycle analysis. The recovery from the Great Recession, more than a decade old at this writing, has been historically weak. I argue in this section that this fact is best explained by linking Minsky financial dynamics of the household sector with rising income inequality.

The extent to which today's economy operates below its trend prior to the Great Recession is historically unprecedented. Per capita real GDP in the third quarter of 2019 is 9.4% below the growth trend established between the previous business cycle peaks (from the second quarter of 2000 to the first quarter of 2006). Going back to 1960, real per capita GDP at a cycle peak was never more than 3.5% below the previous peak-to-peak growth trend. While in early 2020 the current cycle has yet to hit its peak, there is no indication that per capita real GDP will come anywhere close to its previous peak-to-peak growth trend before the next recession begins. Perhaps

[20] My perspective on these events is best summarized in Cynamon et al. (2013).

more striking, 2017 real GDP was about 12% below the 10-year-ahead Congressional Budget Office forecast of the economy's potential output made in 2007.[21] In 2019, a 12% gap between what the US actually produced and the past trend amounts to $2.6 trillion, or about $20,000 per year *for every American household.* Something happened to the growth trend of the U.S. economy after the Great Recession and it was very big.

The household sector mirrors this remarkably weak aggregate recovery. Consider the data in Fig. 6.7. The dotted line shows the trend of real household demand established between a peak in 2000 and a peak in 2006. Economic performance in those years was not especially strong, even with this growth in real demand from the household sector. The figure also shows household demand back to 1990 does not deviate substantially from this trend, especially at cycle peaks. Of course, the collapse of the Great Recession is quite evident in Fig. 6.7. No one now denies this was a true crisis. The key point here, however, is that household demand never really recovers.

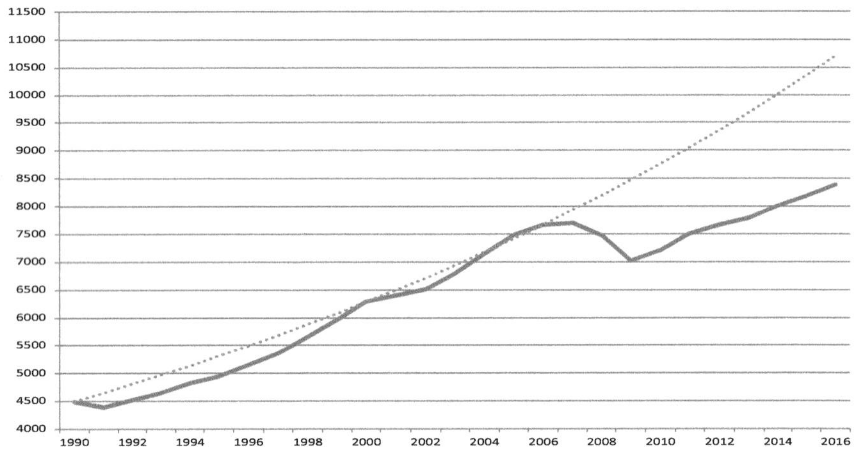

Figure 6.7 Trend versus actual real household demand. *Solid line*: real household demand (billions of 2009 dollars). *Dotted line*: trend of real household demand established between peaks in 2000 and 2006. The trend is extend both back to 1990 and forward to 2016.

[21] The 2007 Congressional Budget Office forecast accounts for the demographics of the baby-boom generation. Extending the forecast beyond its 10-year horizon ending in 2017 implies this gap has not closed through 2019. For more analysis of the recent stagnation of the US economy and further references, see Cynamon and Fazzari (2017b).

Indeed, it doesn't even keep up with the earlier trend and the gap between trend and actual grows over time to over 20% by the final observation of our household demand data in 2016. One can argue sensibly that the trend from the early 2000s is not really relevant to assessing economic performance more than a decade later. But the economy needed that demand growth to sustain something like adequate performance in the early years of the 21st century, demand growth that was lost in the crisis and has yet to be found. Fig. 6.8 tells a similar story over a longer sweep of history. The figure plots the profile of per capita real household demand starting with the peak of each business cycle going back to 1973. The profiles continue until the next recession (or 2016 for the most recent cycle). The data show in historical perspective both how deep the Great Recession collapse was and how anemic the recovery has been.

The remarkable extent to which US income inequality has risen since about 1980 is widely discussed. And the drag on aggregate demand growth from rising inequality has been a consistent theme in post-Keynesian research for decades.[22] The basic idea is that high-income households recycle less of their income back into spending, that is, the rich have a lower propensity to consume. Therefore, a persistent rise of inequality can explain

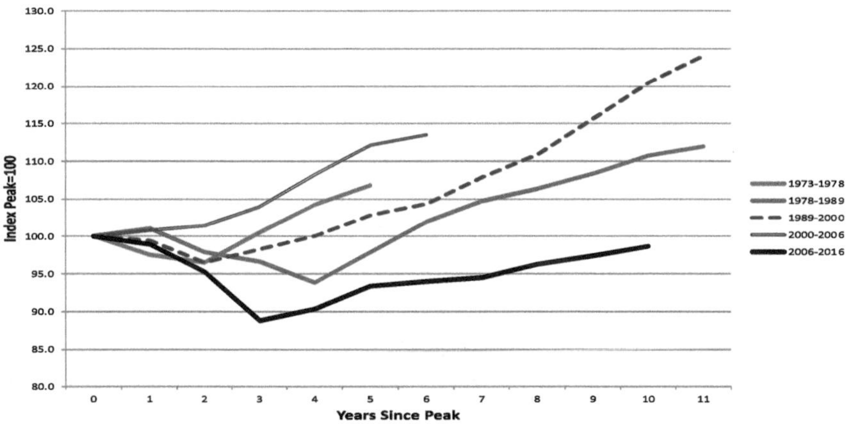

Figure 6.8 Business cycle profiles of real household demand. Real household demand indexed to 100 at the peak of each cycle. Profiles extend until the next recession, or through 2016 for the most recent cycle.

[22] For a recent extensive survey, see Hein (2014).

demand stagnation. But this simple explanation must confront a fundamental historical inconsistency. Inequality began to increase around 1980 along a steady, but rather slow trend. The cumulative effects over nearly 4 decades are dramatic, but this is not an event that happened quickly. In contrast, as Fig. 6.7 shows, the collapse in household demand was a crisis event, concentrated mostly in just 2 years. Furthermore, for most of the Consumer Age period prior to the Great Recession household demand was reasonably *strong,* despite rising inequality. But even as the excesses of household finance have cleared somewhat in the aftermath of the crisis, household demand growth remains weak. Here is where inequality potentially takes center stage: now that unsustainable household borrowing no longer props up household demand, the chickens of inequality-induced demand drag have come home to roost. High and rising economic inequality explains secular stagnation of household demand, stagnation that was hidden during a nearly three-decade Minsky cycle.

What further evidence can be used to explore this hypothesis? In Cynamon and Fazzari (2016) we decompose household financial and spending activity into two broad groups, the bottom 95% and top 5% of the income distribution. Fig. 6.9 shows the ratio of debt to disposable income for these two groups. The increase in household debt is almost entirely concentrated in the bottom 95%. This fact supports the idea that households with mostly

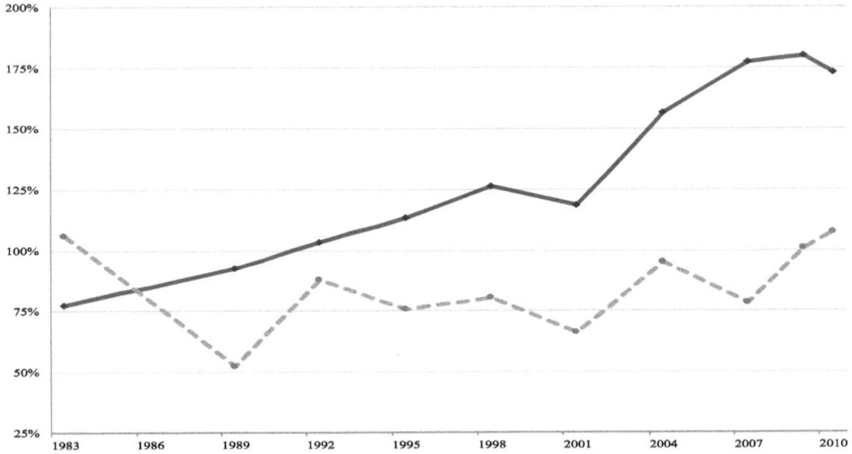

Figure 6.9 Inequality and household debt-income ratios. *Solid line*: household debt to disposable income for the bottom 95% of the income distribution. *Dotted line*: debt to disposable income for the top 5%.

stagnant income, constituting the vast majority of the population, were also the ones who were borrowing in a way that offset the demand drag from slow income growth.

Fig. 6.10 shows the ratio of consumption to disposable income for the bottom 95% and top 5%.[23] The volatility of the consumption ratio for the affluent group may look surprising, but it has a clear explanation in standard economic theory. The top 5% group smooths consumption when incomes fall. This smoothing leads to peaks in the consumption ratio during recessions, most obviously in the Great Recession when the spending rate of the top 5% temporarily exceeds the ratio for the bottom 95%. The dynamics of the consumption ratio for the bottom 95% are very different. For this group, the ratio seems to rise modestly through 2005 with no evidence of consumption smoothing. Then, in the crisis years, the consumption rate *falls* for the bottom 95%. The decline may not look all that dramatic, but note that this decline is in the *opposite* direction of what conventional household consumption theory would predict.

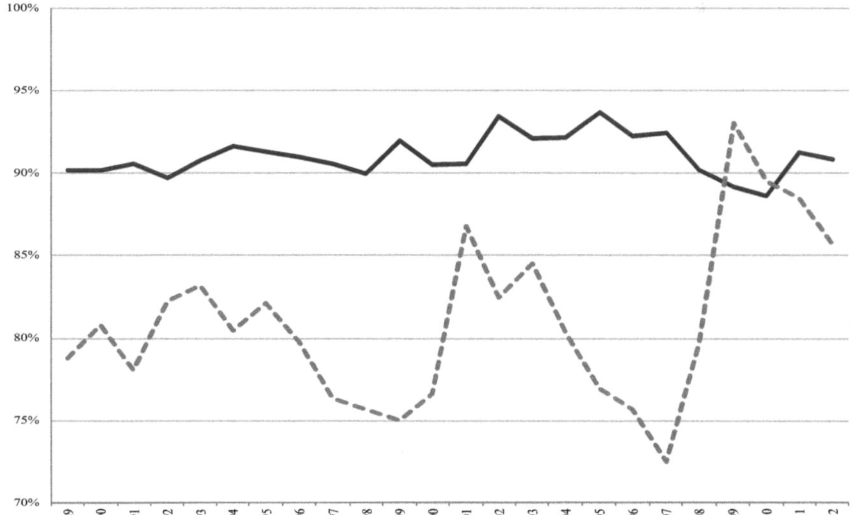

Figure 6.10 Inequality and consumer spending rates. *Solid line*: personal consumption to disposable income for the bottom 95% of the income distribution. *Dotted line*: personal consumption to disposable income for the top 5%.

[23] Because of data availability, this decomposition is based on NIPA personal consumption expenditures rather than the adjusted household demand variable presented in earlier figures.

The bottom 95% follows Minsky dynamics rather than consumption smoothing. They borrowed heavily in the Consumer Age. When financial fragility finally brings the system to its knees and cuts off lending, consumption spending relative to income declines for the bottom 95%.

It was the bottom 95% whose income stagnated in the Consumer Age, who borrowed unsustainably up until the eve of the Great Recession, and who cut back their spending rate (rather than increasing it as predicted by consumption smoothing) in the crisis. This evidence links rising inequality to the Minsky explanation for the period from about 1980 to 2010. The secular stagnation in the aftermath of the crisis, as shown in figures in 6.7 and 8, comes in large part from weak household demand, presumably from the bottom 95% again as the top 5% has continued to do quite well in the aftermath of the crisis.

We provide additional support for the argument that the demand-drag effect of inequality was revealed after the Minsky crisis in Cynamon and Fazzari (2015). We calibrate a simple demand-led growth model with different propensities to consume and different tax rates across income groups. Results show that the rise of inequality since 1980 can explain a decline in the growth path of aggregate demand of about 10%, in the neighborhood of the output gap relative to the previous trend that has persisted over the past decade. Again, the argument is *not* that inequality caused all of the decline in household demand since the Great Recession. Instead, Minsky dynamics masked demand drag from rising inequality until the crisis. The recession pushed household demand down to a lower growth path reflecting the long-term rise of inequality, and there it remains. With the addition of the inequality effect to the implications of the financial instability hypothesis, Hyman Minsky meets secular stagnation.

Conclusion

This chapter argues that Minsky's theory of cyclical financial instability, when its locus is shifted from business investment to household spending, provides a compelling explanation of the path of the US economy from the early 1980s through the Great Recession years. In addition, the combination of Minsky's theory with rising income inequality reveals how the shrinking share of income earned by the high spending parts of economy, that is, almost everyone except the affluent, can explain the weak "secular stagnation" path of the economy from the Great Recession through 2019.

The shift in focus from firms to households may change some details of the basic Minsky analysis. For example, a Minsky crisis is usually associated with a kind of "cleansing" of financial excess. If the financially fragile units are firms, they cease to exist due to bankruptcy or merger into other units. The process is brutal, but effective, in eliminating financial fragility and setting the stage for a new expansion. Of course, households also go bankrupt and face foreclosure and repossession of durable assets, etc. But the households do not go away. They remain in the economy and carry their damaged credit records with them. This change could be partly responsible for the slow recovery, magnifying the effect of rising inequality. Another factor to keep in mind is household demand constitutes a much larger share of the economy than investment. While investment remains more volatile than consumption, a given percentage shock to consumption has a much bigger effect on aggregate economic activity. When consumption is the driving force of economic cycles, the effects are likely to be dramatic, as the Great Recession demonstrated.

Changing the locus of Minsky dynamics from business investment to household demand is not trivial. And adding inequality dynamics to the analysis is a further significant addition to the basic Minsky cycle analysis. But despite these changes, the broad Minsky perspective provides the right framework to interpret the details of financially driven macroeconomic events. The discussion here also shows how effective application of Minsky's theory requires attention to historical specificity. Each cycle has unique characteristics that cannot be fully captured in any single generic model. As Tymoigne and Wray (2014, page 7) write "[Minsky] rejected the idea that an economic theory can apply to all economic systems past and present, and argue that a careful analysis of the existing socio-political-economic institutions is necessary to formulate a meaningful analysis." But despite historical specificity, cycles have a family resemblance. The core concepts of borrowers' risk, lenders' risk, financial validation, and financial fragility play a role in guiding macroeconomic dynamics as described in the first two sections of this chapter. This kind of analysis of historical cases informed by a few core concepts was Minsky's own primary method of study. This approach proves itself relevant again to help us understand the dramatic macroeconomics of the US economy over the past several decades that, according to mainstream analysis, were not supposed to happen.

References

Akerlof, G.A., 1970. The market for 'lemons:' quality uncertainty and the market mechanism. Quarterly Journal of Economics 84 (3), 488–500.

Bernanke, B.S., Gertler, M., Gilchrist, S., 1996. The financial accelerator and the flight to quality. Review of Economics and Statistics 78 (1), 1–15.

Crotty, J.R., 1990. Owner-manager conflict and financial theories of investment demand: a critical assessment of Keynes, Tobin and Minsky. Journal of Post Keynesian Economics 12 (4), 519–542.

Crotty, J.R., 1996. Is the new Keynesian theory of investment really Keynesian? Journal of Post Keynesian Economics 18 (3), 335–357.

Crotty, J.R., 1994. Are Keynesian uncertainty and macrotheory compatible? Conventional decision making, institutional structures, and conditional stability in Keynesian macromodels. In: Dymski, G., Pollin, R. (Eds.), New Perspectives in Monetary Macroeconomics: Explorations in the Tradition of Hyman Minsky. University of Michigan Press, Ann Arbor, pp. 105–142.

Cynamon, B.C., Fazzari, S.M., 2008. Household Debt in the Consumer Age—Source of Growth and Risk of Collapse, vol. 3. Capitalism and Society (BE Press, pp. 1–30.

Cynamon, B.Z., Fazzari, S.M., 2013. The end of the consumer age. In: Cynamon, B.Z., Fazzari, S.M., Setterfield, M. (Eds.), After the Great Recession: The Struggle for Economic Recovery and Growth. Cambridge University Press, New York, pp. 129–157 (Chapter 6).

Cynamon, B.C., Fazzari, S.M., 2015. Rising inequality, demand and growth in the US economy. European Journal of Economics and Economic Policies 12 (2), 170–182.

Cynamon, B.Z., Fazzari, S.M., 2016. Inequality, the great recession and slow recovery. Cambridge Journal of Economics 40 (2), 373–399.

Cynamon, B.Z., Fazzari, S.M., 2017a. Household income, demand, and saving: deriving macro data with micro concepts. Review of Income and Wealth 63 (1), 53–69.

Cynamon, B.Z., Fazzari, S.M., 2017b. Secular Demand Stagnation in the 21st Century U.S. Economy, Institute for New Economic Thinking Conference Paper. https://www.ineteconomics.org/research/research-papers/secular-demand-stagnation-in-the-21st-century-u-s-economy.

Cynamon, B.Z., Fazzari, S.M., Setterfield, M., 2013. Understanding the great recession. In: Cynamon, B.Z., Fazzari, S.M., Setterfield, M. (Eds.), After the Great Recession: The Struggle for Economic Recovery and Growth. Cambridge University Press, New York, pp. 3–30 (Chapter 1).

Davidson, P., 1991. Is probability theory relevant for uncertainty? A post Keynesian perspective. Journal of Economic Perspectives 5 (1), 129–143.

Dymski, G.A., 2010. Why the subprime crisis is different: a Minskyian approach. Cambridge Journal of Economics 34, 239–255.

Fazzari, S.M., 2009. Modern business behavior: the theory of the active firm. In: Goldstein, J.P., Hillard, M.G. (Eds.), Heterodox Macroeconomics: Keynes, Marx, and Globalization. Routledge, New York, pp. 101–111 (Chapter 7).

Fazzari, S.M., 2020. Was Keynesian economics ever dead? If so, has it been resurrected. Review of Keynesian Economics 8 (1), 46–60.

Fazzari, S.M., Variato, A.M., 1994. Asymmetric information and Keynesian theories of investment. Journal of Post Keynesian Economics 16 (4), 351–369.

Fazzari, S.M., Variato, A.M., 1996. Varieties of Keynesian investment theories: further reflections. Journal of Post Keynesian Economics 18, 359–368.

Fazzari, S.M., Ferri, P., Variato, A.M., 2020. Demand-led growth and accommodating supply. Cambridge Journal of Economics. https://doi.org/10.1093/cje/bez055. Forthcoming, published online as.

Fazzari, S.M., Ferri, P., Greenberg, E., 1998. Aggregate demand and micro behavior: a new perspective on Keynesian macroeconomics. Journal of Post Keynesian Economics 20 (2), 527–558.

Fazzari, S.M., Hubbard, R.G., Petersen, B.R., 1988. Finance constraints and corporate investment. Brookings Papers on Economic Activity (1), 141–195.

Fazzari, S.M., Mott, T., 1987. Post-Keynesian investment theory: a study of firm data 1970-1982. Journal of Post-Keynesian Economics 9 (2), 171–187.

Hein, E., 2014. Distribution and Growth after Keynes. Edward Elgar, Northhampton, MA.

Jorgenson, D.W., 1963. Capital theory and investment behavior. American Economic Review 53, 247–259.

Kregel, J., 2013. Trying to serve two masters: the dilemma of financial regulation. In: Cynamon, B.Z., Fazzari, S.M., Setterfield, M. (Eds.), After the Great Recession: The Struggle for Economic Recovery and Growth. Cambridge University Press, New York, pp. 86–103 (Chapter 4).

Lavoie, M., Seccareccia, M., 2001. Minsky's financial fragility hypothesis: a missing link?. In: Ferri, P., Bellofiorie, R. (Eds.), The Economic Legacy of Hyman Minsky, vol. 2. Edward Elgar, Cheltenham, U.K., pp. 76–96

Mason, J.W., Jayadev, A., 2014. Fisher dynamics' in US household debt, 1929–2011. American Economic Journal: Macroeconomics 6 (3), 214–234.

Minsky, H.P., 1975. John Maynard Keynes. Columbia University Press, New York.

Minsky, H.P., 1986. Stabilizing an Unstable Economy. Yale University Press, New Haven, Connecticut (Page numbers refer to the 2008 second edition published by McGraw Hill).

Modigliani, F., Miller, M.H., 1958. The cost of capital, corporation finance, and the theory of investment. American Economic Review 48 (3), 261–297.

Mott, T., 2010. Kalecki's Principle of Increasing Risk and Keynesian Economics. Routledge, Abingdon, U.K.

Myers, S.C., Majluf, N.S., 1984. Corporate financing and investment decisions when firms have information that investors do not. Journal of Financial Economics 13, 187–221.

Ndikumana, L., 1999. Debt service, financing constraints and fixed investment: evidence from panel data. Journal of Post Keynesian Economics 21 (3), 455–478.

Stansbury, A., Summers, L.H., August 23, 2019. Whither central banking? Project Syndicate.

Stiglitz, J.E., Weiss, A., 1981. Credit rationing in markets with imperfect information. American Economic Review 71 (3), 393–410.

Summers, L.H., 2014. US economic prospects: secular stagnation, hysteresis, and the zero lower bound. Business Economics 49 (2), 65–73.

Tymoigne, E., Wray, L.R., 2014. The Rise and Fall of Money Manager Capitalism. Routledge, Abingdon, UK.

CHAPTER SEVEN

Demand, distribution, productivity, structural change, and (secular?) stagnation

Michalis Nikiforos
Department of History, Economics and Society, University of Geneva, Geneva, Switzerland

Introduction

Secular stagnation refers to the tendency of the real GDP growth rate in the United States and other capitalist economies to decrease and remain low. Indeed, as we can see in Fig. 7.1A, the US economy experienced robust growth in the 3 decades between 1940 and 1970. However, the average real GDP growth rate never recovered from the "stagflation" crisis of the 1970s. If anything, the average growth rate decreased slightly in the 1980 and 1990s, and then collapsed in the first 2 decades of the new millennium. The average real GDP growth rate for the 2000 and 2010s was below 2%.

The trend in productivity is not as clear. In the same figure, we can see that the growth rate of productivity decreased in the 1970 and 1980s, then recovered in the following 2 decades, and has collapsed together with the growth rate of output after the Great Recession of 2007–09.

Fig. 7.1B presents the trajectories of real GDP in every postwar economic recovery. Two things stand out. First is that the last three recoveries have clearly been the slowest in the postwar period.

Second, the current recovery, which started in the third quarter of 2009, is the slowest of them all. Fig. 7.1C shows that labor productivity's growth in the current recovery is also the slowest among all postwar recoveries (a fact that corroborates the collapse of productivity in the 2010s in Fig. 7.1C). Finally, despite the low productivity growth, the increase in the employment-to-population ratio also stands out as the slowest among all postwar recoveries (Fig. 7.1D).

Handbook of Economic Stagnation
ISBN: 978-0-12-815898-2
https://doi.org/10.1016/B978-0-12-815898-2.00005-7

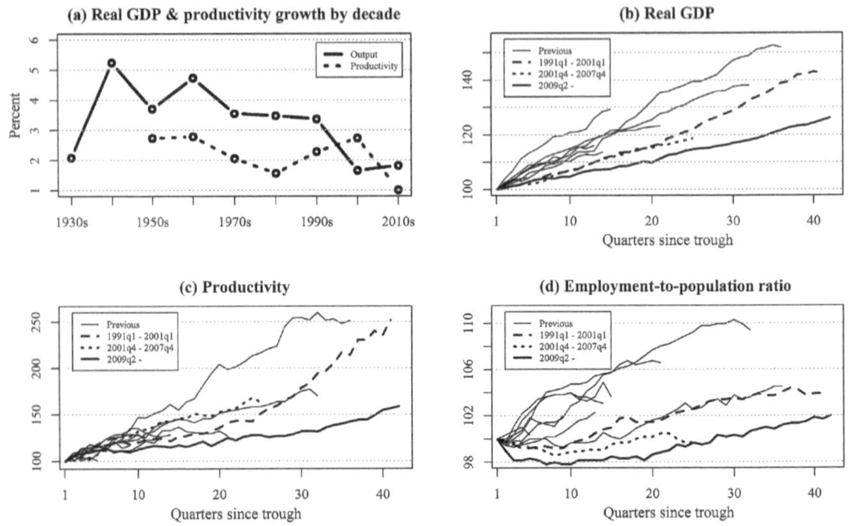

Figure 7.1 ***Main macroeconomic variables.*** Note: Panel (A) presents the average growth rate of the two variables by decade. Panels (B)—(D) present the trajectories of the respective variables in each postwar business cycle (trough to peak). The value for each cycle's trough is normalized to 100. *Source: Bureau of Economic Analysis.*

The term "secular stagnation" was coined by Alvin Hansen (1938, 1939) in response to the Great Depression and the sharp downturn of 1937—38. Hansen proposed a demand-based explanation for the US economy's tendency to stagnate. Investment opportunities, according to his explanation, had declined because of the decline in the expansion of the markets, slower population growth, and new technologies that were less capital intensive. Hansen framed his theory in terms of Knut Wicksel's loanable funds approach for the determination of the interest rate (e.g., Hansen, 1939, 5) and for that reason he has been the starting point of recent New Keynesian discussions of stagnation. Joseph Schumpeter (1939) criticized Hansen's explanation and attributed the downturn to the New Deal policies that were hostile to businesses (and the heroic Schumpeterian entrepreneur). Part of this "stagnation circle" at Harvard at this time, first as a student and then as an instructor, was Paul Sweezy, who wrote extensively on stagnation in the following decades, but from a more Marxian vantage point (e.g., Baran and Sweezy, 1966; Sweezy, 1982). Finally, another important contribution in the postwar period was made by Joseph Steindl (1952).[1]

[1] For a history of the idea of secular stagnation, see Backhouse and Boianovsky (2016).

However, the postwar period's relatively robust growth led to a demise in the interest in stagnation. It was only after the recent crisis and the developments summarized in Fig. 7.1 that there has been a revival of interest and contributions discussing the prospect of stagnation in the US economy. Two approaches have been put forward by neoclassical economists. First, Robert Gordon (2017) provides a purely supply side explanation, where the slowdown in output and productivity growth is due to an exogenous slowdown in innovation. On the other hand, New Keynesian economists (e.g., Summers, 2014; Krugman, 2014) have offered demand-based explanations. As usual in New Keynesian models, demand plays a role because of nominal rigidities—in this case it was the so-called zero lower bound of the interest rate.

The present paper provides an alternative explanation that emphasizes the role of demand in the slowdown of output growth, but in a more straightforward way and without resorting to nominal rigidities. It will be argued that the US economy experienced three main shocks to demand between the 1980 through the 2010s. First, there was a decrease in the US economy's net exports, as foreign producers managed to outcompete American producers. Second, starting in the 1980s, the traditional Keynesian macroeconomic management of the economy was abandoned in favor of fiscal conservatism; the fiscal policy of the 1990s and the 2010s has no precedent in the postwar US economic history. Finally, another important change in recent decades has been the increase in income inequality. From a demand point of view, the increase in inequality implies the transfer of income shares from households with a high propensity to consume to households with a low propensity to consume and puts negative pressure on consumption. To the extent that redistribution does not lead to increases in investment or exports that compensate for the decrease in consumption (which has been the case recently), the increase in inequality also has a negative effect on aggregate demand.

It is also important to note that the negative effects of these developments on demand were compensated for, especially until the crisis of 2007, with the private sector's debt-financed expenditure. In the aftermath of the crisis, households' debt overhang is another factor that contributes to slow consumption growth.

These changes also have important consequences for productivity growth. As emphasized by a long line of economists going back to Adam Smith, changes in the growth rate of output affect technical change. Hence, a negative demand shock that leads to a decrease in output growth can also have secondary negative effects on productivity growth. Second, as emphasized by Karl Marx, and more recently by the theory of induced technical change, the main motive for the introduction of labor-saving technical change is the cost of labor. When the cost of labor stagnates, the incentive for capitalists to introduce new production techniques with higher labor productivity diminishes. Hence, besides its demand effect, the increase in inequality also accounts for the slowdown in productivity. Moreover, overindebted firms are also less likely to innovate as they struggle to repay their debt.

Finally, two more related aspects of the US economy's structural transformation are worth mention. One of them is the financialization of the US economy, which has increased the size and influence of the financial sector. An important aspect of this process has been the decoupling of investment from cash flows. Over the last 4 decades, corporations increasingly use their profits on paying dividends and share buybacks instead of investment. This has an obvious effect on demand and productivity growth. Second, the same period has also seen an increase in the monopoly power of large corporations. Large monopolies contribute to stagnation because they tend to invest less, they have less incentive to innovate, and, because of entry barriers, they also have a negative effect on other firms' innovation.

Neoclassical explanations of secular stagnation

A recent well-known explanation of the slowdown in output and productivity growth has been provided by Gordon (2017) in his book, *The Rise and Fall of American Growth,* which examines the US economy's growth performance over the last one-and-a-half centuries. Gordon argues that in the century after the Civil War (1870—970) there was synchronous technological advancement on many different fronts: the advent of electricity and indoor plumbing; the introduction of trains, motors, and later airplanes in transportation (replacing horses as the main transportation means since antiquity); the improvement in telecommunications; and the introduction of assembly-line production. These changes revolutionized production and formed the basis for the rapid output and productivity growth over this period, and, together with other improvements, such as medical advances or the introduction of air conditioning—only an American could give such a central role to air conditioning—led to a rapid improvement in living standards and an increase in life expectancy by 27 years (from 45 to 72 years) over the same period.

However, Gordon argues these tautochronous technological changes in the century after the Civil War were a historical coincidence. He attributes the slower growth of productivity and output of the last 50 years to technical change being concentrated only in the information and telecommunication sectors, and, as a result, not having the all-encompassing and revolutionary effect of the previous period. He concludes that there is no reason to expect that in the future technical change will accelerate and criticizes this belief as naive techno-optimism. Finally, he attributes part of the slowdown in output growth to demographic factors.

Gordon's argument is consistent with the neoclassical approach to growth. In the steady state of the canonical neoclassical growth model (Ramsey, 1928; Solow, 1956), the growth rate of output is determined by the natural growth rate—the sum of (Harrod-neutral) technical change and population growth—both of which are exogenous. Hence, the rapid growth of the period 1870–970 was due to a coincidental exogenous increase in the natural growth rate. In turn, the secular stagnation of the last 50 years is the result of a decrease in the natural rate, which is also exogenous.

Gordon's book is a very interesting presentation of the US economic history of the last century and a half; however, his main argument suffers on many fronts. First, it completely disregards the role of effective demand and focuses entirely on supply side factors. As Keynes and Kalecki emphasized, we cannot understand the workings of a modern capitalist economy without reference to demand. For example, it is very hard to make sense of the recent crisis and the slow recovery that has followed without an examination of demand factors.[2] Second, there is a long economic tradition that goes back to Smith and Marx, which emphasizes the endogenous character of technical change. From this point of view, the rapid technical change of the last two centuries in the United States and other capitalist economies is not exogenous, but rather due to some basic characteristics of capitalist accumulation. Hence, we should try to understand what factors have contributed to the slowdown of technical change. Finally, and this is also related to the importance of demand, the slowdown in productivity growth is not as dramatic as the slowdown in output growth. As Fig. 7.1A shows, there is a lot of diversity within the period from the

[2] For a methodological discussion of this, which argues that the relevance of aggregate demand in the short and long run is an essential feature of capitalism, see Nikiforos (2018).

1970s until 2014; in the 2000s, despite the slow output growth, productivity growth was comparable with that of the early postwar decades.

The role of aggregate demand as a determining factor for the past 40 years of secular stagnation has been highlighted by New Keynesian authors like Lawrence Summers (2014) and Paul Krugman (2014). As in every New Keynesian model, the starting point of their analysis is neoclassical; hence, the role of demand is introduced through nominal rigidities. In particular, the rigidity that gained prominence in the postcrisis years—because of the aforementioned contributions of Krugman and Summers, and other works such as Krugman (1998) and Eggertsson and Krugman (2012)—was the so-called zero lower bound of the nominal interest rate, which, within a neoclassical framework, does not allow the loanable funds market to clear.

It is beyond the scope of the present paper to provide an extensive critique of the New Keynesian theory or the loanable funds approach to the determination of the interest rate. It suffices here to say that the hype around the zero lower bound evaporated after the Bank of Japan and the European Central Bank introduced negative interest rates, showing that in reality there is no such rigidity.

In what follows, I provide an explanation of stagnation based on demand factors but without having to resort to any nominal rigidity. These demand factors interact with distribution, productivity, and other structural changes that have taken place over the last several decades and provide a more satisfactory explanation of the slowdown of output and productivity growth.

Demand effects

A good starting point for understanding the structure of an economy and the sources of aggregate demand is provided by the financial balances (or the net lending) of its three major institutional sectors—private, government, and foreign—in conjunction with the growth rate. As was emphasized by Wynne Godley (e.g., Godley, 1999), basic accounting principles imply that the three balances sum to zero: if one sector runs a deficit then at least one other has to run a surplus.[3]

The US economy's three balances for the period 1960–2019 are presented in Fig. 7.2. A few observations can be made. First, the growth rate slowdown in the last 4 decades coincides with an increase in the current

[3] For a more detailed discussion, see Nikiforos and Zezza (2017, especially Section 4).

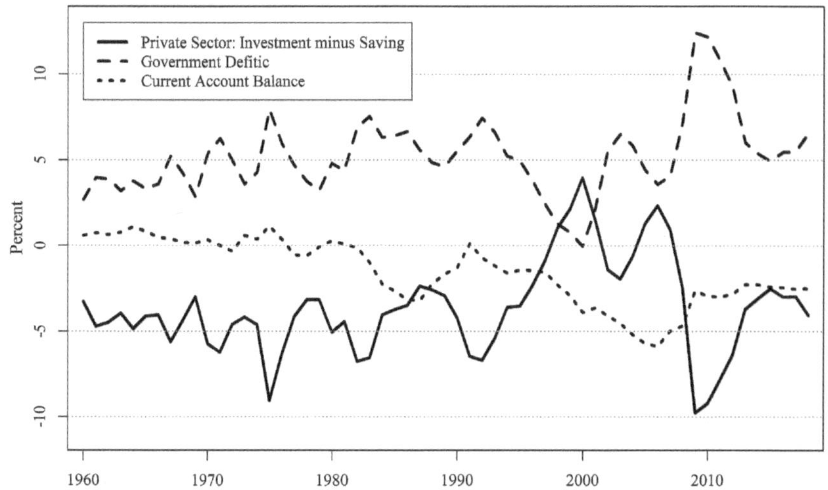

Figure 7.2 Financial balances of the three institutional sectors of the US economy. *Source: Bureau of Economic Analysis.*

account deficit. The current account deficit increased in the first part of the 1980s, but reverted back toward zero by the end of the decade. Starting in the early 1990s, there was a monotonic increase in this deficit, which lasted until the eve of the Great Recession in 2006 when the economy started to slowdown. The current account deficit increased from around zero in 1990 to around 6% in 2006.

As one would expect, and as confirmed in Fig. 7.3, the reason behind the current account deficit's deterioration is the deterioration of the trade deficit of a similar magnitude. This increase in the trade deficit was due to foreign competitor firms' successful invasion of markets in the United States and abroad. To a certain extent, it was also related to technological change over that period, but it was also implicitly encouraged by US trade policy, as "free trade" was used as a way to undermine the power of labor and trade unions.

This increase in the trade deficit was a major drag on aggregate demand, which contributed to the slowdown of the growth. Besides these demand effects, the prolonged increased in the trade deficit implied a demise of American manufacturing, which had important consequences for regions of the country whose economy was based on it. In turn, this had important political repercussions.

In the period after the 2007-09 crisis, the current account deficit has not increased to its previous levels. This is mostly due to the shale gas extraction

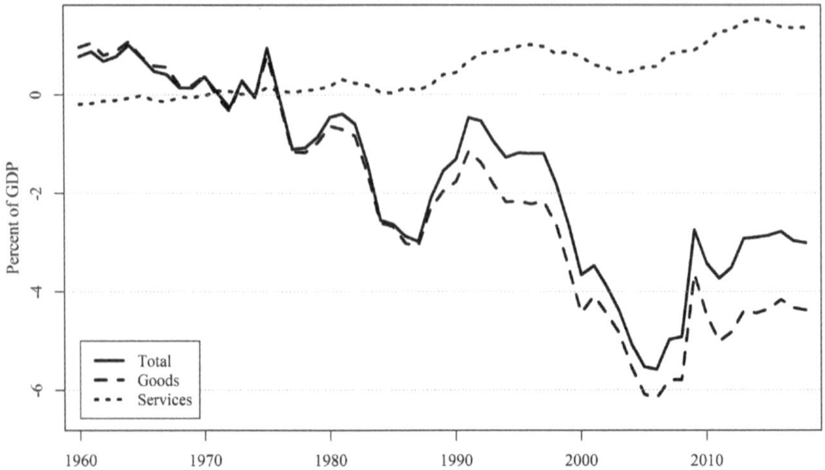

Figure 7.3 Trade balance of the US economy. *Source: Bureau of Economic Analysis.*

methods that were successfully applied after 2011 and have led to the decrease in the trade deficit of petroleum goods to close to zero (from 3% before the crisis). Otherwise the trade deficit of goods other than petroleum has returned to its precrisis levels.[4]

Another major source of deficient aggregate demand has to do with the US government's generally conservative fiscal stance in the last 4 decades. Going back to Fig. 7.2, we can see that in the first 3 decades of the sample, government was a net borrower and government deficit fluctuated procyclically around 5% of GDP. Things changed in the 1990s, starting in 1992, when the deficit was around 7.5% of GDP; the government's fiscal stance became increasingly restrictive and 2000 was the only year in—at least postwar—US history that the government balance was positive.

After the crisis of 2001, government's net lending increased and remained high. This is mostly due to the period's low growth rates and the increase in defense expenditures to fund the wars in Afghanistan and Iraq. Nondefense expenditure remained subdued.

Government deficit increased with the crisis of 2007—09 and remained relatively elevated for a fairly long time due to the slow recovery (it has also increased recently due to the 2017 tax cuts). However, as Fig. 7.4 shows, the post-2009 recovery stands out as the recovery with the slowest growth rate

[4] For a discussion, see Papadimitriou et al. (2019, 4—5).

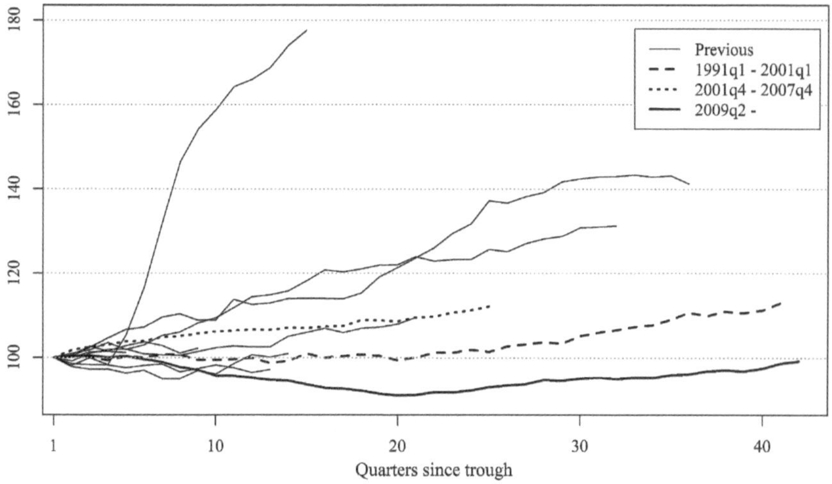

Figure 7.4 ***Government expenditure in postwar US recoveries.*** Note: The figure presents the trajectories of real government consumption expenditures and gross investment in each postwar business cycle (trough to peak). The value for each cycle's trough is normalized to 100. *Source: Bureau of Economic Analysis.*

in real government expenditure. As of 2019Q3, more than 10 years into the recovery, real government expenditure is still slightly below its level at the beginning of the recovery.

If demand from government expenditure and net exports is deficient, then growth can only come about through private expenditure. In fact, as the current account deficit increased and government deficit decreased, growth became dependent on the private sector becoming a net borrower. Fig. 7.2 shows that until the early 1990s the private sector was a net lender, with some cyclical fluctuations in its position. In the 1990s, as the balance of trade turned very negative and the government consolidated its budget, the private sector became a net borrower for the first time in the postwar period. This situation persisted until the eve of the Great Recession (with an exception in the early 2000s). It was actually this reversal in the private sector's stance—essentially the increase in its saving rate—that triggered the slowdown and then the crisis.

Importantly, accounting consistency also implies that net borrowing leads to accumulation of net financial liabilities. Therefore, given the US economy's aforementioned structural characteristics, growth is dependent on the private sector accumulating debt. If we want to use Hyman Minsky's (1992) classification, growth is dependent on the private sector moving from

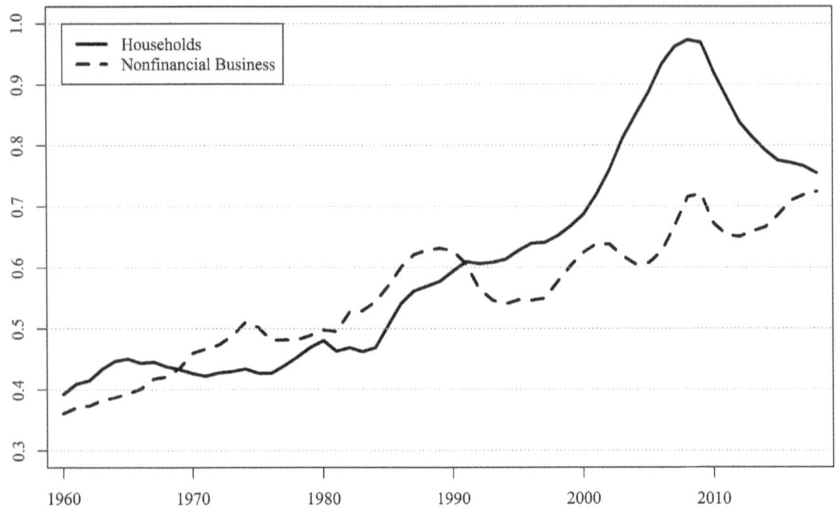

Figure 7.5 Ratio of liabilities of the private sector to GDP. *Source: Bureau of Economic Analysis; Federal Reserve Board.*

a hedge, to a speculative, and then a Ponzi position. Indeed, this is how growth was sustained until 2007. Fig. 7.5 shows that since the mid-1980s and until the recent crisis there was a rapid increase in the private sector's total debt-to-GDP ratio—especially that of households. As Godley (1999) pointed out such a process is unsustainable, and sooner or later has to stop.

The crisis of 2007–09 marked exactly the stop of this process, when households finally increased their saving. In the aftermath of the crisis, households did not increase their indebtedness and, as Fig. 7.1 showed, the economy stagnated. The debt that allowed the economy to grow is now an overhang that contributes to stagnation in its own right.

It is also worth mentioning that such a process of increasing indebtedness is usually accompanied by some sort of asset bubble, another Minskyan process. The bubble—as long as it lasts—makes the balance sheets of both the lenders and borrowers look better and allows the process to continue for longer. The asset bubbles that have become endemic in the United States over the last decades (e.g., the stock market bubble of the 1990s or of the present days, the real estate bubble of the 2000s, etc.) can be understood along these lines.

To sum up the argument of this section, given some of its structural characteristics—which have led to a decrease in net export demand—and the pervasive fiscal conservatism that has prevailed in Washington over the last 4 decades, the US economy faces a dilemma between stagnation and financial instability. The economy can avoid stagnation at the cost of private sector balance sheets becoming more fragile—a fragility that will eventually become in itself a contributing factor to stagnation, as has been happening since the early 2010s.

Income distribution

Another major structural change that has taken place in the United States over the last 4 decades is the increase in income inequality. Fig. 7.6 presents several aspects of this increase. Panel (A) shows that starting in the late 1970s the share of income of the top 10% of the population started increasing and is now at a higher level that in the late 1920s, when it had reached its previous peak. Panel (B) shows that the increase in income inequality is also visible if we focus on the wage share, which has also decreased the last decades. If we exclude the share of wages of the top 10% of the population, the decrease is much bigger: the wage share of the bottom 90% has decreased by close to 13% of GDP compared to the early 1970s. Panel (C) presents another way of seeing the decline in the wage share. It shows that in the early postwar decades the real wage was growing at the same pace as labor productivity. Since the early 1970s, the real wage has been increasing much slower. In the 25 years between 1947 and 1972, the real wage doubled, while in the almost 50 years that followed it only increased 50%. This implies a rate of increase that is four times slower than in the previous period. Finally, panel (D) shows that the average real income of the bottom 90% has stagnated over the same period; today it is slightly *below* its level from the early 1970s.

From a macroeconomic point of view, this increase in inequality implies a redistribution of income from households with a high propensity to consume to households with a low propensity to consume. Therefore, ceteris paribus, it leads to a decrease in consumption and aggregate demand. On the other hand, an increase in inequality can lead to an increase in aggregate demand, if it has a strong effect on investment and net exports. It was already shown that this has not been the case with net exports; investment has also not been very responsive to the increase in profit margins, at least in the last few decades.

Fig. 7.7A shows that the effects of inequality on consumption are visible. As one would expect, since consumption is by far the largest component of aggregate expenditure, consumption's trajectories in postwar recoveries are

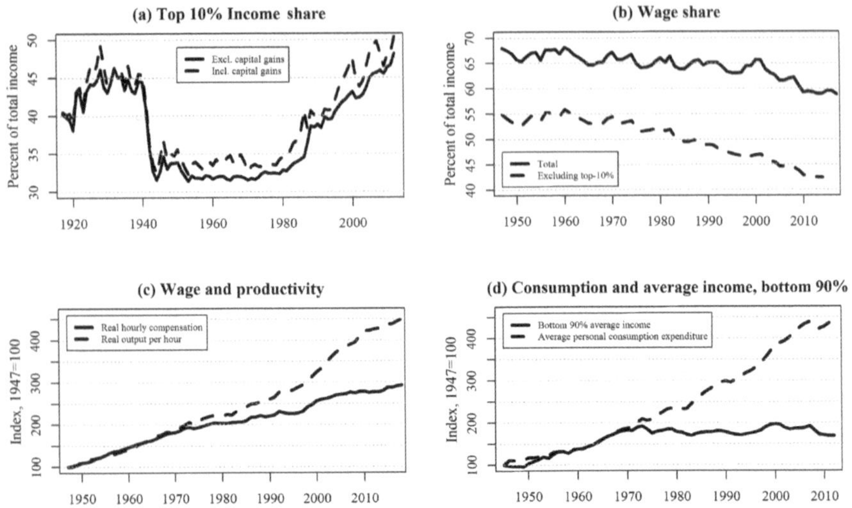

Figure 7.6 Income distribution. *Sources: Bureau of Economic Analysis; Bureau of Labor Statistics; Alvaredo et al. (2016).*

similar to GDP in Fig. 7.1B: the last three recoveries have been the slowest, and the current one has been by far the slowest of them all.

Given the magnitude of the increase in inequality, the decrease in consumption should be even larger. Going back to Fig. 7.6D, we can see that up until the early 1970s, average consumption expenditure increased at the same rate as the income of the bottom 90%. Afterward, the latter stagnated but consumption kept increasing. It is thus obvious that to the extent that this increase in consumption did not come from the households in the top 10% income bracket, it had to come through borrowing on behalf of the bottom 90% of households.

Indeed, as Fig. 7.7B shows, the increase in households' debt-to-income ratio was very unevenly distributed. As it was explained above, the aggregate increase was enormous and unsustainable, but the increase in the bottom 90% of households' debt-to-income ratio is stunning. When the crisis started in 2007, their debt-to-disposable-income ratio reached 1.6. On the other hand, the ratio did not increase for the households at the top, as the increase in their incomes counteracted the increase in the stock of debt.

Edward Wolff (2012, 23), in a paper with a painstakingly detailed examination of the balance sheets of the American "middle class," confirms that the increase in indebtedness was related to consumption expenditures: "Where did the borrowing [of the middle class] go? Some have asserted

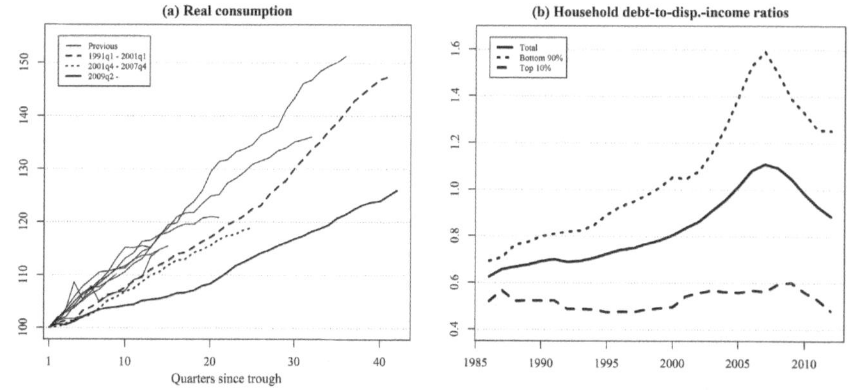

Figure 7.7 ***Consumption and household–debt decomposition.*** Note: Panel (B) presents the trajectories of real personal consumption expenditure in each postwar business cycle (trough to peak). The value for each cycle's trough is normalized to 100. *Sources: Bureau of Economic Analysis; Federal Reserve Board; Taylor et al. (2013).*

that it went to invest in stocks. However, if this were the case, then stocks as a share of total assets would have increased over this period, which it did not [...]. Moreover, they did not go into other assets. In fact, the rise in housing prices almost fully explains the increase in the net worth of the middle class [...]. Instead, it appears that middle class households, experiencing stagnating incomes, expanded their debt in order to finance normal consumption expenditures."

This kind of behavior of middle- and lower-income households can be explained in two ways. First, as some basic services (such as education or health care) became more expensive, households had to borrow in order to finance the consumption of this service. Second, emulation effects à la Veblen (1973) and Duesenberry (1949) might have also played a role.[5]

No matter what the behavioral explanation is, this discussion adds another layer to the dilemma described in the previous section. The increase in inequality puts heavy downward pressure on consumption and demand. Thus, there has to be a choice between debt-financed consumption, which makes the balance sheets of middle- and lower-income households more fragile and eventually leads to a financial crisis, or stagnation. The American economy and society chose the first path in the decades before the crisis.

[5] A more detailed discussion of the behavioral explanations of the increase in debt-financed expenditure, together with a formal treatment of the relation between distribution, growth, and debt within a stock-flow consistent framework, can be found in Nikiforos (2016a).

In the period after the crisis, when the debt-financed consumption did not happen, consumption, demand, and output stagnated. Also, in this case, the debt overhang is now an additional factor contributing to stagnation.

Endogenous technical change

Starting in the very first chapters of *The Wealth of Nations*, Smith (1999) emphasizes the endogenous nature of technical progress. Increases in labor productivity—as a result of economies of scale achieved through a higher division of labor—are limited by the extent of the market. Smith describes a virtuous cycle where technical progress allows for a larger sized market, which in turns allows for more technical progress.

These ideas—which were also discussed by Alfred Marshall (1898) and Allyn Young (1928)—underlie what later came to be known as the Kaldor-Verdoorn law (Verdoorn, 1949; Kaldor, 1957) as well as Gunnar Myrdal's (1957) principle of circular and cumulative causation. Petrus Verdoorn (1949) provided an empirical examination of output growth's effects on productivity growth, while Nicholas Kaldor (1957) defined a technical progress function where productivity growth is a function of the capital–labor ratio's growth rate. Myrdal is more concerned with development's institutional aspects, but his main idea is similar, as he describes a virtuous (or vicious) cycle among development and technical and institutional change.

Another important tradition in the theory of technical change that also goes back to classical political economy—especially Ricardo (1951) and Marx (1976)—emphasized the introduction of techniques of production with higher labor productivity as a way to save labor and increase profitability. More generally, from this point of view, the cost of factors of production is an important determinant for technical change; the more expensive a factor of production is, the more incentive firms have to introduce new techniques of production that economize on it. For example, when labor becomes more expensive—and the wage share increases—firms have a stronger incentive to introduce labor-saving technical change by adopting techniques with higher labor productivity.

These approaches to technical change, in conjunction with the discussion on demand and distribution in the previous sections, provide a better way to understand the slowdown in the rate of productivity growth compared to Gordon's (2017) neoclassical approach, where productivity growth's rise and fall is exogenous.[6] To begin with, as it was explained in the previous sections, deficient net export, government expenditure, and consumption demand (the latter because of the increase in inequality) lead to a decrease in the growth rate of the economy. Based on the Kaldor-Verdoorn law, this decrease can, in turn, have second-round negative effects on productivity growth. Moreover, to the extent that productivity growth contributes to demand growth (because, e.g., it encourages investment), this process can lead to a vicious circular and cumulative process with lower output and productivity growth.

A second factor that is responsible for the slowdown in productivity growth is the stagnation in wage cost (see Fig. 7.6B and C and the discussion in the previous section). Given this dramatic decrease in the cost of labor, firms have a much weaker incentive to adopt labor-saving production techniques.

Interestingly, Gordon (2017) says that much in Chapter 16 of his book—in a discussion that contradicts the book's main thesis. The chapter examines the factors that contributed to the "Great Leap Forward of the American level of labor productivity that occurred in the middle-decades of the twentieth century" (p. 535), which Gordon calls "one of the greatest achievements in all of economic history." He identifies two main factors for the great leap. First are the New Deal institutions and strong labor unions, which led to increases in the real wage. Gordon (2017, 541−3) mentions several transmission channels through which higher wages translated into productivity increases (such as the effect of higher wages and shorter hours on reducing worker's fatigue and increasing their productivity). However, he concludes that: "the main upward stimulus to productivity must have come from the impetus of higher hourly wages, particularly in the 1930s, that led firms to economize on the use of labor. This helps us understand the explosion of productivity during World War II."

[6] It is important to note here that the steady state growth rate is not exogenous in all neoclassical growth models. In the so-called endogenous growth approach that was developed in the early 1990s, the neoclassical model was transformed to produce endogenous growth through some externality-producing mechanism (Lucas, 1988; Romer, 1990; Barro, 1990; Rebelo, 1991). These models have some severe implications for the neoclassical approach to growth. The most important is that because of the externalities, the neoclassical production function is turned into an AK production function (with no decreasing returns to each factor of production), and therefore, the long-run growth rate is not the same as the natural growth rate—which brings us back to the issues raised by Harrod (1939). Second, because of the externalities, market mechanisms cannot guarantee efficient resource allocation. Efficient allocation requires the intervention of a "benevolent central planner."

Gordon makes his argument with the use of a neoclassical production function, where an increase in real wage causes a substitution of labor for capital. However, it is well-known that this is equivalent to a process where the increase in the real wage induces labor-saving technical change.[7]

The second factor Gordon (2017) identifies is World War II. Because of the increase in government expenditure: "as early as 1941, the economy was straining against a shortage of capacity [...], the owner of a leading machine tool supplier shook his head at the backlogs stating that '*demand is infinite*'" (Gordon, 2017, 549; emphasis added).

In turn, this increase in demand and growth led to increases in productivity in the manufacturing of war equipment, which then persisted when companies switched back to peacetime production. Gordon (2017, 537) also mentions that "the war created household saving that after 1945 was spent on consumer goods that had been unavailable during the war." In other words, the government deficit during the war was mirrored by a private sector surplus that led to an increase in their financial assets, allowing for the increase in consumption after the war.

Gordon calls the assertion that the war was the most important contributor to the great leap "the most novel aspect of the chapter." Although the novelty of this argument is questionable—these points have been repeatedly made by several heterodox economists—its essence is in line with the present paper's argument. Gordon describes a situation where high government expenditure demand and increases in wages led to improvements in productivity, in line with the discussion of this section's previous paragraphs. Also, the aforementioned effect of wartime government deficits on household balance sheets is basically the opposite of what has been happening over the last 4 decades and was discussed in the previous sections.

Monopoly capital and financialization

For reasons of completeness of the argument, the role of two more factors should be touched upon very briefly. First, it seems possible that a contributing factor to secular stagnation is the US economy's increasingly oligopolistic and monoplisitic—and monopsonistic—structure. This is an issue that has been recently emphasized by neoclassical economists (e.g.,

[7] Gordon (2017, 541) calls his explanation "basic economic theory." However, it is noteworthy that this explanation contradicts the neoclassical theory of distribution.

Teulings and Baldwin, 2014; Summers, 2016; Philippon, 2019). Probably without realizing, these economists recycle arguments that were put forward several decades ago by Josef Steindl (1952) in his *Maturity and Stagnation in American Capitalism* and Paul Baran and Paul Sweezy (1966) in *Monopoly Capital*. Both books emphasize how the emergence of large oligopolies and monopolies increases the share of profits and therefore savings, while at the same time the increases in demand are not enough to match this increase in savings.

According to Steindl, in oligopolistic markets firms tend to operate with excess capacity—which discourages the entrance of new firms in the market—because there is no market mechanism to eliminate it. In competitive markets, the elimination of excess capacity takes place through price-cutting, which forces less competitive firms out of the market, but in oligopolistic markets firms have the power to set the prices. In turn, this excess capacity weakens investment incentives and leads to stagnation.[8]

Baran and Sweezy also emphasize the surplus absorption problem that tends to increase under monopolies. Aside from investment, they also examine the role of aggregate demand's other sources, such as capitalist consumption, the sales effort, civilian, and military government expenditures, etc., and they conclude that overall demand will not be sufficient to realize the surplus and therefore the monopoly-capital economy will tend to stagnate. The insights provided by Steindl and Baran and Sweezy fit within the framework outlined above and are relevant for understanding the structure of the US economy today, the increase in income inequality, and investment's nonresponsiveness to the increases in the profit margins.

Another important and related development has been the US economy's so-called financialization. Financialization has many different dimensions: changes in corporate governance and sources of profits, as well as the importance of financial motives, markets, institutions, and elites, etc. It is beyond the scope of this paper to go into the details of all these.[9] A few things are important here. First, part of the financialization process is related to the financial sector's increasing concentration; hence, the arguments on monopoly capital can be conditionally extended.[10] Second, financialization is

[8] Hansen (1954) wrote a favorable review of the book.

[9] For a discussion of financialization, see Boyer (2000), Lazonick and O'Sullivan (2000), Stockhammer (2004), Epstein (2005), Orhangazi (2008), and Lazonick (2014, 2015).

[10] Sweezy (1997), in one of his last published articles, referred to the "financialization of the capital accumulation process."

related to the increase in income inequality. Finally, part of financialization has been the decoupling of cash flows and accumulation, as it becomes increasingly attractive or even imperative for firms to channel their profits into financial markets and share buybacks, or to distribute them. These aspects of financialization are part of the story outlined above and contribute to economic stagnation.

Related to that, nonfinancial corporations are now more indebted than ever (see Fig. 7.5, above). Importantly, this debt accumulation has also been decoupled from investment and borrowed funds have, to a large extent, been used for share buybacks. Besides the record level of indebtedness, according to a recent report by the Bank for International Settlements (BIS, 2019), the leverage of US corporations is also above its pre-2007 level. In the same report, it is also mentioned that the percentage of issuers with BBB corporate debt (the lowest investment grade rating) and the share of mutual fund portfolios comprised of BBB bonds have also increased. Moreover, the number of firms whose cash flows are not enough to cover interest payments on their debt—what Minsky (1992) called Ponzi firms and what some more recent literature calls zombie firms (Caballero et al., 2008; McGowan et al., 2017; Banerjee and Hofmann, 2018)—is also elevated despite the last decade's record low interest rates. Finally, at the same time, and despite the very slow recovery, the stock market valuation is higher than its level in the early fall of 1929, and, according to some measures, also higher than its level in the late 1990s.[11] These processes are also clearly unsustainable and when they are over they will be another factor contributing to the US economy's stagnant state.

Instead of conclusion: stagnation, is it secular?

The present paper discussed a set of interrelated and mutually reinforcing factors that can explain the stagnation of output and productivity growth of the last decades. The role of demand was emphasized, and it was explained that the US economy has been experiencing deficient aggregate demand because of net export's weak performance, the fiscal conservatism that has dominated (most of) the last 4 decades, and the increase in income inequality, which puts downward pressure on demand. It was also stressed that because of these developments the US economy's growth before the

[11] For a more detailed discussion of the data, see Papadimitriou et al. (2019, 2020).

crisis rested on the private sector's increasing indebtedness, especially households at the bottom of the distribution. This debt that allowed the US economy to grow before the crisis is now another factor contributing to stagnation.

It was also explained that the slowdown in productivity growth is better explained based by endogenous productivity theory, as opposed to the exogenous approach adopted by Gordon (2017). In particular, two approaches to technical change are relevant: the Kaldor-Verdoorn law and the induced technical change hypothesis, which posit that labor productivity responds to the growth rate of output and the increase in the cost of labor. These approaches to technical change taken together with the aforementioned demand factors provide a consistent explanation for the stagnation of demand, output, and productivity. Finally, it was argued that two related factors that contribute to stagnation are the US economy's increasingly oligopolistic and financialized structure.

A last question to be answered is if the stagnation we are experiencing is *secular* or not. In other words, are there endogenous forces that can pull the economy out of its current stagnant state or should we expect it to last for a long time (unless by accident or an exogenous factor)? As it was explained above, Gordon's (2017) answer is that there are no endogenous forces. The "rise of American growth" was exogenous in the first place and the current stagnant conditions are the norm. Sweezy (1982) reaches the same conclusion, albeit working within a very different theoretical framework. In an article entitled "Why Stagnation?" he concludes with a discussion of "whether or not the history of capitalism has been characterized by a long cycle of some 50 years' duration (what Schumpeter called the Kondratieff cycle)." He suggests that although "it is the nature of an investment boom to exhaust itself, [...] the stagnation phase of a long wave does not generate any 'forces of reversal.' If and when such forces do emerge, they originate not in the internal logic of the economy but in the larger historical context within which the economy functions." Thus, Sweezy also argues that solutions to stagnation are exogenous and coincidental rather than endogenous.

In two recent papers (Nikiforos 2016b, 2019), I express a rather different opinion. Although I agree that there are no strictly speaking economic forces that can pull an economy out of stagnation, I argue that crisis and stagnation act as catalysts for endogenous political-economic responses. As Karl Polanyi (2001) argued, crisis induces *spontaneous reactions* that try to resolve it. Indeed, after the recent crisis there have been different manifestations of these sorts of reactions. Income inequality has been at the center of different movements—such as Occupy Wall Street, Black Lives Matter, and the #MeToo movements, as well as teacher's strikes that have taken place across the country—and it has become one of the main issues of political discourse. The dominance of fiscal conservatism and free trade ideology has also been questioned, and people and politicians are becoming increasingly critical of financial institutions and large monopolies. As it was discussed in this paper, these issues that were in the margins of public discourse until recently are the main factors that have led to stagnation.

Moreover, to the extent that history is a useful guide for the future, it teaches us that the forces of reversal exist. To a large extent, the American economy was pulled out of the crisis of the early 20th century by forces of this kind: the progressive era of the turn of the century; the emergence of strong labor unions and other forms of labor and civic activism; and the establishment of New Deal institutions that led to the breakup of large monopolies, ended the era of *haute finance* (as Polanyi called the financialization of the time), promoted a more equitable distribution of income, and led to the adoption of a generally expansionary fiscal policy.

By this, I do not mean to suggest that we should subscribe to historical determinism. Each era has its own peculiarities and has to invent its own specific mechanisms, policies, and institutional arrangements. The "forces of reversal" exist as tendencies, but the reversal itself that will pull the economy out of stagnation may or may not happen. People's actions (or inaction) play a crucial role in the determination of the actual path that history follows.

References

Alvaredo, F., Atkinson, A.B., Piketty, T., Saez, E., Gabriel, Z., 2016. Distributional National Accounts (DINA) Guidelines: Concepts and Methods Used in WID.World. World Inequality Database. WID.world Working Paper No 2016/1.

Backhouse, R.E., Boianovsky, M., 2016. Secular stagnation: the history of a macroeconomic heresy. The European Journal of the History of Economic Thought 23 (6), 946–970.

Banerjee, R., Hofmann, B., September 2018. The rise of zombie firms: causes and consequences. BIS Quarterly Review 67–78.

Baran, P., Paul, S., 1966. Monopoly Capital. Monthly Review Press, New York.

Barro, R.J., 1990. Government spending in a simple model of endogenous growth. Journal of Political Economy 98 (5, Part 2), S103–S125.

BIS (Bank for International Settlements), 2019. Annual Economic Report. Bank for International Settlements, Basel.

Boyer, R., 2000. Is a finance-led growth regime a viable alternative to Fordism? A preliminary analysis. Economy and Society 29 (1), 111–145.

Caballero, R.J., Hoshi, T., Kashyap, A.K., 2008. Zombie lending and depressed restructuring in Japan. American Economic Review 98 (5), 1943–1977.

Duesenberry, J., 1949. Income, Saving, and the Theory of Consumer Behavior. Harvard Economic Studies. Harvard University Press, Cambridge, MA.

Eggertsson, G.B., Paul, K., 2012. Debt, deleveraging, and the liquidity trap: a Fisher-Minsky-Koo approach. The Quarterly Journal of Economics 127 (3), 1469–1513.
Epstein, G.A., 2005. Financialization and the World Economy. Edward Elgar Publishing, Northampton, MA.
Godley, W., 1999. Seven Unsustainable Processes: Medium-Term Prospects and Policies for the United States and the World. Technical report. Levy Economics Institute of Bard College, Annandale-on-Hudson, NY.
Gordon, R.J., 2017. The Rise and Fall of American Growth: The U.S. Standard of Living since the Civil War. The Princeton Economic History of the Western World. Princeton University Press, Princeton, NJ.
Hansen, A.H., 1938. Stagnation or Full Recovery. Norton, New York.
Hansen, A.H., 1939. Economic progress and declining population growth. The American Economic Review 29 (1), 1–15.
Hansen, A.H., 1954. Growth or stagnation in the American economy. The Review of Economics and Statistics 36 (4), 409–414.
Harrod, R., 1939. An essay in dynamic theory. Economic Journal 49 (193), 14–33.
Kaldor, N., 1957. A model of economic growth. The Economic Journal 67 (268), 591–624.
Krugman, P., 1998. It's Baaack: Japan's slump and the return of the liquidity trap. Brookings Papers on Economic Activity 1998 (2), 137–205.
Krugman, P., 2014. Four observations on secular stagnation. In: Teulings, C., Baldwin, R. (Eds.), Secular Stagnation: Facts, Causes and Cures. CEPR Press, London.
Lazonick, W., 2014. Profits without prosperity. Harvard Business Review 92 (9), 46–55.
Lazonick, W., 2015. Stock Buybacks: From Retain-and-Reinvest to downsize-and-distribute. Center for Effective Public Management of Brookings Institution Report. Brookings Institution, Washington, DC.
Lazonick, W., O'Sullivan, M., 2000. Maximizing shareholder value: a new ideology for corporate governance. Economy and Society 29 (1), 13–35.
Lucas, R.E., 1988. On the mechanics of economic development. Journal of Monetary Economics 22 (1), 3–42.
Marshall, A., 1898. Principles of Economics, fourth ed. McMillan and Co, London. 1890.
Marx, K., 1976. Capital: A Critique of Political Economy, vol. I. Penguin Books, London, 1867.
McGowan, M.A., Andrews, D., Millot, V., 2017. The walking dead?: zombie firms and productivity performance in OECD countries. In: OECD Economic Department Working Papers No 1372. Organisation for Economic Co-operation and Development, Paris.
Minsky, H., 1992. The financial instability hypothesis. In: Levy Economics Institute Working Paper No. 74. Levy Economics Institute of Bard College, Annandale-on-Hudson, NY.
Myrdal, G., 1957. Economic Theory and Under-developed Regions. G. Duckworth, London.
Nikiforos, M., 2016a. A nonbehavioral theory of saving. Journal of Post Keynesian Economics 39 (4), 562–592.
Nikiforos, M., 2016b. Distribution-led growth in the long run. Review of Keynesian Economics 4 (4), 391–408.
Nikiforos, M., 2018. Distribution-led growth through methodological lenses. In: Forum for Macroeconomics and Macroeconomic Policy (FMM) Working Paper 24-2018. IMK at the Hans Boeckler Foundation, Macroeconomic Policy Institute, Düsseldorf, Germany.
Nikiforos, M., 2019. Induced shifting involvements and cycles of growth and distribution. In: Levy Economics Institute Working Paper No 924. Levy Economics Institute of Bard College, Annandale-on-Hudson, NY.
Nikiforos, M., Zezza, G., 2017. Stock-flow consistent macroeconomic models: a survey. Journal of Economic Surveys 31 (5), 1204–1239.

Orhangazi, Ö., 2008. Financialisation and capital accumulation in the non-financial corporate sector: a theoretical and empirical investigation on the US economy: 1973–2003. Cambridge Journal of Economics 32 (6), 863–886.
Papadimitriou, D.B., Nikiforos, M., Gennaro, Z., 2019. Can redistribution help build a more stable economy?. In: Strategic Analysis. Levy Economics Institute of Bard College, Annandale-on-Hudson, NY.
Papadimitriou, D.B., Nikiforos, M., Gennaro, Z., 2020. Prospects and Challenges for the US Economy: 2020 and beyond Strategic Analysis. Levy Economics Institute of Bard College, Annandale-on-Hudson, NY.
Philippon, T., 2019. The Great Reversal: How America Gave up on Free Markets. Harvard University Press, Cambridge, MA.
Polanyi, K., 2001. The Great Transformation: The Political and Economic Origins of Our Time. Beacon Press, Boston, 1944.
Ramsey, F.P., 1928. A mathematical theory of saving. The Economic Journal 38 (152), 543–559.
Rebelo, S., 1991. Long-run policy analysis and long-run growth. Journal of Political Economy 99 (3), 500–521.
Ricardo, D., 1951. On the principles of political economy and taxation. In: Sraffa, P., Dobb, M.H. (Eds.), The Works and Correspondence of David Ricardo, vol. 1. Cambridge University Press, Cambridge, UK, 1817.
Romer, P.M., 1990. Endogenous technological change. Journal of Political Economy 98 (5), S71–S102.
Schumpeter, J.A., 1939. Business Cycles. McGraw-Hill, New York.
Smith, A., 1999. The Wealth of Nations. Penguin Books, London, UK, 1776.
Solow, R.M., 1956. A contribution to the theory of economic growth. The Quarterly Journal of Economics 70 (1), 65–94.
Steindl, J., 1952. Maturity and Stagnation in American Capitalism. Basil Blackwell, Oxford.
Stockhammer, E., 2004. Financialisation and the slowdown of accumulation. Cambridge Journal of Economics 28 (5), 719–741.
Summers, L.H., 2014. U.S. Economic prospects: secular stagnation, hysteresis, and the zero lower bound. Business Economics 49 (2), 65–73.
Summers, L.H., March 30, 2016. Corporate profits are near record highs—why is that a problem? Financial Times. https://www.ft.com/content/12afa3ed-ec33-3440-965d-da6ce1292a50.
Sweezy, P.M., 1982. Why stagnation? Monthly Review 34 (2), 1–10.
Sweezy, P.M., 1997. More (or less) on globalization. Monthly Review 49 (4), 1–4.
Taylor, L., Rezai, A., Kumar, R., de Carvalho, L., Barbosa, N., 2013. US Size Distribution and the Macroeconomy, 1986–2009. Schwartz Center for Economic Policy Analysis (SCEPA), The New School, New York. Technical report.
Teulings, C., Baldwin, R., 2014. Secular Stagnation: Facts, Causes, and Cures. A Vox-EU.Org eBook. CEPR Press, London.
Veblen, T., 1973. The Theory of the Leisure Class. Houghton Mifflin Company, Boston, 1899.
Verdoorn, P.J., 1949. Fattori che regolano lo sviluppo della produttivita del lavoro. In: Pasinetti, L.L. (Ed.), Reprinted in English as "On the Factors Determining the Growth of Labor Productivity", vol. 2. Oxford University Press, Oxford. Italian Economic Papers.
Wolff, E.N., 2012. The Asset Price Meltdown and the Wealth of the Middle Class. NBER Working Paper No. 18559. National Bureau of Economic Research, Cambridge, MA.
Young, A.A., 1928. Increasing returns and economic progress. The Economic Journal 38 (152), 527–542.

CHAPTER EIGHT

Economic stagnation in the Euro Area

Leon Podkaminer
The Vienna Institute for International Economic Studies, Vienna, Austria

Preface

Output growth in countries that later formed the Euro Area (EA) has been slowing down secularly. The growth deceleration correlates with the tendency for the suppression of wages which set in after the demise of the Bretton Woods arrangements—amid the materializing economic paradigm change. Liberalizations of private capital flows were soon followed by more ominous internal policy changes including labor market flexibilizations and downsizing the welfare state institutions. Under the Maastricht Treaty (which sanctioned the reemerging liberal paradigm, with the emphasis on fiscal continence) European economic integration, crowned by the introduction of the common currency, advanced strongly. However, economic performance has failed to improve. The monetary policy for the EA, based on the "one-size-fits-all" principle, has perverse growth and inflation effects across the Area and facilitates the rise of cross-country trade (and payment) imbalances. The inability to nominally devalue the currency condemns the external deficit countries to protracted recessions. It is crucially important that wages in the EA are kept depressed by the fierce competition imposed on its EA partners by Germany which abides by its long-term strategy of keeping wages trailing behind labor productivity. The "internal devaluation" which Germany's partners are forced to follow assumes that the whole EA could become a "larger Germany". But this is a mirage as it postulates the existence of a "rest-of-the-world" ready to keep indebting itself versus EA indefinitely. Sooner or later the weak growth led by high and rising export surpluses must come to an end on account of the recurring protectionist sentiments in the net-importer countries, and/or on account of excessive debts accumulated by them. Eventually a robust output growth could only be sustained by robust growth of domestic demand. With the present trends governing the functional income distribution, robust growth in

Handbook of Economic Stagnation
ISBN: 978-0-12-815898-2
https://doi.org/10.1016/B978-0-12-815898-2.00018-5

domestic demand can only come in the form of persistent fiscal deficit spending. But a radical change on fiscal matters is unlikely to happen anytime soon. The EU will thus remain a stagnant area convulsed by recurring economic (and then social and political) crises. Sooner or later, these crises can give rise to further Exits or could even precipitate the dissolution of the Union.

Secular growth slowdown in the Euro Area: evidence

Under the provisions of the Maastricht Treaty (in force since 1992), European economic integration has been further advanced. The introduction of the Euro crowned the process of internal liberalization of trade and capital flows within the European Union's EA. A huge area of ever freer movements of goods, capital, labor, and services emerged. There are many possible measures of advances in economic integration. Perhaps the most unproblematic is the share of mutual trade in the EU's aggregate GDP. The share of intra-EU exports of goods in the combined GDP of the original 12 EA countries[1] was less than 7% in 1960, rising to close to 13% by 1989. Since 2003 that share has ranged between 20% and 23%.

Just as internal economic liberalization, international integration is assumed to be conducive to economic growth (even if it is now often admitted that it may have unwelcome—supposedly transient—distributional effects). Closer integration is commonly expected to promote faster productivity growth—through increased competition and more efficient utilization of scarce resources. Faster productivity growth is held a necessary condition for faster output growth.

European integration has failed to deliver on this promise. Output growth has been slowing down secularly, since around the mid-1970s (Fig. 8.1). Thus, the slowdown cannot be considered to be a recent development that has occurred accidently, following the 2007–09 global "events." Prior to the final abandonment (in 1973) of the Bretton Woods arrangements the (per capita) GDP growth was quite high: on average 3.5% per annum for West Germany and 4.8% for the remaining 11 countries

[1] Since 2006 seven more EU member states (predominantly small or very small East and South European) have joined the Euro Area, at different times. The essential macroeconomic indicators for the enlarged EA differ only marginally from those for the EA12—but the available statistics for the former are much shorter. This justifies consideration, in this essay, of EA12 rather than of the whole Euro Area.

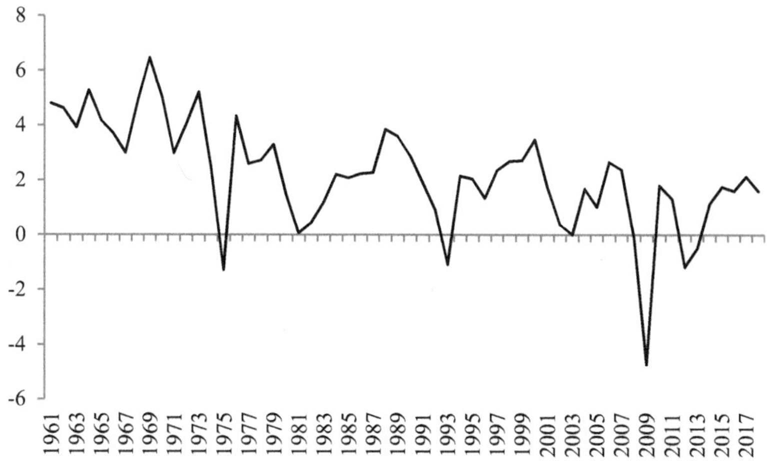

Figure 8.1 Growth rates of real per capita GDP Euro Area (EA12), 1961–2018. *Source: AMECO, own calculations.*

of the future Euro-Area group considered collectively. But growth slowed down already during the years 1974–90 (with average growth rates at 2.2% and 2.3%, respectively). During 1991–2019, the average yearly per capita growth rate for Germany is 1.3% and 1.1% for the remaining 11 countries.[2] As can be seen the growth rates follow declining trends which—if continued—would push the EA into permanent recession. In addition, growth has become increasingly volatile, with violent ups and downs, and outright recessions around 1993, 2003, 2008–09, and 2012–13. One may bear in mind that the short-lived earlier recessions (in 1975 and 1981) could have been, at least partially, the aftermaths of the oil embargoes s severely affecting the "supply side." Beyond energy shortages materially affecting production, the oil shocks had negative consequences for inflation, income distribution and private investment, depressed on account of heightened uncertainties about the future energy supplies and prices.

The deep slumps in 1993 and 2008–09 cannot be viewed as "exogenous shocks." These slumps were endogenous: consequences of malfunction of the economic "mechanisms" consciously designed by the European economic elites. The 1993 recession was primarily the consequence of the crash of the original Exchange Rate Mechanism (which had been expected to

[2] The attention given to Germany is not only due to this country's economic weight—about 30% of GDP of EA12. As will be shown later, since the early 2000s the German internal economic policies have played an important role in affecting growth in its EA partners.

pave the way for the switchover to the Euro); in 2008—09, the recession was due to the near-collapse of the EU's financial sector operating by the rules enacted by the EU policy-makers. The second-dip recession of 2012—13 was provoked by the fiscal consolidation hysteria gripping the Euro-Area decision-makers.[3] The introduction of the Euro (legal tender since 1998), the full internal trade liberalization (Single European Market, since 1993), and a plethora of other "agendas" and "programs" supposed to perfect the functioning of the Area have done nothing to smooth out (and accelerate) GDP growth.

The GDP growth slowdown is associated with a deceleration of growth of private consumption (Fig. 8.2). That is not surprising—private consumption is the major GDP component. In the long (and medium) run, fast GDP growth is hardly possible without fast growth of consumption. Private

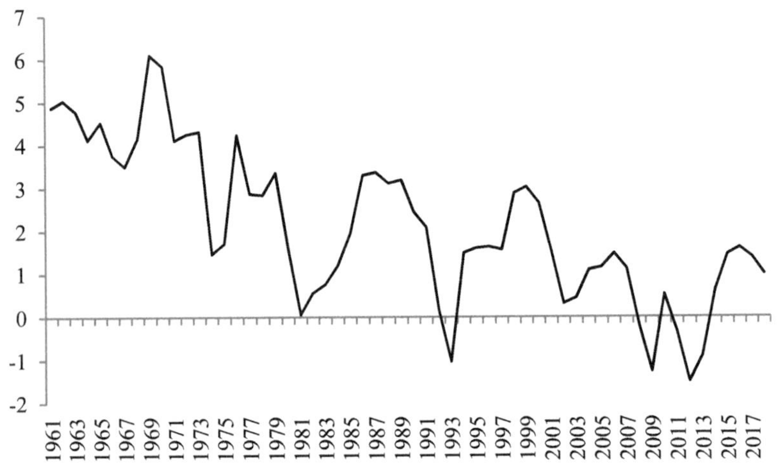

Figure 8.2 Growth rates of per capita private consumption Euro Area (EA12), 1961—2018. *Source: AMECO, own calculations.*

[3] The German unification (1991) was obviously an exogenous shock. However, the unification itself did not push Germany (and the rest of EA11) into recession. In 1991 the West German per capita GDP increased by 3.8%. Such a development was quite natural given East Germany's urgent investment needs. However, the overrestrictive macroeconomic policy response to the unification-related fiscal deficits constituted another endogenous (and negative) shock contributing to the deep German recession in 1993 and slowing down Germany's (and overall EA12) growth later on (see Bibow, 2001).

consumption tends to lead GDP: the slowdown of growth of consumption tends to be followed by a slowdown of GDP growth. Dynamic private consumption is essential for the overall output dynamism. In the last instance it is the secular slowdown of private consumption growth which is responsible for the secular weakening of output growth. As wages—the labor incomes—are the major determinant of private consumption, the examination of what has been happening to wages is necessary for the understanding of the secular slowdown of output growth.

A short digression: the slowdown of private consumption growth is linked to the slowdown of growth of fixed capital formation

For EA12, the slowdown of growth of private per capita consumption has been fairly closely associated with the slowdown of growth of per capita gross fixed capital formation. For the entire period 1961–2019, the coefficient of correlation between the yearly rates of growth of the two items is 0.75. The average growth rate of per capita gross fixed capital formation was 5.1% (years 1961–73), 1.5% (1974–90), and 1.02% (1991–2018). (Much the same tendencies prevail in Germany).

That a "strong" private consumption appears a precondition for strong capital formation cannot be a surprise. Perhaps it may be a surprise (at least to a more "mainstream-oriented" economist) that a weakening propensity to invest does not reflect the prevailing profitability of fixed assets. For EA12 the net return on net capital stock (AMECO item APNDK) was, on average, 11% larger for the years 1991–2018 than for 1961–74. Again, similar tendencies characterize Germany. Ceteris paribus, high profitability seems to have discouraged fixed capital formation. This "paradox" is easy to rationalize: high profitability emerges under repressed wages. But repressed wages mean weak consumer demand growth which, when rationally expected, must discourage fixed business investment.

Falling wage shares: not quite a "natural development"

After 1974, the monetary policies gave priority to combating high inflation which was ignited by the oil price shocks. Consequently, until approximately 2001 (and throughout much of the 1980s in particular), the interest rates were often quite high in the EA. As such they may have played a role in slowing down the growth of consumption directly—by suppressing the demand for consumer credit and raising the attractiveness of depositing households' idle monetary savings with the banks. But interest rates, quite low or even negative in real terms, could not have had much of a direct negative effect after 2001.

The deceleration of growth of private consumption has had more to do with the tendency which set in around the mid-1970s: the gradual change in the functional distribution of income. As can be seen (Fig. 8.3), the GDP wage shares kept falling from 1975 through 2007 and have stabilized at depressed levels afterward.

The suppression of the wage shares (and thus the rise in the shares of nonwage incomes—and of profits in particular) has been one factor behind the expanding income inequality and, by implication, behind the suppressed consumption propensities. In addition, the consumption propensities have been suppressed by other, related, developments: high unemployment (Fig. 8.4) and the ongoing, since the mid-1970s, evolution of the tax systems. "Flattening" of the personal income tax systems as well as falling taxation of profits have added to growing inequality in disposable incomes. The tendency for the substitution of indirect for direct taxation has

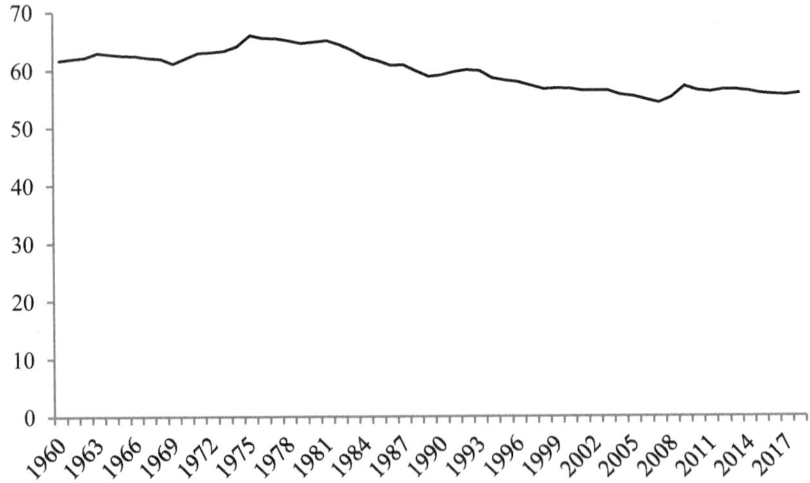

Figure 8.3 The GDP wage share (adjusted) Euro Area (EA12), 1960–2018. *Source: AMECO.*

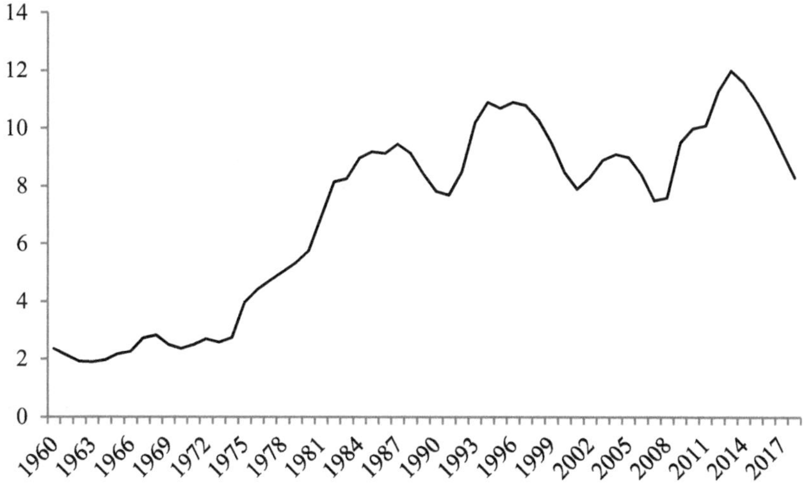

Figure 8.4 Unemployment rate Euro Area (EA12), 1960–2018. *Source: AMECO.*

additionally reduced the overall progressivity of the national taxation systems—with obvious consequences for the overall income inequality levels and the private consumption propensities.[4]

It is certainly possible to claim that the secular decline in the wage share is a natural development reflecting diminishing "marginal productivity" of labor.[5] An alternative explanation is that labor started to lose to "capital" because the basic paradigms of the post-war economic systems were no longer generally accepted. The demise of the Bretton Woods arrangements was the first sign of the materializing paradigm change. Liberalizations of private capital flows and the flexibilization of the exchange rates were followed by more ominous *internal* policy changes initiated in the UK and the USA and then gradually emulated in the major continental European countries. Advancing external liberalizations (of trade and capital flows—also vs. the rest of the world) were thus synchronized with progressing internal liberalizations. The latter stipulated more or less wholesale privatizations and financialization of the sectors supplying public services, "unchaining" of

[4] Growing internal income inequalities in individual member countries are associated with strongly increasing (since 2009) dispersion of per capita incomes across the EA12. The Area experiences "sigma divergence" rather than the conventionally expected "sigma convergence."

[5] In arithmetic terms, the contraction of the GDP wage share means that the average labor productivity per employed person has been outpacing average labor compensation per employee. For the EA12, the real unit labor cost (the ratio of compensation per employee to nominal GDP per employee) fell by 23% from 1975 through 2007 (and remained essentially flat afterward).

the financial sectors, "taming" of the trade unions, labor market flexibilizations, and successive rounds of reforms downsizing the welfare state institutions. Industrial policies were replaced by competition policies. The reemerging liberal paradigm prescribing fiscal continence underlies, for example, the dynamics of final government consumption (Fig. 8.5).

Labor was the primary "collateral casualty" of the war on inflation. High and rising unemployment "disciplined" employees and helped to beat them into submission over deteriorating conditions of pay and work.

Despite the eventual victory over high inflation (around 1990), the position of labor has not been improving since. High unemployment whose effective reduction through active fiscal policies is outlawed by the Maastricht Treaty[6] (and the consecutive EU Fiscal "Pacts" reinforcing the Treaty) keeps wages on a short leash. The European Central Bank had played, until the Great Recession, an active role in the repression of wages, thus buttressing high unemployment. The ECB was long guided by paranoid fears of inflation in excess of 2% and repeatedly insisted on "wage moderation"

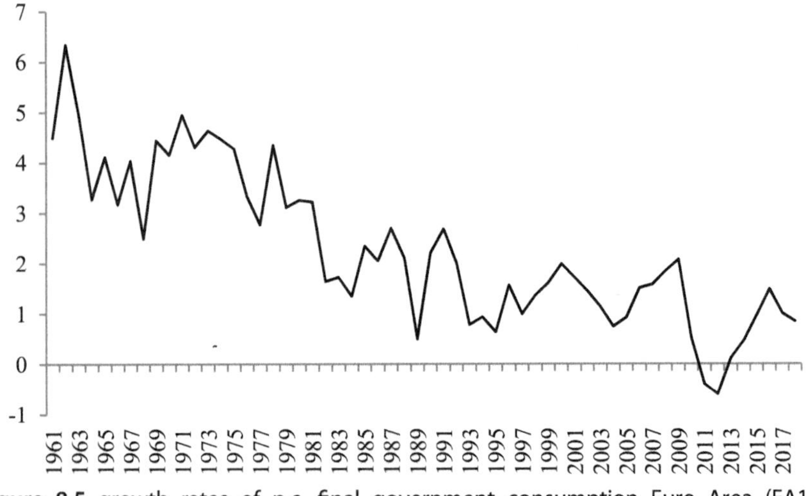

Figure 8.5 growth rates of p.c. final government consumption Euro Area (EA12), 1961–2018. *Source: AMECO, own calculations.*

[6] The Maastricht Treaty, signed in the early 1992, had been designed in the late 1980s and early 1990s. These were the heydays of neoliberal (and monetarist) revolutions whose ideas were reflected also in the "Washington Consensus."

(but not on "profit moderation") as a precondition of price stability (Price stability itself was proclaimed essential for fast and sustainable output growth.)

Of crucial importance is the fact that wages in the EA have been kept depressed by the fierce competition imposed on its EA partners by Germany. The German long-term strategy has been to keep wages trailing behind labor productivity. This cannot be ignored by Germany's partners who must adjust accordingly—or lose out on the competitive race. In an otherwise integrating economic area the internal policy by the dominant member country has far reaching consequences for everyone.

There can be little doubt that globalization (external liberalization vs. the rest of the world) contributes to the repression of wages in the EA through outsourcing/offshoring of production activities to low-wage/low-tax destinations *outside* EA12.[7] But the internal EA competition has been of central importance just because its participants, while structurally very different, are tightly bound together by geography and common EU regulations, share a common currency and are exposed to the same monetary policy.

A somewhat longer digression: supply side developments unlikely to have underlain stagnating output growth

Labor productivity growth has followed a declining trend (see Fig. 8.6). Given the rather undisputable acceleration of technological progress and the rather obvious advances in applied research and innovation activities, the labor productivity growth slowdown is considered a paradox. Some explanations of the paradox suggest that output (and productivity) have been systematically underestimated by the statistics. Others tend to disagree with the mismeasurement thesis without yet offering a coherent explanation of the paradox.

Robert Gordon (2015) is the most vocal representative of the "supply siders" who blames the post-2008 output stagnation itself on the slower growth (since 2004) in potential output "*emanating from the behavior of productivity.*" This seems to suggest that the supply side needs further "structural reforms," stronger deregulation, more labor market flexibility, etc. so as to

[7] Credible threats of outsourcing/offshoring can achieve the required effect of moderating the domestic wage demands without actually relocating activities to remote places. Such threats also help extort tax (and subsidy) concessions from the fiscal authorities.

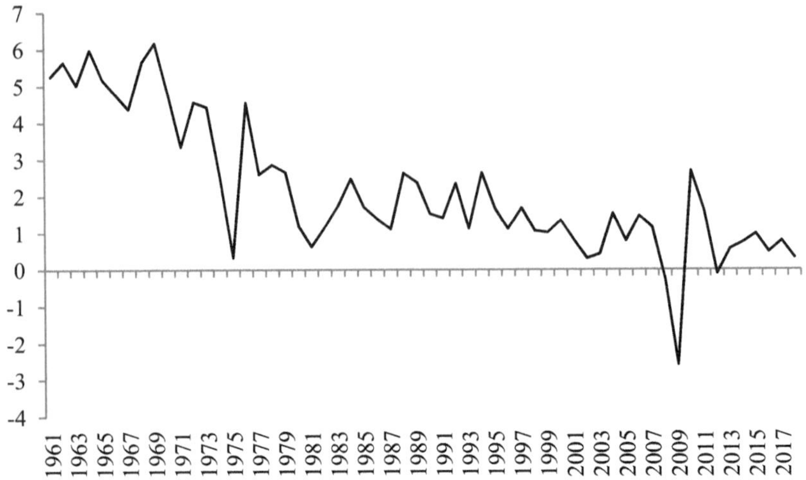

Figure 8.6 Growth rate of labor productivity (real GDP per employed person) for EA12 1961–2018 (%). *Source: AMECO.*

strengthen productivity growth and thus contribute to faster growth of output. By implication, the supply side views on the roots of the secular stagnation (whether in the EU, USA, or at the global level) really ignore the possibility of stagnation emanating from the orientation of the macroeconomic policies followed, or from the prevalence of neoliberal maxims on, for example, the beneficial effects of labor market (de)regulation or of free international trade and capital flows.

However, the results of an econometric examination (Podkaminer, 2017) of the links between labor productivity and output growth for various groups of countries indicate that, generally, productivity growth does not "cause" growth of output. Much more often the causation seems to be running in the opposite direction: from output (or its growth rate) to productivity (or its growth rate).[8] This finding, though inconsistent with the mainstream ideas on the sources of long-term economic growth, is reminiscent of the classical Kaldor-Verdoorn Law. The progressing slowdown in output growth (also at the global level), initiated around the mid-1970s (amid the wholesale change of economic policy paradigms), has been mirrored—and followed—by the progressive slowdown in productivity

[8] Only in two EA12 countries (Greece and Ireland), the productivity dynamics may have played a role in determining the dynamics of output.

growth (the indisputable acceleration of technological innovations notwithstanding).

It is also rather obvious that the growth slowdown cannot be attributed to intensified shortages of exhaustible natural resources. The secular decline in commodities' terms-of-trade indicates that commodities are becoming less scarce, not more.

The noxious of restrictive EU fiscal policy rules and the common monetary policy

For many authors, the principles introduced by the Maastricht Treaty and later reiterated in a series of Fiscal Compacts or Pacts did not bode well for the future. In their opinion, these policies pave the ground for the eventual economic disintegration of the EA and the whole European Union (see e.g., Laski and Podkaminer, 2012; de Grauwe, 2013; Podkaminer, 2015, 2016; Hein and Truger, 2017). Even if the EA has escaped disintegration so far (thanks to unconventional measures risked by Mario Draghi, the Italian chair of the European Central Bank) it is paying a high price—in the form of anemic, erratic, and uneven (across the EA) growth. Combined with the common currency (and the common monetary policy long embodying the tradition of German central banking), the Maastricht fiscal policy rules have additionally weakened economic performance of the Union (and of its EA core in particular).

The vicious dynamics behind the developing economic drama can be concisely described as follows. The first to consider is the set of fiscal rules setting very narrow limits for public sector deficits. The fiscal rules were to apply universally—without much regard for national specificities. Thus, a country (such as Germany) capable of producing output much in excess of the needs of its private sector (be it private consumption or private investment) cannot rely on the public sector for absorbing the potential excess private sector savings by means of deficit spending. Such a country is thus left with no other easy option than to attempt to run trade surpluses—to find abroad the outlet for its excess output. Trade surpluses become a way of supporting domestic growth (and of keeping its own unemployment in check). Of course, for a country to be capable of running trade surpluses there must be some countries capable of running trade deficits. It is understood that for countries running trade deficits this implies not only the accumulation of foreign debt—but also the suppression of domestic output growth and rising unemployment.

At this stage, it is important to consider the way the common currency facilitated the rise of cross-country trade (and payment) imbalances. One currency, one monetary policy and one policy interest rate have very different economic implications for various members of the same country group. The policy interest rate has been tuned to the *average* inflation rate calculated for the whole area. That would be fine if inflation (and inflation histories) were similar across the whole area. However, in fact they have been very different.[9] In consequence, for countries with inflation persistently higher than the average, the real interest rates have tended to be low (or even negative) while—at the same time—the real interest rates may be prohibitively high in countries with much lower inflation. As Fig. 8.7 shows, from the late 1990s (switchover to the common currency) until 2008 (the collapse of the real estate booms in the Southern Eurozone countries) the real short-term interest rates in Germany were consistently

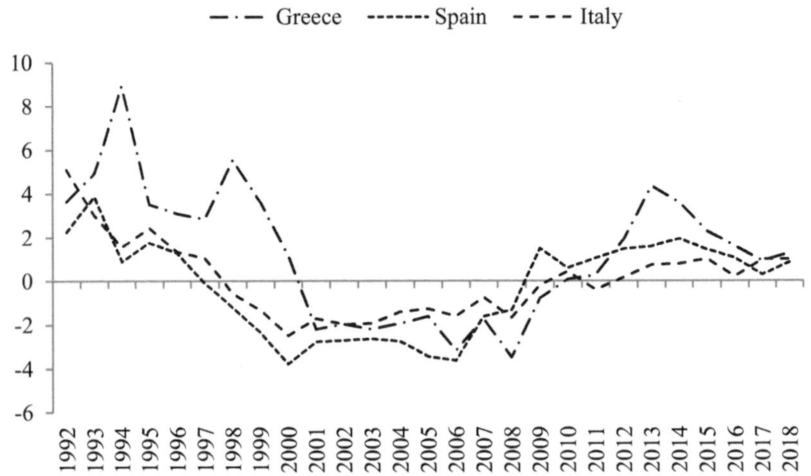

Figure 8.7 Real short-term interest rates for Greece, Spain and Italy (percentage-point differentials over Germany), 1992–2018. *Source: AMECO, own calculations.*

[9] For many decades inflation used to be much higher in, for example, Italy than in Germany. As late as 1996 Italian inflation (measured as the GDP deflator) was still 4 percentage points higher than the German. Later on the differential narrowed—since 2010 the GDP deflator has been larger for Germany (not much, about 0.5 percentage points in 2018). Despite the convergence in the recorded inflation rates the Italian inflation qualitatively still differs rather radically from its German equivalent. The former has materialized under the prolonged stagnation, the latter under comparatively stable (if unimpressive) growth. An eventual return of faster growth in Italy is quite likely to involve the return to much higher, historically attested, rates of inflation.

higher than in Spain and Italy. But the Southern periphery countries enjoyed lower real interest rates entirely on account of their inflations being much higher than in Germany. The same applied to other high-inflation countries (e.g., Ireland). As long as the governments of the Eurozone member states and their national banking systems enjoyed the same level of credibility, the cross-country differentials in short-term real interest rates on commercial loans were approximating also the differentials on the long-term government bonds. In other words, until 2008 credit to the German private as well as public sectors used to be much more expensive, in real terms, than elsewhere. Such differential developments favoring Germany's partners could not persist indefinitely. As soon as the boom supported by low real interest rates in the South collapsed (under the weight of accumulating internal and foreign debts), the nominal (and thus real) interest rates in countries that had had higher inflation became high (in many cases excessively high). It is at this stage that the initial boom fed by low interest rates turned into a (balance-sheet) recession initially engulfing the debtor countries and eventually also their creditors.

The moral to this story is that the principle "one size fits all" underlying the ECB's interest rate determination does not work in practice. The common monetary policy has been destabilizing output growth and inflation: fueling inflation (and pushing up growth, usually financed by accumulating debt and involving misallocation of real resources) in countries experiencing a boom and higher inflation, while suppressing inflation (and output growth) in countries experiencing deflation and stagnating output growth.

At this stage, the existence of the common currency becomes crucially important. As a consequence of differential developments in real interest rates (and inflation), countries with traditionally low inflation (and weak growth in wages, such as Germany or Austria) have been gaining cost-competitiveness advantages versus their higher-inflation partners. Of course, the shared currency precludes nominal depreciation (be it spontaneous or managed by the national authorities) by the higher-inflation partners. For countries fully in charge of their national currencies such depreciations are often the cheapest and most efficient way of responding to the erosion of external competitiveness. Italy's pre-Euro era experience is a case in point. After 1973, the Italian Lira kept steadily devaluing against the German Mark—from 182 Lira/DM in 1973 to 740 in 1988 (on average about 10% per year). That did not affect Italy's output growth (which was fairly strong during that period) while securing sizable current account surpluses all along.

Real effective exchange rate of Germany's EA partners: from relative appreciation to relative depreciation

As can be seen (Fig. 8.8) in three major EA12 countries, the real effective exchange rates (based on unit labor costs)[10] declined initially (since 1995, i.e., during the "probationary" run-up to the switchover to the Euro). In Italy, the same (albeit weaker) tendency came to the fore 2 years later. However, since 2000, upon the formal switchover to the Euro, real appreciation—driven primarily by rising unit labor costs—restarted in France, Spain, and Italy—but was kept at bay in Germany. Since 2000—03, the German unit labor cost index has been virtually constant. That outcome was deliberately engineered by the German government under its "Agenda 2010" which was implemented since 2003. The Agenda stipulated far reaching reforms of the labor market institutions (including the unemployment insurance system and the Labor Codes). The purpose of the

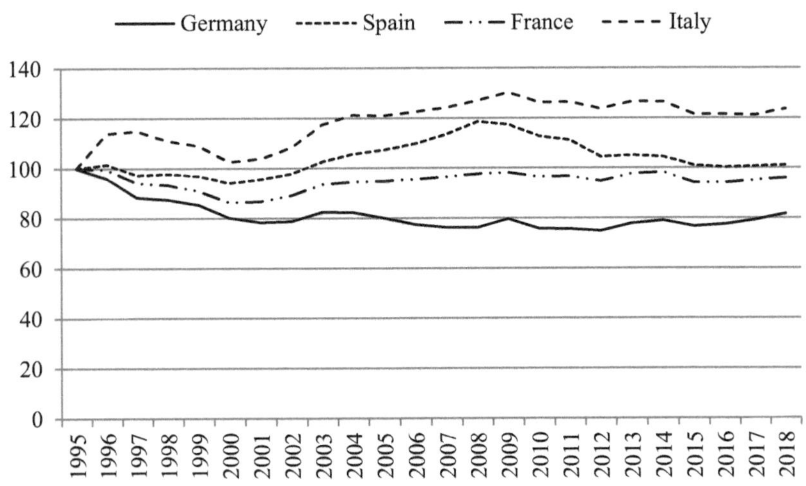

Figure 8.8 Real effective exchange rates, 1995—2018 (1995 = 100). *Source: AMECO, own calculations.*

[10] The nominal effective exchange rates of individual EA countries can develop differently (because of eventual differences in the structure of trade with countries outside the EA and the eventual nominal exchange rate developments vs. the currencies of such extra-EA countries). Abstracting from such differences in the nominal effective exchange rates, the real effective exchange rates from Fig. 8.8 primarily reflect the cross-country differences in the nominal unit labor costs developments.

Agenda was to combat high unemployment—essentially by *increasing* the labor supply (through restricted access to unemployment benefits) and by suppressing growth in wages (starting in the public sector). Without the drastic measures introduced, the German real effective exchange rate could have joined the upward trend seen in other EA countries.

In the three major EA12 countries (but especially in Italy and Spain as well as in Portugal and Ireland), unit labor costs had grown vigorously until 2008–09—with the predictable effects for their external competitiveness versus Germany. Consequently, the private sectors of Germany's trading partners ran external deficits and accumulated high debts to foreign and domestic parties.[11] (In due time large portions of the excessive private sector debts accumulated had to be taken over by national governments seeking to rescue their commercial banking systems. That created the—misleading—impression of public sector profligacy and spurred the paroxysms of fiscal consolidation in 2011–13.)

The debt and competitiveness consequences of the prolonged real appreciation inevitably stopped the appreciation itself. Relative to Germany the real effective exchange rates of EA12 countries peaked during the crisis. Afterward they started to depreciate. The dynamics of relative (to Germany) real effective exchange rates for the three largest EA12 countries is shown in Fig. 8.9.

The enforced postcrisis adjustments in real effective exchange rates have moved (still rather slowly) the individual EA countries to the conditions prevailing in Germany where wages have been engineered to fall far behind labor productivity. However, in Germany, these conditions were consciously shaped as a central part of the national economic strategy seeking to run the highest trade and current account surpluses possible. For most EA partner countries, the adjustments are enforced by the necessity to regain competitiveness and to stop accumulation of debts.

The adjustments prove very costly in terms of output foregone. During the postcrisis period (2010 through 2018), the average per capita GDP for EU11 grew by a miserable 0.8% per year, less than even in Germany (1%). The unemployment rate for EU11 fell rather moderately, from 11.1% in 2010% to 10.2% in 2018. German unemployment rates stood at 7% and 3.4%, respectively (In, 2008 the unemployment rates for EU11

[11] Actually, for an individual EA country all domestic debt (accumulated by private or public sector alike) constitutes foreign debt. The Euro may be a national legal tender—but in the last instance its issue is the sole prerogative of the sovereign "extraterritorial" European Central Bank.

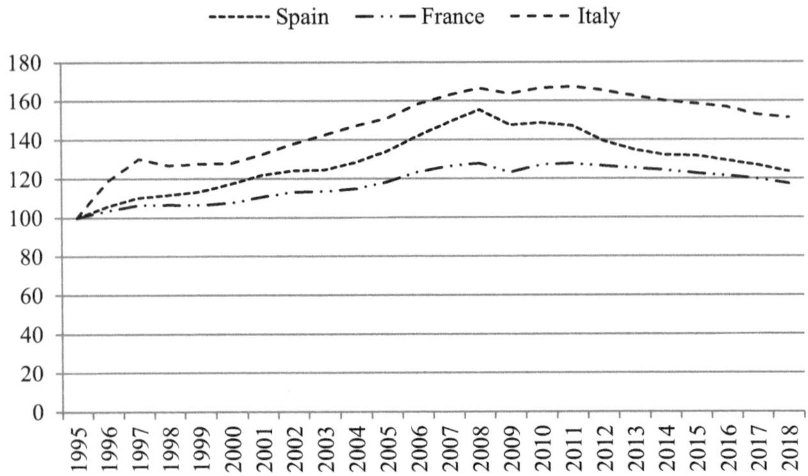

Figure 8.9 Real effective exchange rates relative to Germany, 1995–2018. *Source: Own calculations. The curves in Fig. 8.9 are calculated as ratios of the curves in Fig. 8.8 (for Spain, France and Italy) over the curve for Germany.*

and Germany were almost equal, at about 7.6%). However, gains (in terms of falling nominal unit labor costs) have proved hard to achieve. The gaps between German and its EA11 partners' real effective exchange rate indices remain huge (Fig. 8.9).

Nonetheless, in terms of external balance, the progress achieved on the real effective exchange rate is quite spectacular. After years of large foreign borrowing (2004–11), the EA11 group considered collectively has become capable of working out large surpluses, thus emulating Germany in this respect (Fig. 8.10).

The limits of "internal devaluation"

The concerns over cross-country trade and payment imbalances which are threatening the disintegration of the EA and a collapse of the common currency (with some countries reintroducing national currencies) underlies many policy initiatives such as the *Euro Plus Pact* (European Council, 2011). The Pact prioritizes fostering competitiveness and convergence across the EA in terms of unit labor costs. The same idea has been reiterated since (e.g., European Commission, 2015).

One specific policy strategy often considered to strengthen weaker Eurozone partners is "internal devaluation." Internal devaluation involves a set of actions (including some labor market reforms) which would result

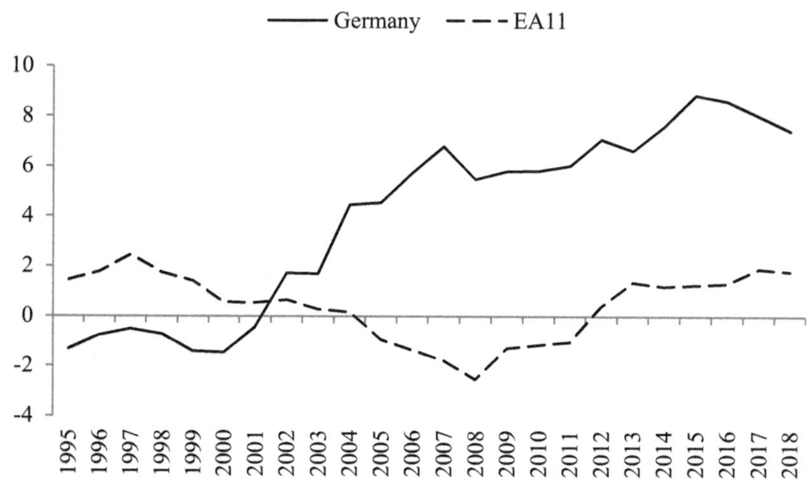

Figure 8.10 Net lending, total economy: Germany and the rest of the Euro Area (EA11) Percent of GDP, 1995–2018. *Source: AMECO.*

in a sufficiently strong deflation in wages (and prices, in due course). Of course, the suppression of wages (and thus of domestic demand) is a bitter medicine if only because it is almost certain to provoke a recession—or at least stagnation—of unforeseeable depth and length. It took Portugal 10 years to regain the per capita real GDP level of 2007. Things are looking even worse for Greece and Italy where the current (2019) per capita GDP levels are still below (by 20% and 7%, respectively) the peak values recorded in 2007. Internal devaluation of a sort has been actually taking place since 2008–09 (Fig. 8.9). It has helped on the "external front" but has naturally failed to overcome the weakness of output growth.

A more attractive alternative to internal devaluation is believed to involve the achievement of competitiveness gains through policies promoting much faster growth of labor productivity. Of course, faster growth of labor productivity (e.g., through a fast change in the structure of production and improved quality of exportable goods and services) cannot be a bad idea though it is not quite clear how this could be effectively engineered (without resorting to an industrial policy of a sort). The spectacular failure of the Lisbon Agenda (2000–10) and other such EU policy initiatives promising speedy structural change, technological breakthroughs and quality improvements—and thus advances in productivity—is a case in point. Besides, as already mentioned, the causality seems to be running from faster output growth to faster productivity growth rather than vice versa. A more concrete trouble with the "productivity alternative" is that in the long run the EA11 has on the whole performed *better* than Germany in terms of labor productivity growth. Ironically, from 2003 through 2010 (precisely when Germany was out-competing the rest of EA) productivity growth was much stronger in EA11 than in Germany.[12] Germany's supercompetitiveness cannot be squared with evidence on its relative productivity performance. It derives from its restrictive wage (and fiscal) policies which suppress economic growth not only in Germany.

As long as Germany firmly adheres to its restrictive wage and fiscal policies (and there is no indication these might appreciably soften anytime soon) other EA countries would have to follow suit.[13] That would doom them to slow growth secularly: Italy is the point in case. With depressed wages and stagnant consumption (and therefore stagnant investment in fixed assets) growth could rely only on expansion of trade surpluses. But EA11 has already become a huge rising-surplus country (and Germany has been such a rising-surplus country for 15 years now). Yet, this is not visibly helping to speed up growth.

The second trouble with the internal devaluation strategy is that it rests on the tacit assumption that the whole EA could become a "larger Germany"—on a *permanent* basis. But this postulates the existence of a "rest-of-the-world" ready to keep indebting itself versus EA indefinitely (and at an accelerating speed which would have to be consistent with the positive EA output growth). Rather obviously, the "rest-of-the-world" is unlikely to obligingly serve the needs of EA permanently. Sooner or later growth led by high export surpluses must come to an end on account of the recurring protectionist sentiments in the net-importer countries, and/or on account of excessive debts accumulated by these countries.

[12] The average yearly rate of growth of labor productivity in the whole EA11 was 5.4% and 4% for Germany (years 1961–73), 2.1% versus 1.7% (years 1974–90), 1.3% (years 1991–2003, both EA11 and Germany) and 0.7% versus 0.5% (years 2003–10). Only after 2010 Germany performed better than EA11 (0.9% vs. 1%). But after 2010 the competitive position of EA11 has been improving versus Germany (depreciating real effective exchange rates relative to Germany). Consequently, EA11 switched from being a current account deficit to a current account surplus area.

[13] A meaningful relaxation of the wage policies in a country that has managed to "devalue internally" would reproduce the conditions that gradually led to the earlier crisis: from an eroding real effective exchange rate to diminishing external competitiveness, disappearing external surpluses and, finally, to the accumulation of debts sooner or later necessitating another "shock therapy" and more or less lengthy and painful recession.

Suppression of fiscal deficits critically contributing to stagnant EA output growth

The conventional wisdom underlying the fiscal policies in most high-income countries stresses the need to restrict public-sector financial deficits. This is particularly the case with the European Union. The EU Growth and Stability Pact "lays down the obligation for Member States to adhere to the medium-term objective for their budgetary positions of close to balance or in surplus" (European Council, 2005). The Fiscal Compact agreed upon by the majority of EU leaders is designed to strengthen "fiscal discipline" across the EA (and beyond). It goes even further, imposing the obligation to reduce public sector debt/GDP ratios. Given the sluggish pace of nominal GDP growth, that requirement actually imposes the obligation to run budgetary *surpluses*. Thus, the taxation of the private sector (net of transfers to the same) should be persistently higher than the income earned by the private sector on sales of goods and services to the public sector. The private sector would then have to "bleed" for many years to come—for the sake of "sound public finances." The "sound public finances" are deemed indispensable for the long-term dynamism of the private sector itself.[14]

The fact that despite the best efforts of fiscal authorities around the world the public financial balances almost always and everywhere end up in deficits squares with the tendency of the private sectors to work out *positive* excess saving (i.e., saving in excess of capital formation). This is no accident: the fundamental macroeconomic identity states that the private sector's excess saving equals the (national) net external lending plus the financial deficit of the public sector. Given the private sectors' preference for running some positive excess savings (and the relative unimportance of external imbalances, at least in the longer run), the public sectors must run fiscal deficits secularly.

The policy aiming at balanced public finances enforced on EA implies that its private sector's excess saving is not allowed to materialize. The excess savings are to be "preemptively" taxed away. Under confiscatory fiscal policies seeking to wipe out parts of the potential excess private saving, it is unreasonable to expect any faster rise in private investment (or even in

[14] The consecutive German governments have been the most ardent adherents of the fiscal prudence gospel. There is a quasi-religious principle behind the German (and Swiss) economic policy. The German word for debt is "Schuld," which also denotes "guilt." Clearly, public debt is to be shunned by all means.

private consumption). Of course, Germany has been able to run very large fiscal surpluses. But this outcome is due to Germany's huge external surpluses. Since 2012, the EA11 has also been working out large external surpluses. But these have so far proved insufficient for absorbing the EA11 excess private savings. At 1.2% of GDP, the fiscal deficit for EA11 was still (in 2018) far from being negligible.

Fig. 8.11 shows the dynamics of the fiscal balances and the excess private savings for the Germany and the rest of EA (EA11) since 1995. As can be seen, in 2000 the fiscal balance for Germany (and for EA11 considered collectively) was close to zero. In 2007, the fiscal balance for EA11 was also close to zero (but Germany ran a sizable fiscal surplus).

Admittedly, the developments culminating in the years 2000 and 2007 were unsustainable. Much of the private investment went into risky (or speculative) activities (e.g., residential construction) that had failed to pay off, leaving large segments of the whole EA private sector (combined) deeply indebted to other segments of the same. Similarly, the expanding private consumption had been disproportionately driven by debt owed to other parts of the private sector (rather than being backed by rising wages and other regular household incomes). The *internal* private-sector debt/credit excesses were followed by the painful private sector "deleveraging" (and "balance-sheet recessions") characterized by depressed private investment, increased private saving (depressed consumption out of the disposable income) and—consequently—increased excess savings of the private sector (the latter equal to the increased public sector fiscal deficits) reaching their local maxima in 2003 and 2010.

Figure 8.11 Private sector excess savings and government fiscal deficit as percentage of GDP: Germany and EA11, 1995–2018. *Source: Own calculations based on AMECO.*

The recent (post-2010) developments are not all that different. Although the fiscal deficit for the entire EA11 combined is quite low almost all private excess saving takes the form of external surpluses—representing net lending to the rest of the world. For this reason, the post-2010 developments are also unsustainable. As soon as the net lending to the rest of the world (backing the EA11 and German external trade surpluses) comes to an end, the excess private saving could only be maintained by sufficiently large fiscal deficits—just as it was the case after the collapse (in 2000 and 2007) of previous booms.

The future remains uncertain

The deep ("systemic and structural") tendencies underlying the behavior of private sector saving and investment are likely to be strengthening in the future. It is rather difficult to envision a decisive rise in the wage share, or a decline in income inequality. If anything, the combined effects of progressing globalization (outsourcing production to low-wage and low-tax countries) and technological change (expansion of "intelligent machines" reducing the demand for labor) will support falling wage and investment shares, rising income inequality, and saving rates. Potential excess private saving would then increase in line with the progressing income concentration. Sufficiently relaxed fiscal policy would be an important countervailing force in such circumstances. By "deficit spending," it would supply the highly desired financial wealth (i.e., public debt) to the private sector (or rather to its rich segment).

Rejection of the fiscal consolidation provisions is vitally important for countries such as Germany whose private sectors have been induced to save much in excess of their investment. Without the ability to run trade surpluses (which can never be sustained indefinitely) such countries eventually either experience stagnation, or else allow public sector deficits which would be capable of generating (and absorbing) the excessive private savings.

The EU cannot prosper under selfimposed limitations that have little economic justification, theoretical and practical. The belief in the benefits of fiscal "prudence" is the backbone of these limitations. The ubiquitous acceptance of the "beggar thy neighbor" practices with respect to the national wage and tax policies also plays a destructive role. Unless the basic paradigms of economic policy are radically overhauled, the EU will remain a stagnant area convulsed by recurring economic (and then social and political) crises. Sooner or later these crises will give rise to further exits or could even precipitate the dissolution of the Union.

Whether the radical change happens before it is too late is of course highly uncertain. In any case, it should be the duty of European politicians—and economists—to voice their concerns over the overall orientation of the economic policies of the European Union—and of Germany in particular.

References

Bibow, J., 2001. On the "Burden" of German Unification. Levy Institute Working Paper 328.

de Grauwe, P., 2013. Design Failure in the Eurozone: Can They Be Fixed? LEQS Paper 57.

European Council, March 24–25, 2011. The Euro Plus Pact. Stronger Economic Policy Coordination for Competitiveness and Convergence, Annex I to European Council Conclusions.

European Council, 2005. Council Regulation No. 1055/2005 Amending the Growth and Stability Pact. (The Same Requirement Features in the More Recent (2012) Fiscal Compact, Article 3, Point 1(a)).

European Commission, 2015. The Euro Plus Pact: How Integration into the EU Framework Can Give New Momentum for Structural Reforms in the Euro Area, EPSC Strategic Notes, Issue 3.

Gordon, J.R., 2015. Secular stagnation: a supply-side view. American Economic Review: Papers & Proceedings 105 (5), 54–59.

Hein, E., Truger, A., 2017. Opportunities and limits of rebalancing the Eurozone via wage policies: theoretical considerations and empirical illustration in the case of Germany. PSL Quarterly Review 70 (283), 421–447.

Laski, K., Podkaminer, L., 2012. The basic paradigms of EU economic policy making need to be changed. Cambridge Journal of Economics 36 (1), 253–270.

Podkaminer, L., 2015. The euro area's secular stagnation and what can be done about it. A post-Keynesian perspective. Real World Economics Review (70), 1–16.

Podkaminer, L., 2016. Economic disintegration of the European Union: not unavoidable, but probable. Acta Oeconomica 66 (S1), 49–60.

Podkaminer, L., 2017. Labour productivity growth slowdown: an effect of economic stagnation rather than its cause. Acta Oeconomica 67 (S), 67–77.

PART B

Secular stagnation in the global south

CHAPTER NINE

Inequality, stagnation, financialization, and the Global South

Yılmaz Akyüz
Former Director, UNCTAD and Former Chief Economist, South Centre, Geneva, Switzerland

Introduction

The failure of large-scale bailout operations, historically low interest rates and rapid expansion of liquidity to bring about a robust recovery from the Great Recession caused widespread pessimism about the growth prospects of the US economy. It triggered a search for ex post facto explanations, including a thesis that it faced secular stagnation due to a structural demand gap caused by vanishing investment opportunities and excessive savings (Summers, 2013).[1] While there is little dispute about the deceleration of accumulation and growth, what is sorely missing from this account is the role of growing inequality and financialization as major causes of inadequate demand and sluggish accumulation, and of liberal policies in bringing these about, including financial deregulation and ultra-easy monetary policies pursued to overcome stagnation—issues several Keynesian economists had emphasized long before the Great Recession.

The combination of stagnation, ultra-easy money and financialization has had far reaching consequences for emerging economies (EMEs). It has generated exceptionally favorable global financial conditions for them, creating an unprecedented surge in capital inflows in a search-for-yield, accelerating their integration into international finance, and deepening their linkages with mature markets. This has aggravated their vulnerability to

[1] Summers (2019) reiterated his position recently, arguing that events of the last 5 years confirm that secular stagnation is real and spreading and that fiscal not monetary policy will play a major role in stabilization policy going forward. The global savings glut argument of Bernanke and the liquidity trap hypothesis of Krugman effectively attempt to answer the same question of inadequate demand at exceptionally low interest rates.

Handbook of Economic Stagnation
ISBN: 978-0-12-815898-2
https://doi.org/10.1016/B978-0-12-815898-2.00004-5

external shocks and entailed significant resource transfers to advanced economies through financial channels.

This chapter explores these issues, drawing on Akyüz (2017, 2018, and 2021). First, it briefly discusses the role of inequality and financialization in stagnation in advanced economies and that of policies in bringing these about. This is followed by an examination of spillovers to EMEs, consequences for their external vulnerability and resource transfers to advanced economies.[2]

Inequality, stagnation, and financialization

In sharp contrast with a long-standing belief that income shares stay relatively stable in the course of economic growth, there has been a secular downward trend in the share of wages in GDP in all major economies. This downward trend started in the 1970s in most countries and is more pronounced in the US and Japan than other advanced economies. During 1970–2014, the labor share declined by around 10 percentage points in the US and Japan and six to seven percentage points in Germany and the UK (ILO, 2015). Growth in real compensation of workers weakened after the 1970s and stayed behind output per worker. This trend continued in the new millennium: in 10 advanced economies, between 2000 and 2013 labor productivity rose by 17% while real wage index rose by some 6% (ILO/OECD, 2015).

Evidence from EMEs is more nuanced, but there is a pronounced decline in the wage share in Asia. In China, the decline started in the 1990s with its growing integration into the global economy. Although this was reversed after 2010 as a result of efforts to establish a buoyant domestic consumer market, the wage share in GDP in China remains lower than that in major advanced economies by 5–10 percentage points. The decline in the wage share in all these economies is also accompanied by a well-documented increase in the concentration of wealth, resulting also in growing inequality in the distribution of asset incomes.[3]

Occasionally, technological change is emphasized as the main reason for the decline in the share of labor, but this is highly controversial

[2] The countries examined here include G20 EMEs (Argentina, Brazil, China, India, Indonesia, Mexico, Russia, South Africa, and Turkey) and four advanced economies (the United States, the United Kingdom, Japan, and Germany).

[3] For the global picture, see Alvaredo et al. (2018) and Fine et al. (2019).

(Stockhammer, 2009; Goodhart and Erfurth, 2014). Three other factors appear to have played a much greater role. First, liberal policies have weakened labor while augmenting the market power of large corporations. Second there is a close relation between financialization—the increased size, scope, and influence of finance—and growing inequality, notably in the US. A financialization index combining the financial sector's total financial assets as a percent of GDP, the shares of the financial sector in total corporate profits, total employment and employee compensation shows a 3.5-fold increase between the early 1980s and 2015 and is highly correlated with the increase in the shares of the top income classes in GDP in the US (Soons, 2016; see also Palley, 2007; Greenwood and Scharfstein, 2013; and Smith, 2016). Finally, globalization has shifted the balance between labor and capital. The integration of China, India, and the countries that constituted the Soviet Union into the global economy has added 1.5 billion workers to economically active persons competing in world trade without a commensurate increase in the global capital stock (Freeman, 2010).

In terms of the Gini coefficient, the US and the UK come at the top of the list in inequality. This is partly because financialization has gone much further in the Anglo-American world. Furthermore, there are still important differences in the erosion of labor markets institutions, declines in union density and collective bargaining coverage as well as employment protection and minimum wage legislation, with the US and the UK again coming at the top in terms of market orientation (Freeman, 2008; Jaumotte and Buitron, 2015; ILO, 2015). These differences in financial and labor market policies and institutions and in taxation explain much of the intercountry variations in income and wealth distribution.

Whatever its proximate causes, the growing gap between labor productivity and wages means that the purchasing power of workers over the goods and services they produce has been falling. This together with the increasing concentration of wealth and asset incomes results in underconsumption and structural demand gap—thus, inequality is not only a social but also a macroeconomic problem. Although sustained declines in wages would reduce the cost of production and increase the surplus in the hands of the capitalist class, they would also limit the extent of the market since wages are the most important component of aggregate demand. Wage suppression thus creates the classical-Marxian problem of monetary *realization* of profits—a reason why Keynes also rejected declines in wages as a recipe for unemployment. This demand gap cannot be constantly filled by investment regardless of the rate of interest since that would ultimately lead to overcapacity.

When investment is raised beyond a certain point, demand constraint would start to bite and profitability would fall, and this would in turn deter investment. This also implies that there may be no inconsistency between falling share of wages and falling profitability of investment.

Sluggish wages also reduce price pressures and allow and encourage central banks to create credit and asset bubbles to overcome stagnation without fear of inflation. This is all the more so because, with unrelenting fiscal orthodoxy, monetary policy has become the main instrument to stimulate economic activity. In the US, for instance, over the past three cycles, the Federal Reserve has been quite restrained in raising policy rates at times of expansion while cutting them drastically during contractions, creating a downward bias in interest rates (Borio and Disyatat, 2014; Palley, 2016). Thus, the "coincidence of a declining wage share and declining real interest rates is not … accidental" (Goodhart and Erfurth, 2014: 4).

This process creates destabilizing interfaces between debt and interest rates. Lower wages and reduced inflationary pressures lead to lower interest rates which, together with financial deregulation, encourage rapid accumulation of debt and asset bubbles. This, in turn, makes it difficult for central banks to raise policy interest rates without causing disruptions in financial markets, thereby making low interest rates selfreinforcing. Indeed, the downward bias in real interest rates in G7 countries has been associated with a strong upward bias in debt as a proportion of GDP since the mid-1980s, suggesting that ultra-easy monetary policies made possible by sluggish wages and low inflation have created a debt trap (Borio and Disyatat, 2014; Hannoun and Dittus, 2017).

This implies that inequality can lead to excessive credit expansion and financial fragility. This would happen when declining wages in conditions of low interest rates create an urge to borrow and access to finance is facilitated by deregulation and implicit government guarantees. The two major crises in the US, the Great Depression and the Great Recession, were both preceded by a sharp increase in inequality and a similarly sharp increase in household debt leverage (Kumhof and Rancière, 2010). It is argued that in the run-up to the subprime crisis, growing inequality in the US created political pressure to foster easy credit to assuage the less wealthy and reduce consumption inequality despite rising income inequality (Rajan, 2010). Several empirical studies undertaken since the Great Recession also link financial fragility to inequality (Amountzias, 2019).

The financial boom-bust cycles generated to reignite growth by monetary easing and deregulation exacerbate the stagnation problem by creating waste and distortions on the supply side and reducing potential growth, and by redistributing to the top and widening the structural demand gap. During booms, the financial sector crowds out real economic activity as cheap credit diverts resources to low-productivity sectors such as construction and real estate (Cecchetti and Kharroubi, 2015). Misallocations created by the booms are exposed during the ensuing crises when the economy would have to make a shift back to viable sectors and companies, but this is impeded by credit crunch and deflation (Borio et al., 2015).

Second, boom-bust cycles aggravate the underconsumption problem by increasing inequality. In the US, for instance, the crisis has impoverished the poor, particularly those subject to foreclosures, while policy interventions have benefitted the rich. In the recovery, the top 1% captured 58% of total growth as their income grew by 27% against 4.3% growth of the income of the remaining 99% (Saez, 2015). In every year from 2008 onwards, real hourly wages stayed behind hourly labor productivity and the share of wages fell both during the contraction and subsequent recovery (Dufour and Orhangazi, 2016). Since the onset of the global crisis, the real incomes of about two-thirds of households in 25 advanced economies were flat or fell and this proportion was over 80% in the US (Dobbs et al., 2016).

These imply that when credit and asset bubbles burst and the economy contracts, even a bigger bubble may be needed for recovery and growth. In the US, the bursting of the Savings and Loans bubble of the 1980s was followed by a bigger (technology or dot-com) bubble in the 1990s which came to an end at the turn of the century, followed by the subprime bubble and a bigger bust, leading to even more aggressive interest rate cuts and liquidity expansion.

Inadequate demand is also at the heart of the secular stagnation thesis of Summers (2013). According to this while investment opportunities have started to vanish because of slowdown in population growth and innovation, greater income and wealth inequality has increased the supply of loanable funds, thereby raising the level of investment needed to achieve full employment. As a result, the rate of interest that equates savings and investment at full employment level of income has declined significantly and even become negative, impairing the ability of monetary policy to provide adequate demand stimulus to raise employment. While aggressive monetary policy action is necessary to fight stagnation, it is argued, the main line of response is to be found in public investment, exports and supply side reforms to improve private investment opportunities.

The secular stagnation thesis has been criticized on several grounds by economists in both the Keynesian and Marxian traditions (Despain, 2015; Hein, 2015; Keen, 2014; Magdoff and Foster, 2014; Palley, 2016; Stiglitz, 2018; Wray, 2013) as well as some BIS economists (Borio and Disyatat, 2014; Borio et al., 2015; Cecchetti and Kharroubi, 2015). For the issue at hand, it is notable that the demand gap is described by secular stagnationists in terms of vanishing investment opportunities rather than underconsumption caused by wage suppression and wealth concentration, and their effects on demand and profit expectations are largely ignored. Inequality is portrayed as causing excess supply of loanable funds or excess savings rather than underconsumption. There is no proper recognition that wage suppression is at the heart of declining inflation and interest rates and no mention of the role of liberal policies in generating demand gap and slowing accumulation by suppressing wages and encouraging financial bubbles and financialization as a remedy to stagnation. In the same vein, the solution proposed fails to address the root cause of the problem by reversing the secular decline in the wage share and growing wealth concentration.

Spillovers to the Global South

Sluggish growth, declining wages, weak inflation, falling interest rates, and rising indebtedness are now common features of major advanced economies. These have played a major role in growing penetration of financial capital and firms from advanced economies into EMEs, deepening their integration into global finance. Sluggish growth and declining interest rates have created a search for yield in high-risk, high-return investment globally, including in EMEs with greater profit opportunities and capital gain prospects. This process accelerated significantly in the new millennium. The outcome is externally driven, subordinated financialization in EMEs, superimposed on a relatively underdeveloped economic structure.

The deepened integration is manifested by a rapid growth of external balance sheets, gross external assets, and liabilities, of EMEs. After recurrent crises in EMEs, nonresident capital inflows surged in the early 2000s, mainly thanks to the policies which culminated in the subprime crisis in the US and the debt crisis in the Eurozone. The surge surpassed the previous post-war booms in capital inflows. After a sharp decline during the collapse of Lehman Brothers in September 2008, inflows recovered quickly thanks to ultra-easy monetary policies pursued in the US and Europe in response to the crisis. Subsequently they have manifested a certain degree of instability according to news about the direction of monetary policy in the US, and slowed after 2010 as per cent of GDP, but there has been no generalized reversal (bust) so far. In fact, for EMEs taken together, nonresident capital inflows have never been negative since the 1980s, implying a constant increase in their gross external liabilities.

Over 85% of gross external assets and liabilities of G20 EMEs outstanding in 2016 was accumulated after 2000.[4] Gross external assets and liabilities as a proportion of GDP increased in almost all of them. The net foreign asset positions (NFAP) have been negative except in surplus economies, China and Russia, which accumulated external assets partly from current account surpluses partly from nonresident capital inflows. In deficit, EMEs gross foreign assets came entirely from capital inflows: that is, their external balance sheets are highly leveraged.

Integration has deepened not so much through expansion of cross-border lending and borrowing as through increased penetration of international financial capital and firms in credit, deposit, currency, bond, equity, and property markets of EMEs. This is also accompanied by changes in the structure of their external balance sheets, notably currency, capital, and sectoral compositions of their gross liabilities. It has resulted not only from the drive of financial capital to penetrate more lucrative markets, but also further financial liberalization in EMEs themselves. Not only have domestic financial markets been opened to nonresidents, but also residents have been allowed significant freedom in their access to international financial markets as borrowers and investors. These have not only strengthened the traditional cross-border financial linkages of EMEs, but also resulted in an unprecedented foreign presence in their markets, exerting a strong influence on their liquidity and valuation dynamics and creating new channels in the transmission of impulses from international financial markets.

First, in order to reduce vulnerability to external debt crises, most EMEs have sought to move from debt to equity finance on grounds that equity liabilities are less risky and more stable, liberalizing foreign direct investment (FDI) regimes and easing access to equity markets. As a result, nonresident holding of equities as a percent of market capitalization rose sharply, exceeding the levels in many major advanced economies. For G20 EMEs together, the share of equities in total gross external liabilities increased

[4] For evidence cited in this section, see Akyüz (2017 and 2021).

from less than 40% to close to 60% during 2000–16 while the share of external debt fell by a corresponding amount.

On the assets side, there has also been a shift from debt to equities mainly due to a surge in FDI abroad by several EMEs, including Brazil, Russia, and South Africa where FDI now accounts for between 30 and 40% of gross external assets. Outwards FDI also increased rapidly in China, but its share in gross external assets remains relatively low and much of it concentrated in the Global South (UNCTAD, 2014). The net equity position of G20 EMEs is negative and has deteriorated since 2000 because inward FDI in these economies grew much faster than their outward FDI.

Second, until recently, external debt liabilities of EMEs were predominantly in reserve currencies as they were unable to issue external debt in local currency, suffering from the so-called original sin problem (Eichengreen et al., 2003). Many governments have sought to reduce their exposure to the exchange rate risk by opening local bond markets to nonresidents and borrowing in local currencies. This, together with increased willingness of international lenders to assume the exchange rate risk and come under domestic jurisdiction in return for significantly higher yields, has resulted in a significant increase in the share of domestic-currency in total external debt of several EMEs (Klingebiel, 2014; IMF/WB, 2016). In many of them, the share of foreign holdings in local bonds and deposits came to exceed the levels observed in reserve-currency countries, notably the US. Some EMEs have also been able to issue local-currency debt in international markets and have established local-currency offshore bond markets (Mizen et al., 2018).

Third, while governments in major EMEs have rarely resorted to international borrowing in reserve currencies, there has been a large build-up of corporate external debt in dollars since the global crisis (Alfaro et al., 2017; Lund et al., 2018). In EMEs as a whole the external debt of nonfinancial corporations came to exceed external sovereign debt (Bell, 2017). They have also issued debt in international markets through their subsidiaries. When financial institutions are included, the private sector accounts for around 75% of total external debt liabilities of EMEs and these are largely in reserve currencies.

Fourth, international banks have shifted from cross-border lending to EMEs to local lending by establishing subsidiaries. As a result, there has been a visible increase in the share of foreign banks in EMEs even though the crisis in the US and Europe resulted in a certain degree of withdrawal.

Local-currency claims of international banks in EMEs rose from 15% of their total claims in the mid-1990s to 40% by 2008. Local lending by foreign banks to EMEs in all currencies is now greater than their cross-border lending.

Finally, the composition of external debt liabilities of EMEs has also changed from bank loans to bonds. This is partly due to opening of domestic bond markets to nonresidents. However, international lending to EMEs, notably to nonfinancial corporations, has also shifted from bank loans to bond issues. As a result, EMEs have become more susceptible to conditions in international bond markets than in international banking as was the case in earlier crises.

External vulnerabilities of EMEs

The deepened international financial integration of EMEs and significant changes in the structure of their external balance sheets entail far-reaching consequences for their external vulnerability. In particular, the internationalization of domestic equity and bond markets and increased foreign presence in the banking system have created new vulnerabilities, adding to those resulting from interruptions to access to international capital markets.

Because of lack of a strong local investor base, equity markets in EMEs are not sufficiently deep and liquid. As a result, the entry and exit of even relatively small amounts of foreign capital tend to result in large price swings. Furthermore, because of increased access to markets abroad, local investors in EMEs have been acting with a global perspective. Thus, stock prices in EMEs are now closely correlated with capital inflows and prices in mature markets. Even in countries with little foreign presence, such as China, equity prices have become highly susceptible to changes in the global risk appetite.

Opening local bond markets and borrowing from nonresidents in local currency have no doubt allowed the sovereign to pass the currency risk to lenders. However, it has also led to a significant exposure to interest rate shocks and loss of autonomy in controlling domestic long-term rates, heightening their sensitivity to fluctuations in debt markets of major advanced economies (Sobrun and Turner, 2015). It has reduced the capacity of local bond markets to act as a spare tyre at times of stress in international debt markets. Because they are not deep and liquid enough, "even the small amount of foreign investment going into the long end of the yield curve can have a large marginal impact" (Pradhan et al., 2011, 15–16). Foreign holdings reach several multiples of average daily trading volume and this creates "'a systemic liquidity mismatch' between the potential for portfolio outflows from emerging market economies and the capacity of local institutions and market makers (in particular international banks) to absorb these flows" (IMF, 2014: 36–7). As argued by Morgan Stanley (2014: 3), foreign ownership in the domestic bond markets now constitutes The Achilles' heel of EMEs.

Whether in local currency or dollars, foreign ownership of debt is a key indicator of external vulnerability. This has become evident in the Eurozone crisis where problems emerged not in countries with large stocks of debt but large foreign holdings (Gros, 2011). The US has always been uneasy about foreign holdings of its treasuries. While about one-third of US treasuries are held by nonresidents, this proportion is much higher in many EMEs, particularly if debt issued in foreign currencies is included. More significantly, unlike US treasuries the externally held local-currency sovereign debt of EMEs is not in the hands of foreign central banks but in the portfolios of fickle investors, making them much more susceptible to changes in global risk appetite and interest rates.

Greater presence of foreign banks in EMEs also aggravates their external vulnerability. It is now increasingly recognized that "these groups are highly interconnected internationally and may expose individual countries to the risk that shocks in other countries will spill over into their domestic financial systems" (Fiechter et al., 2011: 5). They are known to have acted as a conduit of financial instability in advanced economies, transmitting credit crunches to host countries (He and McCauley, 2013). They have also greater room to engage in regulatory arbitrage by shifting operations back and forth between host and home countries (Sarma and Prashad, 2014; Stein, 2010).

Finally, the shift in the composition of external debt liabilities of EMEs from international bank loans to bond issues also entails new vulnerabilities. Evidence suggests that while the sensitivity of both international bank loans and bond flows to changes in US interest rates increased after the global crisis, this was more marked for bond flows (Avdjiev et al., 2017). This implies a significant increase in the scope of US monetary policy to generate variations in lending conditions for EMEs, both in international bond issues and through its impact on their local bond markets.

Resource transfers

The deepened integration of EMEs into global finance has also resulted in growing resource transfers through financial channels. It has generated an external balance-sheet structure of low-yielding assets and high-yielding liabilities, thereby entailing net investment income transfers abroad. It has also enhanced the susceptibility of value of their external assets and liabilities to variations in currency and financial markets, making them increasingly prone to capital losses.

Although debtor-creditor relations within the Global South have been deepening, a very large proportion of gross external financial positions of EMEs is still with advanced economies (Milesi-Ferretti et al., 2010). EMEs do not have large positions in the currencies or assets of each other. China has the largest claims vis-à-vis other EMEs, but these are still less than a quarter of its total gross assets. Thus, income and capital losses incurred by EMEs have their counterparts mainly in gains of advanced economies, notably the US.

Net investment income positions

With the expansion of external balance sheets, international investment income flows gain added importance in the current account relative to trade. Generally, countries with positive NFAP are expected to earn net investment income. However, a positive NFAP is neither necessary nor sufficient for a country to run surplus on investment income because there are often large differences between yields on assets and liabilities. EMEs run deficits on net international investment income not only because their liabilities exceed assets, but also because their assets bring lower yields than liabilities. Even some EMEs with positive NFAP such as China and Russia are in red in net investment income. During 2000–16, the average yield on external liabilities of G20 EMEs exceeded the average yield on their external assets by 2.6 percentage points. By contrast, the yield differential was positive in all major advanced economies. They all earned higher yields on their assets and paid lower yields on their liabilities than G20 EMEs. The US has enjoyed the highest yield differential and ran a surplus on its international investment income balance despite a large negative NFAP.

Average yields on gross external assets and liabilities depend on their compositions. Equities generally carry higher risk than debt but they also earn higher return. There is a strong positive correlation between the share of equities in gross external assets and liabilities and average returns on total assets and liabilities (Lane and Milesi-Ferretti, 2003). A reason why the average yield on gross external assets of EMEs is lower than the average yield paid on their gross external liabilities is the higher share of equities in total liabilities than in total assets. This is also a reason why EMEs earn lower yields on their total assets and pay higher yields on their total liabilities than advanced economies.

As late-comer outward investors, EMEs earn less on their FDI assets than they pay on FDI liabilities. For 2000–16, the average yield differential between FDI assets and liabilities of G20 EMEs was −3.5 percentage points against +3 points in advanced economies. The US had the higher yield differential on FDI than all others, and this is a major factor why it has a positive international investment income balance despite having a large and growing negative NFAP (Curcuru et al., 2013; Darvas and Hüttle, 2017).

EMEs also earn less on their debt assets than they pay on their debt liabilities. An important part of their gross debt assets consists of low-yielding international reserves while their debt liabilities carry sizable risk premium, including in surplus EMEs with strong NFAP, captured mainly by lenders in advanced economies. The shift from foreign-currency to local-currency debt by EMEs has also widened the interest differential between debt liabilities and assets since governments are charged sizable credit spreads when they borrow in their own currency (Du and Schreger, 2016). Compensation needs to be paid for the exchange rate risks passed onto creditors, and debt issued under local jurisdiction carries higher default risk than debt issued in international financial centers.

Since EMEs pay higher rates on external liabilities than they earn on external assets, they would need a positive NFAP to avoid deficits on net international investment income. Otherwise, they would have to run a trade surplus to balance the current account. If not, the NFAP would deteriorate, raising the deficit on international investment income. The deficit can increase further since the risk premium for EMEs tends to vary inversely with the NFAP. A vicious circle can thus emerge whereby investment income deficits weaken the NFAP which in turn raises the risk premium and hence investment income deficits. As the NFAP deteriorates, it could become increasingly difficult to attract foreign capital even by offering higher yields. In other words, the risk-return profiles of gross assets and liabilities of EMEs do not only entail significant resources transfers to advanced economies, but they also pose a potential threat to financial stability.

Wealth transfers

For EMEs cross-border wealth transfers resulting from capital gains and losses have also become important because structural changes in their external balance sheets amplified the susceptibility of the value of their gross external assets and liabilities to variations in assets prices and exchange rates. As a result, changes in monetary and financial policies and conditions in reserve-currency countries now affect EMEs not only through their impact on capital *flows*, but also by altering the value of their outstanding *stocks* of gross international assets and liabilities. For debt, valuation changes occur primarily from exchange rate variations while asset price changes are more important for equities. However, these two sources of capital gains and losses are not always independent of each other and tend to be highly correlated (Lane and Shambaugh, 2010). In EMEs, they are both strongly influenced by capital flows and they reinforce each other.

Valuation changes now have a significantly greater impact on NFAP than current account balances.[5] During 2000–16, the NFAP of G20 EMEs changed in the opposite direction to the current account balance in the majority of years. The coefficient of correlation between current account balances and year-to-year changes in the NFAP was 0.2. For major advanced economies, there was effectively no correlation. It is particularly weak or negative in economies with a significant degree of financialization. Among advanced economies, this is the case in the US and the UK relative to Germany and Japan and among the EMEs it is the case in the financially more open and liberal economies of Brazil, Indonesia, Mexico, South Africa, and Turkey compared to China, India, and Russia.

Earlier studies found relatively strong correlations between current account balances and year-to-year changes in the NFAP in EMEs (Lane and Milesi-Ferretti, 2001). The subsequent weakening is the outcome of their deepened integration of EMEs into the international financial system, the growing importance of autonomous capital flows relative to current account balances and significant changes in the composition of their assets and liabilities toward instruments more susceptible to price and exchange rate changes.

Capital gains and losses redistribute global wealth among countries since a country's foreign assets are liabilities of another country. For the reason already cited, capital losses (gains) incurred by EMEs have their counterpart

[5] For evidence cited in this section Akyüz (2021).

mainly in gains (losses) of advanced economies. During 2000–2016, G20 EMEs together had a cumulative capital loss of over $1900 billion. Much of this was incurred by two surplus economies, China and Russia, while many other G20 EMEs enjoyed small capital gains. By contrast, collectively the four major advanced economies had a cumulative gain of some $1550 billion. This was mainly due to gains by the US and the UK as Japan and Germany also incurred losses during that period.

There is indeed a strong negative correlation between yearly net capital gains and losses of emerging and advanced economies considered here.[6] An inverse relation is also found when capital gains and losses are estimated separately on gross external assets and liabilities. Capital gains on gross external assets (liabilities) of advanced economies are strongly correlated with capital losses of EMEs on their liabilities (assets). These are also reflected by an inverse relation between year-to-year changes in the NFAP of emerging and advanced economies. During 2000–16, deteriorations (improvements) of the NFAP of G20 EMEs were closely associated with improvements (deteriorations) of the NFAP of advanced economies due to disparate effects of valuation changes.

During 2000–16, the average return differential between external assets and liabilities, including both investment income yields and capital gains and losses, was −5.3 percentage points for G20 EMEs but +1.6 percentage points for advanced economies. On average, G20 EMEs earned 3.5 percentage points less on their gross assets and paid 3.4 percentage points more on their gross liabilities than advanced economies. The US enjoyed higher return differentials than other advanced economies.[7]

The large gap between the rates of return on gross external assets and liabilities of EMEs and advanced economies implies significant resource transfers from the former to the latter. Using the average return differentials for 2000–16, wealth and income transfers, estimated here as the carry cost of "borrowed" gross assets (i.e., net cost of assets accumulated from additional liabilities, excluding liabilities incurred to finance current account deficits) reach 2.3% of the combined GDP of nine G20 EMEs per year. About

[6] The North-South trade-offs in external wealth distribution is also supported by estimates in Gourinchas et al. (2012) for bilateral gains and losses resulting from currency and price changes triggered by the global crisis.

[7] For a similar result for 1990–2015, see Adler and Garcia-Macia (2018).

half of this was income losses due to yield differentials and half wealth transfers due to capital losses. Resource transfers were lower after the 2008 crisis (2.0% of GDP per annum) than before (2.6%).

Conclusions

Major advanced economies, notably the US, have so far ignored the root causes of chronic demand gap and sluggish accumulation but resorted to policies designed to generate growth through credit and asset bubbles. This has widened the demand gap by aggravating inequality and reduced potential growth by creating supply side distortions. It has also served to redirect financial capital and firms toward EMEs in a search-for-yield, deepening their integration into an inherently unstable international financial system. It has generated new sources of vulnerability to external shocks and significant resource transfers to richer economies. The fortunes of EMEs are now increasingly shaped by financial impulses resulting from self-seeking policies of the US through their impact on capital flows and valuation of their external assets and liabilities. The solution calls for a fundamental reform of the international monetary, including the elimination of the exorbitant privilege enjoyed by the US as the issuer of the dominant reserve currency.

References

Adler, G., Garcia-Macia, D., 2018. The Stabilizing Role of Net Foreign Asset Returns. IMF Working Paper 18/79.

Akyüz, Y., 2017. Playing with Fire. Deepened Financial Integration and Changing Vulnerabilities of the Global South. Oxford University Press.

Akyüz, Y., 2018. Inequality, financialization and stagnation. The Economic and Labour Relations Review 1–18.

Akyüz, Y., 2021. External balance sheets of emerging economies: low-yielding assets, high-yielding liabilities. Review of Keynesian Economics 9 (2), 232–252.

Alfaro, L., Asis, G., Chari, A., Panizza, U., 2017. Lessons Unlearned? Corporate Debt in Emerging Markets. Harvard Business School Working Paper 17-097.

Alvaredo, F., Chancel, L., Piketty, T., Saez, E., Zucman, G., 2018. World Inequality Report 2018. Harvard University Press.

Amountzias, C., 2019. An investigation of the effects of income inequality on financial fragility: evidence from Organization for Economic Co-operation and Development countries. International Journal of Finance and Economics 24 (1), 241–259.

Avdjiev, S., Gambacorta, L., Goldberg, L.S., Schiaffi, S., 2017. The Shifting Drivers of Global Liquidity. BIS Working Paper 644.

Bell, A., March 9, 2017. Four Things to Know about Emerging Market Corporate Debt. Goldman Sachs.

Borio, C., Disyatat, P., June 25, 2014. Low Interest Rates and Secular Stagnation: Is Debt the Missing Link? Vox.

Borio, C., Kharroubi, E., Upper, C., Zampolli, F., 2015. Labour Reallocation and Productivity Dynamics: Financial Causes, Real Consequences. BIS Working Paper 534.

Cecchetti, S.G., Kharroubi, E., 2015. Why Does Financial Sector Growth Crowd Out Real Economic Growth? BIS Working Paper 490.

Curcuru, S.E., Thomas, C.P., Warnock, F.E., 2013. On Return Differentials. Board of Governors of the Federal Reserve System International Finance Discussion Papers Number 1077.

Darvas, Z., Hüttle, P., 2017. Returns on Foreign Assets: Exorbitant Privileges and Stabilizing Adjustment. Bruegel Working Paper 07.

Despain, H.G., 2015. Secular stagnation. Mainstream versus marxian traditions. Monthly Review 67 (4).

Dobbs, R., Madgavkar, A., Manyika, J., Woetzel, J., Bughin, J., Labaye, E., Kashyap, P., July, 2016. Poorer than Their Parents? Flat or Falling Incomes in Advanced Economies. Report. McKinsey Global Institute.

Du, W., Schreger, J., 2016. Local currency sovereign risk. Journal of Finance 71 (3), 1027–1069.

Dufour, M., Orhangazi, O., 2016. Growth and distribution after the 2007–2008 US financial crisis: who shouldered the burden of the crisis? Review of Keynesian Economics 4 (2), 151–174.

Eichengreen, B., Hausmann, R., Panizza, U., 2003. Currency Mismatches, Debt Intolerance and Original Sin: Why They Are Not the Same and Why it Matters. NBER Working Paper 10036.

Fiechter, J., Ötker-Robe, l., Ilyina, A., Hsu, M., Santos, A., Surti, J., 2011. Subsidiaries or Branches: Does One Size Fit All? IMF Discussion Note SDN 11/4.

Fine, D., Manyika, J., Sjatil, P.E., Tacke, T., Tadjeddine, K., Desmond, M., 2019. Inequality: A Persisting Challenge and its Implications. McKinsey Global Institute Discussion Paper. June.

Freeman, R.B., 2008. Labor Market Institutions Around the World. CEP Discussion Paper 844. LSE.

Freeman, R.B., March 5, 2010. What Really Ails Europe (And America): The Doubling of the Global Workforce. The Globalist.

Goodhart, C.A.E., Erfurth, P., November 3, 2014. Monetary Policy and Long-Term Trends. Vox.

Gourinchas, P.-O., Rey, H., Truempler, K., 2012. The financial crisis and the geography of wealth transfers. Journal of International Economics 88 (2), 266–283.

Greenwood, R., Scharfstein, D., 2013. The growth of finance. Journal of Economic Perspectives 27 (2), 3–28. Spring.

Gros, D., May 24, 2011. External versus Domestic Debt in the Euro Crisis. Vox.

Hannoun, H., Dittus, P., 2017. Revolution Required: The Ticking Time Bombs of the G7 Model. Amazon Digital Services.

He, D., McCauley, R.N., 2013. Transmitting Global Liquidity to East Asia: Policy Rates, Bond Yields, Currencies and Dollar Credit. BIS Working Paper 431.

Hein, E., 2015. Secular Stagnation or Stagnation Policy? Steindl after Summers. Working Paper 846. Levy Economics Institute of Bard College.

ILO, 2015. Global Wage Report 2014/15. Wages and Income Inequality, Geneva.

ILO/OECD, 2015. The Labour Share in G20 Economies. Report Prepared for the G20 Employment Working Group.

IMF, 2014. Global Financial Stability Report. April, Washington D.C.

IMF/WB, December 14, 2016. Staff Note for the G20 IFAWG: Development of Local Currency Bond Markets.

Jaumotte, F., Buitron, C.O., 2015. Inequality and Labor Market Institutions. IMF Staff Discussion Note 15/14.

Keen, S., January 13, 2014. Secular stagnation and endogenous money. Real-World Economics Review (66).
Klingebiel, D., November 20, 2014. Emerging Markets Local Currency Debt and Foreign Investors. Recent Developments. The World Bank Treasury. Pension & Endowments Departments.
Kumhof, M., Rancière, R., 2010. Inequality, Leverage and Crises. IMF Working Paper 268.
Lane, P., Milesi-Ferretti, G., December, 2001. The external wealth of nations: measures of foreign assets and liabilities for industrial and developing countries. Journal of International Economics 55, 263–294.
Lane, P., Milesi-Ferretti, G., 2003. International financial integration. IMF Staff Papers 55 (Special Issue), 82–113.
Lane, P., Shambaugh, J.C., March, 2010. Financial exchange rates and international currency exposures. American Economic Review 100 (1), 518–540.
Lund, S., Woetzel, J., Windhagen, E., Dobbs, R., Goldstein, D., June 2018. Rising Corporate Debt. Peril or Promise? McKinsey Global Institute Discussion Paper.
Magdoff, F., Foster, J.B., May, 2014. Stagnation and financialization. The nature of the contradiction. Monthly Review 66 (01).
Milesi-Ferretti, G.M., Strobbe, F., Tamirisa, N., 2010. Bilateral Financial Linkages and Global Imbalances: A View on the Eve of the Financial Crisis. IMF Working Paper 10/257.
Mizen, P., Packer, F., Remolona, E., Tsoukas, S., 2018. Original Sin in Corporate Finance. New Evidence from Asian Bond Issuers in Onshore and Offshore Markets. Centre for Finance, Credit and Macroeconomics Working Paper 18/04. University of Nottingham.
Morgan, S., June 18, 2014. Has This Been a "Good" Rally for EM? What if EM Central Banks Had Tightened Policy Instead? The Global Macro Analyst, Morgan Stanley Research, London.
Palley, T.I., 2007. Financialization: What it Is and Why it Matters. Working Paper 525. The Levy Economics Institute of Bard College.
Palley, T.I., 2016. Zero Lower Bound (ZLB) Economics: The Fallacy of New Keynesian Explanations of Stagnation. Macroeconomic Policy Institute Working Paper 164.
Pradhan, M., Balakrishnan, R., Baqir, R., Heenan, G., Nowak, S., Oner, C., Panth, S., 2011. Policy Responses to Capital Flows in Emerging Markets. MF Staff Discussion Note 11/10.
Rajan, R., 2010. Fault Lines: How Hidden Fractures Still Threaten the World Economy. Princeton University Press, Princeton.
Saez, E., June 25, 2015. Striking it Richer: The Evolution of Top Incomes in the United States (Updated with 2014 preliminary estimates). UC Berkeley.
Sarma, M., Prashad, A., 2014. Do Foreign Banks in India Indulge in Cream Skimming? Discussion Paper 14-01 CITD, School of International Studies, JNU.
Smith, N., April 20, 2016. How Finance Took over the Economy. Bloomberg View.
Sobrun, J., Turner, P., 2015. Bond Markets and Monetary Policy Dilemmas for the Emerging Markets. BIS Working Paper 508.
Soons, O.C., 2016. Inequality and Financialization. Senior Honors Projects. Paper 492.
Stein, H., 2010. Financial liberalization, institutional transformation and credit allocation in developing countries: the world bank and the internationalisation of banking. Cambridge Journal of Economics 34 (2), 257–273.
Stiglitz, J.E., August 28, 2018. The myth of secular stagnation. Project Syndicate. https://www.project-syndicate.org/commentary/secular-stagnation-excuse-for-flawed-policies-by-joseph-e-stiglitz-2018-08.
Stockhammer, E., 2009. Functional Income Distribution in OECD Countries. IMK Studies 5/2009. Duesseldorf.

Summers, L.H., November 8, 2013. Policy Responses to Crises. IMF Economic Forum, Washington.

Summers, L.H., April 15, 2019. Secular Stagnation and the Future of Global Macroeconomic Policy. Speech given at the Peterson Institute for International Economics.

UNCTAD, 2014. Bilateral FDI Statistics 2014. Geneva.

Wray, L.R., November 21, 2013. Bow Down to the Bubble: Larry Summerian Endorses Bubbleonian Madness and Paul Krugman Embraces the Hansenian Stagnation Thesis. New Economic Perspectives.

CHAPTER TEN

Does the liberal policy regime condemn Latin America to quasi-stagnation?

Luiz Carlos Bresser-Pereira[1], Carmem Feijó[2], Eliane Cristina Araújo[3]
[1]Getúlio Vargas Foundation, São Paulo, SP, Brazil
[2]Fluminense Federal University, Niterói, RJ, Brazil
[3]State University of Maringá, Maringá, PR, Brazil

Introduction

Latin American countries are quasistagnant since 1980. Recently a director of the Council of the Americas asked "how will the 'lost second decade'" continue to translate into political instability? At the root of the regional turmoil is economic failure. According to the Economic Commission for Latin America and the Caribbean—ECLAC, the period 2014–20 will be the slowest growth in Latin America in 70 years. Indeed, Latin America is deindustrializing, experiencing quasi-stagnation, and falling behind for 40 years, while the East Asian countries that began to grow after the Second World War (South Korea, Taiwan, and Singapore) are today rich countries.

There are many causes on the supply side why Latin-America have been quasistagnant (here represented by Brazil, Mexico, Argentina, Chile, and Uruguay) from the 1980s while East Asian tigers, although undergoing some reduction in their growth rates, have continued to grow fast. Among these causes, the priority given to education and the substantially higher degree of inequality in Latin America than in East Asia are the more mentioned. These are real problems; they explain why from 1950 to 1980 East Asian tigers were already growing faster than Latin-American countries, but they do not explain why from the 1980s Latin America became quasistagnant compared to East Asia. Besides the micro, we must also look for the new macroeconomic facts that explain this change. In a recent paper, Bresser-Pereira et al. (2020) compared the two group of countries and argued that the "liberalization trap" (not the "middle-income

Handbook of Economic Stagnation
ISBN: 978-0-12-815898-2
https://doi.org/10.1016/B978-0-12-815898-2.00008-2

country trap") was this historical new fact. Did the trade and financial liberalization play a major role in explaining the Latin American quasistagnation?[1]

Policy regimes may be developmental or liberal.[2] The policy regime is developmental or Keynesian when it involves a moderate intervention of the state in the economy; it is liberal when such intervention is limited to the minimum.[3] In the two regions, there was a major change of the policy regime from a developmental to a liberal one, but the adoption of a liberal policy regime represented a radical change in Latin America, while it was milder in East Asia. Before 1980, they did not suffer from the Dutch disease problem and were already open economies exporting manufactured goods, while the most successful countries in Latin America, like Brazil and Mexico, were only able to export manufactured goods because they neutralized their Dutch disease with import tariffs.

The relative stagnation of Latin America may be shown by comparing the growth of the GDP per capita from 1980 to 2018 in the region with the growth in the rich countries, and in the East Asian countries. In a catching up figure (Fig. 10.1), where the GDP per capita of the United States in these 40 years are 100% and the lines show the evolution of the average GDP per capita in this period in the East Asian and Pacific countries and in Latin America and Caribbean we see graphically this falling behind.

Considering the last 40 years of quasistagnation, in the first 10 years, the cause was obviously a major foreign debt crisis. What about the other 30 years? Since the end of the 1980s, the Latin American countries engaged in liberal reforms, one after the other, in consonance with the Washington Consensus: trade liberalization, financial liberalization, privatization not only of competitive but also of the monopolist sectors of the economy, generalized deregulation. Reforms that are supposed to make the countries return to fast growth, but one after the other they fail to achieve what was promised. The liberal reformers have always a ready explanation: the reforms have not liberalized as much as it was necessary; more reforms would be required.

[1] Bresser-Pereira et al. (2020).

[2] We define developmentalism as the alternative form of organizing capitalism to economic liberalism. When the economic policy regime is liberal the role of the state is reduced to the minimum; when it is developmental, it is assumed a moderate state intervention and a national perspective (Bresser-Pereia, 2017).

[3] Note that we are using the word "liberal" in its original or academic meaning, not in the American or colloquial meaning.

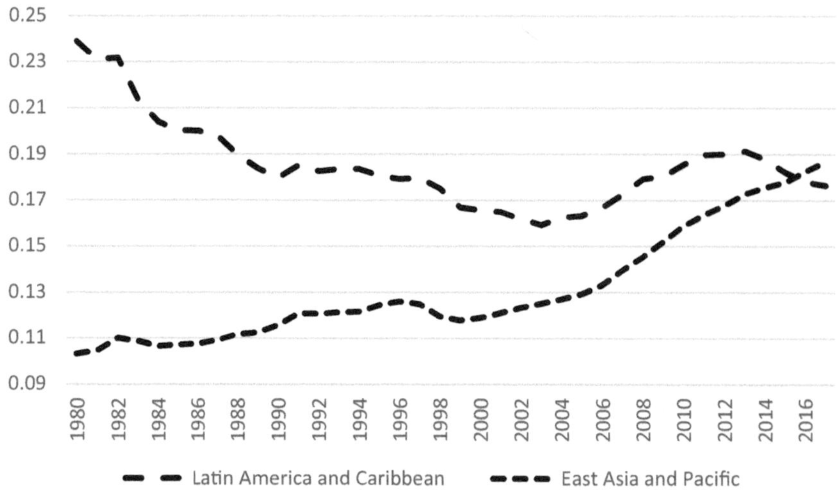

Figure 10.1 GDP per capita of Latin America and Caribbean and East Asia and Pacific in relation to the U.S. GDP per capita (constant 2010 US$): 1980–2017. *Source: World Development Indicators.*

In this paper, our hypothesis is that in the Latin American countries, given the stage of their economic growth and the fact that they are commodity exporters that suffer from the Dutch disease, economic liberalism is unable to assure economic growth and catching up. While, between 1930 and 1980, they adopted a developmental policy regime and were successful in industrializing and growing, in the 1980s they have fallen in the grips of a major financial crisis, which opened room to economic liberalism. Turned dominant from around 1990, the liberal policy regime condemned Latin America to quasistagnation.

We know that this is a bold hypothesis, but we believe that we have strong arguments in its favor. Before coming to them, however, we must make some simple assumptions. First, according to the new-developmental approach, when the exchange rate tends to be overvalued for several years within an exchange rate cycle between two currency crises, it is determinant of investment. The explanation for this is simple. In their decision to invest the companies take into consideration such exchange rate, realize that its planned investment although technically competitive is economically noncompetitive (the exchange rate disconnected the company from its demand), and do not invest or reduce their investment to the minimum.[4]

Second, we understand that heterodox policymakers as well as the orthodox policymakers behind either the developmental or the liberal policy regime are reasonably competent economists. If they are liberal, they believe that the state should limit itself to guarantee property rights and contracts and keep the fiscal account balanced; if heterodox, that the state should additionally intervene moderately in the economy keeping the five macroeconomic prices right (interest rate, exchange rate, wage rate, inflation rate, and profit rate), maintaining balanced the fiscal account except when countercyclical fiscal policy is required, maintaining firmly balanced, if not showing a surplus, the current account, investing in the infrastructure, and making selective industrial policy.

Given these assumptions and what we understand by either liberal or new-developmental policy regimes, in the following section we will present the reasons why economic liberalism is unable to lead the Latin American countries to growth and catch up. We will discuss, first, the fact that Latin American countries interrupted their industrialization before it was consolidated, second, the growth with foreign savings policy, third, the use of an exchange rate anchor to control inflation, fourth, the high level of the interest rate around which Latin American central banks manage their monetary policy, fifth, the problems involved with the Dutch disease, and sixth, the rejection of capital controls, seventh, the rejection of industrial policy, and eighth, public savings. In the conclusion we say a few words about the political economy involved.

First, nonconsolidated industrial development

All countries that formed their nation-state and industrialized, beginning with England in the second half of the eighteenth century did that in the framework of a developmental policy regime.[5] Nevertheless from the 1980s, in the framework of the Washington Consensus, the rich countries pressed the Latin American countries to change from a developmental to a liberal policy regime before they had arrived to a strong level of economic development or of productive sophistication to resist to trade liberalization.

[4] Bresser-Pereira (2012, 2014), Bresser-Pereira et al. (2014b).

[5] The Industrial Revolution happened in the context of Mercantilism, the first historical developmentalism.

Classical developmental emerged as a new discipline in the post-war period, when ECLAC prominent economists, such as Prebisch and Furtado, to name a few, put forward a theoretical interpretation for the unequal development among the nations. Efforts to understand the economic development process of less developed countries led to the policy recommendation in favor of the industrialization of nonindustrialized countries, aiming at improving their economies' participation in trade flows. Industrialization policy would follow a developmental strategy known as import substitution. In Latin America, this strategy had been observed since the II World War until late 1970s, and this is the period of the highest growth rate in the continent.

In practice, late industrialization gave periphery countries highly heterogeneous and less diversified productive structures, in contrast to the more homogeneous and highly diversified structure of the central economies. Their productive structure would be characterized as "immature" and to attain a maturity phase, as conceived by Kaldor (1966), industrialization should be completed. Kaldor suggests four development phases in the industrialization process,[6] and argues, in the wake of the Keynesian tradition, that the maturing of an "immature" economy is based on the growth of aggregate demand. From this perspective, the capital accumulation generated by the industrialization process is the key variable of economic development, since it speeds up technological change to the benefit of the entire economy—as reflected in lower unit costs and higher-quality export products, enabling domestic producers to compete on foreign markets.

The industrialization process, based on import-substitution and state intervention in the Latin American economies, faced a chronic balance of payment problem associated with a high preference for immediate consumption before industrialization had been fully completed. In this sense, from a structuralist theoretical perspective, the economic history of Latin American economies is marked by adjustments in the growth rate caused by external constraints. This restriction is generally present because most countries have failed to overcome a pattern of productive specialization based on the exploitation of natural resources. Although developed economies such as the United States, Canada, and Australia, are examples of countries that have begun their development trajectory based on the exploitation of natural resources and raised the highest and most sustainable levels of

[6] See Feijó and Lamônica (2012).

development, their growth was not suddenly interrupted by trade liberalization as happened in the Latin American economies from the 1980s.

The industrialization strategy based on import substitution and state intervention in Latin America was abandoned after the external debt crisis of the 1980s, and the process of overcoming it spanned roughly the whole decade. The severity of the liquidity crisis that hit the highly indebted Latin American economies, following the sharp increase in the international interest rates and the default of the Mexican economy in 1981, left them with little room for maneuver and the "reorientation to the market" phase started.[7] The way out of the long economic recession that followed the debt crisis (known as the "lost decade") is associated with the economic opening implying trade and capital liberalization, privatization, and financial deregulation, which became the main economic policy recommendation of the Washington Consensus. The management of monetary and fiscal policies, on their turn, became chiefly subordinated to the views of the international financial markets. This subordination implied narrowing policy space for implementing developmental policies aiming at completing the industrialization process. In a word, the process of trade and financial integration of the Latin American economies from the 1980s onwards caught these economies in the process of catching up and implied the loss of autonomy for economic authorities to implement "effective countercyclical macroeconomic policies consistent with longer-term development objectives and developmental policies" (Ocampo and Vos, 2008: 29). The management of countercyclical fiscal policy, a low and stable long-term inflation rate, low real interest rates, and a competitive real exchange rate along the time proved to be difficult targets to be accomplished for most of the Latin American economies.

Fig. 10.2 compares the share of the exports in the trade flow of both Latin America and Caribbean and East Asian and Pacific economies to illustrate the point about the difference in the evolution of the productive structures of both regions. While in 1960 the share of exports of goods and services of the Latin America and Caribbean was a little lower (7.3%) than the East Asian and Pacific region (10.2%), but not very distant, in the following decades the difference increases steadily. This is a clear indication that the East Asian and Pacific countries have well succeeded in the process

[7] In the words of Bresser-Pereira (2002:6): "After 1982, when the debt crisis broke, macroeconomic instability emerged as the central economic problem. Latin American countries had no alternative but to adjust and reform."

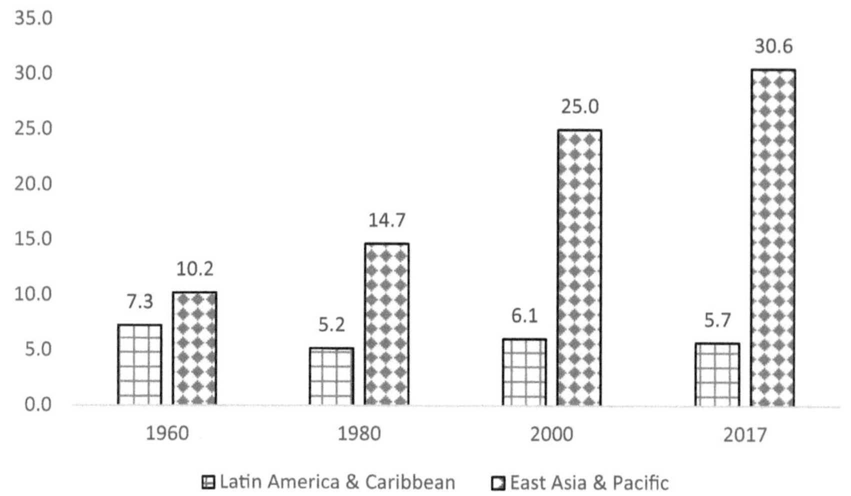

Figure 10.2 Share of exports of goods and services (current US$) of Latin America and Caribbean and East Asia and Pacific regions in world exports: selected years (%). *Source: World Development Indicators.*

of catching up, and the Latin American and Caribbean countries are falling behind and becoming less industrialized, relatively.[8]

Second, growth with foreign savings

The liberal theories and the corresponding liberal orthodoxy argue that the total savings rate can be increased by resorting to foreign savings. According to this thesis, the absorption of foreign savings complements domestic ones, increasing the economy's total savings. Actually, this view is an expression of exchange rate populism. It ignores that foreign savings rather replace than add to domestic savings. It does not consider that the capital inflows that are required to finance the current account deficits (the "foreign savings") appreciate the national currency and make the local companies not competitive, thus discouraging investment, while it increases the acquisitive power of salaried people and rentiers, thus stimulating consumption.

[8] According to UNIDO (https://stat.unido.org/database/MVA%202021,%20Manufacturing) in 1990 the share of manufacturing value added in total GDP in Asia was 18.1% and 16.5% in Latin America. In 2018 these shares were 22.5% and 12.8%, respectively, which illustrates how deep deindustrialization has advanced in Latin America since the 1990s. For a discussion on Latin America deindustrialization, see, among others, Palma (2005).

Our assumption in this paper is that, under normal circumstances, the rate of substitution of foreign for domestic savings tends to be high,[9] and this is what has been happening in Latin America since the 1990s. According to ECLAC, based on the consolidation of national accounts figures, from 1990 until 2018, the correlation between domestic and external savings is negative (−0.6). During this period, the share of domestic saving as a percentage of GDP was 19.7%, with little oscillation, and the average share of external savings was 1.9%.

To illustrate how the strategy to grow with foreign savings in Latin America has implied less economic growth, Fig. 10.3 illustrates with the trend line that when the economies show positive foreign saving, their GDP per capita growth rate is lower than when the opposite is observed. Therefore, the Figure shows that the GDP per capita growth has been negatively correlated with foreign savings in the Latin American economies since the 1990s.

According to the arguments of new developmentalist theory, especially those of Bresser-Pereira (2014, 2017) and Bresser-Pereira et al. (2014b), the strategy of growth with current account deficits, besides leading countries to

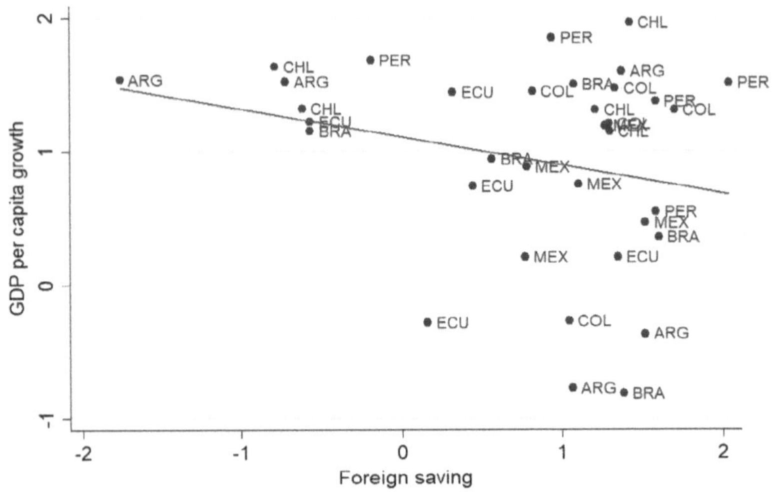

Figure 10.3 Latin America: Foreign Savings and GDP per capita growth: 1990–2018. *Source: IMF database.*

[9] See Bresser-Pereira et al. (2014a) for an empirical study on Brazil.

a balance-of-payment crisis, is associated with the long-term appreciation of the domestic currency. A consequence of the overvaluation is that it makes uncompetitive the companies that produce tradable noncommodity goods and services adopting the best available technology, thus discouraging investment and stimulating consumption. The deficits correspond to a long-term appreciated exchange rate because countries engaged in this strategy require an *additional* foreign currency inflow to finance them, which appreciates the country's currency.

Historical evidence of the dynamic Asian countries shows a very different growth performance. The Asian countries, in general, show current account surpluses, a correspondingly competitive exchange rate, and high rates of investment and domestic savings. Therefore, their growth strategy is based on "foreign dissaving," despite the common wisdom saying that capital-poor countries should receive savings from capital-rich ones. China, Malaysia, and Taiwan illustrate the case, as do Indonesia, South Korea, Malaysia and Thailand, which endured the 1997 balance-of-payments crisis when they abandoned this policy and resorted to foreign savings. A clear relation, therefore, exists between the exchange rate and growth, as well as between trade surpluses and accelerated growth.

Third, anchor to control inflation

Liberal orthodoxy views as legitimate to control inflation through the use of an exchange rate anchor, that is, the appreciation of the national currency. They are critical of the populist politicians that uses the prices of the state-owned enterprises, but feel comfortable in using "the price of the country" (the exchange rate) to control inflation. The majority of Latin American economies experienced high inflation and monetary instability during the 1980s, as Table 10.1 shows. Because of that, inflation control was crucial for Latin American economies to resume growth in the 1990s. Often, exchange rate-based anchors were the means used to achieve price stability in the region.

Although inflation came down quickly in countries that adopted exchange rate-based stabilization, it led to imbalances over the longer-term that increased countries' vulnerability to financial crises. The appreciation of the exchange rate proved harmful to the manufacturing sector, and it discouraged exports of manufacturing goods and generated deficits in the

Table 10.1 Latin America and selected countries: inflation rate (consumer prices).

Period	LA and Caribbean	Argentina	Brazil	Chile	Colombia	Ecuador	Mexico	Peru
1980–89	170.7		328.1	21.4	23.4	34.0	69.0	481.3
1990–99	130.2		843.2	11.8	22.1	39.0	20.4	807.9
2000–09	6.0	8.6	6.9	3.5	6.3	17.8	5.2	2.6
2010–18	5.3	11.2	6.1	3.0	3.8	2.8	4.0	2.9

Source: IMF—World Economic Outlook Database, October 2019.

trade balance and the current account balances. The result was an increase in the fragility of the Latin American economies which left the countries susceptible to exchange rate crises.

Unlike in Latin America where there was a recurring trend of currency overvaluation cycles in the 1980 and 1990s, the Asian countries concentrated on their export-led growth strategy with permanent stimulus to the export sector, avoiding exchange rate appreciation. While the former used the exchange rate as a stabilization tool, the latter used the exchange rate as a stimulus to the export sector.

Fourth, high level interest rate

The use of an exchange rate anchor to control inflation and the growth with foreign savings policy are made operational by increasing the level of the interest rate around which the central bank conducts its monetary policy. Monetary authorities search to legitimizing such high interest rates with the need to cool off aggregate demand, ignoring or not realizing that such usually interest rate level is not really required to control inflation but to attract foreign capitals which cause exchange rate appreciation. Indeed, to increase the interest rate is an obvious and legitimate policy to keep the prices right; but why move the interest rate down from, for instance, 7% percent level, instead of 3% level—a legitimate level considering, for instance, a 1% international interest rate and a 2% country risk?

During the 1980s and early 1990s, liberal policymakers adopted high real interest rates in Latin America which was a main cause for the overvalued exchange rate in the long term. A direct impact of exchange rate appreciation is on the price of tradable goods, discouraging exports. An indirect effect is on the domestic prices, through the relative decrease in the prices of imported goods, mainly raw materials and inputs. Also, if the appreciation trend persists, it induces the substitution of domestic products for similar imports.

According to the new developmentalism, the tendency to the overvaluation of the exchange rate is built over a succession of appreciation and depreciation cycles. The cycle starts with an exchange rate crisis that leads to depreciation. Because interest rates are historically higher in Latin American countries, the exchange rate appreciates again, and it stabilizes for some years in an overvalued bottom level, corresponding to a current account deficit and increasing foreign debt. Only a financial bubble explains why the creditors take time to react. But they eventually lose confidence, suspend the roll-over of the debt, and another currency crisis closes the cycle.

For the new developmentalism theory, following the Keynesian tradition, interest rates, around which the Central Bank makes its monetary policies, should be kept at a low level, while the exchange rate should be competitive. If this virtuous combination between the interest rate and the exchange rate is achieved and sustained, then it is expected that the competent noncommodity producers should be made competitive using the best technology available in the world. On its turn, the wage rate should grow with productivity, not more than that, so that the profit rate would be satisfactory for competitive enterprises, especially those in the manufacturing sector.

Fifth, neutralization of the Dutch disease

The trade liberalization adopted by the Latin American countries in the framework of the Washington Consensus involved the abandonment of the mechanism that neutralized the Dutch disease on the domestic market (high import tariffs, which all countries adopted) and on the foreign markets (export subsidies, which only Brazil adopted). Import tariffs are usually understood as protectionism except in the case of the infant industry; the new-developmental approach adds a second condition: import tariffs on manufactured goods are not protectionist when they neutralize the Dutch disease and, thus, assure to the manufacturing industry equal conditions of competition in relation to the manufacturing industries of other countries.

One of the main contributions of New Developmentalism on growth theory is to identify that most developing countries face a major economic disadvantage that may impair their catching up process: the Dutch disease.

According to Bresser-Pereira (2008: 48), "the Dutch disease is the chronic overvaluation of the exchange rate caused by the abundance of cheap natural and human resources whose exports are compatible with an exchange rate lower than the one that would pave the way for the non-commodity tradables industries." To measure the Dutch disease, the new developmentalism defines two equilibrium exchange rates—current and industrial—that when they diverge, the economy would be facing the disease. According to Bresser-Pereira (2018: 6):

The current equilibrium is dependent on the value of the foreign money and on the international price of the commodities exported. The industrial equilibrium is the exchange rate that the companies producing manufacturing goods (or, more generally, tradable noncommodity goods and services) utilizing state-of-the-art technology require to be competitive. The Dutch disease can be defined as the difference between the two equilibriums.

This definition of Dutch disease has interesting implications. First, it indicates that the "disease" imposes restrictions on the manufacturing sector to attain the stage of maturity to boost long-term growth. Second, it brings to the forefront of the explanation for the unequal development of nations the management of the macroeconomic policies, in particular, the role of the exchange rate in the catching-up process of developing economies. Therefore, for the new developmentalism, the Dutch disease is the result of short-term commodities booms and long-term Ricardian rents that make viable exports of such commodities at an exchange rate more appreciated than the one required by the country's existing or potential companies producing tradable noncommodity goods and services.

Before the 1980s debt crisis, the policymakers in Latin America did not know the Dutch disease but knew that growth involved industrialization. Thus, intuitively or pragmatically adopted high import tariffs that neutralized it. This mechanism is not the ideal way of neutralizing the disease, because it just neutralizes it on the domestic market, but it is politically more feasible, particularly when the exported commodity is agricultural and involves a large number of producers.

On the other hand, the import tariffs should not be seen as protectionist, as are not protectionists the tariffs deriving from the infant industry argument. They just create equal conditions of competition for the local companies. The difference is that in the case of the infant industry, the tariffs are necessarily temporary, while in the case of the Dutch disease, they will be required while the disease is in action.

Given the new developmentalism approach, import tariffs play an essential role in fostering structural change to increase long-term growth rates. Therefore, import tariffs are instruments to neutralize the Dutch disease, and not only a way to protect the infant industry, as usually pointed out in the economic literature. If adequately administered, they would work to protect domestic markets and, therefore, contribute to sustaining demand for local producers.

The Latin America and Caribbean region is traditionally exporter of commodities, and therefore a region prone to Dutch disease. In 1990, according to ECLAC database, 66.8% of the total exports of goods from the region were of primary goods. Although this share is being reduced, reaching 48.2% in 2018, the deindustrialization process has been advancing in the continent: the manufacturing sector share in total value added decreased from 20.3% in 1990 to 14.3% in 2018.

Sixth, capital controls

The liberal orthodoxy rejects the capital controls which are often strongly required, not so much to avoid capital flight (because the competently heterodox policy will reject current account deficits and will not engage in net foreign debt), but to limit the capital inflows that unduly appreciate the national currency.

Capital controls are one of the most controversial issues in the macroeconomic debate since Keynes's publication of the *General Theory*, in 1936, in the sense that it reflects the contemporaneous debate on the efficiency of the markets as opposed to governmental regulation to better coordinate the functioning of modern economies (Carvalho and Sicsú, 2004). More recently, since the neoliberal wave of the 1990s, the core of the debate is around the degree of autonomy that monetary authorities in developing countries have when capital flows are loosely regulated.[10]

Rey (2015:1), in an influential paper based on empirical evidence, concluded that developing economies, financially integrated and without currency convertibility, are more sensitive to the global cycle because "whenever capital is freely mobile, the global financial cycle constrains

[10] See, also, Kregel (2008), Ocampo and Stiglitz (2008) and Arestis (2016).

national monetary policies regardless of the exchange rate regime."[11] This is so because capital flows tend to have a pro-cyclical nature. In practical terms, in the absence of capital controls, when international liquidity is plentiful, excessive international flows tend to appreciate the currencies of these economies. Otherwise, when the international cycle is reversed, the currencies of these economies tend to suffer sharp depreciation.

Free capital movement has at least two consequences for developing economies that have limited capacity to issue liabilities in their own currency, both negative. A first negative externality is to exacerbate exchange rate volatility. Several consequences follow from this. Given the importance of the exchange rate as a signal to the general operating conditions of the economy, its volatility induces a significant deterioration in public expectations, that is to say, the variation in the exchange rate may fuel adverse expectations among residents and nonresidents about the soundness of the economy. Moreover, as observed by Carvalho and Sicsú (2004), even minor fluctuations in the exchange rate reduce the predictability of firms' financial operating costs, increasing uncertainty, and lowering investment incentives. As a result, the cost of capital in these economies tends to rise with increased volatility. Also, the imbalances created by the free movement of capital are not transitory, because the pricing system is not flexible enough to adjust the productive structure, once relative prices change due to exchange rate fluctuation.

To increase policy autonomy and reduce exchange rate volatility, most developing countries, including Latin America, after the currency crises that occurred in the second half of the 1990s have adopted a strategy of accumulating international reserves for precautionary purposes. Carvalho (2008) shows that the accumulation of reserves works as a "liquidity cushion" to protect economies against adverse short-term changes in the balance of payments and allows for the accommodation of sudden demands for foreign currency. According to the author, the accumulated reserves can give some "breath" for economic authorities to try to avoid the worst consequences of a sudden stop.

[11] On this, Carvalho (2008: 273) states: "It is consensual among economists that opening the capital account of the balance of payments reduces the domestic autonomy in the choice of goals and instruments for monetary policy. In fact, it is practically a tautology, since opening the capital account increases international financial integration and this means precisely that the national economy becomes part of some bigger economic unit."

However, regardless the strategic importance of the accumulation of large volumes of foreign reserves for developing economies, in most cases, the accumulation of reserves is not a choice, but a consequence of the capital inflows that are beyond the control of the economic authorities. In some other cases, reserve growth may be the result of the expansion of net exports, resulted from a boom in commodities.[12] In short, the accumulation of high levels of reserves in a volatile environment of capital flows is an important instrument, though far from a sufficient one, to counterbalance the uncertainty surrounding the behavior of the capital account in developing economies financially integrated.

The new developmentalism identifies a second negative externality of free capital movement in developing economies: the long-term overvaluation trend of the exchange rate. This externality might be considered the most damaging effect of the free capital movement on developing economies because if, on the one hand, the increased volatility of the exchange rate turns long-term decisions more uncertain as mentioned, on the other, when the exchange rate is overvalued in the long-term, decisions will be indefinitely postponed. As put in Bresser-Pereira (2018:2): "The exchange rate acts as a *switch* that grants or withholds *access* to existing demand, be it international or domestic." (italics in the original).

The trend toward the overvaluation of the exchange rate in developing countries financially integrated occurs because the exchange rate does not just oscillate around the equilibrium. As claimed by Bresser-Pereira (op. cit), after a balance of payment crisis, the exchange rate depreciates sharply. However, because interest rates are higher in developing economies, international capital ends up returning, setting up a valuation trajectory. This trajectory will reach a floor, and due to the Dutch disease, the level of the exchange rate will be the lowest that the more efficient commodity exporters can tolerate. For how long can the overvaluation cycle last? According to the new developmentalism, the exchange rate can remain substantially overvalued for several years, affecting resources allocation in the long run. Growth rates will be reduced.

[12] Besides, the management of foreign reserves as a policy instrument imposes restrictions on domestic policies, since the impact of capital flows should be sterilized. If economies work with relatively high rates of interest, consequently the cost of sterilization will be higher, and this cost is reflected in an increase in the burden of public debt.

Given this perspective, capital controls,[13] together with the accumulation of reserves, are essential instruments to widening policy space, and increase growth potential of developing economies.[14] Carvalho (2008) registers three groups of measures of capital controls. The first group should apply to inflows by nonresidents. This would inhibit the inflow of short-term financial capital, searching for interest rate arbitrage opportunities. A second group of capital account regulations should control outflows by residents. As noticed by Carvalho, based on the empirical observation of the balance of payment crisis in the late 1990s, residents are the first group of investors to promote capital flight. A last group of regulations should limit the possibility of domestic firms that sell to local markets to issue liabilities in foreign currencies. This would avoid the problem of exchange rate mismatches between assets and liabilities.

Seventh, industrial policy

The liberal orthodoxy rejects industrial policy which is much required if a country is really involved into a national project of growth. New Developmentalism's microeconomics involves a clear distinction between the competitive and the noncompetitive sectors of the economy. In the noncompetitive sector, which includes the infrastructure and basic inputs companies and the large commercial banks "too big to fail," there is no market and the state is supposed to coordinate with the use of planning and strong regulation. In the competitive sector, the coordination by market is much superior to the one by state, but in some industries, for some time, industrial policy is necessary if the country is really committed to growth.

New developmentalism advocates industrial policy as an instrument to enhance long-term growth rates. Therefore, to improve aggregate productivity, industrial policy should focus on all activities that produce dynamic effects on the economy as a whole. Latin American economies are latecomers among the industrialized economies, and therefore, industrial

[13] Chile is a well succeeded example of capital controls established in the late 1980s.

[14] It should be added that new developmentalism also proposes the creation of a sovereign fund (following the Norway example) to be built with the revenue of an export tax imposed on export of commodities. The creation of this fund would prevent capital inflow and therefore contribute to fighting the appreciation trend of the exchange rate. On the other hand, the tax on export of commodities would be the instrument to neutralize the Dutch disease. This tax would increase the cost of production of commodities and, in this sense, it would make the current equilibrium exchange rate to converge to the industrial equilibrium.

policies are necessary to promote the diversification and to reduce heterogeneity in their productive structure.

Also, new developmentalist approach advocates that industrial policies should be well-coordinated with macroeconomic policies. In this sense, industrial policy should be seen as an essential complement to the macroeconomic policy regime, which should aim at keeping the five main macroeconomic prices "right."[15] Following these orientations, the economy should be able to induce capital accumulation and simultaneously allow policy space for the implementation of appropriate industrial and technological policies to accelerate the catching-up process.

The advancement of the deindustrialization process in Latin America since the 1990s strongly suggests that industrial policies are relevant to restore a higher growth trajectory. According to Nassif et al. (2018), in the structuralist and new developmentalism approach, industrial policy is defined as the combination of governmental incentives at the sectoral level, with horizontal policies.[16] In the first case, it is included tariff protection on imports, subsidies within limits imposed by the World Trade Organization, and, most important, long-term public credit for investment projects and innovation. As well remarked by Ocampo et al. (2009:153), public funding should be considered a significant instrument of industrial policy, as international agreements have not yet limited development banking.[17] In the second case, horizontal industrial policies should target investment in infrastructure and research and development.

Among all instruments of industrial policy, tariffs are wrongly the most polemic. New Developmentalism rejects protectionism, but, as we saw when we discussed the Dutch disease, it advocates in favor of tariffs when they are a means to neutralize the disease in relation to the domestic market. Thus, it is not only the infant industry argument, but also the neutralization of the Dutch disease argument that legitimize industrial policies based on tariffs on the imports of manufactured goods.

[15] See Bresser-Pereira (2019:46–47) for an explanation for the "right" levels of the macroeconomic prices.

[16] Ocampo (2005) also advocates in favor of horizontal and sectorial industrial policies, as the dynamic of productive structures results from the interaction between activities, firms, **sectors,** and institutions.

[17] It should also be mentioned that Hausmann and Rodrik (2003) argue in favor of public credit as a better instrument to support innovative firms in comparison to the use of tariff protection. Tariff protection, according to the authors, would not be so efficient, because, in practice, it is difficult to separate true innovators from imitators.

A different orientation for the industrial policy should be applied to noncompetitive sectors, including the basic infrastructure inputs and the financial industry. In these cases, the coordination by the market is much inferior to the one by the state, which should step in with strong and transparent regulation.

Eighth, public savings

Liberal orthodoxy disregards the importance of public investment. It believes legitimate to transfer to the private sector the monopolist infrastructure public services, using the argument that "private are more efficient than public companies." This is false. To privatize the infrastructure is to lose control of the investments required for growth. The investor in the privatized monopolies is not really business entrepreneurs. When they get hold of a company, they are usually made responsible for the investment. They do the minimum possible, they delay the investments, and they increase the prices in the first opportunity while the quality of the services deteriorate.

There are two main approaches in the economic literature that address the role of fiscal policy and analyze its impact on the determination of private investment: the neoclassical approach and the Keynesian approach. The first is opposed to activist fiscal policy, assuming that exits a crowding-out effect between public and private investment. It also stresses the inflationary consequences of fiscal expansion and the problems related to the expansion of public debt. The second approach, based on the principle of effective demand of John Maynard Keynes (1936) and Michal Kalecki (1954), is in favor of contracyclical fiscal policy, and control on public debt.

Concerning the crowding-out effect, the idea is that a rise in investment by the public sector can inhibit private investment, assuming that the use of physical inputs and financial savings by the public sector will limit the availability of these resources to the private sector. Also, public investment would pressure up the price of inputs and, above all, interest rates. Interest rates should rise because it is assumed that public expending is to be financed through increased compensation for public bonds. If so, credit would be reduced to the private sector that would then reduce investments. This is how the crowding-out effect would work. Besides, expansionary fiscal policies bring up inflationary risks, as well exposed in the neoclassical synthesis model set up by Hicks (1937), as well as in the monetarists and new-classical models.

Differently, public spending increases the level of activity, what leads to higher aggregate savings—instead of reducing the loanable funds available to private agents (Neto and Vernengo, 2004–5). According to Keynes's investment theory, the private decision to invest in capital goods depends on long-term expectations of profits which are driven by the "animal spirits." Short-term interest rates or cost-of-capital variables play no role on decisions that involve the "animal spirits." On this, Fazzari (1994/1995: 232) based on a detailed examination of the behavior of US individual firms on investment, concludes: " .... there is little if any loss to investment from possible deficit induced increases in interest rates, while there may be substantial gains for investment caused by the economic stimulus resulting from deficit."

Gavin and Perotti (1997) analyzed the fiscal policy in Latin American countries from 1970 to 95 and found that it had been procyclical, and particularly so in periods of low growth. Alberola et al. (2016) investigated the relationship between fiscal policy and the cycle in Latin America and also concluded that fiscal policy is procyclical. According to the authors, the main explanation for that is financing conditions "Worsening financing

Table 10.2 Public and private Investment-to-GDP ratio (%), selected regions 1990, 2000, 2010, 2015.

Public investment

Region	1990	2000	2010	2015
East Asia & Pacific	9	14	14	11
Eastern Europe & Central Africa	3	2	3	3
Latin America & Caribbean	4	3	4	4
Middle East & North Africa	5	4	8	7
South Asia	6	5	6	4
Sub-Saharan Africa	4	4	5	5

Private investment

Region	1990	2000	2010	2015
East Asia & Pacific	13	12	22	26
Eastern Europe & Central Africa	19	10	11	12
Latin America & Caribbean	10	14	15	15
Middle East & North Africa	8	9	11	11
South Asia	10	12	18	18
Sub-Saharan Africa	9	9	12	13

Note: *EAP*, East Asia and Pacific; *ECA*, Eastern Europe and Central Asia; *LAC*, Latin America and Caribbean; *MNA*; Middle East and North Africa; *SAS*, South Asia; and *SSA*, Sub-Saharan Africa. Based on Castellani et al. (2019).

conditions, which tend to coincide with difficult economic times, constrain fiscal policy. Favorable financing conditions, more prominent in good times, favor fiscal profligacy" (Alberola et al., 2016).

Table 10.2 shows for selected regions and years that public investment-to-GDP ratios have remained relatively stable. Latin America and the Caribbean is the region with the second-lowest public investment-to-GDP ratio. Also, the share of private investment-to-GDP increased throughout the period, from 10% in 1990 to 15% by 2015, confirming that private investment drove the increase in total investment in the region, while public investment remained stable.

Conclusion

In this paper, we offered eight arguments why liberal policy regimes, which became dominant in Latin America from the 1990s, are incapable of making the region to grow and catch up. On the contrary, what we are seeing is quasistagnation. We did not include in our discussion the political economy involved. We say now, in this conclusion, a few words on this subject. In contemporary capitalism, the orthodox policymakers represent mainly the interest of rentier capitalists (who live out of interests, dividends, and real estate) and financiers, who manage the wealth of rentiers and act as their organic intellectuals, while the heterodox hope to represent the interest of the working or salaried classes. The policies defended by liberal policymakers reflect such political economy. The ideal would be that they were "neutral" policymakers above the class interests, but we know that this is impossible.

The class commitments cause major distortions in the policymaking process. The commonsense distinction between right and left policymaking is between the state spending more or less than it should, between fiscal populism and austerity. Actually, fiscal discipline is a condition for long-term growth. Fiscal populism is contradictory to the idea of the state achieving public savings to finance its required investments. When a developing country faces a macroeconomic disadjustment, the effective policy is a combination of fiscal adjustment with currency depreciation. The fiscal adjustment hits more the poor than the rich; the depreciation, more the rich, less the poor. Austerity is a way of doing excess fiscal adjustment and no currency depreciation; it is to recover the competitiveness of the country by reducing just the wages of workers instead of also the profit and wealth of the rentier capitalists by depreciating the currency.

Differently from fiscal populism, exchange rate populism is not a problem of choice, but a question of destiny for liberal orthodoxy. Since the liberal economist believes that the market coordinates well the exchange rate, he rejects exchange rate policy. Besides, he believes that to try to grow with foreign indebtedness is the right thing to do. Thus, when the current account deficits show up, he sees them as natural. They are not; current account deficits are the main cause of loss of economic competitiveness and of cyclical financial crises. Together with high interest rates, they are in the core of the financialization process.

Summing up, a liberal policy regime is incompatible with growth in the Latin American countries. Economic liberalism is bad also for rich countries and for countries that do not suffer from the Dutch disease. Policy regimes are either liberal or developmental. A Keynesian policy regime is a developmental regime to the extent that it defends a moderate state intervention. The fact that the regime is developmental does not mean that it will work well. It depends on the capability of the policymakers. This, however, is not the case of the liberal policy regimes. They count too much with the coordinative capability of markets, ignoring that they are unable to coordinate the noncompetitive sectors of the economy and to keep right the five macroeconomic prices. In consequence, they adopt the policies that we discussed in this paper, which are inimical of growth and catching up.

When we compare the developmental and the liberal phases of the economic history of the rich countries, considering, for instance, England and France, we see that growth was faster in the two developmental phases (the Mercantilist 1700—1830 phase and the 1945—75 Golden or Keynesian phase, than the two liberal phases: the 1830—1929 phase and the 1980—2018 neoliberal phase). If this is true to rich countries, is truer to developing countries and still truer to Latin American countries.

References

Alberola, E., Kataryniuk, I., Melguizo, A., Orozco, R., 2016. Fiscal Policy and the Cycle in Latin America: The Role of Financing Conditions and Fiscal Rules. BIS Working Papers No 543. Available at: https://www.bis.org/publ/work543.pdf.

Arestis, P., 2016. Financial liberalization, the finance—growth nexus, financial crises and policy implications. In: Arestis, P., Sawyer, M. (Eds.), Financial Liberalisation. International Papers in Political Economy. Palgrave Macmillan, Cham.

Bresser-Pereira, L.C., 2019. Macroeconomia novo-desenvolvimentista. In: Feijo, C., Araujo, E. (Eds.), Macroeconomia Moderna: lições de Keynes para economias em desenvolvimento. Elsevier and Associação Keynesiana Brasileira, pp. 45—56, 2018.

Bresser-Pereira, L.C., Araujo, E., Gala, P., 2014a. An empirical study on the substitution of foreign for domestic savings in Brazil. EconomiA (15), 54—67.

Bresser-Pereira, L.C., 2002. Latin America's quasi-stagnation. In: Davidson, P. (Ed.), A Post Keynesian Perspective on 21st Century Economic Problems. Edward Elgar Press, Cheltenham, pp. 01–28.
Bresser-Pereira, L.C., January-March. The Dutch disease and its neutralization: a Ricardian approach. Brazilian Review of Political Economy 28 (1), 47–71.
Bresser-Pereira, L.C., 2012. The exchange rate at the center of development economics. Estudos Avançados 26 (75), 7–28.
Bresser-Pereira, L.C., 2014. The access to demand. In: Papadimitrious, D.B. (Ed.), Contributions to Economic Theory, Policy, Development and Finance: Essays in Honor of Jan A. Kregel. Palgrave Macmillan, London, pp. 196–206, 2014.
Bresser-Pereira, L.C., October 2017. The two forms of capitalism: developmentalism and economic liberalism. Brazilian Journal of Political Economy 37 (4), 680–703.
Bresser-Pereira, L.C., 2018. Neutralizing the Dutch Disease, Working Paper 476, Fundação Getúlio Vargas, São Paulo, May, Available at: https://bibliotecadigital.fgv.br/dspace/bitstream/handle/10438/23921/TD%20476-Luiz%20Carlos%20Bresser%20Pereira.pdf?sequence=1&isAllowed=y.
Bresser-Pereira, L.C., Araújo, E., Peres, S.C., 2020. An alternative view to the middle-income trap. Structural Change and Economic Dynamics 52 (2020), 294–312.
Bresser-Pereira, L.C., Oreiro, L.C., Marconi, N., 2014b. Developmental Macroeconomics. Routledge, London.
Carvalho, F.J., 2008. Macroeconomic policy with open capital accounts. In: Hein, E., Niechoj, T., Spahn, P., Truger, A. (Eds.), Finance-led Capitalism: Macroeconomic Effects of Changes in the Financial Sector, Series of the Research Network Macroeconomics and Macroeconomics Policies, second ed., vol. 11. Marburg, Metropolis, pp. 273–295.
Carvalho, F.J., Sicsu, J., April-June. Controvérsias recentes sobre controle de capitais. Brazilian Journal of Political Economy 24 (2), 163–184.
Castellani, F., Olarreaga, M., Panizza, U., Zhou, Y., 2019. Investment Gaps in Latin America and the Caribbean. International Development Policy, Revue internationale de politique de développement. https://doi.org/10.4000/poldev.2894. Online since 11 March, Avaliable at. http://journals.openedition.org/poldev/2894.
Fazzari, S.M., 1994/1995. Why doubt the effectiveness of Keynesian fiscal policy? Journal of Post Keynesian Economics 17 (2 (Winter)), 231–248.
Feijo, C., Lamônica, M., August 2012. The importance of the manufacturing sector for Brazilian economic development. Cepal Review (107), 107–126.
Gavin, M., Perotti, R., 1997. Fiscal policy in Latin America. In: Bernanke, B., Rotemberg, J. (Eds.), NBER Macroeconomics Annual, vol. 12. MIT Press, pp. 11–72. Available at: https://www.nber.org/chapters/c11036.
Hausmann, R., Rodrik, D., December 2003. Economic development as self-discovery. Journal of Development Economics 72 (Issue 2), 603–633.
Hicks, J.R., April 1937. Mr. Keynes and the classics: a suggested interpretation. Econometrica 5 (2), 147–159.
Kaldor, N., 1966. Causes of the Slow Rate of Economic Growth of the United Kingdom. Cambridge University Press.
Kalecki, M., 1954. Theory of economic dynamics: an essay on cyclical and long-run changes. In: The Capitalist Economy. Allen and Unwin, London.
Keynes, J.M., 1936. The General Theory of Employment, Interest and Money. Prometheus Books, New York, 1997.
Kregel, J., 2008. What can Keynes tell us about policies to reduce unemployment and financial instability in a globalised international economy. METU Studies in Development 35, 161–176.

Nassif, A., Bresser-Pereira, L.C., Feijo, C., 2018. The Case for Reindustrialisation in developing countries: towards the connection between the macroeconomic regime and the industrial policy in Brazil. Cambridge Journal of Economics 42, 355–381.

Neto, A.F.C., Vernengo, M., 2004. Fiscal policy and the Washington Consensus: a post Keynesian perspective. Journal of Post Keynesian Economics 27 (2), 333–343.

Ocampo, J.A., Vos, R., 2008. Policy space and the changing paradigm in conducting macroeconomic policies in developing countries, in BIS papers no. 36 New financing trends in Latin America: a bumpy road towards stability. In: Proceedings of a Joint Meeting Organized by the BIS and the Federal Reserve Bank of Atlanta in Mexico City, May, 2007.

Ocampo, J.A., 2005. The quest for dynamic efficiency: structural dynamics and economic growth in developing countries. In: Ocampo, J.A. (Ed.), Beyond Reforms: Structural Dynamics and Macroeconomic Vulnerability. World Bank Publications, Washington, DC, pp. 3–43.

Ocampo, J.A., Rada, C., Taylor, L., 2009. Growth and Policy in Developing Countries. Columbia University Press, New York.

Palma, G., 2005. Four sources of de-industrialisation and a new concept of the Dutch disease. In: Ocampo, J.A. (Ed.), Beyond Reforms. Stanford University Press, Palo Alto, pp. 71–116.

Rey, H., May 2015. Dilemma Not Trilemma: The Global Financial Cycle and Monetary Policy Independence, NBER Working Paper 21162. Revised in February 2018, Available at: https://www.nber.org/papers/w21162.

CHAPTER ELEVEN

Mexico: unequal integration and "stabilizing stagnation"

Robert A. Blecker
Department of Economics, American University, Washington, DC, United States

Dedication

To the memory of Julio López Gallardo and Jaime Ros Bosch.

Introduction

In the 1950 and 1960s, Mexico achieved an "economic miracle" of rapid growth with low inflation and a stable currency, which the government branded as a strategy of *desarrollo estabilizador* ("stabilizing development"). Nevertheless, the seeds of subsequent instability had already been sown, since the Mexican economy was growing faster than a rate consistent with external (balance of payments) equilibrium, resulting in increasing current account deficits by the 1970s (Reynolds, 1978; Ibarra and Blecker, 2016). Between the 1970s and 1990s, the country experienced a series of repeated economic and financial (debt) crises, roughly coinciding with the country's sexennial presidential election cycle. From 1975—76 to 1994—95, a crisis broke out about every 6 years, usually either right before or right after a presidential election. Each time, the balance of payments deteriorated, inflation accelerated, the peso was devalued, and a severe recession occurred.

By the early 21st century, Mexico appeared to have emerged from this destructive cycle of repeated crises and reestablished macroeconomic equilibrium. According to the conventional wisdom, an inflation-targeting monetary policy kept inflation low and stable, a floating exchange rate secured balance-of-payments equilibrium, and balanced budget rules ensured the absence of large fiscal deficits. External debts were maintained at sustainable levels starting in the late 1990s. A mild recession in 2001 and a more severe one in 2008—09 were provoked by US economic downturns, not generated by domestic policy inconsistencies. Nevertheless, there

Handbook of Economic Stagnation
ISBN: 978-0-12-815898-2
https://doi.org/10.1016/B978-0-12-815898-2.00002-1

were two major problems with this achievement of macroeconomic stability: first, in spite of relatively rapid growth of exports, the domestic economy ceased to grow at a rate adequate for Mexico to converge with the US or other advanced economies; and second, in spite of some gains in reducing absolute poverty and a narrowing of wage inequality, the overall distribution of income became notably more unequal. Parodying the government's claims of past decades, critics have derided the more recent period of anemic long-term growth as a situation of *estancamiento estabilizador* ("stabilizing stagnation").[1]

This chapter will examine why the Mexican economy has entered this phase of long-run or "secular" stagnation. The chapter will focus especially on whether stagnant growth has occurred in spite of, or rather because of, the neoliberal policies (so-called reforms) that were adopted to stabilize the economy in the aftermath of the crises of the late 20th century. Given the long-run nature of the discussion here, this chapter will not attempt to evaluate the economic policies of president Andrés Manuel López Obrador (AMLO), who took office in December 2018, or the impact of the covid-19 pandemic in 2020–21.[2] Rather, this chapter will consider alternative hypotheses about long-run stagnation in Mexico, including "supply-side" explanations proffered by neoclassical economists and "demand-side" explanations given by heterodox economists. This discussion will highlight how the country's supposedly stabilizing monetary and fiscal policies—including a sharp reduction in public investment and infrastructure spending—and a frequently overvalued currency have combined with external constraints that were tightened by trade liberalization to yield the pattern of slow and unequal growth observed since the turn of the millennium.

The growth slowdown in Mexico

Mexico was one of the star growth performers in the post-World War II period, up to the 1970s. The data in Table 11.1 (taken from a database that starts in 1961) show that Mexico's average annual growth rate of total gross

[1] The earliest appearance of this phrase that the author has found is the following from Suárez Dávila (2005, p. 43): "Many analysts agree that history will characterize the economic policy of president [Vicente] Fox as one of 'stabilizing stagnation'" (this and all other translations from Spanish were done by the author). The author thanks Juan Carlos Moreno-Brid for supplying the reference and Gerardo Esquivel for confirming it.

[2] For an early evaluation of AMLO's economic policies, see Moreno-Brid (2019).

Table 11.1 Mexico's average annual growth rate compared with major global regions and North American countries, selected periods 1961–2018 (in percent per year).

	Total GDP			Per capita GDP		
	1961–79	**1980–99**	**2000–18**	**1961–79**	**1980–99**	**2000–18**
Mexico	6.6	2.9	2.2	3.5	0.9	0.8
Latin America and Caribbean	5.8	2.4	2.6	3.2	0.5	1.4
Middle income	5.5	3.0	5.4	3.2	1.2	4.2
East Asia and Pacific	6.6	4.4	4.5	4.4	2.9	3.7
South Asia	3.5	5.5	6.3	1.2	3.2	4.8
Sub-Saharan Africa	4.3	1.8	4.5	1.6	−1.0	1.7
European Union	4.3	2.3	1.6	3.6	2.0	1.3
Canada	4.8	2.6	2.1	3.2	1.5	1.1
United States	3.9	3.2	2.1	2.7	2.1	1.2

Notes: Mexico is included in the Middle income and Latin America and Caribbean groups. Data for Canada start in 1962.
Source: World Bank, *World Development Indicators Database*, last updated October 2, 2019, accessed October 7, 2019, and author's calculations.

domestic product (GDP) of 6.6% was on a par with that of the East Asia and Pacific region and above-average for all Latin America and Caribbean and middle income countries (groups in which Mexico is included) for the period 1961–79. Given its relatively high population growth at that time, Mexico's per capita GDP growth rate of 3.5% per year was a little less spectacular, but still above-average for those two comparable groups and only a little less than the per capita growth of East Asia and Pacific. During the period of most frequent crises (1980–99), Mexico's average annual per capita growth fell to only 0.9% per year. Although this was a period in which many other developing countries also experienced crises and slower growth, Mexico slipped further behind East and South Asia at that time.

Since 2000, the middle income countries as a whole and several key developing regions have recovered their growth compared to the previous 2 decades, but Mexico stands out as a striking exception. With annual growth averaging only 2.2% for total GDP and 0.8% for per capita GDP in the 2000–18 period, Mexico is far below the corresponding averages for East Asia and Pacific, South Asia, Sub-Saharan Africa, and all middle income countries, and is also (more modestly) below the average for Latin America and Caribbean. In what will be argued below is more than a coincidence, the growth of Mexico's total GDP for the 2000–18 period is almost exactly the same as that of its fellow members of the North American

Free Trade Agreement (NAFTA), Canada and the United States (2.2% per year for Mexico vs. 2.1% for each of the latter). Also, although most of developing regions have accelerated their growth in the most recent period, compared to the last 2 decades of the twentieth century, all of the advanced economies shown (United States, Canada, and European Union) exhibit signs of long-run stagnation in the most recent period (as discussed elsewhere in this book).

A key consequence of Mexico's economic stagnation is its lack of long-run convergence with the US economy. As a middle-income emerging economy, Mexico aspires to raise the average income level of its citizens toward that of the advanced, high income countries, in Mexico's case especially its richer neighbor to the north. As shown in Fig. 11.1, Mexico's labor productivity (output per worker) and, to a lesser extent, real GDP per capita (output per person) increased as percentages of US levels during the miracle years between 1950 and 1970, indicating a process of convergence during that period. After some fluctuations in the early-to-mid 1970s, these

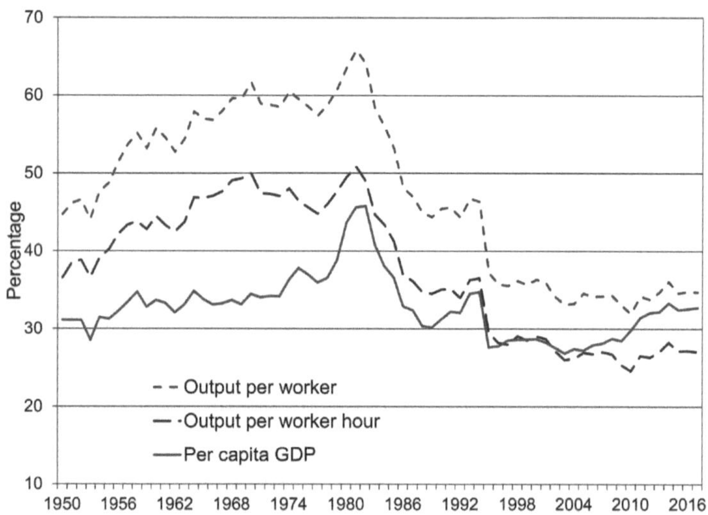

Figure 11.1 Mexican per capita GDP and labor productivity as percentages of US levels, in purchasing power parity terms, annually, 1950–2017. Notes: GDP per capita is measured by expenditure-side real GDP at chained purchasing power parity exchange rates (PPPs), in millions of 2011 US dollars, divided by population. Labor productivity is measured by output-side real GDP at chained PPPs, also in millions of 2011 US dollars, divided by either total employment ("workers") or total worker hours (average annual hours multiplied by total employment). *Source: Author's calculations based on Penn World Tables v. 9.1, accessed October 10, 2019. See Feenstra et al. (2015) for a description of this dataset and the methodology.*

percentages briefly peaked during the (unsustainable) oil boom and foreign borrowing binge of 1978–81, before collapsing during the debt crisis and "lost decade" of the 1980s and falling again during the peso crisis of 1994–95. Since then, Mexico's GDP per capita has recovered somewhat, relative to that of the US, but as of 2017 (the last year for which these data were available), it was about the same percentage of the US level (33%) as it was 50 years earlier in 1967. Even more strikingly, as of 2017 Mexico's average productivity (output per worker or per worker hour) relative to the US level had not recovered even to the same percentage as before the peso crisis (1994), and remained notably lower than it was 67 years earlier in 1950. Thus, Mexico has actually diverged from the US in terms of labor productivity, while in terms of GDP per capita it simply has not converged.[3]

This is not to deny that any progress has been made in the Mexican economy. In absolute terms, per capita GDP continued to exhibit positive albeit sluggish growth during the post-1980 period, as shown in Table 11.1. Mexico has become a world-class exporter in several sectors, especially the automotive industry, telecommunications equipment, and other electronic goods. Moreover, productivity has increased rapidly in large firms and export-oriented manufacturing—but real wages in those industries have not followed suit, and average productivity in the economy as a whole has been held down by low and even falling productivity in other sectors, especially services and the informal sector (Moreno-Brid and Ros, 2009; Bolio et al., 2014; Levy, 2018).

Alternative explanations for Mexico's slow growth

The term "secular stagnation" has not been widely applied to the Mexican case, but essentially the same idea has been explored in a large literature seeking to explain the country's slow average growth rate over the past 3 decades (see, among others, Moreno-Brid and Ros, 2009; Arias

[3] The differences between the labor productivity (output per worker or per hour) and per capita GDP series shown in Fig. 11.1 are worth explaining. Between 1950 and 1980, Mexico's labor productivity performed better (it was higher and more rapidly increasing, relative to the US) than its per capita GDP because Mexico had very rapid population growth at that time, resulting in a young population and relatively slower growth of the labor force and employment compared to population. In more recent decades, the country's population growth has slowed down but the proportion of the population of working age has increased, while there has been considerable "informalization" of the labor force, resulting in the worse performance of labor productivity relative to GDP per capita (both compared to the US) since the late 1990s.

et al., 2010; Hanson, 2010; Ros, 2013; Levy, 2018; López, 2018). In this section, we turn to the competing explanations for Mexico's weak growth performance in the postliberalization era—starting with the late 1980s, when Mexico started to open its economy but still faced significant macroeconomic instability, and focusing mainly on the period after 2000, when the country finally achieved conventional macro stability yet failed to recuperate its growth.

The conventional wisdom: supply side causes

According to orthodox or "neoclassical" economics, long-run growth is always determined by supply-side factors; hence, if the Mexican economy has not grown adequately in recent decades, it must be because of supply-side constraints. This kind of thinking has informed many analyses of the Mexican economy, which have identified a never-ending series of candidates for the key supply-side obstacles to Mexican growth. In this view, the country's macroeconomic stabilization and trade liberalization policies cannot be responsible for the slow growth; on the contrary they have supposedly laid the foundations for rapid and sustained growth that—for some *other* reason—has not occurred. A fairly standard rendition of this view is the following:

> *Implicit in Mexico's bet on economic openness was the idea that its advances in trade policy, coupled with the macroeconomic stability achieved through improvements in fiscal and monetary policy, would be sufficient to drive economic growth. Unfortunately, the export-fueled motor has not proven strong enough to overcome the significant drag created by multiple structural deficiencies and has instead propelled a part of Mexico forward while leaving much of the country behind .... Weaknesses in the Mexican education system, insufficient energy and transportation infrastructure, a lack of access to credit, the still-limited rule of law, and a misalignment of incentives in the social insurance and tax regimes have combined to stifle growth and allow inequality to persist.*
>
> ***Wilson (2019, p. 2).***

The reference to part of Mexico being left behind is an allusion to Mexico's developmental "dualism" in the sense of Lewis (1954): the coexistence of a "formal" (modern, capitalist) sector that employs wage labor (*asalariados* or "salaried" employees, in the Mexican terminology) in large, profit-making firms that utilize advanced technology with high and rising productivity, along with an "informal" (traditional, backward) sector in which self-employed workers or very small firms operate with obsolete technology, low productivity, and depressed incomes. In Mexico, the formal sector is legally codified as firms that employ salaried workers are obligated to pay for significant social benefits, such as health care and pension plans, to withhold taxes for their employees, and to respect various worker rights, including protections against arbitrary dismissal (Levy, 2018). However, it is widely recognized that enforcement of these legal requirements is often lax, especially for relatively smaller firms, and even firms that pay for workers' social insurance may choose to stay smaller than the threshold beyond which other tax rates increase (Levy, 2018). In contrast, the informal sector consists of (mostly small) firms that hire salaried workers illegally and hence do not fulfill the legal obligations to their workers, as well as other types of enterprises, such as family firms and self-employment. Since around 2000, the government has created some social programs to benefit informal sector workers, which are paid out of general government revenue rather than by taxes on employers.

The dualism of the Mexican economy "explains" the slow growth of the country's productivity and the low average level of Mexican productivity relative to the US and other advanced economies, but only in an accounting sense. The largest and most globally oriented firms in the formal sector have productivity levels similar to firms in more advanced economies, levels that have risen at rates comparable to more successful national economies, such as those of countries in East Asia and Pacific. In contrast, informal producers—especially the smallest ones—have very low and, in many cases, falling productivity levels. But there is a very large number of informal firms, which employ a significant (and by some measures increasing) portion of the Mexican labor force; hence, their low productivity holds down the national average level of productivity while their sluggish or negative productivity growth diminishes the national average growth rate of productivity (Bolio et al., 2014; Levy, 2018).

The existence of dualism is not a causal factor, however; the central question is what has caused the persistence (and increase) of informality in the contemporary Mexican economy. For neoclassical economists, the answer must lie in the microeconomic incentives created by the government's labor and tax policies. According to Levy (2018), the social insurance costs, tax burdens, and labor regulations (e.g., difficulties in terminating employees) for legally registered formal firms discourage such firms from expanding employment and also induce many firms to operate illegally or not hire salaried workers in the first place. Some firms may choose to stay small in order to evade higher tax rates or to avoid enforcement of the social insurance requirements. Levy also claims that the availability of "free" social services for informal workers, which has increased since 2000, has made informal employment more attractive thereby explaining some of its recent increase.

However, these supposed incentives are not a convincing explanation for persistent or rising informality in Mexico. Ros (2013)—responding in part to earlier arguments of the same author (Santiago Levy)—points out that the timing of when many of the supposedly "distortionary" policies were enacted does not well match the timing of when informality increased the most. Ros also observes that the poor quality and limited availability of many of the social services for informal workers make it unlikely that they would prefer those over the higher quality, more widely available (although still imperfect) services provided to formal sector workers, especially in regard to health benefits. To be sure, the services provided to formal sector workers are uneven in quality and reliability, but those provided for "free" to informal workers are often even worse in quality and availability. Arias et al. (2010) concur that social programs do not explain the increase or persistence of informality in Mexico, and focus instead on regulatory burdens in the formal sector.

Furthermore, the alleged disincentives to formal employment (regulatory and other) have not deterred firms from expanding such employment when the demand for their products is increasing. For example, between 2007 and 2018, employment in Mexican manufacturing rose by 518,800, representing an increase of 16% over the 2007 level. The vast majority of this increase (about 80%) consisted of formal (salaried) jobs in the motor vehicles sector (principally automobiles, auto parts, and aerospace).[4] Clearly, both Mexican firms and foreign firms located in Mexico are willing to pay the costs of hiring significantly more formal-sector employees if the demand for their products increases sufficiently, regardless of the costs or disincentives for doing so. This is not to deny that Mexico should consider redesigning its social insurance system to make it more equitable across all types of workers and to lessen disproportional burdens on law-abiding formal sector firms, but the incentives created by that system are not a sufficiently strong obstacle to the expansion of formal sector employment when demand conditions warrant it. Rather, as two scholars of the Mexican economy conclude,

[4] Author's analysis of data from Instituto Nacional de Estadística y Geografía (INEGI), Encuesta mensual de la industria manufacturera (EMIM), accessed April 28, 2019, at https://www.inegi.org.mx/sistemas/bie/.

> *Thus what appears to have happened is simply that as the economy was unable to absorb the new entrants to the labor force into the high-productivity sectors, the expanding labor force found its way into the low-productivity activities of the services sector .... In other words, what explains the strong productivity slowdown is a massive increase in underemployment in the tertiary [services] sectors of the economy that is also reflected in the well-documented decline in the share of wage and salary employment in the total labor force and the increase in the size of the informal sector ....*
>
> ***Moreno-Brid and Ros (2009, pp. 234–235).***

Similar considerations apply to other supply side explanations that have been offered. For example, there is no doubt that the Mexican economy has a high degree of concentration that results in high price-cost margins that make certain goods and services very expensive, for example, in telecommunications services.[5] In many cases, this monopoly power resulted from the way that state enterprises were privatized by being sold off to small groups of wealthy, well-connected investors in the early 1990s (González, 2019). To the extent that such monopoly power raises prices for consumers, it can certainly reduce consumer welfare. But as Hanson (2010) argues, the causal connection between high prices of some goods and services and slow long-run growth is far from clear.

Ros (2013, pp. 80–81) notes that Mexican prices of telecommunication and internet services actually decreased (relative to averages for all OECD countries) after 2000, making high prices in that sector an unlikely culprit for relatively slow growth in the post-2000 period. He also observes that indicators of industrial concentration are not good predictors of which sectors in the Mexican economy have relatively high prices compared to other countries; some more expensive inputs come from less concentrated industries, and conversely. Levy (2018) notes that competition policies improved under the administration of president Enrique Peña Nieto (2012–18), yet growth did not accelerate during that period. Moreover, some of the large, oligopolistic companies that have high profit margins nevertheless are also among the most technologically advanced (e.g., providers of internet and cell phone services), so they are unlikely candidates for explaining low or stagnant productivity. Where high degrees of industrial concentration could

[5] For an extensive analysis of monopoly power in the Mexican economy and how it has contributed to "low growth which is distributed unfairly," see González (2019).

be relevant is in explaining low investment rates and scarce credit supply, as discussed below.

Another commonly cited supply side culprit is alleged deficiencies in "human capital" formation in Mexico.[6] Most observers recognize that this cannot be because of a lack of schooling. As Ros (2013), Levy and Székely (2016), and Levy (2018) all agree, educational levels (e.g., average years of schooling) of the Mexican labor force have risen dramatically in the past few decades and are similar to those of other middle-income countries. Also, although the quality of the Mexican education system does not rank highly in international comparisons, the same authors concur that it has nonetheless improved in recent decades. If anything, the supply of highly educated labor has grown faster than the demand, as evidenced by the large numbers of workers employed in occupations that do not require the skills they were trained in and the decreasing wage premium for more educated workers since the late 1990s (Levy, 2018). Levy argues that human capital is "misallocated" in Mexico, but stresses that it has not failed to increase, at least in terms of educational attainment; he also argues, convincingly, that workers who are underemployed relative to their educational preparation do not receive the on-the-job training and upgrading of their human capital that they would receive if they were employed in jobs that would better utilize their skills.

However, some of the structural problems noted in some branches of the conventional literature do constitute genuine obstacles to Mexico's economic growth. One important one is the highly concentrated nature of the financial system. After the 1994—95 financial crisis, the government of president Ernesto Zedillo (1994—2000) opened the banking system to foreign ownership, after which the vast majority of the banks were purchased by foreign banks, a small number of which control most of the banking activity in the country (Calomiris and Haber, 2014; González, 2019). These banks make most of their profits from charging exorbitant fees for banking services, rather than from lending to business firms. Although the solvency of the Mexican banking system has improved since it was opened up to foreign ownership, Mexico still has one of the world's lowest ratios of bank credit to the private sector as a percentage of GDP, for a

[6] Ros Bosch (2013, p. 89) cites studies from the OECD and a private sector research institution, both of which focus on the allegedly low quality of the Mexican educational system.

country of its per capita income level. In effect, large, globally oriented companies can get finance from international capital markets, but small and medium-sized firms have difficulty getting funds for expansion, and funding for startups is even more scarce. These financial constraints are a contributing factor to the dualistic character of the country's economy, as well as to depressed levels of private domestic investment.

The second genuine obstacle is the set of social pathologies that go under the rubric of the lack of "rule of law": the legacy of government corruption, the power of organized crime, the heightened level of violence, the entry of drug cartels into extortion rackets and human trafficking, the subornation of large parts of the government (especially at the state and local level, but also at the federal level) by the cartels, and the impunity of public officials who are able to escape prosecution or punishment. Recent administrations have made some efforts to create a more independent judiciary, but their militaristic approach to controlling the cartels has only escalated the level of violence and fomented more bloody turf battles among them. Ros (2013, p. 122) observes that rising violence and crime have had "at least three important economic consequences: the direct cost associated with spending on security by private firms and the government; the negative effect on tourism, especially international [tourists]; and the adverse impact on foreign direct investment."

Large multinational corporations in the export sector are able to operate within enclaves where they provide their own security, but smaller firms that operate in the domestic economy are often faced with the choice of paying "protection" money to the cartel extortionists, being killed, or abandoning their homes and businesses and fleeing from their cities and towns (Navarro, 2019). As González (2019, p. 21) argues, the failure of the Mexican state to maintain a "monopoly on the use of force in the country's territory" since the demise of the 70-year reign of one-party rule in the 1990s has led to this explosive increase in violence while undermining the growth of the economy. He argues that this problem has worsened since 2000, in which case it could help to explain why Mexico's growth has deteriorated since then. On the other hand, the causality about organized crime could also go the other way: youth who see few opportunities for well-paying jobs in the formal sector as a result of economic stagnation are more prone to be recruited into the cartels and criminal activity.

The main explanation: focusing on the demand side

Although some of the structural issues flagged in the literature thus represent genuine obstacles to Mexico's economic growth, the standard discussions completely miss out on the importance of demand-side constraints. Contrary to the conventional wisdom, the slowdown in Mexico's growth in the past few decades has occurred at least partly as a result of, and not in spite of, the policies adopted to promote macroeconomic stabilization and trade liberalization. This is not to deny that it is desirable for Mexico to prevent macroeconomic crises or to become globally competitive. Rather, the point is that the ways in which Mexico has accomplished these goals have made their achievement come at the cost of downward pressures on aggregate demand in the domestic economy, and sometimes even disappointing growth of export industries.

Fiscal, monetary, and exchange rate policies

By the early 2000s, Mexico had settled on a mix of fiscal and monetary policies that was supremely contractionary, not only in not sustaining high levels of output and employment in the short run, but also in failing to promote rapid growth of the capital stock and potential output for the long run (Ros, 2013). On the fiscal side, the government adopted balanced budget rules, which limit expenditures to increase in tandem with tax revenues, while failing to adopt a "fiscal reform" that would significantly raise tax revenue and thereby permit more robust levels of government spending consistent with a balanced budget. Mexico has one of the lowest ratios of tax revenue to GDP of any OECD country, and also ranks low on this indicator among other Latin American middle-income countries. Given its lack of monetary autonomy and the low position of the peso in the global currency hierarchy (Castillo Polanco and Schmidt, 2019), Mexico does need to finance most of its government expenditures through taxation, at least on average over the business cycle (although it ought to be able to do more deficit financing during recessions).

As a result, government spending has not been increased to levels that could begin to address the country's structural deficiencies in areas such as infrastructure, technology, health, and sanitation. In fact, since the debt crisis of the 1980s, the rate of public investment (government investment spending as a share of GDP) has declined notably and has never recovered to its pre-1980s levels (Ros, 2013, pp. 126–129). Moreover, the fiscal policy regime is strongly procyclical, as the balanced budget rules force the government to contract spending precisely when it is most needed during a downturn or recession (Esquivel, 2010; Ocampo, 2011). Hence, the state sector fails to provide the kind of demand stimulus cum investment in public capital that the Mexican state used to provide during the years of rapid state-led expansion between the 1940s and 1970s. Moreover, inadequate public investment in infrastructure increases costs for the private sector and hence weakens private investment, thereby exacerbating supply-side deficiencies in productive capacity.

On the monetary side, starting in the late 1990s and early 2000s, Mexico adopted a very strict form of inflation targeting, in which the central bank (Banco de México) focused solely on inflation objectives and paid no attention to other objectives, such as employment, growth, or a competitive exchange rate (Esquivel, 2010). Unlike in the past, when Mexico had either a fixed or managed exchange rate, after the mid-1990s the peso was allowed to float (although the exchange rate was still influenced to some extent by central bank intervention in the foreign exchange market). Instead of using the exchange rate as a nominal anchor to control inflation, as the government had done (with frequently disastrous results) in the past, now the exchange rate was made flexible and the central bank's interest rate manipulation would become the means of controlling inflation.

In the early years of this regime, monetary policy operated in an asymmetrical fashion by tightening policy when the peso tended to depreciate but not loosening policy when the peso tended to appreciate (Galindo and Ros, 2008). The result was a sharp real appreciation of the peso in the early 2000s to levels not seen since just before the currency crises of 1975–76 and 1982–83, as can be seen in Fig. 11.2. Not surprisingly, Mexico's export growth slowed dramatically in the 2000–07 period when the peso was at a high level, while the Chinese yuan was also undervalued at the time (Blecker, 2014). However, as Fig. 11.2 also shows, the peso depreciated modestly in real terms after 2008, and more sharply in 2016–18. The latter depreciation helped Mexican exports to remain competitive in the uncertain atmosphere created by the inauguration of Donald Trump as US president in 2017 and the subsequent renegotiation of NAFTA.

Aside from its impact on export performance in the short run, the real exchange rate also affects capital accumulation (investment in real productive assets) in the Mexican economy. Ibarra and Ros (2019a) find that a real depreciation of the peso has a significant, positive effect on the accumulation rate (net investment relative to the capital stock) in tradable goods

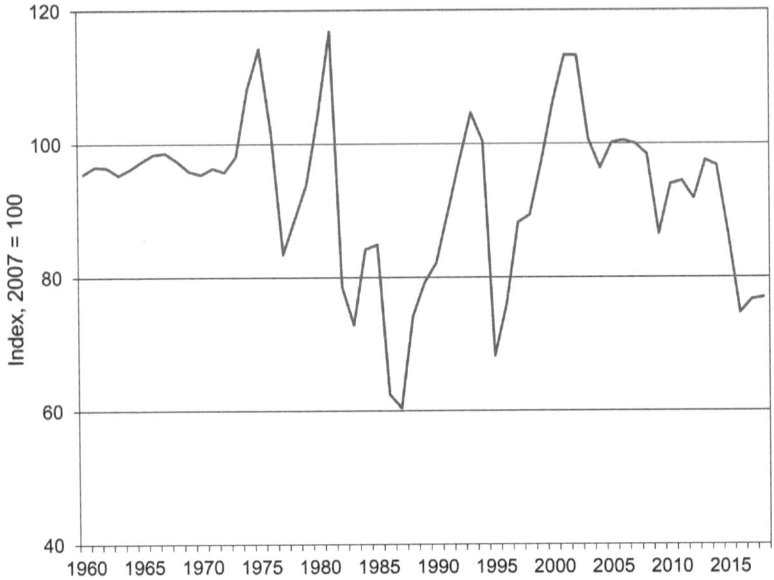

Figure 11.2 Real effective exchange rate (REER) of the Mexican peso, annually, 1960–2018. Notes: This graph shows the annual REER index for Mexico relative to 66 countries. This index is expressed as the real value of the country's currency, so a higher number indicates a real appreciation of the Mexican peso (higher relative prices of Mexican goods). *Source: Bruegel, "Real effective exchange rates for 178 countries: a new database," methodology described in Darvis (2012), updated October 4, 2019, accessed December 1, 2019, https://bruegel.org/publications/datasets/real-effective-exchange-rates-for-178-countries-a-new-database/.*

industries and in the manufacturing sector, a negative effect on accumulation in nontradable sectors, and a net positive effect on aggregate accumulation (since the positive effects on tradable goods and manufactures outweigh the negative effects on nontradables). For the tradable goods and manufacturing sectors (which, of course, have considerable overlap), Ibarra and Ros (2019a) find that the real exchange rate operates through a profitability channel: a real depreciation raises relative prices and profits for the goods produced in those sectors. However, the impact of a real depreciation on investment in nontradable goods sectors is negative because a real depreciation raises the relative price of imported capital goods, while it lessens the relative profitability of those activities. Since the peso has been at a relatively high real value for most of the period since macroeconomic stability was achieved in the late 1990s and early 2000s (up to 2014), peso overvaluation has to be counted as one of the chief contributors to disappointing export performance and stagnant output growth in Mexico at that time.

The peso did fall in value after 2014, however, and by 2016–18 its real value was down to low levels not seen since the postcrisis years of the mid-1980s and mid-1990s (see Fig. 11.2). This depreciation undoubtedly helped to sustain Mexico's exports and industrial production in the short run in the face of Trump's various threats (e.g., to withdraw the US from NAFTA or close the US-Mexican border); it also (along with other factors) helped Mexico to capture some of the export business that left China as a result of his "trade war" with the latter country (Townsend and Martin, 2019).

Nevertheless, past overvaluations of the peso are likely to have caused persistent damage to the Mexican economy. Ibarra (2018) finds that the impact of changes in the real exchange rate on capital accumulation in Mexico is asymmetrical: an appreciation causes capital accumulation to decrease by more than a depreciation causes it to increase, especially in the manufacturing sector and tradable goods industries, and to a lesser extent in the economy as a whole.[7] This suggests that the cumulative negative impact of periods of appreciation has outweighed the cumulative positive impact of periods of depreciation. Possible reasons for this asymmetry are not hard to find. Looking at the data in Fig. 11.2, one can see that most real depreciations in Mexico have been short-lived, so risk-averse investors would be wise to wait and see if the peso will appreciate again before committing to long-term investment projects. Furthermore, using quarterly data, Ibarra finds that the effects of a real depreciation on aggregate investment in Mexico are negative in the short run but positive in the long run.[8] Thus, a depreciation of the type seen in the last few years shown in Fig. 11.2 would have to persist for several more years to start to have a long-run payoff at the aggregate level, and furthermore, would have to be sustained long enough to undo the continuing damage to capital accumulation from past periods when the peso was higher in value.

[7] In the nontradable sector, Ibarra (2018) finds that the effect of the real exchange rate on capital accumulation is symmetrical, with a depreciation reducing investment by about the same amount as an appreciation raises it. He also finds an asymmetrical effect of the production growth rate, which has a negative effect when it is low that is much bigger (in absolute value) than its positive effect when it is high. The latter result suggests that economic stagnation is self-perpetuating in Mexico, since periods of low growth diminish capital accumulation by more than periods of rapid growth stimulate it. Furthermore, Ibarra finds that the total investment rate was permanently diminished (after controlling for other factors) after the crises of 1994–95 and 2008–09.

[8] López et al. (2011) found that a currency depreciation has contractionary effects on Mexican output in the short run, using detrended data; they did not test for long-run effects.

The external constraint

Openness to international trade can be desirable for many reasons, such as creating incentives for tradable goods industries to become more efficient and competitive, attracting inflows of foreign direct investment, and providing low-cost, high-quality goods for domestic consumers. Nevertheless, the high degree of openness that Mexico has achieved since the late 1980s also implies dependency on foreign market conditions for national exports, which for Mexico almost entirely means the growth of the US economy. Roughly 80% of Mexico's exports are sold in the US market, representing an unusually high degree of dependency on a single export market for a country's of Mexico's size and level of development. In spite of many efforts to diversify the markets for Mexican exports (e.g., through numerous international trade agreements with countries outside North America), the percentage of those exports that is sold in the US market has remained within a range of about 70–90% throughout the past few decades. Moreover, Blecker (2009) found that the sensitivity of Mexico's economic growth to US economic growth only became statistically significant after the two countries (along with Canada) joined NAFTA in 1994, so that sensitivity is a direct product of Mexico's regional economic integration with the US economy.

Castillo Polanco and Schmidt (2019, p. 370) argue that the Mexican economy is subject to a balance-of-payments (BP) constraint because

> *Under the present institutional framework, the Mexican financial system cannot self-finance a sustained growth of aggregate demand because expansions require a concomitant [in]flow of [US] dollars .... without US$ inflows, an increase in domestic credit will induce an increase in the interest rate which can constrain the expansion or engender a recession.*

Applying the theory of BP-constrained growth originally developed by Thirlwall (1979), and extending this model to incorporate the important role of imports of intermediate goods in the production of Mexican exports, Ibarra and Blecker (2016) estimated the equilibrium growth rate of the Mexican economy consistent with BP equilibrium as a function of the average US growth rate for various historical periods between 1960 and 2012. For the most recent period covered in that study (2001–12), Ibarra and Blecker came up with a range of estimates for Mexico's BP-equilibrium growth rate of between 1.7% and 2.9% per year, based on average US growth of 1.6% per year during that period. Mexico's actual average annual growth rate of 2.0% in 2001–12 was within this range, which signifies that output was growing at a pace that would not cause rising trade (current account) deficits by stimulating too much demand for imports. Indeed, although this growth was below historical and international norms, as discussed earlier, this was a period in which Mexico had only very small and stable deficits on current account.[9]

But the 1.6% annual growth rate of the US economy in 2001–12 occurred during a period of secular stagnation, as discussed elsewhere in this volume. Using Ibarra and Blecker's model, it is possible to calculate what Mexico's BP-equilibrium growth rate would have been if the US economy had grown at a rate closer to its historical average. To err on the conservative side, let us assume (counterfactually) that the US had grown exactly twice as fast (3.2% per year) in the 2001–12 period, which would still have been slightly below its average annual growth rate of 3.4% from 1960 to 2000. If the US growth rate had thus doubled, Mexico's BP-equilibrium growth rate for 2001–12 would have been in a range of 2.6–5.2% per year, meaning that the country could have grown about twice as fast (say around 4% per year) without incurring rising current account deficits.[10]

It is also important to note that Mexico's industrial production has become tightly integrated into regional supply chains in North America since the formation of NAFTA. In the early years of NAFTA (1994–2000), this proved advantageous to Mexico as the US economy was temporarily booming, while Mexico also enjoyed the benefits of a depreciated exchange rate (see Fig. 11.2) and the newly enacted NAFTA tariff preferences. As shown in Table 11.2, Mexican industrial production (especially for manufactures, which were export-oriented) grew relatively rapidly in those years, in spite of the peso crisis of 1994–95 which holds down the averages for the whole period (especially for total industry, which also includes nontradable sectors such as construction, mining, and utilities).

[9] Mexico's current account deficit averaged about 1.0% of GDP between 2001 and 2012, with only small fluctuations and no upward or downward trend during that period. Author's calculations based on data from International Monetary Fund, World Economic Indicators, October 2019 database, accessed November 23, 2019, at https://www.imf.org/external/pubs/ft/weo/2019/02/weodata/index.aspx.

[10] Author's calculations based on the model in Ibarra and Blecker (2016); see also López (2018) for similar calculations. Of course, there is no guarantee that Mexico would actually have grown twice as fast in reality, simply because its BP-equilibrium growth rate would have been that much higher. Nevertheless, given how much Mexico's growth depends on the dynamism of its exports to the US market, it is likely that actual growth would also have been boosted to some extent by faster growth of the latter.

Table 11.2 Growth of Mexican and US industrial production, all industries and manufacturing only, selected periods, 1981–2019 (average annual percentage rates).

	All industries		Manufacturing only	
	Mexico	**United States**	**Mexico**	**United States**
January 1981–December 1993	2.2	2.1	–	2.6
January 1994–December 2000	3.8	5.1	5.2	5.9
January 2001–December 2007	1.3	1.4	0.7	1.8
January 2008–February 2019	0.5	0.5	1.7	0.1

Notes: Data shown are averages of 12-month growth rates based on monthly indexes. Separate data for the manufacturing sector for Mexico are not available before 1993.
Source: Author's calculations based on industrial production indexes from Instituto Nacional de Estadística y Geografía (INEGI), https://www.inegi.org.mx/sistemas/bie/, for Mexico, and Board of Governors of the Federal Reserve System, https://www.federalreserve.gov/data.htm, for the US, both accessed April 24, 2019.

But what the promoters of North American integration did not count on was the severe slowdown in US industrial production after 2000. Essentially, the US industrial structure with which Mexico was seeking to integrate shrank, as approximately five million US manufacturing jobs were lost after 2001 (Blecker, 2014). Indeed, after that time, Mexican industries became more integrated into global as well as regional supply chains, as they began to source more of their imported inputs (intermediate and capital goods) from Asia rather than from the US. But in terms of exports, Mexican industries are still strongly dependent on the US market.

As a result, Mexico's industrial growth slowed down tremendously starting in 2001. In terms of total industrial production, the slowdown in Mexico almost exactly mirrors that in the US in both subperiods shown (2001–07 and 2008–19). Interestingly, however, the two countries diverge slightly in terms of manufacturing output, with Mexico slowing down more in 2001–07 and the US slowing down more in 2008–19. The reasons for this reversal have to do with the timing of Chinese competitive effects, which hurt Mexican exports mostly in the 2001–07 period (see Gallagher et al., 2008), and also with Mexico's exchange rate, which was severely overvalued during that period, as shown in Fig. 11.2. After 2008, the China effect was ameliorated by a combination of Chinese currency appreciation and rising Chinese wages, as well as a depreciated Mexican peso (especially after 2014). Nevertheless, in spite of this slight discrepancy, the overall picture shown in Table 11.2 is one in which Mexico's industrial output grows more slowly after 2001, more or less in step with a similar slowdown in US industrial production.

Putting all these factors together, the combination of contractionary macropolicies, inadequate public investment, a frequently overvalued currency, and tightened external constraints has fostered the stagnation of Mexican growth observed since 2000. Furthermore, this stagnation has, in turn, exacerbated many of the structural problems discussed earlier. In particular, slow growth of formal sector output and employment has pushed many Mexican workers into the less-productive informal sector, resulting in the persistence of dualism and the slow growth of average productivity in the economy as a whole (Moreno-Brid and Ros, 2009; Ros, 2013). Also, the lack of adequate jobs at good wages in the formal sector has contributed to the appeal of criminal economic activities, which offer potentially higher rewards (albeit with heightened risks) compared with many informal sector activities. Instead of resulting from misplaced incentives at the microlevel or supply side constraints, however, informalization and the consequent sluggishness of overall productivity growth are mainly effects, rather than causes, of the slow growth of output and depressed accumulation rate, whose origins lie mainly in the impact of the macroeconomic and trade policy regimes on the demand side.

Inequality and the falling labor share

The relationship between income distribution and secular stagnation in Mexico is complex and surely bidirectional in causality. To begin with, different indicators of income distribution give very different impressions of whether the Mexican economy has become more or less unequal since the 1990s. On the one hand, standard measures of wage inequality (such as the skilled labor premium) and personal inequality (such as Gini coefficients based on household survey data) show diminishing inequality since the late 1990s, which reversed previous worsenings (see, e.g., Lustig et al., 2013). On the other hand, there has been a clear fall in the overall share of labor (compared with capital) in national income since the late 1990s (Ibarra and Ros, 2019b), while adjustments to the survey data to correct for missing information on upper-income strata reveal that personal inequality has actually worsened too (Del Castillo Negrete, 2015; Esquivel, 2015; Cortés and Vargas, 2017).

In terms of causality running from stagnation to inequality, the slow growth of labor demand (employment) in the formal sector has contributed to preventing wages from rising in proportion to labor productivity in the modern sector of the economy, especially for manufactured and tradable goods, thus helping to explain the fall in the labor share of value added in those activities. Other factors, including the rising degree of monopoly power in the economy (González, 2019) along with the decline in the bargaining strength of labor unions (Bensusán and Middlebrook, 2012) have also contributed to increased profit margins and the falling labor share. The informalization of the labor force, which as we have seen is largely a result of stagnation in the formal sector, also contributes to overall inequality at the household level.

In regard to the opposite direction of causality, the literature to date has focused on the effects of the functional distribution of income between capital and labor income (or profits and wages[11]) on capital accumulation and output growth. Ibarra and Ros (2019a) found that higher profit rates have a positive effect on capital accumulation (investment) in all major sectors of the Mexican economy, although more strongly so in manufacturing and tradable goods than in nontradable goods and services. Onaran and Galanis (2012) found that private domestic demand (the sum of personal consumption plus domestic investment) is wage-led in Mexico, but net exports are strongly profit-led (because higher labor costs reduce the trade balance). According to their estimates, the negative effect of a higher wage share on net exports dominates the positive effect on domestic demand, so that total private aggregate demand in Mexico is profit-led.

There are two important qualifications to this last finding. First, the predominance of the negative effect on net exports is a function of the large share of foreign trade in the Mexican economy; if the economy were refocused on domestic activity, the positive effects on domestic demand would become proportionately larger. And second, a simultaneous increase in the wage share in Mexico and its trading partners (especially the US) would be expansionary, because in this situation Mexico would not lose international competitiveness, so the negative effect on net exports would be muted (Onaran and Galanis, 2012). However, most of these studies have focused on short-run effects; more research is needed to confirm how distribution affects output in the long run in the Mexican economy.[12]

[11] In empirical data, there is not an exact correspondence between labor income and total wages (compensation of employees) or between capital income and total profits because labor and capital income include imputations for the returns to these factors in self-employment and proprietary enterprises, whereas wages and profits are received only in capitalist enterprises (Ibarra and Ros, 2019b). In our discussion here, we simplify by referring to these pairs of concepts interchangeably due to space constraints.

[12] Vargas-Sánchez and Luna (2014) found that Mexican output (GDP) is wage-led in the long run but profit-led in the short run.

Conclusions

Mexico's neoliberal reforms and macroeconomic stabilization policies of the 1980 and 1990s were based on a strong, and unrealistic, assumption. That is, if the country would open its economy to international trade, get inflation under control, privatize state enterprises, and avoid repeated crises, the economy would automatically and smoothly grow and expand. The architects of these policies paid no attention to where the aggregate demand would come from to sustain high and rising levels of formal-sector employment. In reality, the macroeconomic policies that they adopted operated systematically to depress domestic aggregate demand, while trade liberalization made Mexico uniquely dependent on one source of external demand: the US market. Furthermore, the monetary policies adopted to suppress inflation frequently led to real overvaluation of the peso, which undermined the export-led growth that the government was supposedly trying to achieve. While there were other, structural obstacles, especially the monopolized banking system and the increased levels of criminal activity and violence, the demand-side constraints have been the most binding restrictions on Mexico's growth at the macro level.

Mexico's economic stagnation is thus fundamentally rooted in a fatal flaw in the neoliberal policy regime its government has pursued since the liberalizing reforms of the late 1980s. This regime deliberately suppressed wages (relative to productivity) in order to make export industries internationally competitive, thereby compressing domestic consumption, while relying on the US economy to serve as the main source of demand stimulus. When the US economy, where 80% of Mexico's exports are sold, entered a period of secular stagnation after 2000, even the export engine naturally faltered and the Mexican economy correspondingly sank into a period of stagnation. In addition, the monetary, fiscal, and exchange rate policies adopted to stabilize the macroeconomy since the late 1990s have mainly operated to depress domestic demand further. Moreover, the macro and trade policies were frequently in conflict with each other, as the monetary policies often caused the peso to be overvalued, thereby limiting the growth of export sales, investment in tradable goods industries, and the expansion of formal sector employment. And ironically, the paucity of public infrastructure investment under the neoliberal regime has only worsened, rather than alleviated, supply-side deficiencies.

There is arguably also a deeper flaw in the strategy of regional economic integration that Mexico adopted under NAFTA. The viability of this strategy would ultimately depend on the expansion of the US consumer market for Mexican exports, while the US was also opening itself up to trade with China and other countries as well as Mexico. But US wages (especially for less educated workers) were adversely affected by rising imports of manufactured goods—especially from China, but also, albeit to a lesser extent, Mexico (Autor et al., 2016; Hakobyan and McLaren, 2016). As discussed elsewhere in this volume and earlier sources (e.g., Setterfield, 2013), the resulting depression of US consumer demand was temporarily offset by the build-up of household debt prior to the financial crisis and Great Recession of 2008–09, which proved to be unsustainable in the aftermath of that crisis and the sluggish recovery that followed.

In the face of these challenges, Mexico needs to rebalance its economic strategy to put greater emphasis on expansion of the internal market (domestic demand)—without abandoning exports, but not making them the chief source of stimulus as they have been since the late 1980s. Strengthening the internal market requires, above all, a significant redistribution of income to bolster the purchasing power of workers and the emerging middle class. It also requires a more robust role for the state, especially through public investment in infrastructure and expenditures on basic social needs (education, health, sanitation, etc.), as well as an industrial policy that can promote innovation and productivity. In the Mexican context, such a program of expenditures needs to be accompanied by a long-overdue fiscal reform that would enhance the taxation capacity of the government. To facilitate all of this, Mexican monetary policy needs to shift toward a pro-investment stance and should focus especially on preventing the peso from becoming overvalued so that the balance of payments does not become an obstacle to the success of a new policy regime. Other, structural reforms may be important too, for example, in the financial sector and social insurance, but if demand constraints remain binding, none of those reforms will stimulate long-run growth any more than previous rounds of reform have up to the present.

Acknowledgement

The author would like to thank Eric Hershberg, Carlos Ibarra, and participants in a session at the May 2019 conference of the Latin American Studies Association (LASA), Boston, Massachusetts, for comments on earlier versions of this chapter.

References

Arias, J., Azuara, O., Bernal, P., Heckman, J.J., Villarreal, C., 2010. Policies to Promote Growth and Economic Efficiency in Mexico. Institute for the Study of Labor (IZA), Bonn, Germany, February. Discussion Paper No. 4740.

Autor, D.H., Dorn, D., Hanson, G.H., 2016. The China shock: learning from labor-market adjustment to large changes in trade. Annual Review of Economics 8, 205–240.

Bensusán, G., Middlebrook, K.J., 2012. Organized Labour and Politics in Mexico: Changes, Continuities and Contradictions. University of London, Institute for the Study of the Americas.

Blecker, R.A., 2009. External shocks, structural change, and economic growth in Mexico, 1979–2007. World Development 37 (7), 1274–1284.

Blecker, R.A., 2014. The Mexican and U.S. economies after twenty years of NAFTA. International Journal of Political Economy 43 (2), 5–26. Summer.

Bolio, E., Remes, J., Lajous, T., Manyika, J., Ramirez, E., Rossé, M., 2014. A Tale of Two Mexicos: Growth and Prosperity in a Two-Speed Economy. McKinsey Global Institute, San Francisco.

Calomiris, C.W., Haber, S.H., 2014. Fragile by Design: The Political Origins of Banking Crises and Scarce Credit. Princeton University Press, Princeton.

Castillo Polanco, L.A., Schmidt, T.P., 2019. The process of endogenous liquidity in developing economies: the case of Mexico. Review of Keynesian Economics 7 (3), 369–387.

Cortés, F., Vargas, D., 2017. La evolución de la desigualdad en México: viejos y nuevos resultados. Revista de Economía Mexicana, Anuario UNAM 2, 39–96.

Darvas, Z., March 15, 2012. Real Effective Exchange Rates for 178 Countries: A New Database. Bruegel. Working Paper 2012/06. https://bruegel.org/publications/datasets/real-effective-exchange-rates-for-178-countries-a-new-database/.

Del Castillo Negrete, M., 2015. La magnitud de la desigualdad en el ingreso y la riqueza en México. UN, CEPAL, Serie Estudios y Perspectivas, Mexico City.

Esquivel, G., 2010. De la inestabilidad macroeconómica al estancamiento estabilizador: el papel del diseño y la conducción de la política económica. In: Lustig, N. (Ed.), Crecimiento Económico y Equidad, vol. 9, Los Grandes Problemas de México. El Colegio de México, Mexico City, pp. 35–77.

Esquivel, G., 2015. Desigualdad Extrema en México: Concentración del Poder Económico y Político. Mexico City: Oxfam Mexico. https://www.oxfammexico.org/sites/default/files/desigualdadextrema_informe.pdf.

Feenstra, R.C., Inklaar, R., Timmer, M.P., 2015. The next generation of the Penn world table. American Economic Review 105 (10), 3150–3182. Available for download at: www.ggdc.net/pwt.

Galindo, L.M., Ros, J., 2008. Alternatives to inflation targeting in Mexico. International Review of Applied Economics 22 (2), 201–214.

Gallagher, K.P., Moreno-Brid, J.C., Porzecanski, R., 2008. The dynamism of Mexican exports: lost in (Chinese) translation? World Development 36 (8), 1365–1380.

González, F.E., 2019. Mexico under Misplaced Monopolies: Concentrated Wealth and Growing Violence from the 1980s to the Present. Routledge, London and New York.

Hakobyan, S., McLaren, J., 2016. Looking for local labor market effects of NAFTA. Review of Economics and Statistics 98 (4), 728–741.

Hanson, G.H., 2010. Why isn't Mexico rich? Journal of Economic Literature 48 (4), 987–1004.

Ibarra, C.A., 2018. Asymmetric real-exchange-rate effects on capital accumulation: evidence from non-linear ARDL models for Mexico. Latin American Economic Review 27. https://doi.org/10.1186/s40503-018-0057-x. Article 10.

Ibarra, C.A., Blecker, R.A., 2016. Structural change, the real exchange rate and the balance of payments in Mexico, 1960–2012. Cambridge Journal of Economics 40 (2), 507–539.

Ibarra, C.A., Ros, J., 2019a. Profitability and capital accumulation in Mexico: a first look at tradables and non-tradables based on KLEMS. International Review of Applied Economics 33 (3), 426–452.

Ibarra, C.A., Ros, J., 2019b. The decline of the labor income share in Mexico, 1990–2015, 122. World Development, pp. 570–584.

Levy, S., 2018. Under-Rewarded Efforts: The Elusive Quest for Prosperity in Mexico. Inter-American Development Bank, Washington.

Levy, S., Székely, M., 2016. ¿Más escolaridad, menos informalidad? un análisis de cohortes para México y América Latina. El Trimestre Económico 83 (4), 499–548.

Lewis, W.A., 1954. Economic development with unlimited supplies of labour. The Manchester School 22 (2), 139–191.

López, J., 2018. Growth dilemmas in open middle-income economies: a reflection on Mexico's recent experience. Review of Keynesian Economics 6 (3), 333–351.

López, J., Sanchez, A., Spanos, A., 2011. Macroeconomic linkages in Mexico. Metroeconomica 62 (2), 356–385.

Lustig, N., López-Calva, L.F., Ortiz-Juarez, E., April 2013. Declining inequality in Latin America in the 2000s: the cases of Argentina, Brazil, and Mexico. World Development 44, 129–141.

Moreno-Brid, J.C., 2019. The demise of neoliberalism in Mexico today: if so, so what? World Economic Association. WEA Commentaries 9 (1), 7–12. https://www.worldeconomicsassociation.org/files/2019/04/Issue9-1.pdf.

Moreno-Brid, J.C., Ros, J., 2009. Development and Growth in the Mexican Economy: A Historical Perspective. Oxford University Press, New York.

Navarro, A., 2019. El narco se roba la tranquilidad de San Miguel de Allende. El Financiero/Bloomberg, December 3. https://elfinanciero.com.mx/bloomberg-businessweek/carteles-se-apoderan-de-ciudad-mexicana-llena-de-extranjeros.

Ocampo, J.A., 2011. Macroeconomy for development: countercyclical policies and production sector transformation. CEPAL Review 104 (August), 7–35.

Onaran, Ö., Galanis, G., 2012. Is aggregate demand wage-led or profit-led?. In: National and Global Effects. Conditions of Work and Employment Series, No. 40. International Labour Office, Geneva.

Reynolds, C.W., 1978. Why Mexico's "stabilizing development" was actually destabilizing (with some implications for the future). World Development 6 (7–8), 1005–1008.

Ros, J., 2013. Algunas Tesis Equivocadas Sobre el Estancamiento Económico de México. El Colegio de México and Universidad Nacional Autónoma de México, Mexico City.

Setterfield, M., 2013. Wages, demand and US macroeconomic travails: diagnosis and prognosis. In: Fazzari, S.M., Cynamon, B.Z., Setterfield, M. (Eds.), After the Great Recession: The Struggle for Economic Recovery and Growth. Cambridge University Press, Cambridge, pp. 158–184.

Suárez Dávila, F., 2005. Del "estancamiento estabilizador" hacia una política activa de financiamiento del desarrollo. Economía UNAM 2 (6), 43–54.

Thirlwall, A.P., 1979. The balance of payments constraint as an explanation of international growth rate differences. Banca Nazionale del Lavoro Quarterly Review 32 (128), 45–53.

Townsend, M., Martin, E., 2019. U.S. and China Got into a Trade War and Mexico Won. Bloomberg. March 27. https://www.bloomberg.com/news/articles/2019-03-27/who-is-winning-trump-s-trade-war-with-china-so-far-it-s-mexico. (Accessed 2 December 2019).

Vargas Sánchez, G., Luna, A., 2014. Slow growth in the Mexican economy. Journal of Post Keynesian Economics 37 (1), 115–133.

Wilson, C., 2019. A New Administration Confronts a Changing World: Mexico's Economic Competitiveness Strategy at a Geopolitical Inflection Point. Brookings, Washington.

CHAPTER TWELVE

The stagnation of the Mexican economy is here to stay*

Arturo Huerta G.
Facultad de Economía, UNAM, Mexico City, Mexico

Macroeconomic policies for maintaining "stability" are detrimental to endogenous conditions for growth

The low rate of economic growth in the Mexican economy (an average annual rate of 2.4% from 1982 to the present; 2.1% during the last 10 years; and 0 during 2019) derives from free-market policies for goods and capital, and from the predominating macroeconomic "stabilization" policies (so-called).

The free movement of capitals requires that the country acts to stabilize the exchange rate. A country that lacks the endogenous conditions to keep its currency stable will find itself obligated to raise interest rates and implement fiscal-austerity policies to contract domestic demand and employment, thereby avoiding pressures upon prices, salaries, and the external sector. By these means, the country promotes capital inflows that ensure exchange-rate stability.

Stability of the exchange rate does not allow for flexibility of economic policies to foster growth

Fiscal austerity and exchange-rate stability are favored (despite assertions that the country works with a flexible exchange rate), because these conditions of "stability" are said to be necessary for economic growth. This explanation hides the true purpose of such measures, which is to favor the financial sector and limit the government's size and participation in the economy.

* The present article is part of the Research Project of the PAPIIT of the UNAM, IN305419, "Free Trade versus Protectionism: their consequences for economic growth and macroeconomic variables".

Handbook of Economic Stagnation
ISBN: 978-0-12-815898-2
https://doi.org/10.1016/B978-0-12-815898-2.00011-2

Exchange-rate stability reduces competitiveness and the capacity for economic-policy management that is needed to ease monetary, fiscal, exchange-rate, and credit policies in favor of economic growth. The government sees itself obligated to promote capital inflows through high interest rates and fiscal austerity and to reduce the fiscal deficit to avoid demand pressures on supply and imports to reduce pressure on the exchange-rate parity.

Fig. 12.1 reflects the absence of changes in the exchange rate and thus shows that the exchange-rate parity has not adjusted itself to changes in price differential between the US and Mexico. As a result, that parity, together with national production and productivity differentials, are at a disadvantage with respect to imports. Hence, pressures remain upon the trade deficit and economic growth.

Because the exchange rate must be maintained stable, the government cannot lower the interest rate and expand public spending in favor of employment and productivity growth. Those measures might stoke fears of inflation and devaluation. Instead, the government implements policies that contract demand and increase idle capacity, along with the external commercial deficit, thereby also reducing the private sector's profits, increasing that sector's indebtedness, and diminishing its capacity to spend and invest.

The resulting decrease in public and private investment is detrimental to productivity and technological development. National production is made less competitive vias à vis imports; a disadvantage that undermines the dynamics of accumulation, accentuates deindustrialization and productive backwardness, and reduces the economy's potential for growth. Thus, the

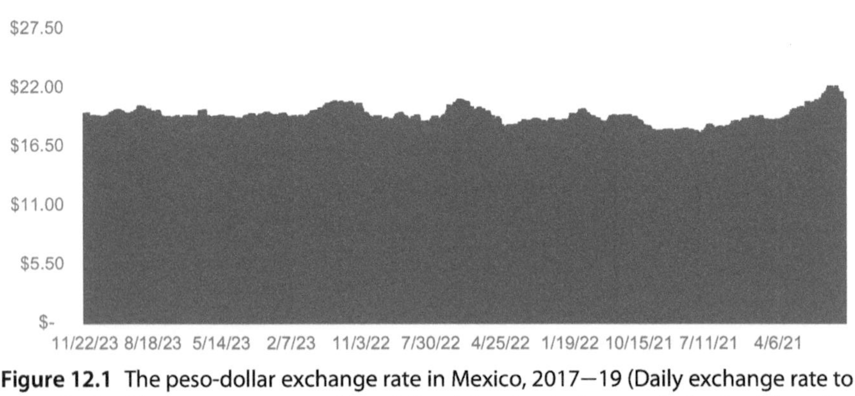

Figure 12.1 The peso-dollar exchange rate in Mexico, 2017—19 (Daily exchange rate to pay off the Mexican government's public obligations). *Source: Author's elaboration based on Banxico data.*

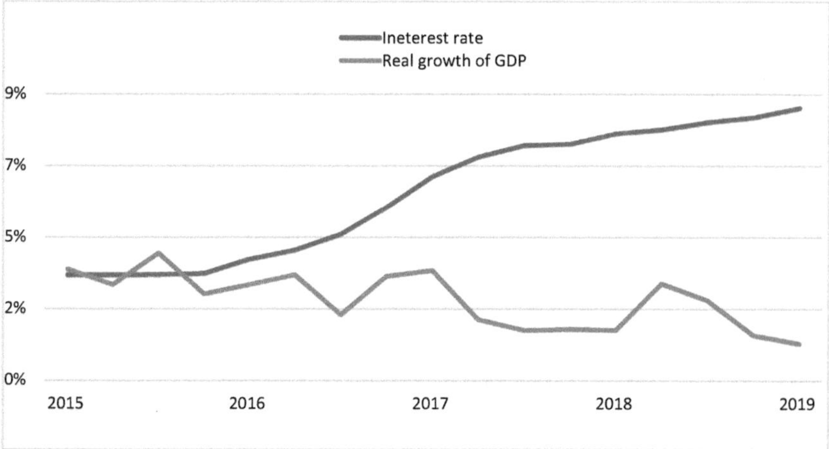

Figure 12.2 Real Growth of GDP in Mexico versus Quarterly interest rates, 2015Q1-2019Q1. *Source: Author's elaboration based on Banxico data.*

economy falls into increasing dependence on capital inflows, reducing the viability of measures for relaxing the economic policy to resume growth.

The cost of stabilizing the exchange rate through high interest rates, fiscal austerity, and low salaries is the stagnation and economic recession that are taking shape in the Mexican economy (Fig. 12.2).

The government's policy for stabilizing the exchange rate, and for lowering inflation, the fiscal deficit, and the amount of debt has brought about economic stagnation that will end in recession and crisis

The Ministry of Finance works with selfimposed primary fiscal surplus targets (which excludes payment of debt service) that amounts to 1% of GDP in 2019 and 0.7% of GDP in 2020 (Fig. 12.3). By doing so, demand pressures upon prices remain low, and the Ministry of Finance can make payments on the debt and reduce it, thereby earning the approval of financial markets.

The Ministry of Finance considers debt harmful. Moreover, because of the priority given to exchange-rate stability, the Ministry of Finance does not use the national currency to finance government spending. As a result, the economy ends up in the worst of all possible worlds, with no source of financing other than tax collection. By opting to restrict its capacity for spending and investment in this way, the Ministry of Finance has configured

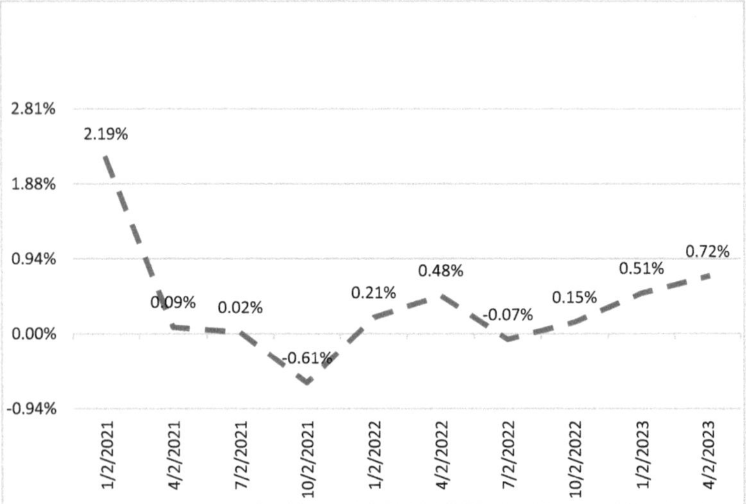

Figure 12.3 Fiscal targets as % of GDP in Mexico, 2017Q1-2019Q2. *Source: Author's elaboration based on data from INEGI and Banxico.*

a growth that consists of simple reproduction. That is, the government spends only as much as it collects—a situation that does not drive the dynamics of the economy, but instead maintains the economy stagnant. If the Ministry of Finance works with a fiscal surplus (i.e., spends less than it collects), the economic activity contracts.

The combination of fiscal austerity and free trade with no tariffs on the majority of imports contracts domestic demand (or allows it to leak outside the country) and acts in detriment to decisions regarding investment and economic growth. The government, instead of implementing expansionary fiscal policy to counteract the payment of external debt owed to nonresidents, so that economic growth might be stimulated, decides to maintain the fiscal austerity that protects exchange-rate stability and keeps inflation low, at the cost of giving a low priority to the objectives of employment and growth. Josef Steindl wrote in 1976 that "… in the past there was a general conviction that the government would intervene to avoid a generalized depression; this reduced uncertainty and operated in favor of greater, more-stable private investment. This confidence has been broken. This is the other reason why the function of expected profits has been displaced downward" (1979).

When the government persists in reducing its fiscal deficit and the amount of debt, while the central bank insists upon stabilizing the exchange rate through high interest rates to reduce demand and attract foreign capital, the result is stagnation, unemployment, low salaries, foreign-trade deficit, and increased idle capacity. This context discourages potential investors and impedes potential economic growth, with the further result of exacerbating economic, political, and social problems.

The context of stagnation configured by the predominating antiinflationary economic policies compromises the macroeconomic stability desired by the government, because the contraction of economic activity reduces tax revenues, thereby maintaining pressure upon public finances. Added to that difficulty are the productivity differentials between Mexico and the United States—its principal trading partner (see Fig. 12.4), and the productivity backwardness that exists in the Mexican economy (see Fig. 12.5).

To maintain a stable exchange rate, and avoid exerting pressure upon it, the central bank proceeds to increase the interest rate to attract capital. In this way, the central bank continues the policies that produced a vicious circle, for they are detrimental to accumulation and growth. Thus, pressures of the private and external sectors upon public finances increase, by generating conditions in which the debt cannot be repaid.

The economy becomes more dependent upon capital inflows to finance the external debt and to avoid devaluation, so that free movement of goods and capital may be maintained. Thus, the economic policy cannot be eased to foster economic growth.

Despite the inflow of capital, the problem continues because that flow is directed primarily toward the financial sector, resulting in backwardness of the productive sector and an imbalance between the two sectors, in addition

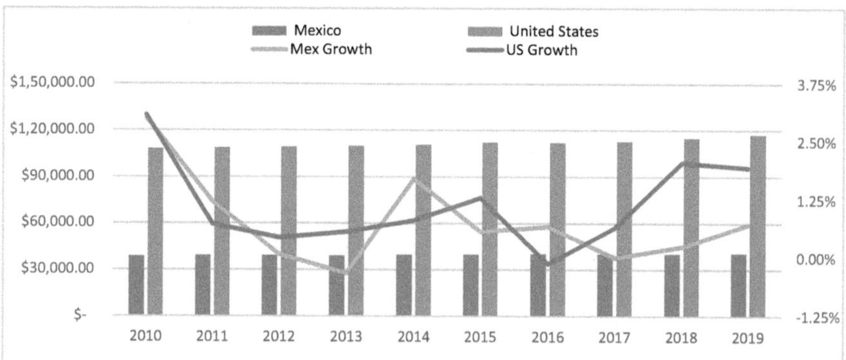

Figure 12.4 Labor Productivity in Mexico and the US in constant 2011 PPP prices, and Growth Rates, 2010–19. *Source: Author's elaboration based on World Bank data.*

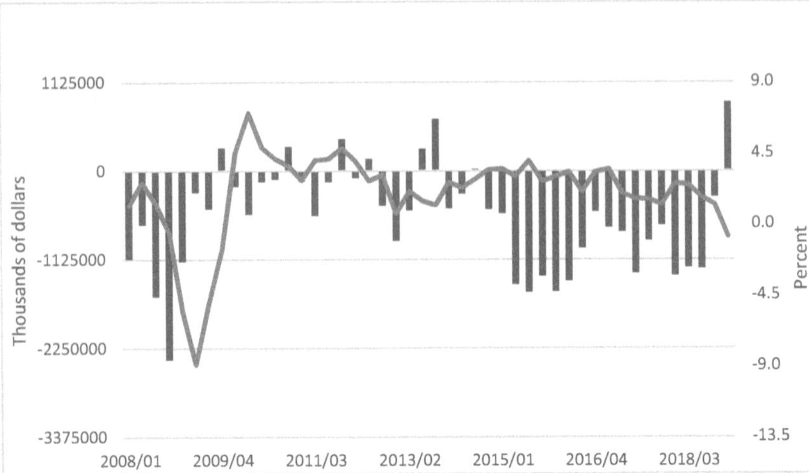

Figure 12.5 Trade Balance (*line*) versus % change in GDP (*bars*). *Source: Author's elaboration based on INEGI data.*

to the negative effects of the policy that was formulated to promote the capital inflows. Such a policy puts the brakes on economic activity, reduces competitiveness, and increases the foreign trade deficit. Those effects, in turn, reduce Mexico's capacity to make payments on its debt. Therefore, Mexico must continue the policies that attract capital inflows. This dynamic places the economy in a highly vulnerable context, subject to external variables and markets, including the perception of international capital about the domestic economy. The Mexican economy is subject to having policies imposed on it by international ratings agencies that allow access to international markets. For this reason, Mexico finds itself implementing restrictive monetary and fiscal policies, as well as accentuating the transfer of the economy to foreign hands.

The economy may still be unable to attract international capital inflows, for at least three reasons: the country now has fewer attractive national assets to offer; the national economy is decelerating; and the ratification of the Mexico-America-Canada Treaty (T-MEC) continues to be delayed. In addition, the mounting current-account deficit compromises repayment of financial obligations.

When external variables are unfavorable, whether because of reduced capital inflows or because of falling international prices for oil and exports, the economy lacks internal conditions for overcoming such a situation. This vulnerability makes external imbalances unsustainable and renders the government unable to maintain exchange-rate stability and the free movement of goods and capital.

The fiscal and taxation policy

The new government (which began on December 1, 2018) has decided to continue with the policy of exchange-rate stability and fiscal austerity and has tried to reduce the amount of debt. Also of note is the decision to not increase taxes, and to not establish new taxes for 3 years. These measures limit capacity to spend and invest, because the sovereign currency is not used for spending to not destabilize the exchange rate. As a result, the government has no fiscal policy to drive economic growth and generate employment. Instead, it attempts to attain a condition of primary fiscal surplus by reducing public spending. The government believes that foregoing a tax increase will stimulate the private sector to invest but does not consider the negative effects that a contraction of public spending and a primary surplus will have on demand, and in the dynamics of accumulation, as in investors' decision-making.

Without growth of individual and business incomes, taxes cannot be increased, nor can new taxes be established, because investment, consumption, and economic activity would be reduced even further. Taxes should be increased in periods of strong economic growth, not during economic recessions. Taxes take purchasing power away from the sectors that are subject to them. If the government limits the amount of its spending to the amount it collects, then that amount will be equal to the amount that the private sector has ceased to spend. Therefore, the government's spending will have no impact whatsoever to promote greater demand and economic activity. And if the government collects taxes to make payments on the debt, and not to increase spending and investment, then economic activity will be restricted because of reduced spending by the sectors that are subject to those taxes.

It will not be through tax increases that the government will obtain the resources needed to reduce the amount of debt and to reactivate and the economy and revitalize its spending capacity.

Fiscal austerity, together with a high interest rate and free trade, reduces the incomes of businesses, individuals, and the government, and therefore restrict consumption, investment, and ultimately economic activity. When that activity contracts, the country's financial problems worsen, thereby comprising growth, investment, and the nation's capacity to make payments on its debt. In such a context, the national and foreign banks restrict the availability of credit during times of low economic growth, as can be seen in Fig. 12.6. The low availability of credit feeds causes a further decrease in growth of employment and the national economy. The drop in value

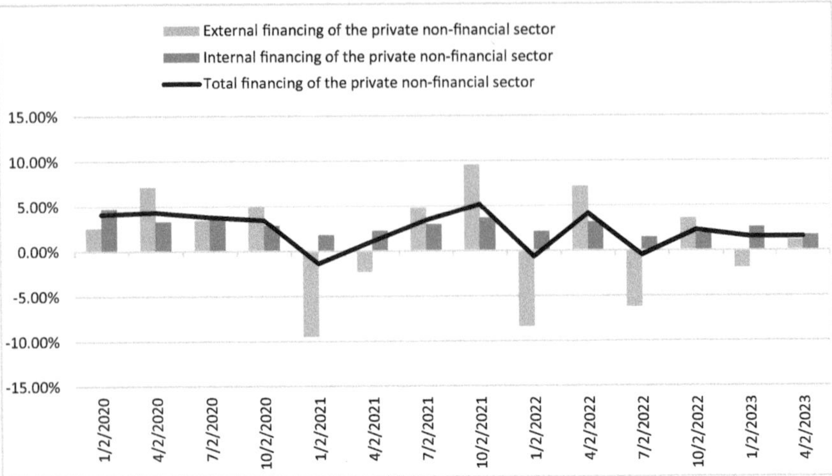

Figure 12.6 Total Domestic and Foreign Financing of Mexico's Private Sector (previous quarter % change), 2016Q1-2019Q1. *Source: Author's elaboration based data from Banxico and INEGI.*

of the Mexican Stock Market, by 15.6% in 2018, followed by an increase of on 4.2% as of November 22, 2019 affects the financial position of shareholders because their capital is not growing, nor is their capacity to make payments on debt improving, so that the shareholders might improve their position for taking on debt and investing.

The government will not succeed in reducing the amount of debt by reducing public spending

The government's policy of cutting public spending and investment to produce a primary fiscal surplus and reduce the amount of debt will not succeed, because that policy contracts demand and the degree to which productive capacity is utilized. As a consequence, investment is discouraged, and economic activity decelerates. Incomes of businesses and individuals then fall, and the government ends up collecting less tax revenue. This dynamic caused Mexico's revenue from the income tax and value-added tax to be lower, to this point, in 2019. Thus, pressures upon public finances continue, making it unlikely that Mexico will reach its goal of having a primary surplus equal to 1% of GDP during 2019. Nor will the amount of public debt be reduced. The same will occur in 2020, for which the government foresees an economic growth rate of 1.5%—2.5%. That rate will not be attained, and the government will collect less tax revenue, and will have trouble obtaining a surplus equal to 0.7% of GDP.

The public sector, businesses, and families will not be able to reduce the amount of debt in a context of stagnation. With the policy of high interest rates and primary surplus, there is no possibility whatsoever of economic growth, nor of making payments on the public and private debt.

The government must increase spending to stimulate demand and drive economic activity to improve the income of business and individuals, which will then enable the government to collect greater tax revenues. In this way, the government's spending will pay for itself and reduce the amount of debt.

Trade agreements have not been favorable toward economic growth

The Mexican economy is faced with a foreign-trade deficit because of low levels of productivity and the broken chains of production that resulted from opening up trade, for example, by the appreciation of the exchange rate, and the almost total lack of tariffs on 95% of the products imported from countries with which Mexico has trade agreements. In addition, Mexico's production and export of crude oil has fallen, along with oil prices, while Mexico's imports of oil products have increased (See Fig. 12.7.).

Faced with the stability and appreciation of the exchange rate, businesses attempt to improve their competitive position by reducing wages and salaries. Unemployment favors capital by weakening the workers' bargaining power and clearing the way for labor reforms that reduce the workers' benefits and salaries. The businesses that gain most from this situation are the transnational exporters. In contrast, businesses that produce for the domestic

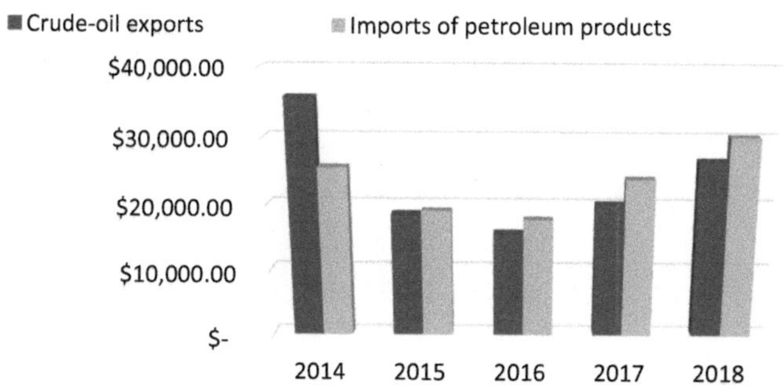

Figure 12.7 Mexico's export of Crude oil and Import of Oil products (UDS million), 2014–18. *Source: Author's elaboration based on Pemex data.*

economy see lower consumer demand. Mexico has the lowest minimum wages in Latin America.

Mexico's domestic companies cannot grow externally because they are not competitive—a disadvantage accentuated by US protectionist policies, the deceleration of the world economy, and the efforts of countries worldwide to reduce their respective trade deficits, thereby intensifying the trade war.

Despite Mexico's low salaries, many of its domestic companies have seen reduced profit margins and domestic-market shares. The companies' products end up being displaced by imports, resulting in deindustrialization. For example, the manufacturing's share of the GDP fell from 23% in 1980 to 18.3% in 2018. The growth in manufactured exports has been commanded by transnational businesses, but that dynamic does not radiate to local industry because of high import coefficients, and the transfer of transnationals' profits to those companies' places of origin.

In Fig. 12.8, it can be observed that the flows of Foreign Direct Investment from 2015 until the second quarter of 2019 do not reflect high levels or rates of growth. That observation, in turn, reflects the limits of the strategy of external-directed growth. Those low growth rates, combined with protectionist policies established by the US (and the delays in signing the T-MEC in Canada and the US Congress), maintain uncertainty that discourages investment by transnational exporting companies, thereby contributing to the context of stagnation of the national economic activity.

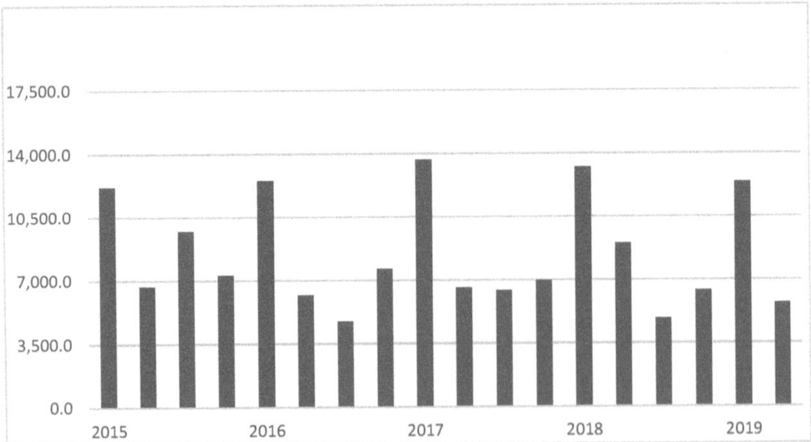

Figure 12.8 Quarterly flow of domestic foreign investment in Mexico (USD millions), 2015Q1-2019Q2. *Source: Author's elaboration based on data from the* Secretaría de Economía.

Mexico continues to promote trade agreements without having the levels of productivity and competitiveness against imports. In 2019, the Trans-Pacific Partnership came into effect. Therefore, pressures upon the foreign-trade deficit will continue and will reduce investment and business's profits, along with job creation, leaving even fewer possibilities for raising salaries and improving distribution of income.

Income inequality is harmful to economic growth

Income inequality contracts consumption by most of the population, and thus diminishes demand, investment, and employment. The proportion of wages and salaries in the economy continues to decline. That fell from 41% of GDP in 1976, to 26.2% in 2018 (data from the INEGI) because of unemployment, underemployment, and low salaries, which in turn had resulted from the predominate policy of fiscal austerity, high interest rates, and free trade. The increase in the percentage of profits in the national income has not translated into faster growth of productive investment because of the contraction of the internal market and the low competitiveness of internal production. Instead, investors opt for the financial sector, and for strategic sectors that the government has opened to private investment, but without increasing productive capacity.

Families and businesses will continue to see restricted growth of their incomes because of the continuing high interest rates, budget cuts, trade deficit, and low competitiveness caused by a strong peso and a cheap dollar. Therefore, the families' and businesses' investment options will also continue to be limited.

Despite establishing its social policy of *Jóvenes Construyendo el Futuro* (Young People Constructing a Future) and pensions for the elderly, the new government will not succeed in increasing demand because low salaries and underemployment will continue. So will underemployment and the informal economy, thus increasing income inequality and the policy of maintaining the primary budget surplus. This combination of factors will hinder growth of demand and economic activity. Together, the rates unemployment (3.74%), underemployment (7.6%), and participation in the informal economy (59.8%) add up to 71.14% of the economically active population as of the third quarter of 2019 (Data from the *Encuesta Nacional de Ocupación y Empleo.*).

The minimum-wage increase that took effect in January 2019 did not counteract this phenomenon. Salaries will remain low and will rise more slowly than the productivity. Consequently, the demand, too, will grow slowly, thus discouraging investment, job creation, and economic activity.

Without growth of formal employment and salaries, neither demand nor economic activity will increase. The government must increase spending to increase demand so that the private sector can invest and create jobs. There are no growth-promoting policies in place for employment, better salaries, or regulating and supervising the banking and financial sectors.

Public investment is falling, and there is insufficient internal and external demand for growth

Fig. 12.9 reflects the lack of growth in consumption, public spending, net exports, and investment (public and private) from 2017 to the first quarter of 2019. Because of lack of growth in those areas, conditions do not exist for growth of demand. The lack of growth in those areas was the result of fiscal austerity, high interest rates, exchange-rate stability, and the foreign-trade deficit, plus unemployment and low salaries. This situation has increased the amount of idle capacity and has reduced both private investment and the growth potential of the economy—a feedback effect that further contracts the internal market and maintains economic stagnation.

The prevalence of the primary fiscal surplus since 1983 has caused public investment to fall significantly (from 13.1% of GDP in 1981% to 2.4%

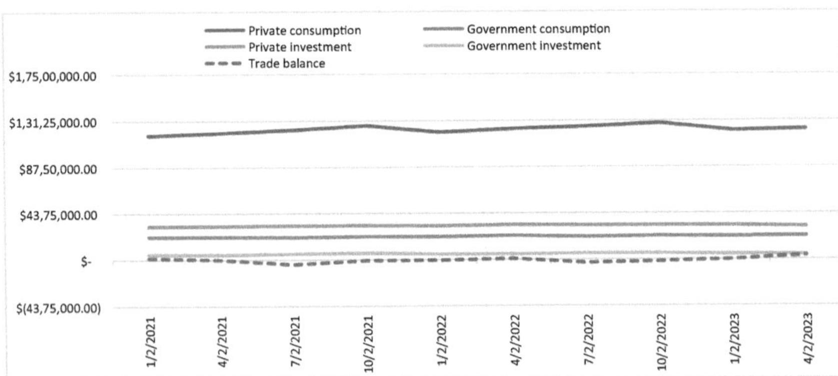

Figure 12.9 Public and private investment, consumption, and trade balance in Mexico (millions of 2013 pesos), 2017Q1-2019Q2. *Source: Author's elaboration base in data from Banxico.*

in 2019). Private investment now occurs where the government has stopped investing. However, gross fixed investment as a percentage of GDP has not increased.

The leakage of demand toward imports (imports were 37.9% of GDP in 2018) derives from free trade, predominance of a strong exchange rate, and the Mexican economy's low levels of productivity. This leakage reduces the internal multiplier effect of the demand and is detrimental to investment and economic growth.

In this context of uncertainty, investors delay their investment decisions, thereby configuring a stagnation of the Mexican economy. The uncertainty has multiple causes: the new government's economic policy, the cancellation of the new airport; the fall of the stock market in 2018; the delay in signing the T-MEC in the US and Canada; the deceleration of Mexico's economy and world trade; and the high rate of internal interest.

The new government's decision to strengthen the position of the State in the oil and electrical sectors reduces the possibilities that big businesses have for investing in those sectors. If no other profitable investment options are available, and the national economy does not show promise of growing, then big businesses do not invest—a decision that also manifests itself in lower demand for stocks in the equities market.

When demand does not grow, and the interest rate (7.5%) is higher than the growth rate of national income (0.0%), there is no investment. Economic growth is not at all viable. Businesses in that context do not solicit capital for investment because they do not have an assured flow of income to cover repayment of loans. The bank, for its part, does not extend credit because the bank is uncertain that loans will be repaid. As a result, the amount of credit extended by the commercial bank grows slowly, as shown in Fig. 12.6.

When investment diminishes, economic activity contracts, and with it the income and profits of the private sector along with the income of individuals. Profits, according to Kalecki (1971), depend upon investment. Therefore, profits are reduced when investment falls. In addition, profits depend upon the situation of the foreign sector: when that sector runs a deficit, profits fall because domestic businesses are replaced by imports. In the same sense, the fiscal surplus is harmful to the private sector's income and profits because in that case the government withdraws more from the economy than the government puts into it.

When the financial position of the private sector deteriorates, consumption and investment contract. Low growth of investment has brought lower productivity growth and productive capacity, plus pressures upon the foreign trade deficit, thus inhibiting the dynamics of accumulation and economic activity.

There is no prospect of increasing consumption while employment and salaries do not increase, and while income distribution does not improve. In addition, public spending and investment will not increase while the fiscal-austerity policy continues. Nor is there any possibility of reducing leakage of demand toward imports while Mexico continues with free trade, low productivity, appreciation of the national currency, and national productive backwardness.

There is no countercyclical fiscal policy

The Mexican government cannot implement countercyclical policies to resume economic growth when exports, consumption, or private investment are falling. According to the predominating theoretical perspective that determines decisions about investment, the government does not proceed to increase public deficit spending to increase demand in order to drive private investment and job creation, for fear of inflation and devaluation. Nor can the central bank lower the interest rate to stimulate growth, because the bank does not want to provoke capital flight, which could devalue the national currency.

When the exchange rate is maintained stable, and accompanied by high interest rates and fiscal austerity, it is not possible to counteract the negative effects (upon the national economy) of the foreign-trade deficit and the contraction of the private sector's investment and consumption. This is because these factors are the cause of such problems. The predominating fiscal and monetary policies act procyclically. Therefore, economic activity and the stock market continue to decline, and capital flees the country in search of better investment options. As a result, the stability of the exchange rate and the free movement of capital are called into question.

The economy places itself in a position of greater disadvantage in the face of external shock, given the greater deterioration that such policies caused to the productive sphere. In spite of that disadvantage, monetary and tax authorities do not modify their policy, in order to please financial markets.

Lower economic growth potential is detrimental to job creation, salaries, and the public wellbeing

As economic activity slows, the economy's growth potential is harmed, thereby placing the economy in a condition of weakness when it faces external shocks. The economy is not in a condition to increase employment and salaries to improve the population's standard of living because productive capacity is insufficient. This situation could lead to pressures upon prices and imports.

Mexico does not have highly productive sectors of production that absorb labor and raise salaries. The country has not had a macroeconomic policy or industrial policy of the type that would drive technological and industrial development, or development of value chains, or improve labor conditions.

It will be difficult for Mexico to overturn the condition of lower growth potential that the predominant economic policy has configured. Therefore, the slowing of economic activity will not be temporary.

Deceleration of the world economy

The worldwide spread of fiscal-austerity policies has reduced countries' economic growth. That reduction has translated into slower growth of imports by some countries and has thus affected the exports of others. This situation accentuates the present decline of world trade and causes economies to not grow toward the internal market, or the external one. From the foregoing, the government recognizes that reducing the interest rate has not been sufficient to reactivate the economy. However, the government has not dared to relax fiscal policy for fear of falling further into debt. The government does not recognize that it cannot make payments on its debt and reduce it if the government does not spend more. In contrast, economies like those of the US and China are relaxing their fiscal policies to make their economies more dynamic. Germany, too, has seen itself forced to increase spending in the face of that country's decelerating economy. However, the announced spending appears to be insufficient for restoring economic growth. If fiscal-austerity policies continue to predominate in most countries, then conditions will not exist for reverting the deceleration of the economic dynamic.

Uncertainty regarding Brexit, added to stagnation in the Euro zone and the slowing of China's economy, affect not only equity markets but world trade and the world economy. The repercussions manifest themselves in the form of lower international prices for oil and other raw materials, thereby pressuring both the foreign-trade balances of countries that export such goods, and the exchange rates of those countries' respective currencies. In the case of Mexico, the drop in the international price of oil stands out: after reaching USD 77.73 per barrel on October 3, 2018, the price of Mexican mixed crude oil fell to USD 51.83 on 14 December of that year, then to USD 49 on November 13, 2019.

The fragility of the economy when it depends upon capital inflows

If the new government stops offering attractive assets to foreign investors (as previous governments did via structural reforms that privatized and foreignized the economy), and also stops making the economy attractive for capital inflows (by not offering investors conditions of growth, profitability, and repayment), then capital inflows will become insufficient for dealing with the deficit of the current account for balance of payments. The exchange rate and equity market will then come under pressure. In response, the central bank will maintain a high interest rate to attract capital and prevent capital outflow, at the cost of slowing the economy and accentuating problems of insolvency. However, the problem will persist because investors will worry about how to ensure repayment of their investments when the economy is in recession.

The Mexican economy has neither productive conditions, nor the economic-policy management needed to deal with external shocks

The national economy's combination of low productivity, productive backwardness, pressures upon the external sector, and high levels of indebtedness put it in a weak position in the face of free trade, a decelerating world economy, and the vagaries of international financial markets. Fig. 12.10 shows how the total public and private debt has almost doubled from the first quarter of 2010 to the first quarter of 2019, while the activity of the economy grew at an average annual rate of only 2.1% during the same period. As can be seen, public debt grew more than private debt.

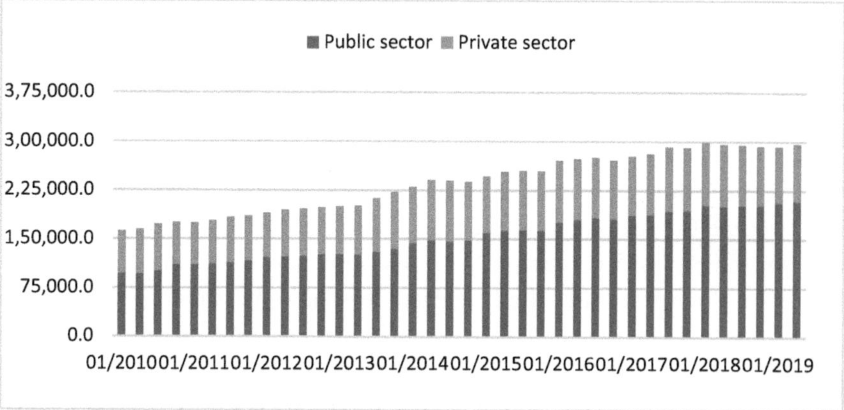

Figure 12.10 Quarterly public and private debt—domestic and external (USD million), 2010–19. *Source: Author's elaboration based on data of the* Secretaría de Hacienda y Crédito Público.

Fig. 12.11 shows that since 2010, the internal debt has been increasingly acquired by foreign investors, who take advantage of the interest-rate differential with which the Bank of Mexico operates.

Exchange-rate stability, like free movement of goods and capital, is maintained by capital inflows because the economy does not have endogenous conditions to do so by other means. As a result, the economy becomes vulnerable to the behavior of foreign capital.

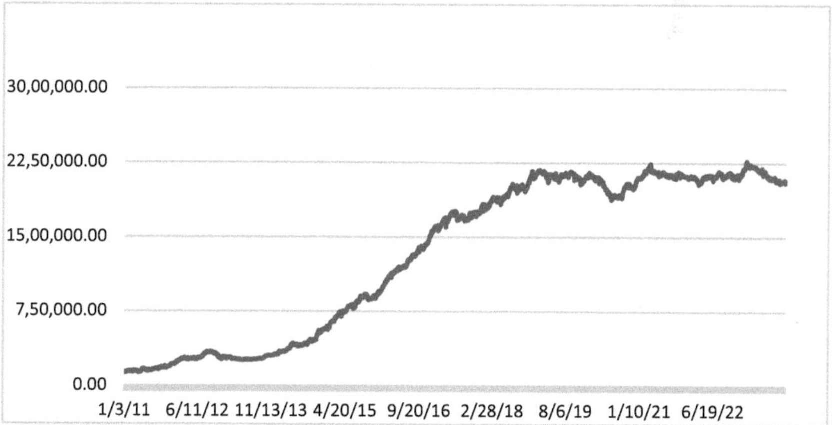

Figure 12.11 Mexican government debt held by foreigners (daily balance, millions of pesos), 2007–19. *Source: Author's elaboration based on Banxico data.*

The repercussions that the dynamics of the rest of the world will experience because of the deceleration of world commerce and the trade war between the US and China will depend upon how governments respond in this context. The Mexican economy has neither productive conditions, nor the economic-policy management needed to deal with external shocks.

The challenge is not only to avoid the slowing of economic activity, but to overcome the structural problems of deindustrialization and of the loss of food sovereignty in basic grains. Both phenomena worsen the foreign-trade deficit and compromise the capacity to make payments on financial obligations.

The impossibility of continuing with the predominating neoliberal policy

If the economy does not have conditions for adjusting the current-account deficit, and/or to ensure the flow of resources for facing that deficit, then the country will not be able to maintain free trade, free movement of capital, or the convertibility of the national currency to stabilize the exchange rate.

It is not possible to proceed with a primary fiscal surplus when the economy does not grow. In a context in which the foreign-trade deficit and private sector do not increase their consumption and investment, because of the financial problems that they face, the government cannot continue prioritizing the primary fiscal surplus that has brought the economy to stagnation and recession, as may be seen in Table 12.1.

There are no prospects for productive development advancing, because of high interest rates and because the policy of fiscal austerity and budget-cutting tends to predominate. Mexico's budget for science and technology is 0.5% of GDP and will not increase in 2019 or subsequent years (according to announcements in the *Criterios Generales de Política Económica* (General Criteria for Economic Policy))—a situation that separates us increasingly from the other countries in the OECD, whose investment in science and technology averages 2.7% of GDP.

Table 12.1 Quarterly GDP at constant prices (Rate of growth with respect to the previous trimester).

2018 trimesters				2019 trimesters		
1st	2nd	3rd	4th	1st	2nd	3rd
1.3	−0.2	0.4	−0.1	−0.1	−0.1	0.0

Source: Author's elaboration based on INEGI data.

The need to operate with a flexible exchange rate

A sovereign country must not subordinate itself to financial markets, because the policies that those markets can impose for stabilizing exchange rates impede monetary, fiscal, and exchange-rate policies that favor growth. If the country operated with a flexible exchange rate, sovereign management of economic policy would be regained. The central bank is perfectly capable of lowering the interest rate, and the government can expand public spending in favor of employment and the productive sector to reduce pressures upon both the external sector and the requirements for capital inflow.

Mexico needs a fiscal deficit that favors the productive sector to adjust the external deficit and drive the dynamics of the economy

For the growth to resume, either the Ministry of Finance needs to operate with a fiscal deficit, or the public sector needs to operate with a deficit, or the economy needs to achieve a foreign-trade surplus and improve the financial conditions of the private sector (businesses and families) to increase consumption and investment. The problem is that the economy lacks the conditions to achieve a foreign-trade surplus, given the context of free trade, nominal exchange-rate stability, low levels of productivity, pronounced backwardness of national productivity, and the deceleration of international trade. The private sector has debt limits and will not invest if demand and the sector's profits do not grow. The problem is that the government imposes limits upon itself, favors fiscal austerity, and does not wish to increase the public debt, all for fear of the inflation and exchange rate devaluation. In such a context, the private sector has little hope of seeing increases in sales and incomes that might motivate it to increase investment. Nor can the government improve its financial position and reduce the amount of debt.

The government cannot continue to speak of sound finance and reduction in the public debt to justify fiscal austerity and the primary surplus, while simultaneously operating according to the neoliberal thesis that fiscal deficits and public debt are bad. Fiscal policy must be evaluated according to its impact upon the real economy and the situation in which the private sector and external sectors find themselves. If the private sector has a financial deficit and is not investing; and if the economy runs a foreign-trade deficit at the same time that a decrease in growth of exports is oncoming because of US protectionist policies, new terms imposed by the new T-MAC, and slowing of the global economy; then the Mexican government must operate with a fiscal deficit in order to foster technological development. For example, to produce substitutes for imports to reduce the foreign-trade deficit, improve the financial position of the private sector (businesses and families), and drive the dynamics of the economy.

When the national income increases, the government collects more in taxes, which would reduce the public deficit that drives growth and would avoid increasing the debt. To increase its spending, the government need not incur more debt or raise taxes; it just needs to spend, so that it may drive economic activity. The government collects in taxes that which it spends, not the other way around. It is spending that generates income. If the government does not spend more, it cannot collect more in taxes and cannot make payments on its debt (Wray, 2012, Chapter 4).

If the government should need to issue debt when it falls into fiscal deficit, this situation will not turn out badly if the debt serves to bolster productive growth and job creation, both of which will generate income to cover payments on the debt and to reduce it.

While the economy is not growing, public finances will not improve, nor will the amount of debt be reduced. Just as the Mexican government runs a fiscal deficit that derives from making payments on the debt, the government is perfectly capable of operating with a spending deficit that favors the productive sector and employment. The current stagnation has, itself, created, the unemployment and idle capacity that enable the government to expand public spending independently of the government's fiscal deficit or levels of indebtedness. Productive capacity will be available to respond the increased public spending. In this regard, Mitchell has said, "If there is a new crisis, there will be a massive fiscal space defined by idle resources in the non-governmental sector that have remained unemployed because non-governmental spending has collapsed" (2018).

Deficit spending must bolster the economy's growth potential so that productive capacity will be available to reduce imports and satisfy the increase in demand that will be generated by greater public spending. In addition, deficit spending of this sort will make possible an increase in the added value of national exports, and a reduction in the foreign-trade deficit, thereby improving incomes of businesses and individuals so that the country's economy may emerge from the recessive context into which it has fallen. As a result, the government will be able to collect more taxes and reduce the fiscal deficit to foster economic growth, and thus will not fall into debt. Fiscal policy requires a monetary policy that accommodates expansion of public spending to foster economic activity.

It is monetary policy that must subordinate itself to the objectives of growth and employment that are being pursued by the employment policy—not the other way around, as has been occurring. Operating with a fiscal deficit would not be a problem for the government if the government used that deficit to foster national production. Nor would refinancing the debt be a problem if that debt were in the national currency.

Regarding the existing foreign debt, a foreign-trade surplus is needed to make payments on it, but the national economy has no prospect whatsoever of producing that surplus. Therefore, the government must rethink how to pay that debt to avoid slowing economic growth and that rethinking should be directed toward import-substitutions that would save foreign exchange to cover payments.

References

Kalecki, M., 1971. Selected Essays on the Dynamics of the Capitalism Economy. Cambridge University Press.

Mitchell, B., 2018. Precarious Private Balance Sheets Driven by Fiscal Austerity Is the Problem in. www.bilbo.economicoutlook.net/blog/. September 17.

Steindl, J., March 1979. Stagnation theory and stagnation policy. Cambridge Journal of Economics 3 (Issue 1).

Wray, R., 2012. Modern Money Theory: A Primer on Macroeconomics for Sovereign Monetary System. Palgrave Macmillan.

CHAPTER THIRTEEN

The Brazilian economic recession and stagnation and an Agenda to ensure macroeconomic stability and social development

Fernando Ferrari Filho[1,2]
[1]Department of Economics, Federal University of Rio Grande do Sul, Porto Alegre, Brazil
[2]National Council of Scientific and Technological Development, Brasília, Brazil

Introduction

From 2010 to 2014, the Brazilian economy moved from a situation of reasonable economic growth,[1] low unemployment and inflation rates, and improved macroeconomic fundamentals to another, during the period 2015–18, of recession and stagnation, higher unemployment rates, volatile inflation rates, and fiscal vulnerability.[2]

On the one hand, the reasons for Brazil's economic success in the former period were Luiz Inácio Lula da Silva's response to the 2007–08 global financial crisis and major recession of 2009,[3] which involved implementing countercyclical fiscal and monetary policies, and the economic policies during the first term of the Dilma Rousseff government, which slightly altered the course of the macroeconomic tripod.[4] On the other hand, the economic problems in the period 2015–18 were related to the orthodox economic policies, mainly fiscal policy, explicitly contractionary, adopted by the

[1] The annual average economic growth rate, calculated by the author based on Table 13.1, was 3.4%.
[2] Based on the figures of Table 13.1, from 2015 to 2018 the annual average GDP growth was −1.1%, the annual average inflation rate was 5.9%, the unemployment rate increased from 5.3% (January 2015) to 11.6%t (December 2018) and the nominal fiscal (primary plus financial) deficit over GDP was 9.1% in 2015, 9.0% in 2016, 7.8% in 2017 and 7.1% in 2018. The average rates were calculated by the author.
[3] In 2009, GDP fell 0.2%.
[4] Implemented in 1999, the Brazilian macroeconomic tripod (i.e., inflation targeting regime, fiscal surplus and flexible exchange rate) is based on the New Macroeconomic Consensus (NCM) framework.

Handbook of Economic Stagnation
ISBN: 978-0-12-815898-2
https://doi.org/10.1016/B978-0-12-815898-2.00015-X

governments of both Rousseff (from January 2015 to August 2016) and Michel Temer (from September 2016 to 2018).[5]

Given that, this chapter has two objectives: first, it describes and analyses the reasons for the Brazilian economic recession, between 2015 and 2016, and stagnation, 2017 and 2018; second, it outlines an agenda to restore macroeconomic stability and social development, defined as sustainable economic growth, stable inflation, fiscal and external equilibria, and improved income distribution.

Besides this introduction, the chapter is divided as follows: section two presents the economic policies and the economic performances of the Rousseff and Temer governments; section three proposes an Agenda for the Brazilian economy, based on Keynesian and Institutionalist approaches; and section four concludes.

Chronicle of a crisis foretold

In October 2014, in a very close-run election, Rousseff was re-elected President of Brazil. After taking office in January 2015, her administration's first year was marked by two features that contributed to Brazil's economic crisis and stagnation. The first was "Operation Carwash" (*Operação Lava Jato* in Portuguese),[6] that is, a political factor that not only worsened economic agents' decision-making expectations, but also, partly, explained the abrupt and deep recession that engulfed Brazil in 2015 and 2016. The second arose when the government, abandoning the countercyclical macroeconomic policies implemented largely after the global financial crisis and major recession in 2009, decided to introduce some orthodox fiscal and monetary policies, mainly to gain any market confidence.

Exploring the second feature, as Table 13.1 shows, by the end of 2014, the Brazilian economy was beginning to show signs of an impending crisis:

[5] At the start of the second Rousseff government, the administration was paralyzed by the orthodox economic policies and, moreover, by a political crisis that resulted in the impeachment of President Rousseff.

[6] A criminal investigation by the Federal Police to investigate money laundering and corruption in public enterprises, such as Petrobras (Brazil's largest corporation). The investigation grew into a major scandal, because it implicated politicians and leading entrepreneurs in important private companies. In sum, it revealed structural corruption in the political and economic system.

Table 13.1 Some macroeconomic indicators of the Brazilian economy.

Year	GDP growth rate (%)	Unemployment rate (%)	Inflation rate (%)	Primary fiscal result/GDP (%)	Nominal fiscal deficit/GDP	Basic interest rate, end of period (%)	Trade balance (US$ billion)	Risk country (EMBI, %))	Average exchange rate, end of period (R$/US$)
2010	7.6	6.7	5.91	2.7	2.6	10.75	20.2	189	1.67
2011	4.0	6.0	6.5	3.1	2.6	11.0	29.8	223	1.87
2012	1.9	5.5	5.84	2.4	2.4	7.25	19.4	142	2.05
2013	3.0	5.4	5.91	1.9	1.4	10.0	2.6	224	2.36
2014	0.5	4.8	6.41	−0.6	−6.7	11.75	−3.9	260	2.65
2015	−3.5	6.8	10.67	−1.9	−9.1	14.25	19.6	523	3.95
2016	−3.3	11.5	6.29	−2.5	−9.0	13.75	47.7	328	3.26
2017	1.3	12.7	2.95	−1.7	−7.8	7.0	67.0	240	3.31
2018	1.3	12.3	3.75	−1.6	−7.1	6.5	58.3	276	3.88

Based on IPEADATA (2020) and IBGE (2020).

GDP increased only 0.5%, inflation rose to 6.41%, the primary fiscal result over GDP was - 0.6%,[7] the trade balance surplus decreased to US$ 2.6 billion, the Brazil risk (as measured by Emerging Markets Bond Index—EMBI) increased to 260 basis points and capital outflows intensified.

In this context, Rousseff decided that her government would introduce economic changes to tackle the approaching economic crisis. The idea was to apply a tighter macroeconomic policy to reduce aggregate demand and thus curb accelerating inflation, as well as to introduce fiscal austerity measures to mitigate the public deficit and guarantee service of outstanding public debt. The theoretical thrust of Rousseff's macroeconomic policies was thus given by the roots of the NCM.

As her Minister of Finance, Rousseff appointed Joaquim Levy (Ph.D. in Economics from the University of Chicago), who was tasked with achieving a huge short-term fiscal adjustment. Fiscal policy was dominated by the following measures: public expenditures were cut; some taxes (on financial loans, company financial revenues, manufactured goods and automotive exports) were increased; subsidies for companies were reduced; social benefits (unemployment and sickness insurance, for instance) were cut; and public and administered prices were raised dramatically. The impact of this fiscal policy on the economy was contractionary because it replaced public investment and social benefits by payments to rentiers.

Monetary policy followed orthodox guidelines and was also explicitly recessive, as the basic interest rate (Selic) set by the Central Bank of Brazil (CBB) was raised to reduce and control inflation.[8] It is important to mention that in Brazil, in general, a rising interest rate punishes both firms, which need credit to operate, and workers, who not only need credit to buy goods, but also lose jobs when firms face difficulties. Moreover, high interest rates cause additional fiscal problems because the financial deficit increases.[9]

At the same time, some liberalizing reforms were enacted, such as social security reform and additional capital account liberalization.

[7] Incidentally, this was the first time the primary fiscal target had not been met since fiscal discipline and the Fiscal Responsibility Law (FRL) were introduced in 2000, providing rules to establish fiscal equilibrium at the three levels (federal, state and municipal) of government and in the three branches (Executive, Legislative and Judiciary). For additional details, see:Tribunal de Contas da União (2020).

[8] At end of 2014, the Selic rate was 11.75%, while in December 2015 it was 14.25% (Table 13.1).

[9] At the end of 2015, the ratio of financial deficit to GDP had increased to 7.2% (Table 13.1).

To sum up, when Rousseff decided to apply orthodox fiscal and monetary policies and implement liberal reforms, completely contrary to what had been done in her first term and promised during her reelection campaign, she turned radically to the right.

The main consequences of this orthodox economic policy were that Brazil's currency, the *real*, weakened dramatically from an average exchange rate of R$ 2.36 per US dollar in 2014 to R$ 3.33 in 2015 (i.e., around 42% depreciation). As a result, annual inflation rose to 10.7%, due mainly to the huge exchange rate depreciation (i.e., the pass-through mechanism from exchange rate to the domestic prices) and public and administered price shocks. In addition, as Table 13.1 shows, GDP fell 3.5%, while the average unemployment rate increased from 4.8 (2014) to 6.8% (2015).

This economic policy strategy based on fiscal austerity and tight monetary measures not only failed to solve Brazil's economic problems, but it deepened them. Thus, Rousseff decided to dismiss Joaquim Levy and introduced some economic policy "flexibilities".

Under the new strategy, monetary policy remained tight aiming to mitigate inflation, while fiscal policy became more "flexible" to stimulate aggregate demand.

By 2016, however, the economic problems had not been reduced. On the contrary, they had worsened, not only because fiscal expansion was carried out in a manner that lacked credibility, using devices (among them, "creative accounting"[10]) that inspired mistrust, but as a result of the political and institutional crisis, which led, in April 17, to Rousseff's suspension and finally, in August 31, the Senate removed President Rousseff from office,[11] considering her guilty of breaking the Brazilian fiscal laws.

As a result, in the same day of the on August 31, 2016, the Vice-President Temer became president in her place for the remainder of the original term (2015–18).

[10] In Brazil, "creative accounting" refers to the use of artificial manners of achieving fiscal equilibrium. The most notorious of these methods, the "fourfold operation," evolved from the exchange of resources between the State and state enterprises. The four public entities involved in the scheme were the National Sovereign Fund, National Treasury, BNDES (public development bank) and Caixa Econômica Federal (public commercial bank). They exchanged assets and loans in such a way that, in the end, the National Treasury amassed the amount necessary to attain the primary balance surplus it had committed to with the Brazilian parliament. For additional details, see Villaverde (2016).

[11] The process to impeach Rousseff began in 2015, when she was charged with violating the FRL.

As his Minister of Finance, Temer appointed Henrique Meirelles, a former chairman of the CBB during Lula da Silva's administration, who implemented a liberal proposal based on fiscal austerity and structural reforms.

Some short-term fiscal austerity measures were taken through a sweeping program to reduce public spending. Later though, in December 2016, the government submitted, and the Brazilian Congress approved, a constitutional amendment establishing the New Fiscal Regime (NFR), designed to achieve tight fiscal consolidation. Under the NFR, for the next 20 fiscal years, the annual variation of nominal public sector expenditures would be pegged to the consumer price index (IPCA), that is, the prior year's inflation. It will thus constrain public spending in line with the government's endeavor to deliver fiscal consolidation forcibly.

At same time, tight monetary policy continued to be applied in order to bring the inflation rate within the range of the inflation targeting regime.

This economic strategy restored "confidence" among economic agents, mainly the International Monetary Fund and international financial investors, because the inflation rate had fallen to 6.29% by year end. Nonetheless, in the real economy, the results were poor: GDP fell 3.3% and unemployment rose to 11.5% (Table 13.1).

It is important to mention that the main cause of the Brazilian recession in 2015–16 was the short-term fiscal adjustment, which impaired the state's ability to galvanize the economy, because the structural adjustment resulted in structural compression of public investments. Moreover, in a scenario of economic recession, the public spending cutbacks contributed to a decline in government revenues. This fiscal policy, which prompted negative expectations among economic agents—not only for fiscal equilibrium, but also the federal government's ability to lead recovery from the recession that had begun in 2015—was thus pro-cyclical.

In 2017, the government proposed, and Congress approved, a labor law reform to radically change Brazil's 1943 Consolidated Labor Laws (*Consolidação das Leis do Trabalho*). The goal of the labor reform was to deregulate the labor market and, as a result, to raise the level of employment. In practice, however, at least in the short run, the labor reform has been unsuccessful.[12] In line with its liberal proposal, the Temer government also proposed a social security reform, but was unable to secure congressional approval.

[12] In 2017 and 2018, the unemployment rates were, respectively, 12.7% and 12.3% (Table 13.1).

During 2017 and 2018, while fiscal austerity policies were in place, the monetary policy operated by the CBB became more flexible, mainly because inflation had fallen substantially, to 2.95% in 2017 and 3.75% in 2018. Accordingly, the Selic rate was 7.0% and 6.5% at the end of 2017 and 2018, respectively (Table 13.1).

With improving fiscal conditions, lower interest rates, a competitive exchange rate (the exchange rate was R$ 3.31 and 3.38 per US dollar at year end 2017 and 2018, respectively) and an international scenario favorable to the Brazilian economy, economic activity recovered, and GDP increased 1.1%, in both 2017 and 2018 (Table 13.1).

In conclusion, recession and stagnation in Brazil from 2015 to 18 can be associated with the following factors: (1) economic policy volatility (expansionary in 2016 and contractionary in 2015, 2017 and 2018) as well the fiscal and monetary policies were essentially pro-cyclical, that is, during the recession the economic authorities (EAs) raised interest rates and tightened fiscal spending[13]; (2) political and institutional crises; (3) huge fiscal deficit and high public debt; and (4) a process of deindustrialization and commodity-dominated exports (also called "re-primarization").[14]

An Agenda for the Brazilian economy

In Chapter 24 of *The General Theory, of Employment, Interest and Money* (GT), Keynes suggested some economic policies designed to mitigate or remedy "[t]he outstanding faults of the economic society in which we live [that] are its failure to provide for full employment and its arbitrary and inequitable distribution of wealth and income" (Keynes, 1936: 372).

The focus of Keynes's suggestions was the power that the State should wield to steer the economic system, given that, if left to the free workings of the market, the economic system, and economic policies themselves (unless there was coordination among them) would contribute not to solving, but to aggravating the major problems of monetary economies. To

[13] Exploring this point, Arestis et al. (2019) argue that during the period 2011—14 EAs presented some "mistakes of the past," in terms of monetary and exchange rate policies, while, from 2015 to 2017, the management of fiscal policy, by EAs, represented the "waste of future opportunities."

[14] This latter point is not explored here, but has been an important cause of Brazil's stagnation since the 1990s. See, for instance, Nassif et al. (2018).

Keynes, the role of the State was thus fundamental to ensure macroeconomic stability and social development. For that purpose, Keynesian macroeconomic policies should be coordinated in such a way as to: (1) manage fiscal policies designed to expand effective demand and reduce social inequalities; (2) make use of more flexible monetary policy, so as to galvanize levels of consumption and investment; and (3) coordinate and regulate the financial and foreign-exchange markets in order to stabilize capital flows and exchange rates.

The "old" American Institutionalists, such as John Commons (1931) and Thorstein Veblen (1889), tried to understand the role of the evolutionary process and the role of institutions in shaping the habits and rules of individuals and society as a whole. Hodgson (2002: 113), for instance, defined institutions as "durable systems of established and embedded social rules that structure social interactions. Language, money, law, [...] firms (and other organizations) are all institutions." Thus, the "economic theory of institutions" considers not only institutions, but also human activity and the evolutionary nature of economic processes. In this context, to Institutionalists, the economic system represents a "continuous process" of change that involves a restructuring of the capitalist economy rather than acquiescence to the automatic mechanisms of the market.

In the light of these Keynesian and Institutionalist understandings about the dynamics of the economies, this section presents an Agenda to restore macroeconomic stability and social development, as stated in the introduction to this chapter. This Agenda, as will be shown, must contemplate both short-term macroeconomic policies and structural-institutional changes.

The short-term macroeconomic policies need to afford favorable conditions to rouse entrepreneurs' animal spirits once and for all. For that purpose, monetary policy must explicitly consider the goal of employment stability together with price stability, fiscal policy must prioritize public investment and social programs, and exchange rate policy must be designed to maintain balance of payments equilibrium.

More specifically:

(i) Fiscal policy should be implemented in such a way as to expand expenditures in both social programs and public investments, especially in infrastructure to boost economic activity. Here, it should be stressed that public—private partnerships are to be encouraged. Moreover, the government should always seek fiscal responsibility, as

Keynes (1980) recommended,[15] although this should not be pursued as an end in itself, but on the criterion of countercyclical fiscal policy management: policy should be expansionary in periods of crisis and recession, while it should be neutral in times of prosperity or economic growth above productive capacity.

(ii) Monetary policy should be guided by employment goals and not only inflation targets.[16] For this purpose, discretionary monetary policy is indispensable. Also, macroprudential measures should be taken to mitigate financial risk and expand liquidity in the economy. Lastly, as regards the financial system, the CBB and EAs should (1) indicate measures to decentralize the system, with a view to reducing bank spreads and democratizing access to credit, and (2) underscore the importance of the public banks, such as the BNDES, Banco do Brasil and Caixa Econômica Federal, and the regional and state development banks, as regards long-term financing for productive investment.

(iii) CBB should administer the exchange rate in such a way as to keep the real effective exchange rate (REER)[17] competitive, so that any speculative actions on the foreign currency market can be contained. To achieve this goal, the National Treasury should buy and sell foreign currency to support exchange rate stability and counter disorderly conditions on the foreign exchange market. In other words, the exchange rate regime must be similar to a managed floating exchange system, which would aim to preserve some flexibility/volatility in the short-term nominal exchange rate, while at the same time maintaining a stable and competitive REER. In addition, capital controls should be used to enhance the CBB's autonomy in setting the nominal interest rate to support domestic objectives, prevent the *real* from appreciating and avert financial and exchange crises. Moreover, the REER proposal is intended not only to maintain balance of payments equilibrium, thus

[15] In 1942, after analyzing *The Beveridge Report* on the United Kingdom's social security budget, Keynes proposed introducing separate "ordinary" and "capital" budgets. He wrote, "the ordinary Budget should be balanced at all times [while] [...] the capital Budget [...] should fluctuate with the demand for employment" (Keynes, 1980: 225).

[16] This does not mean that the CBB would have an inflationary bias. The point is that, considering that inflation in Brazil is connected with supply bottlenecks, inertial behavior and exchange rate pass-through, then it makes no sense to raise interest rates in order to contract demand and, in that way, to control inflation. For a critical analysis of inflation targeting in Brazil, see Araujo et al. (2018).

[17] REER is the weighted average of a country's currency relative to an index or basket of other major currencies adjusted for the effects of inflation.

mitigating external constraints, but also to establish an exchange rate that is not so overvalued as to create disincentives to industry, nor so weak as to reduce wage purchasing power.

In terms of structural-institutional changes, which are so important to expanding supply capacity and potential GDP, the government should, among other things:

(i) Implement a progressive income tax reform (i.e., higher rates of taxation on income and wealth);

(ii) Continue raising the real minimum wage and funding for social programs, such as Family Allowance Program (*Programa Bolsa Família*), so as to improve standards of living among poor people and expand domestic consumption;

(iii) Encourage an institutional environment to galvanize the stock market and, particularly, private corporate debt[18];

(iv) Adopt income policies to regulate wages and prices in line with productivity gains in the economy and the dynamics of market competition;

(v) Expand industrial policy programs to coordinate public and private efforts to mitigate the deindustrialization process and, at the same time, to secure the Brazilian economy a place in the international scenario in a context where Brazil can incorporate the structural and technological changes occurring in the world economy;

(vi) Implement trade agreements with other emerging countries, such as Latin American, Asian, and African countries;

(vii) Invest in innovation, research, and development, and education that are essential for productivity gains in productive sectors;

(viii) Stimulate a cooperative arrangement between public and private sectors, that is, public—private partnership, to aim at expanding the infrastructure projects, such as transport, water and sewerage systems, and education and health systems.

Finally, it is important to emphasize that structural-institutional changes cannot disregard the State's role in the economy, which must be redefined by rebuilding the coordination mechanisms that were dismantled during the 1990s, and, more recently, from 2015 to 2018. In other words, the State according to Keynes (1936: 378) has to "exercise a [...] comprehensive

[18] To achieve these aims, it is necessary to introduce, for instance, investor protection, exposure limits for financial institutions, and risk limits for institutional investors, as well as taxation appropriate to risk profile.

socialization of investment" and, following the "old" American Institutionalists' arguments, has to shape the economic and social behavior of the modern economies. In other words, the State should, once again, exercise its function as a regulator, coordinator and inducer of economic activity, as well as it should have the power to establish a real Welfare State in Brazil.

Conclusion

This chapter showed, first, that the recession and stagnation in Brazil from 2015 to 2018, a period when the cumulative GDP growth rate was −5.5%, were caused by the orthodox economic policies implemented (most importantly, the NFR), as well as by the political and institutional crisis which resulted in the impeachment of Rousseff.

These facts (fiscal austerity, tight monetary policy, and the impeachment process) affected economic agents' decision processes. In other words, following Keynes' idea (1936), in a context of fundamental uncertainty, entrepreneurs, households, and bankers decided to retain money: the recession and stagnation occurred because liquidity preference inhibited economic agents' decisions to spend. Applying Keynes' metaphor to the Brazilian economy:

"unemployment develops, that is to say, because people want the moon [financial assets, mainly public bonds – no risk and high premium and liquidity]; – men cannot be employed when the object of desire (i.e., money) is something which cannot be produced and the demand for which cannot be readily choked off. There is no remedy but to persuade the public that green cheese is practically the same thing and to have a green cheese factory (i.e., a central bank) under public control" (Keynes, 1936: 235).

Secondly, it was proposed an Agenda for the Brazilian economy, based on Keynesian and Institutionalist approaches. This Agenda was designed to ensure macroeconomic stability and social development and it was focused on both short-term macroeconomic policies able to create an institutional environment to influence and stimulate economic decisions, and on structural-institutional changes to expand aggregate supply.

To conclude, we know that to elaborate this Agenda will be, paraphrasing Lennon & McCartney, a "long and winding road," mainly because the current president of Brazil, Jair Messias Bolsonaro, elected in October 2018, is a radical right-wing politician who believes that only a Minimum State and a free-market system are able to solve all Brazilian economic problems.

References

Araujo, E., Araujo, E., Ferrari-Filho, F., April-June. Macroeconomic performance in Brazil under the inflation targeting regime. Investigación Económica LXXVII (304), 72–101.

Arestis, P., Ferrari-Filho, F., Resende, M.F., Terra, F.H.B., 2019. Brazilian monetary and fiscal policies from 2011 to 2017: conventions and crisis. Challenge: The Magazine of Economic Affairs 62 (3), 187–199.

Commons, J.R., December 1931. Institutional economics. American Economic Review 21, 648–657.

Hodgson, G.M., 2002. The evolution of institutions: an agenda for the future theoretical research. Constitutional Political Economy 13, 11–127.

IBGE, 2020. Informações Estatísticas. Available at: http://www.ibge.gov.br. (Accessed 6 July 2020).

IPEADATA, 2020. Séries Históricas. Available at: http://www.ipeadata.gov.br/. (Accessed 6 July 2020).

Keynes, J.M., 1980. Activities 1940-1946: Shaping the Post-War World – Employment and commodities/The Collected Writings of John Maynard Keynes, vol. XXVII. Palgrave Macmillan, London.

Keynes, J.M., 1936. The General Theory of Employment, Interest and Money. Palgrave Macmillan, London, 2007.

Nassif, A., Bresser-Pereira, L.C., Feijó, C., March 2018. The case for reindustrialisation in developing countries: towards the connection between the macroeconomic regime and the industrial policy in Brazil. Cambridge Journal of Economics 42 (2), 355–381.

Tribunal de Contas da União, 2020. The Fiscal Responsibility Law. Available at: https://portal.tcu.gov.br/english/inside-tcu/the-fiscal-responsibility-law/. (Accessed 6 July 2020).

Veblen, T., 1889. The Theory of the Leisure Class: An Economic Study of Institutions. Houghton Mifflin, Boston, 1973.

Villaverde, J., 2016. Perigosas Pedaladas: Os bastidores da crise que abalou o Brasil e levou ao fim o governo Dilma Rousseff. Geração, São Paulo.

PART C

The return of big government and economic prospects after the pandemic

CHAPTER FOURTEEN

The role of big government: an introduction*

L. Randall Wray
Economics, Levy Economics Institute of Bard College, Annandale-on-Hudson, NY, United States

This chapter will look at the arguments for the role a "big government" can play in maintaining adequate aggregate demand to promote sustainable growth. We will focus on the "Domar problem"—the tendency for the supply effects of investment to outstrip the demand effects—as well as problems of inflation and financial instability that arise from investment-led growth.[1]

In a series of articles and books, Harold Vatter and John Walker made the case that the U.S. economy has long suffered from chronically insufficient demand that generates growth below capacity. They extended Evsey Domar's work on the supply side effects of investment spending and provided a comprehensive analysis of the evolution of the U.S. "mixed" economy.

In the *General Theory*, Keynes had addressed the demand-side effects of investment: rising investment generates income that in turn induces consumption spending through the multiplier. Keynes singled out investment as the major "autonomous" component of spending, as it is focused on future sales and expected profits over the life of the plant and equipment. Hence, fluctuations of investment "drive" the economy—or, as Minsky put it, Keynes had an investment theory of the cycle. Because Keynes was most interested in explaining the point of effective demand, he tended to hold constant the productive capacity of the economy. Whether the economy was operating at full capacity or with substantial excess capacity could then be attributed to the level of effective demand itself a function of the quantity of investment. If the economy were operating below full capacity,

* This chapter draws on Levy Economics Institute Working Paper No. 488, "Demand Constraints and Big Government", L. Randall Wray January 2007. http://www.levyinstitute.org/pubs/wp_488.pdf.

[1] See also Pigeon and Wray (2002).

Handbook of Economic Stagnation
ISBN: 978-0-12-815898-2
https://doi.org/10.1016/B978-0-12-815898-2.00009-4

then the solution would be to raise effective demand—either by encouraging more investment, or by increasing one of the other components of demand.

As "Keynesianism" was embraced after WWII, its policy recommendation was reduced to "pump-priming" and "fine-tuning" of effective demand, accomplished through various investment incentives (tax credits, government-financed research and development, countercyclical management of interest rates) and countercyclical transfer payments—combined with continued defense spending on the cold war.

However, Domar (1946) had already recognized the problem with a policy bias toward investment—for not only does investment add to aggregate demand, but it also increases potential supply by adding plant and equipment that increase capacity. He argued that while it takes an increase of investment to raise aggregate demand (through the multiplier), a constant level of net investment will continually increase potential aggregate supply. The "Domar problem" results because there is no guarantee that the additional demand created by an increase of investment will absorb the additional capacity created by net investment. Indeed, if net investment is constant, and if this adds to capacity at a constant rate, it is unlikely that aggregate demand will grow fast enough to keep capital fully utilized. There would need to be an additional source of aggregate demand as the "multiplier" operates only with rising investment. This refutes Say's Law, since the enhanced ability to supply output would not be met by sufficient demand. As such, "more investment" would not be a reliable solution to a situation in which demand were already insufficient to allow full utilization of existing capacity.

Vatter and Walker showed that after WWII, the output-to-capital ratio was at least one-third higher than it had been before the war (Vatter and Walker, 1989). Due to capital-saving technological innovations, it takes less fixed capital per unit of output so that the supply side effects of investment will persistently outpace the demand-side multiplier effects. The only way to use the extra capacity generated by net investment is to increase other types of demand, such as household spending (consumption plus housing investment), government spending (federal, state, and local levels), and foreign spending (net exports). Vatter and Walker believed that growth of government spending would normally be required grow at a pace that exceeds GDP growth in order to avoid stagnation (Vatter and Walker, 1983, 1989, 1997).

This should not be interpreted as endorsement of Keynesian countercyclical "pump-priming" to "fine-tune" the economy. Indeed, Hansen had previously demonstrated that pump-priming would fail (Vatter and Walker, 1997). If government increases its spending and employment in recession, only to withdraw the stimulus when expansion gets underway, it would restore a situation of excess capacity. The larger the government, the harder it becomes to cut back spending because jobs, consumption, income, and even investment all depend on the government spending. According to Vatter and Walker, in a well-run fiscal system, government spending will rise rapidly when investment is rising (to absorb the created capacity) and then will still rise rapidly when investment falls (to prevent effective demand from collapsing). They call this a "ratchet"—rather than countercyclical swings of government spending, "government as a share of the economy should rise indefinitely" (Vatter and Walker, 1997).

Samuelson's "multiplier-accelerator" model added a further complication—as the increase of national income through the multiplier would encourage more investment through the accelerator. This could lead to explosive cyclical growth and collapse. Minsky (1957) addressed this instability by arguing that government could and should play a role in putting in place ceilings and floors to constrain aggregate demand, while also arguing that government should place less emphasis on encouraging investment as a means of maintaining growth and full employment. Instead, he advocated for government-led growth to promote greater financial and economic stability, as well as to foster greater equality.

Minsky thus argued that government-led expansion is preferred—for stability reasons.[2] In an interesting manuscript, Minsky developed a model to examine budgeting for economic stability (Misnsky and Adelaman, 1960). The paper begins with the acknowledgment that "much of the following is related to the principles of functional finance," and explicitly cites Lerner's Economics of Control and Economics of Employment, while admitting that "an old fashioned assumption underlies this paper: that full employment and price stability are compatible." The paper asserts that "national debt is unique ..., for there is no default risk .... [The only risks are] that the interest rate and the price level may change."

Further, the national debt adds net financial wealth to the private sector: "The total wealth of private units equals the value of things in the economy

[2] Wray (2018), http://www.levyinstitute.org/pubs/wp_900.pdf.

plus the value of the national debt." The paper concludes that the best policy combination consists of a low interest rate, with the national debt growing at the same rate as private debt, and with both equal to the rate of growth of productivity. Note that this implies perpetual budget deficits in order to grow national government debt as productivity grows. This is functional budgeting in the sense that it provides safe financial wealth to the private sector that is leveraged as the economy and private debt grow.

A few years later, however, he warned that the traditional Keynesian policy—that promotes investment and high growth—would be unsustainable:

> *The 1960's witnessed the apparent victory of Keynesian policy. However, the successful application of Keynesian policy may result in an economy that is inherently unstable. This instability is not the result of a tendency to stagnate or enter into a deep depression state; rather it is due to a tendency to explode .... [T]o an increasing extent both households and business were expecting next year to be better than this year. This trend in the expectational climate resulted in an explosively increasing demand for private investment in the mid-1960s.*
>
> ***Minsky (2013, 331).***

For this reason, he advocated targeted spending by government, along with policy to shift the gains from growth from high income, high wages, and the most advanced sectors toward the lagging sectors and lower wage workers. In a lot of his writing he emphasized shifting spending away from investment and toward consumption, as well as policy to ensure full employment and growth of wages at the bottom so that household consumption would be financed out of income rather than by debt. To quickly sum up his position:

* economic growth led by the private sector would be financially fragile as private debt would grow faster than ability to safely service it;
* investment-led growth would be especially precarious because it would produce both financial instability as well as inflation
* government-led growth, if spending were carefully targeted to job creation, would promote noninflationary and financially stable growth with full employment and shared prosperity.

Adolf Wagner added yet another argument for favoring big government. He argued that economic development leads to industrialization and urbanization, which generates an absolute, as well as a relative, increase in the demand for more government services (of course, J.K. Galbraith made a similar point). Hence, for political and socioeconomic reasons, government should grow faster than the economy. If it does not, not only will this leave society with fewer publicly provided services than desired, but it will also generate stagnation through the Domar problem.

These arguments concerning secular trends can be supplemented by the Kalecki/Minsky analysis of the role of government over the cycle in sustaining profits. Aggregate profits are equal to investment, plus the government deficit, plus the current account surplus, plus consumption out of profit, and less saving out of wages. When investment falls, profits fall. As Minsky (1986, 1993) put it, past investment undertaken on the expectation of future profits cannot be validated at the lower level of investment, depressing current investment, and further lowering profits through a process of cumulative causation. In a big government economy with a budget that automatically swings in a counter-cyclical manner, deficits are created that attenuate effects on profits.

Capital-saving innovations increase the capacity effects of investment, thus, so long as investment remains above replacement levels, potential aggregate supply rises. To utilize this new capacity, aggregate demand must increase even though investment has fallen to a lower level. Unless another source of demand fills the gap, the government's budget must become more stimulative. This is more easily accomplished with a bigger government because of the larger potential swings of its budget balance relative to the size of the economy as a whole. Minsky argued that government must be at least as large as investment; however, government will have to be larger to the extent that investment swings are large and if automatic swings of the budget are relatively small.

Further, persistent trade deficits will increase the role of government in maintaining profits and demand. Minsky argued that positions in capital assets are financed through a combination of internal and external funds. Growth of investment generally leads to growth of debt; over the course of an expansion, leverage ratios rise (both debt-to-net worth and debt-to-income) and financial positions evolve from largely hedge (interest and principal payments are made as they come due) toward speculative (only interest can be paid) and even Ponzi (interest must be capitalized).

Thus, an expansion led by investment spending will tend to lead to a fragile financial structure (Minsky, 1963). Leverage ratios and fragility will be increased to the extent that expansion also generates a trade deficit (as demand and profits leak to the foreign sector) and a government budget surplus (depressing demand and profits). On the other hand, Minsky (1963) argued that a government-led expansion would not increase fragility because budget deficits would raise private sector income and wealth, generating profits and filling private portfolios with safe and liquid assets. However, profits and robust private balance sheets would be likely to induce investment and risk-taking. Hence, there is an inherent contradiction because financial stability is enhanced by a growing role for government in leading an expansion, but this can generate a run-away inflationary spiral that is held in check only if the government's budget moves sharply toward surplus to suck income, profits, and wealth from the private sector—creating financial instability. For this reason, institutional constraints are needed to limit the natural trend toward fragility. These can be imposed through rules, regulations, and supervision of financial institutions, as well as by lender six of last resort intervention when all else fails. For this reason, the "Big Bank" (central bank) is a natural complement to the "Big Government."

The Domar problem and secular stagnation since 1910!

Unlike many analysts who date the beginnings of secular stagnation to the 1970s (Gordon) or even later in the 1990s (Peterson, 1994), Vatter and Walker concluded that the United States has experienced secular stagnation since 1910, with GDP growth averaging 4% per year before that date, but less than 3% from 1910 to 1990 (Vatter and Walker, 1997). High growth before 1910 could be described as "Keynesian," that is, led by investment. However, the "Domar problem" surfaced by 1910, apparently because investment had become subject to capital-saving innovations that increased capacity effects. This seems to be most true of investment in structures, which was permanently lower after 1910.

Vatter and Walker identified several different regimes in the post-1910 period. While all of them produced slower growth than that experienced before 1910, performance was better in some than in others. For example, the period 1910–29 can be characterized as a "small government," slow-growth laissez faire economy, with the gold standard providing an additional constraint (Minsky, 1993). Its growth rate was just 2.8%, attributed to low investment, especially in structures (Vatter and Walker, 1997). During some periods, other types of spending temporarily made up for lower trend investment—such as military spending during WWI and an installment-debt led consumer durables boom in the late 1920s. However, with a small government there was no sustainable source of demand to allow the economy to grow more robustly.

After 1930, growth of government spending outpaced GDP growth, especially during WWII; this more than made up for lower trend investment so that GDP growth improved. The early postwar "golden age" period (Minsky, 1993 called it a "practical best") followed the dictates of Wagner's Law, while the slow-growth period after the early 1970s suffered the consequences of breaking that law. For example, during 1948–73, real purchases by all levels of government grew at a compounded pace of 4.24%, faster than real GNP growth of 3.67%.2 Government payroll employment grew at a rate of 3.62%, compared with just 1.57% for the civilian labor force. In contrast, after 1973, the rate of growth of real government purchases and payroll employment averaged just 1.8%, while real GNP grew at 2.4% and the civilian labor force at 2%—both figures significantly higher than the comparable government figures.

The important point stressed by Vatter and Walker in all of their studies is that the main constraint on economic growth since 1910 has been chronically insufficient aggregate demand. While they did not dismiss the possibility of supply-side bottlenecks, they insisted that the U.S. economy is, and has been, capable of growing at a 4% rate on a sustained basis. However, aggregate demand has not been held high enough to permit growth at capacity, resulting in secular stagnation. While demand occasionally does meet or (rarely) exceed the necessary level, it is quickly brought back down—often through intentional policy measures, such as interest rate hikes or temporary tax surcharges, or simply due to political opposition to expansion of government at the necessary pace.

What has been needed all along is faster growth of "Big Government"; Vatter and Walker insist that to achieve sustained growth of real GDP at a feasible rate requires only a small increase of investment, but a large increase of government spending (Vatter and Walker, 1997). Interestingly, orthodox economists and policy-makers habitually misread the problem, proposing the wrong policy solution. Conventional wisdom imagines supply side constraints that limit feasible (inflation-adjusted) sustained growth to something on the order of 2%–2.5% per year.[3] However, growth at such a pace leaves capital and labor idle—discouraging investment and productivity growth.

[3] See Kelton and Wray on supposed "speed limits": http://www.levyinstitute.org/pubs/rpt5_98.pdf.

The proposed orthodox solution is always a policy to encourage "more saving" to generate "more investment" that will attenuate the imagined supply constraints. Of course, "more saving" would mean less consumption, increasing idle capacity and hence discouraging investment. Further, if investment were increased through such policy, it would create more excess capacity. Compounding the problem is the resurgence of balanced budget conservatism over the past 4 decades, which likens the federal budget to that of a household that will bankrupt itself if it continually spends more than its income. In addition, ivory tower academics have concocted fanciful tales about the effects of fiscal deficits, running from "crowding-out" of investment, to "debt burdens" on future generations, and finally to "Ricardian equivalents" that imagine that "rational" households increase current saving to pay future taxes.

Vatter and Walker (1997) provide a thorough examination of the evolution of attitudes toward government and its budget. In the early 1930s, the conservative attitude toward government was well-summarized by President Hoover: "Though the people support the government, the government should not support the people" (Vatter and Walker, 1997). The Great Depression, the New Deal, and WWII abruptly displaced that orthodoxy, and helped to push through the Employment Act of 1946 that asserted government responsibility for macroeconomic performance. While government budgeting was never understood, even during the heyday of "Keynesianism," the notion that government must balance its budget over a specified period was not accepted during that early post-war era. Abba Lerner promoted functional finance—the idea that fiscal policy should be formulated to achieve desired results, rather than with a view to balancing the budget—and together with Domar emphasized that far from burdening the population, government debt represents net wealth in the form of safe and liquid assets. In any event, the federal government did run deficits in most years, and as we have seen, government grew faster than the economy until the early 1970s.

However, over the course of the past quarter century, conservative ideology managed a comeback. Vatter and Walker insisted that "the logic of the national debt in a fiscal policy world is a ratchet. Debt never goes down ..." (Vatter and Walker, 1997). Still, conservative orthodoxy had become so dominant by the mid-1990s that President Clinton promised to run perpetual budget surpluses so that all of the federal debt issued since 1837 (the one and only time the U.S. government was debt-free) would be retired. Economists not only applauded the effort, but endorsed the projections! The Fed even held a conference to discuss how monetary policy would be conducted once all the debt was retired. However, the budget surplus threw the economy into a recession that destroyed the tax revenue flow so a large and chronic budget deficit quickly returned.

Still, the prevailing political rhetoric refers to growing debt burdens for our grandchildren and the possible insolvency of our nation's government. Through an ironic ideological about-face, the Democrats became the party of "fiscal responsibility," promising to slash spending and increase taxes should they gain control of government. In a very nice exposition of the bankruptcy of orthodox policy making, Vatter and Walker (1989) examined the projections made by the Council of Economic Advisors in each of the annual Economic Reports of the President, through both Democratic and Republican administrations (1979–86) for the coming year. Vatter and Walker concluded the "expected stagnation was chronically overachieved," with actual GNP growth averaging a miserable 2.0%. Ironically, actual federal purchases grew far above projections, at 3.1% per year, while actual investment averaged a growth rate below projections at 3.2%. In other words, the CEA persistently expected more robust growth, fueled by investment, but the real engine of growth was government spending, albeit at levels that were too low to allow the economy to grow at its true potential of 4% per year.

If the CEA had been able to induce policy-makers to hold growth of government spending below zero, as projected, actual GNP growth would have been even lower, resulting in less inducement to invest, as capacity utilization would have been even further from what was technically feasible.

While the "bigger government" associated with the post-war economy did (perhaps) achieve smaller cyclical amplitude, thanks to the stabilizing influence of countercyclical budget swings, the long-term trend was well below potential output growth and below growth rates achieved in the small government, laissez faire economy of the 19th century. To get back to growth rates closer to potential requires faster growth of government spending.

Conclusion

The argument that J.K. Galbraith made in the early 1960s concerning the relative dearth of public services is only very much stronger today—with unmet needs for universal health care, for universal access to higher education to prepare youth for the "knowledge" economy, and for greater public involvement in finally eliminating the remaining inequalities that result from intransigent racism, sexism, and cultural biases. The biggest existential challenge to humanity today is the unfolding climate catastrophe—a challenge that cannot be met without ramping up the role of government.

As Hyman Minsky used to argue, capitalism was a failed system in 1930. The growth of "Big Government" was singled out by Minsky and by Vatter and Walker as the necessary medicine to build a viable and robust version of capitalism. Minsky always insisted that there are "57 varieties" of capitalism, with different systems appropriate to different historical epochs. The evolutionary or institutional approach taken by Domar, Minsky, and Vatter and Walker, which recognizes the necessity of the "mixed economy," is the alternative that will help us to formulate policy appropriate to today's problems.

References

Domar, E.D., April 1946. Capital expansion, rate of growth, and employment. Econometrica 14 (No. 2), 137—147.

Minsky, H.P., December 1957. Monetary systems and accelerator models. The American Economic Review 47 (No. 6), 859—883.

Minsky, H.P., 1963. Discussion. American Economic Review 53 (2), 401—412.

Minsky, H.P., 1986. Stabilizing an Unstable Economy. Yale University Press, New Haven, CT.

Minsky, H.P., 1993. Finance and Stability: The Limits of Capitalism. The Levy Economics Institute of Bard College. Working Paper #93.

Minsky, H.P., 2013. Ending Poverty: Jobs, Not Welfare. Levy Economics Institute of Bard College, Annandale-on-Hudson, NY.

Minsky, H.P., Adelaman, I., 1960. In: Minsky, H.P. (Ed.), On the National Debt and Economic Growth. Archive, 120. Available at: https://digitalcommons.bard.edu/hm_archive/120.

Peterson, W.C., 1994. Silent Depression: The Fate of the American Dream. W. W. Norton & Co, New York and London.

Pigeon, M.-A., Randall Wray, L., 2002. Demand constraint and the new economy. In: Davidson, P. (Ed.), A Post Keynesian Perspective on Twenty-First Century Economic Problems. Edward Elgar Publishing, Cheltenham, U.K.

Vatter, H., Walker, J.F., 1983. Can the Good Performance of the 1960s be repeated inn the 1980s? Journal of Economic Issues XVII (2), 369—378.

Vatter, H., Walker, J.F., 1989. Why has the United States operated below potential since World War II? Journal of Post Keynesian Economics 11 (3), 327—346.

Vatter, H., Walker, J.F., 1997. The Rise of Big Government in the United States. M.E. Sharpe, Armonk, NY.

Wray, L.R., January 2018. In: Wray, L.R. (Ed.), Working Paper No. 900 "Functional Finance: A Comparison of the Evolution of the Positions of Hyman Minsky and Abba Lerner". Levy Economics Institute and Bard College.

Further reading

Minsky, H.P., 1968. Effects of shifts of aggregate demand upon income distribution. American Journal of Agricultural Economics 50 (2), 328–339. Reprinted in Minsky (2013).

Plotkin, S., Scheuerman, W.E., 1994. Private Interest, Public Spending: Balanced Budget Conservatism and the Fiscal Crisis. Black Rose Books. Reuters, Montreal, 2006.

Vatter, H., Walker, J.F., 1982. The princess and the pea; or, the alleged vietnam war origins of the current inflation. Journal of Economic Issues XVI (2), 597–608.

Vatter, H., Walker, J.F., 1990. The Inevitability of Government Growth. Columbia University Press, New York.

Vatter, H., Walker, J.F., Alperovitz, G., 1995. The onset and persistence of secular stagnation in the U.S. Economy: 1910–1990. Journal of Economic Issues XXIX (2), 591–600.

Wray, L.R., 1994–5. Is Keynesian policy dead after all these years? Journal of Post Keynesian Economics 17 (2), 283–304.

Wray, L.R., 2003. The perfect fiscal storm. Challenge 46 (1), 55–78.

Wray, L.R., 2006a. Neocons and the ownership society. Challenge 49 (1), 44–73.

Wray, L.R., 2006b. Flexible Exchange Rates, Fed Behavior, and Demand Constrained.

CHAPTER FIFTEEN

Secular stagnation: as good as it gets?

Flavia Dantas[1], L. Randall Wray[2]
[1]Economics Department, State University of New York, Cortland, NY, United States
[2]Economics, Levy Economics Institute and Bard College, Annandale-on-Hudson, NY, United States

Introduction

The term secular stagnation was first coined by Alvin Hansen in the 1930s, and frequently used until the 1950s.[1] According to Hansen, in its essence, secular stagnation meant "sick recoveries which die in their infancy, and depressions which feed on themselves and leave a hard and seemingly immovable core of unemployment" (Hansen, 1939, p.4). Hansen and others were concerned with the "external forces" that underlie economic progress, including population growth and technological innovations. Economic maturity meant that fewer investment opportunities consistent with full employment would be available.

While the economic performance of the US economy in the later post-war period proved Hansen's concerns, the early postwar saw relatively high and sustained growth. For the most part, the "Keynesian" economists were confident that "fine-tuning" could sustain effective demand. Nonetheless, theoretical discussions about economic growth continued. After WW II, some like Domar and Harrod were concerned with the conditions necessary to ensure that aggregate demand grew at a sufficient pace with the productive capacity created by new investment. The concern was that the demand effects of new investment would be too small to keep aggregate demand at a sufficient level. Unfortunately, that led to the two Cambridges debate over Neoclassical growth theory—with the battle won by Keynes's followers, but the war won by the Neoclassicals. In any event, economic growth as a topic of discussion was largely sidelined for a generation during capitalism's "golden age"—at least in the rich, developed countries, with economic growth relegated to development economics.

[1] For a historical account of the term, see Backhouse and Boianovsky (2016).

Handbook of Economic Stagnation
ISBN: 978-0-12-815898-2
https://doi.org/10.1016/B978-0-12-815898-2.00012-4

Most recently, concern with subpar growth in developed economies renewed discussions about secular stagnation. Summers revived the term and gave it a slightly different meaning—he defined secular stagnation as "a prolonged period in which satisfactory growth can only be achieved by unsustainable financial conditions."[2] Summers (2014), Eichengreen (2015), and Rachel and Summers (2019) argue that there has been a structural imbalance between saving and investment at positive rates of interest; equilibrium at full employment requires negative real interest rates, but monetary policy is constrained by the zero-lower bound. They point to several causes for the structural increase in the supply of savings and the structural decline in investment. The higher saving rates are a combination of increased life expectancy, concentration of income and wealth at the top, and increased uncertainty. At the same time, the reduction in the inducement to invest is similarly due to several factors: declining population growth, reduced rate of technological progress, lower capital prices (which reduces the demand effect of investment), changes in corporate behavior, and higher retained earnings. For example, according to Summers (2014) output, capacity utilization and employment expanded to satisfactory levels in the previous business cycle (2001–07) only because of the unsustainable upward movement in the share of GDP related to residential investment and loosening of credit standards. What goes up must come down.

Others have focused strictly on supply side forces, specifically, concern with the apparent slowdown in productivity growth and technological innovation. Gordon (2017), for example, argues that the unique set of inventions of the millennia 1870 to 1970 that altered the pace of economic growth in such profound ways is unlikely to return. Since the 1970s, economic innovation has been concentrated in "a narrow sphere of economic activity" such as communication and information processing, which does not transform life in the same fundamental ways as previous innovations had, and thus, limits the opportunity for new investment. The consequence is a significant slowdown in labor productivity and potential GDP growth experienced since the 1970s.

In addition, other "headwinds" make supply side prospects even worse: demographic shifts that cause lower labor force participation and employment rates and the consequent reduction in the total number of hours

[2] See Summers' website (post of June 7, 2007) at http://larrysummers.com/2017/06/07/secular-stagnation/.

worked per capita, lower educational attainment, more inequality, and a rising debt to GDP ratio which will inevitably lead to a future increase in tax rates or a reduction in government transfers. Gordon's position is in stark contrast to the "techno-optimists," who are concerned with technological displacement of even the most specialized, higher education jobs by robots, which would lead to permanently lower consumption and aggregate demand.

In contrast to the above, we argue that the secular stagnation experienced in the US economy since the 1970s is, and has been, a problem of chronic insufficient demand. We do not reject the notion that productivity is important or that supply side constraints might arise (as they recently have with the COVID-19 pandemic), but insufficient aggregate demand has been the primary reason for historically low growth rates observed over the period of analysis in rich, developed capitalist countries such as the United States. However, we also reject Summers' secular stagnation hypothesis—that is, that secular stagnation in the US is caused by an imbalance between saving and investment that has reduced the equilibrium real rate of interest to very low, or even negative territory. Our argument is that slow growth of demand is the cause of slow growth of investment; in addition (as Vatter and Walker argued—see the chapter by Wray), the supply boost to capacity increasingly exceeds the demand side multiplier effect of investment. This compounds the problem of insufficient aggregate demand to operate at full capacity—which reduces the incentive to invest.

There are several causes of chronic insufficient demand in the US and the rest of the industrialized world, including chronic labor underutilization, wage stagnation, rising inequality, current account deficits, improper policy response, and insufficient government spending. Many of these factors have been analyzed in previous contributions to this volume, so we will instead focus on the evidence of chronic insufficient of demand in the U.S. through the lens of labor markets; stagnant worker's incomes, falling participation rates of prime-age men, and relatively slow growth of productivity are all indicative of a problem of insufficient aggregate demand. The fundamental problem is not demographic trends, lack of technological innovations, negative equilibrium real rates of interest, or displacement by robots. We will argue that the slow "recovery" of labor markets following recessions, and especially of the employment rate and labor force participation, is due to a combination of insufficient job creation as well as stagnant wages.

We focus on *two* slow growth episodes experienced by the US economy (early-mid 1970s to mid-1990s, and then post-GFC, but prior to COVID-19). We argue that the US had been suffering from insufficient aggregate demand for several decades before economists like Summers and Krugman took notice. To be sure, stagnation is periodically relieved by short economic bursts—usually brought on by unsustainable asset price bubbles (dot com stocks, commodities, housing prices—a point also made by Summers, and by Fazzari in this volume). But once the bubbles burst, we return to secular stagnation. We also believe that, in absence of fundamental changes, the postpandemic US economy could return to the same pattern.

In this chapter, we first provide an overview of the relationship between growth and labor productivity over the two periods in question. The slowdown in productivity growth since the 1970s has puzzled economists and has been an important part of the secular stagnation argument made economists like Gordon, who believe that low rates of real GDP growth are due to supply side forces. Next, we discuss labor market trends. We focus on labor market participation, especially by prime-age workers. While female participation rates had been rising—which had long boosted overall participation—prime-age male participation has experienced a falling long-term trend. Recessions cause the participation rate of all groups to fall; in recent expansions; however, the recovery of participation rates have been attenuated over expansions—and in the expansion following the Global Financial Crisis (GFC), even rates of prime-age females took a long time to fully recover. So far, they remain depressed in the recovery from the depths of the pandemic.

Some have proposed a basic income guarantee as a solution to current labor market dynamics: just provide income to workers who have been displaced by robots, or who do not have the skills and training required in today's knowledge economy. However, that might raise aggregate demand beyond our limited ability to grow supply constrained output. The result could be stagnation and inflation—with the specter of a late 1970s style stagflation. While we do need more aggregate demand, we will argue that this should take the form of targeted job creation as well as growth of wages at the bottom of the wage ladder. Our recommendation will follow Hyman Minsky's "employer of last resort" proposal developed in the 1960s (see Minsky, 2013) and revived in recent decades as a "job guarantee" program. This would bring workers back into the labor force without fueling the inflation that would be generated by either the basic income guarantee or the old "Keynesian" reliance on "pump-priming."

Secular stagnation and labor productivity growth

Economic growth in most developed countries slowed since early 1970s in comparison to the early postwar period. The U.S. experienced particularly substandard growth over the 1973–96 period and following the FSC (2007–20). For example, while real per capita GDP increased at an annual average of 2.45% over the 1948–72 period, it slowed to an annual average rate of 2% over the 1973–96 period and to less than 1% per year over the 2007–19 period (in 2020, following the COVID-19 pandemic, U.S. per capita GDP contracted by 4%).

These were also periods of particularly weak productivity growth except for the short-lived 1996–2006 period. Fig. 15.1 below shows U.S. labor productivity growth (measured as nominal output per hour worked as published by the Bureau of Labor Statistics) and unemployment rates over the 1970–2021 period. For most of the period since 1972, labor productivity growth remained below the 2.8 yearly postwar average (shown as a horizontal line), while unemployment rates remained comparatively high. Productivity growth in the later period generally exceeded that average only in recoveries—and even then, not by much and not for long.

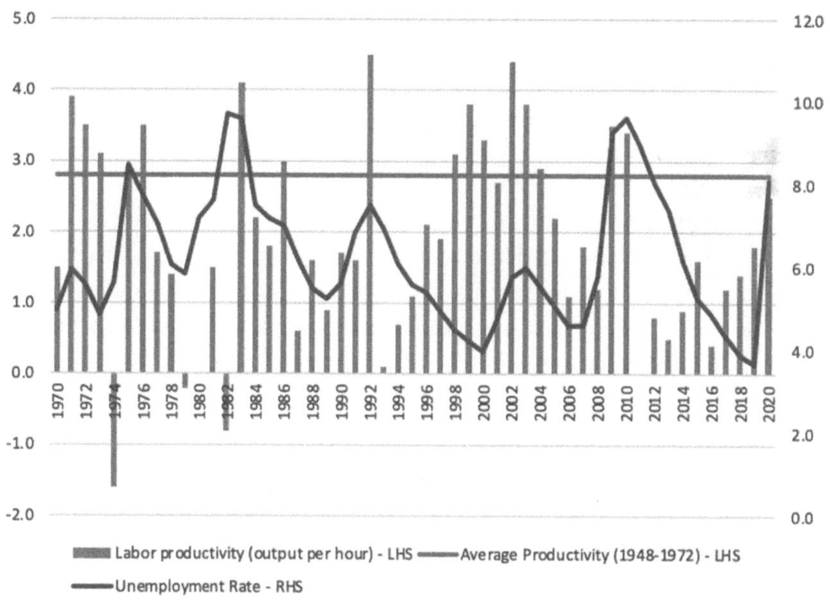

Figure 15.1 US labor productivity growth (nominal output per hour) versus unemployment rate. *Source: Bureau of Labor Statistics and Author's calculation.*

The consensus by the early 1990s was that subpar output growth in the US was a combination of the exhaustion of technological innovation, which permanently reduced labor productivity growth and investment opportunities (previously abundant in the postwar period), lower population growth, and some form of labor market hysteresis (caused by long-term unemployment), all which reduced the growth of the supply potential of the economy, and in turn aggregate demand. All this changed in the last half of the 1990s when the "New Economy" surged ahead with dot.com "innovations," and particularly strong labor markets. By the mid-1990s, unemployment in the US had fallen close to the lower rates that had been last experienced in the 1960s, with growing employment-population ratio and prime-age labor force participation. There was much talk about the new information technology that had suddenly made it possible to grow at rates similar to the postwar period precisely because of faster productivity growth.

The economy stumbled with the dot.com crash and a recession at the end of the 1990s, but growth resumed in the early 2000s with the synergies of the commodities, real estate, and stock market bubbles.[3] In the dozen years between 1995 and 2007, an increase in productivity growth raised potential GDP growth and temporarily attenuated the talk about supply side constraints—as many observers claimed we had entered a "new era" of higher growth, lower unemployment, stable prices, and financial stability. The "productivity boom" did not last for long as the economy crashed into the GFC. Labor productivity, employment and economic growth plummeted, followed by a very slow recovery over the next decade.

According to the orthodoxy, productivity growth is supposed to be the most important determinant of long-run growth, so the slowdown in labor productivity growth revived the secular stagnation debate and the discussions about supply side constraints to economic growth. The main limiting factors are said to be the lack of capital deepening, slowed rate of technological progress, deteriorating educational achievement, and/or experience of the labor force along with other troubling demographics trends. Labor force participation, for example, is supposed to be growing slowly due to lower birth rates and an aging population. In addition, while the US benefitted from rising labor force participation by women from the 1960s through the 1990s, that source of labor had been exhausted by the 2000s.

[3] See Fazzari's chapter in this volume.

Furthermore, structural changes in labor markets have reduced the demand for workers with lower skills and education. For whatever reason, too many young people do not complete enough schooling to meet the needs of modern production processes. Finally, it is claimed that the technological wave created by the computer age has run its course, and no new breakthroughs are on the horizon that would unleash major productivity advances (see Gordon, 2017).

In reality, we believe that the periods of faster growth of per capita GDP and labor productivity were fueled by robust growth in aggregate demand. Economic growth since 1996 has been led by the private sector—especially by household spending fueled by consumption out of wealth, the housing bubble, easy credit expansion, and growing indebtedness of U.S. households.[4]

Growth decomposition: productivity as a residual

By identity, total output is equal to the product of the aggregate number of hours worked and labor productivity (total output per hour). If we adjust output for inflation and divide both sides of the identity by population, then we get the result that real output per capita is the product of labor productivity (real output per hour) and the number of hours worked per capita. By definition, it follows that a slowdown in labor productivity (due, e.g., to a slowdown in technological innovation) or a reduction of hours worked per capita (due, e.g., to consistently high unemployment or low employment rates) will be consistent with a lower real output per capita. The identity by itself does not imply causality, and in fact, most movements in these components are endogenous. For example, an increase in real GDP per capita driven by stronger aggregate demand, all else equal, will increase the demand for labor, and the number of hours worked. If the number of hours worked increases faster than population and real output, then labor productivity will slow down even if technological innovations are abundant.

While economists and policymakers habitually impute great importance to measured productivity growth even over very short periods of time (even quarter over quarter changes are treated as important indicators of changes on the supply side), in practice, measured productivity growth, by itself, cannot tell us that supply side factors are the cause. The reason is that while

[4] See the chapters by Fazzari and by Tymoigne in this volume.

supply side factors (e.g., new technologies) can be important, employment growth (and hence changes in the number of hours worked, and the employment rate) and productivity growth are both driven by growth in GDP, which, in turn, translates into changes in GDP per capita, for a given growth of population. There is thus a strong interdependency among the various terms.

Low growth of per capita hours worked can be attributed in part to slow growth of output per capita; that is, if aggregate demand (the driver of output) does not grow at a pace sufficiently above productivity growth, then employment growth must suffer. Also, low demand discourages full capacity use of both labor and capital, which depresses use of both factors of production and can even depress technological advancement if demand is chronically low and labor is cheap. Firms have little incentive to invest in training of workers or new capital if unemployed workers are plentiful (holding down labor costs) and existing capacity is underutilized.

Fig. 15.2 decomposes growth of real GDP per capita into growth of labor productivity and hours worked per capita. The 1948–72 period was a period of rapid growth in per capita output and labor productivity. Although

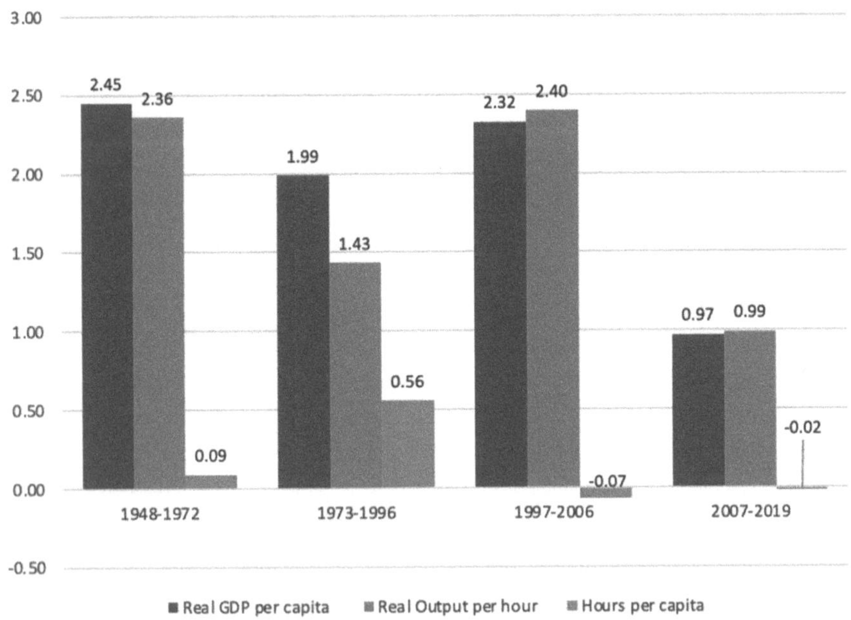

Figure 15.2 Real GDP per capita, real output per hour, and hours per capita. *Source: Bureau of Economic Analysis, Bureau of Labor Statistics, and authors' calculation.*

unemployment rates remained relatively low over that period (averaging around 4.8%), hours worked per capita remained relatively constant due to a combination of a low labor force participation rate (the enhanced flow of women into the labor force had not yet begun) and rapid population growth (averaging 1.5% per year).

This pattern changed over the 1973–96 period: per capita GDP growth and labor productivity slowed down. Despite still robust population growth (averaging 1% per year), the number of hours per capita grew significantly faster than in the previous period reflecting the increase in labor force participation as baby boomers, women, and immigrants joined the labor force. Nonetheless, higher unemployment rates (averaging 6.8% over the period) and the growing gap between productivity and labor compensation (see below) meant that aggregate demand remained chronically insufficient, keeping the overall growth of GDP lower. Essentially, the boost of hours worked per capita approximately offset the fall of productivity growth over this period as compared to the previous period. In some sense, aggregate demand constraints meant that growth of the labor force allowed firms to substitute cheap labor for productivity growth.

In the "new economy boom," all of the economic growth is explained by productivity growth as hours worked per capita were constant. Paradoxically, unemployment over much of this period was low. As we will show below, this does not necessarily mean that labor markets were tight as labor force participation rates and employment rates indicate considerable slack. Aggregate demand grew just fast enough to keep productivity growth up, but not enough to increase hours worked per capita. Finally, growth in the period following the GFC was particularly slow and again insufficient to raise hours worked per capita. All of the growth was "explained" by (slow) productivity growth.

In sum, we believe that the decomposition of growth provides some evidence for the argument that the entire period under analysis experienced insufficient demand. An identity cannot demonstrate causation but can discipline analysis. The sum of productivity growth and hours worked per capita is constrained to equal GDP growth per capita—in the short run and the long run. More labor hours are a substitute for productivity growth, given GDP growth—perhaps not in a behavioral sense, but at least in a mathematical sense. The earliest period examined (1948–72) shows high GDP and productivity growth with virtually no growth of hours worked per capita. This may well be the period in which labor was scarce, due to a variety of constraints (discrimination against women and minorities, immigration policy, stronger unions). However, with the growing labor force participation of women as well as declining unionization rates in the next two periods, labor was probably not scarce. The 1973–96 showed growth of worker hours as well as productivity growth, but with GDP growth substantially slower than the earliest period. The new economy boom saw growth return but with no growth of labor hours per capita, so productivity growth had to "explain" all the growth. It is worth looking at this period to see whether labor might have been the constraining factor. Finally, the post-GFC period sees no growth of labor hours and low growth of both GDP and productivity. This looks, at least superficially, like a period with significant insufficient aggregate demand.

The role played by stagnation of wages

Secular stagnation is also a product of compressed labor compensation, which depresses aggregate demand. Fig. 15.3 shows that growth in real hourly compensation has lagged behind labor productivity improvements since the 1970s. Standard economic theory says that labor productivity and wages should grow together, that is, real wages over time should

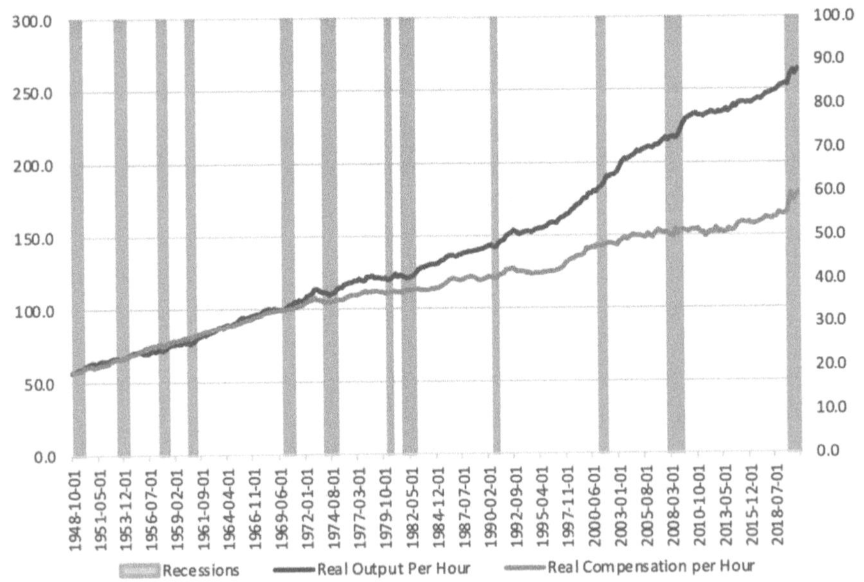

Figure 15.3 Real output per hour and real hourly compensation, nonfarm business sector, 1948.Q1—2021.Q1.

increase with labor productivity—the assumption is that under full employment, workers, and employers have the similar bargaining power so that each walks away from the production process fairly compensated for their contribution. In the real world, capital's control and share has increased since the early 1970s. There are many reasons for the loss of workers' bargaining power: the demise of unions, deregulation, outsourcing of industrial production, and competition with low wage exporters.

In any event, the trend of the wage/labor productivity relation since the early is not consistent with labor market tightness. Indeed, the widening gap would indicate that labor has been so sufficiently abundant over the period that firms did not need to compete for workers by raising wages in tandem with productivity growth. This casts some light on the growth decomposition results in the previous section. Growth of GDP does not seem to have been constrained by the labor supply side. Indeed, even the new economy boom—which did not increase hours worked per capita—did not see a marked improvement of the relation between wages and labor productivity. If labor supply had been a constraint, it seems that wages would have risen faster.

The evidence from wage performance would not seem to indicate that growth was constrained by the supply of labor. Further, if wages are relatively stagnant in comparison with the growth of productivity, that in itself can generate problems of effective demand—as we explain in the next section.

Labor markets—the demand side

Despite the wide-spread belief that supply side factors impinge on the ability of the economy to grow faster over the long run, the evidence is that the US has operated with substantial labor market slack since the mid-1970s, which have kept wages significantly depressed. Insufficient aggregate demand has caused slower productivity growth over most of this period. In this section, we look at labor markets for further evidence of chronic insufficient demand.

Since 1990, all of our recessions have been followed by "jobless recoveries." This was particularly true of the GFC—which required almost a decade for recovery of labor markets. Immediately before the COVID-19 pandemic, the official unemployment rate had finally fallen to historically low levels—3.5% in February 2020. Fig. 15.4 below shows the recovery after the last three recessions of the unemployment rates for three different

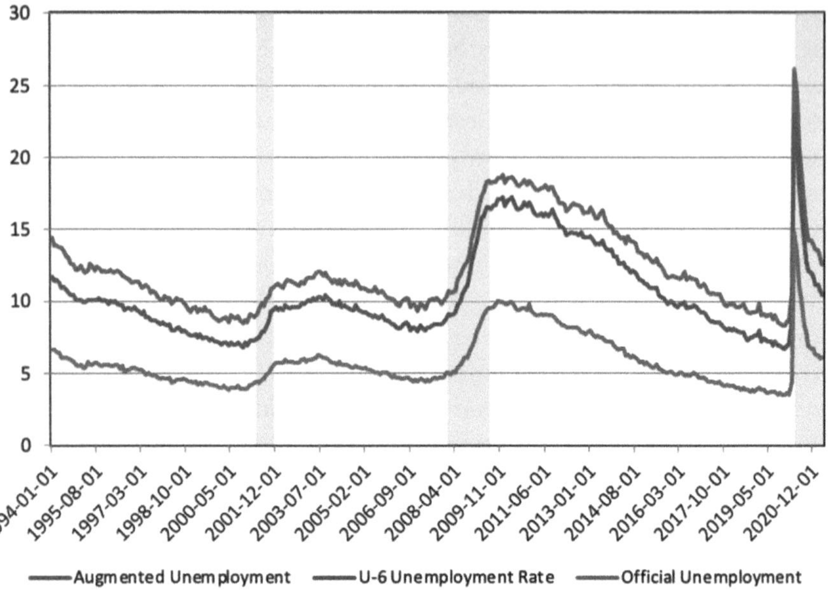

Figure 15.4 U.S. unemployment rates in recovery, 1994–2021.

measures of unemployment: the official unemployment rate, which excludes those marginally attached[5] to the labor force and involuntary part-time workers; the U-6 unemployment rate, which is the broadest official measure published; and our "augmented measure" which adds to the U-6 measure all those not in the labor force who want a job but did not search for one in the previous year.[6]

The official unemployment rate peaked at 10% in October 2009, while the U-6 and the augmented measure continued to increase until April 2010. It took about 75 months for official unemployment rates to return to their prerecessionary levels, and, respectively, 96 and 100 months for the U-6 and

[5] The marginally attached to the labor force are all those who want a job and are available to work now and have actively searched for work in the previous year but not in the previous 4 weeks.

[6] The U-6 measure of the unemployment rate only included the employed part-time for economic reasons and the "marginally attached" to the labor force. To be marginally attached one must want a job, be available to work now, and have searched for work in the previous year (but not in the previous 4 weeks). When we include those individuals not in the labor force who want a job now but did not search for one in the previous year, we get to what we call our augmented unemployment rate. We do not know how many of those would be available to work now (the BLS does not ask the question of availability to this group), but the "search criteria" used in the official measures eliminates all those who have become deeply discouraged, believing a job is not available for them.

our augmented rate to return to their pre-GFC levels. The lengthy recovery of unemployment rates from their pre-GFC peak is a direct consequence of chronic insufficient demand and improper policy response. Further, the discrepancy between the different measurements at any point in time sheds some questions on the official reading of labor markets—our augmented measure shows that around 14.4 million potential workers were at least partially idled before the COVID-19 crisis hit, and around 20.7 million potential workers remained idle as of April2, 021.[7]

Evidence from unemployment rates suggests that secular stagnation has been a problem of chronic insufficient demand for a long time. More troubling, the pattern from the latest recessions has been that even as unemployment rates begin to fall, labor force participation, and the employment-population ratio remain depressed for an extended period. Fig. 15.5 shows that in a downturn the sharp rise of the unemployment rate is associated

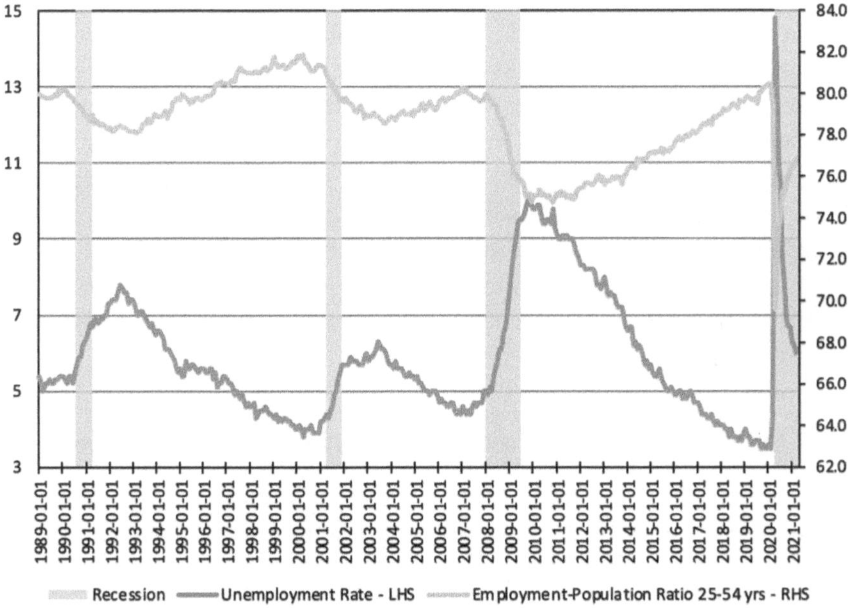

Figure 15.5 Unemployment rate and prime-age employment-population ratio.

[7] The nature of the COVID-19 pandemic's impact on labor markets is, of course, different from that of a usual recession. As social distancing measures eased, the relief bills were enacted, and the relatively successful U.S vaccination response after Biden's election, unemployment rates dropped relatively quickly, though they remain above their prerecessionary levels—particularly the U-6 measure as well as our augmented measure.

with a rapid decline of the employment ratio, but the relatively rapid fall of unemployment in the recovery is not matched by a quick restoration to a higher employment ratio. This is because a greater proportion of the unemployed are leaving the labor force, rather than finding jobs—as was the typical case in recoveries before 1990. When a smaller percentage of the working age civilian population is participating in the labor market, falling unemployment does not necessarily increase the employment-population ratio commensurately.

The typical discourse (e.g., Williams, 2016; Fujita, 2014) is that *decoupling* of the unemployment rate and the employment-population ratio is largely a consequence of changing demographics—such as retirement of baby boomers and younger people going to school for longer periods. An aging workforce has increased retirement rates (both normal age as well as early retirements), while extended schooling postpones movement into the labor force by the young. The combination of these factors is claimed to have generated the decline in the employment ratio and labor force participation. Further, more people of working age are believed to have voluntarily left the labor force, choosing to have more time to care for family members, to obtain more education, or to enjoy leisure. The entry of women into the labor force has allowed more of their husbands to stay at home. Generous social safety nets reduce the costs of exit from the labor force, while skills mismatches make such exits by prime-age males more appealing than taking a job that requires little skill and pays lower wages. These are the arguments frequently made to explain stagnant or falling participation rates.

We turn to the experience of prime age workers to examine these supply side explanations.

Evidence from the experience of prime age workers

Since 1990, the pace of recovery of the prime-age employment ratio (those 25–54 years—who always have the highest labor force participation) has been painfully slow after each recession. Fig. 15.6 shows that after the GFC, it took 141 months for the employment rate to return to its prerecessionary level. More troubling, the pattern from recent recessions has been that even after unemployment rates begin to fall, labor force participation, and the employment-population ratio remain depressed for an extended period.

The pattern of recent decades is that with each recession, more people become excluded—more or less permanently—from labor markets. This

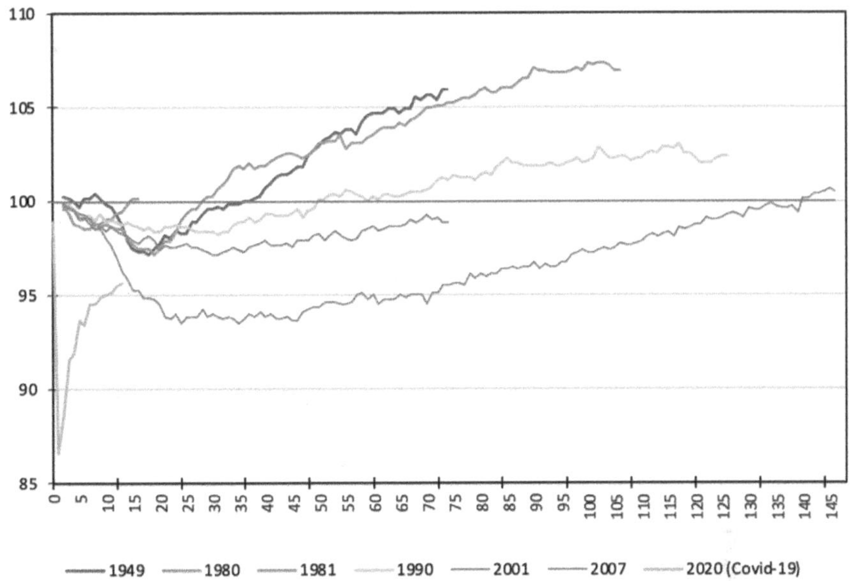

Figure 15.6 Prime-age employment-ratio recovery (# months).

trend is particularly worrisome for prime-age men, who have been leaving the labor force since 1970, presumably as job prospects dimmed. For almost 40 years, rising labor force participation rates of women made up for that. However, as Fig. 15.7 shows, the prime-age labor force participation rate fell off in the GFC and only very slowly recovered over the next 2 decades.

Most workers have not seen significant wage increases—which might explain some of the decline of participation by prime age males. And while structural shifts have partially contributed to the falling participation ratio, they cannot easily explain why participation among prime-age workers remains significantly below prerecessionary levels. The typical explanation for declining labor force participation is age demographics, combined with changing characteristics of the American labor force and other structural forces (see, e.g., Aaronson et al., 2006; Eberstadt, 2016). However, labor force participation for those 55 and over actually has been rising (although the rate might have leveled off in the past few years), partly counteracting the negative impact of an aging population on the overall participation rate.

The erosion of labor force participation for prime-age men has been steady in the U.S. economy since the mid-1960s. Eberstadt (2016), for

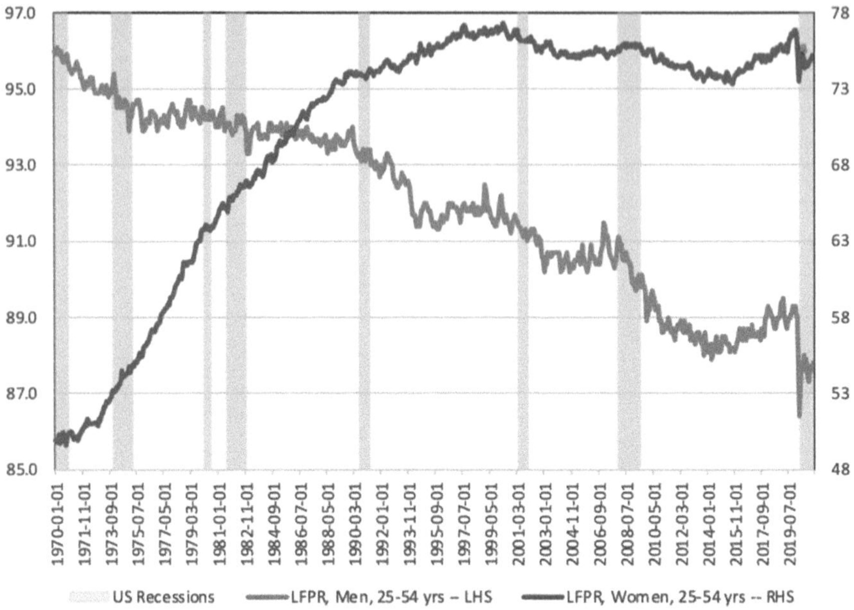

Figure 15.7 Prime-age labor force participation rates. *Source: US. Bureau of Labor Statistics.*

example, calculates that "a monthly average of nearly one in six prime-age men had no paying job of any kind" (2016, p. 213). If current trends continue, in 40 years, one out of four men of prime working age will be out of the labor force (Summers, 2016).

The U.S. does not fare well in international comparisons—in 2018 it had one of the lowest prime-age labor force participation rates among OECD countries. It is hard to make the argument that excessive labor market regulation, or generous social safety nets, are the reason for the lower participation rates in the U.S. since OECD countries with higher labor force participation tend to have more closely regulated labor markets, and more extensive and comprehensive social safety net. Further, the U.S. Congress passed the Personal Responsibility and Work Opportunity Reconciliation Act in 1996, which curtailed or imposed time limits on government assistance to those in need to promote private sector work over "government-dependency" of the able-bodied. Still, performance compared to other OECD countries declined; the US was among only a handful of countries with a falling participation ratio between 1990 and 2018.

Some have attributed the decline of labor force participation to "social shifts" (Williams, 2016) such as changes in personal preferences as more people "traded a second paycheck for spending more time at home, whether it's for childcare, leisure, or simply that it's a better lifestyle fit" (Williams, 2016) or to seek higher educational achievements. While the decline of labor force participation for those between the ages of 16 and 24 reflects the fact that Americans are spending more years in school, it cannot explain why Americans of prime-working age have simply withdrawn from the labor market.

While the social shifts explanation sounds plausible, it is unlikely that a large number of Americans are voluntarily leaving the labor force for personal preferences. In fact, the number of those not in the labor force, who report not wanting a job now has declined for age groups 16–24 and 25–54.[8] Further, the historical trend for married couples with children under 18 shows a significant increase in the percentage of families in which both parents are employed—from 25% in 1960s to almost 61 in May 2016. Neither of these trends is obviously consistent with the "lifestyle changes" argument.

The number of prime-age men who are neither employed nor looking for a job has more than doubled over the past 50 years (Eberstadt, 2016). According to a White House Report, adverse labor supply conditions explain very little of this decline—fewer than 25% of prime-age people not in the labor force have a working spouse, and nearly 36% of them were living in poverty (White House, 2014, 2016). The report also shows that "m-age males without children saw a larger decline of 9.4 percentage points since 1968 compared to 4.9 percentage points among prime-age males with children." (White House, 2014, 2016) That runs counter to the belief that the "supply side" choice to leave the labor force to take care of children can explain much of the movement of prime-age males out of the labor force. Only a quarter of prime-age men who are not in the labor force are parents (falling from 40% in 1968) (White House, 2014, 2016).

Finally, if we compare time-use of prime-age men who are out of the labor force with those who are working, we do not find much evidence that prime-age workers leave the labor force to pursue more education, to care for family members, or to do housework. Rather, the most significant difference in time use between those who are working and those who are out of the labor force is that a larger portion of the day is spent in

[8] See table A.38 of Labor Force Statistics, Current Population Survey, Bureau of Economic Analysis.

socializing, leisure, and relaxing.[9] Also, unemployed men spend almost twice as much time in educational activities as do men who are out of the labor force[10].

While all these data are only suggestive, we believe they support the argument that chronically insufficient aggregate demand produces an insufficiency of jobs and loose labor markets. Measured unemployment is only part of the story, as many work part-time, take contingent work, or leave the labor force. Labor force participation rates rose until the 1990s only because women entered; prime age male participation rates were falling over the entire period under analysis. Redundancy of human labor keeps wage growth low—which further encourages workers to voluntarily leave the labor market. Hence, we face what looks like labor market slack, but one that is tighter than it appears. Stagnant wages and stagnant working hours keep aggregate demand low. This hinders growth and reduces the incentive to invest. Given constrained supply of jobs and wages plus slow growth of productivity, secular stagnation is inevitable.

While it is too early to tell, evidence from the pandemic is that participation rates of women (especially) have fallen greatly. Many speculate that this could be a long-lasting trend as families have weighed the costs (monetary and familial) of working outside the home in a nation that provides little support for working parents. If true, this might paradoxically contribute to even bigger problems with effective demand even as it tightens labor markets at least marginally through exit of some parents—unless wages and monetary support for families rise substantially.

The way forward

Despite the wide-spread belief that supply side factors impinge on the ability to grow faster over the long run, the evidence is that the US has operated with substantial labor market slack since the mid-1970s. If anything, slack has risen in the aftermath of the GFC—probably in part due to labor market hysteresis. This slack—and accompanying downward pressure on

[9] The BLS "American Time Use Survey" showed that in 2014 a typical workweek for those prime-age who were not in the labor force spent on average 240 min more per day socializing, relaxing, or in other leisure activities than those employed, a large portion of which was spent in front of the TV.

[10] On those lines, a disturbing trend is that nearly 31% of the prime-working age men not in the labor force selfreported illegal drug use according to a 2004 survey presented by Eberstadt (2016). These numbers are staggering if compared to only 8% for those who are employed, and 22% for those who are unemployed (Eberstadt, 2016).

wages—reduces the incentive for firms to invest in labor-saving production techniques. That, in turn, reduces the incentive to innovation that raises labor productivity. In other words, lack of effective demand produces a vicious cycle of perverse disincentives that together keep aggregate demand and economic growth low. Unfortunately, policy makers misread this as supply side constraints on growth—as they think that measured productivity is purely a supply side phenomenon. Actually, at any point in time, measured productivity is a residual that heavily depends on the state of effective demand. And that, in turn, is a fundamental determinant of the incentive to invest to increase productivity.

While a growing consensus among mainstream economists asserts that secular stagnation is the "new normal," the evidence for the US, at least, is that substantial labor market slack persisted long after the GFC. This labor could be put to work to increase aggregate demand and economic growth—which would be likely to raise measured (residual) productivity. The problem is that effective demand is too low. While part of the policy solution is to encourage private demand, there is also room for more government spending. Since the private sector will hire the most employable workers first (those with more education, training, and work experience), it is necessary for the government to take up the slack that remains even in a robust expansion.

Also, while today's crisis is affecting supply and demand simultaneously, once the pandemic is resolved and the economy starts to reopen, the level of aggregate demand will remain subdued without significant demand side stimulus. Unemployment rates could remain elevated for years to come, with depressed labor force participation and employment ratios. Wages will continue to lag behind productivity growth with reduced opportunities to participate in the labor force. While there have been attempts to prop up demand with the CARES Act, the Consolidated Appropriations Act, and the American Rescue Plan Act, we still need millions of jobs.

Is there a better way to deal with unemployment, depressed labor force participation, and economic insecurity? History is our best guide. Direct job creation was a fundamental component of the New Deal. History shows that it was not extensive enough—with women, blacks, and minorities sometimes excluded—and the New Deal jobs programs were abandoned once the economy recovered. This time we can make a *new* New Deal jobs program more generous, inclusive, and permanent—with a universal Job Guarantee program (See Wray et al., 2018 for a simulation of such a program.).

We need a direct job creation bill (we can call it a Public Service Employment guarantee, or PSE for short), with the federal government immediately taking over payrolls for all workers laid off and furloughed. It would also offer jobs to those who were already unemployed or who were out of the labor force (people who have been largely left behind by the rescue packages adopted so far). The jobs would pay a basic wage of $15 per hour plus benefits (health care, childcare, and in high rent areas a supplemental housing allowance). Workers would be put on the payroll immediately—as soon as they sign-up—and then gradually matched to job openings. All public and not-for-profit entities would be allowed to submit proposals to offer projects that provide safe work for them to help with the crisis and recovery. As recovery begins, firms can begin to hire workers back into the private sector, and state and local governments can hire workers back into regular public sector jobs.

There are several advantages to such an approach. First, the spending is targeted to those who need jobs—rather than mailing out checks to many who do not—as the early rounds of pandemic relief did. As we now understand, the pandemic has targeted much of its destruction at minorities or those who were already disadvantaged: homeless, unemployed, poor, and low wage service sector and "gig" workers. Those with higher education, more wealth, and greater income are far more likely to have retained their jobs while working from home.

Second, the PSE program can be used to supply workers to needed relief projects—such as packaging meals for isolated, elderly, and sick individuals. These projects will provide socially useful output, and in some cases, may help deal with the potential inflationary pressures resulting from temporary supply shortages. Note also that the program can also provide day care and other services that would enable parents with children to return to work. Indeed, it would be possible to offer-free day for all children through the PSE program once it is ramped up with proper training and facilities.

Third, the PSE program will provide workers as we phase-in Green New Deal (GND) projects. (see Nersisyan and Wray, 2020). Fourth, the PSE will be permanent. As we've shown, recoveries take a long time to regain jobs and they always leave many behind. Even a decade after the Great Recession, we had not fully recovered. In many ways, our society and economy were weaker than they had been in 2007. The PSE will provide jobs for those who will be left behind this time and will continue to provide a jobs safety net for anyone who needs it. We estimate that even at a business cycle peak, the PSE would employ as many as 10 million.

Obviously, this is only an educated guess. But even if it turned out to be an overestimate that would simply mean that the private sector was able to hire more workers out of the PSE program than we have expected. That's a good thing! The PSE will expand whenever the economy slows and shrink whenever the economy expands. It is an automatic stabilizer and a social safety net—by design.

The COVID-19-related health crisis will eventually end, but we will still have a range of problems to resolve: secular stagnation, lack of adequate access to health care, an environmental crisis, an inequality crisis, a poverty crisis, as well as social and political crises to resolve. The PSE is part of a package of reforms we will need as an alternative to the unsustainable economy we had before—a permanent force for crisis preparation, for the GND, and to provide alternatives to destructive consumerism.

References

Aaronson, S., Fallick, B., Figura, A., Pingle, J., Wascher, W., 2006. The recent decline in the labor force participation rate and its implications for potential labor supply. In: Brookings Papers on Economic Activity. Brookings Institution, Washington, DC.

Backhouse, R., Boianovsky, M., 2016. Secular stagnation: the history of a macroeconomic heresy. The European Journal of the History of Economic Thought 23 (6), 946–970.

Eberstadt, N., 2016. Men without Work: America's Invisible Crisis, Kindle Edition. Templeton Press, West Conshohocken, PA.

Eichengreen, B., 2015. Secular stagnation: the long view. American Economic Review 105 (5), 66–70.

Fujita, S., 2014. On the Causes of Declines in the Labor Force Participation Rate. Research Rap Special Report. Federal Reserve Bank of Philadelphia. February 6.

Gordon, R., 2017. The Rise and Fall of American Growth: The U.S. Standard of Living since the Civil War. Princeton University Press, Princeton, New Jersey.

Hansen, A., 1939. Economic progress and declining population growth. The American Economic Review 29 (1), 1–15.

Minsky, H., 2013. Ending Poverty: Jobs, Not Welfare. Levy Economic Policy Institute of Bard College: Annandale-on-Hudson, NY.

Nersisyan, Y., Wray, L.R., January 2020. Can we afford the green new deal?. In: Public Policy Brief No. 148. Annandale-on- Hudson, NY: Levy Economics Institute of Bard College.

Rachel, L., Summers, L., 2019. On Secular Stagnation in the Industrialized World. NBER Working Paper No. 26198.

Summers, L., 2014. U.S. Economic prospects: secular stagnation, hysteresis, and the zero lower bound. Business Economics 49 (2), 65–73.

Summers, L., September 23, 2016. Men Not at Work. Financial Times. Retrieved from: https://www.ft.com/content/eb0c4aa4-80b5-11e6-8e50-8ec15fb462f4.

White House Council of Economic Advisors, July 2014. The Labor Force Participation Rate since 2007: Causes and Policy Implications. Executive Office of the President of the United States. Available at: https://www.whitehouse.gov/sites/default/files/docs/labor_force_participation_report.pdf.

White House Council of Economic Advisors, June 2016. The Long-Term Decline in Prime-Age Male Labor Force Participation. Executive Office of the President of the United

States. Available at: https://www.whitehouse.gov/sites/default/files/page/files/20160620_cea_primeage_male_lfp.pdf.
Williams, J., January 8, 2016. After the First Rate Hike. California Bankers Association, Santa Barbara, CA. Retrieved from: http://www.frbsf.org/our-district/files/Williams-Speech-After-the-First-Rate-Hike.pdf.
Wray, L.R., Dantas, F., Fullwiler, S., Tcherneva, P.R., Kelton, S.A., April 2018. Public Service Employment: A Path to Full Employment. Research Project Report. Annandale-on- Hudson, NY: Levy Economics Institute of Bard College.

Further reading

Dantas, F., Wray, L.R., February 2017. Full employment: are we there yet?. In: Public Policy Brief No. 142. Annandale-on-Hudson, NY: Levy Economics Institute of Bard College.

CHAPTER SIXTEEN

Secular stagnation and the age of ultra-low interest rates

Eric Tymoigne
Department of Economics, Lewis & Clark College, Portland, OR, United States

Post 2007, bond bears trumpeted the doom of US Treasuries.[1] Quantitative easing would lead to higher inflation, large fiscal deficits would take scarce saving away from investors, and the downgrading of the US public debt would make financial market participants more wary of the US Treasury's ability and willingness to service its debt. The combined effects of the three channels were supposed to generate a rapid rise in interest rates. Instead, under the guidance of monetary policy, interest rates fell. Long-term rates fell almost continuously and went negative to reach record low levels in August 2019. The market value of investment-grade bonds that traded at a negative yield in the United States was $17 trillion (about 30% of the total market value) and almost 70% of euro government bonds did the same. Even some European junk bonds started to trade at a negative yield in the middle of 2019.[2] Short-term rates, that follow closely the prevailing the fed funds rate, rose in the second part of the 2010s as the Fed tightened its policy, before falling again the late 2010s.

The trend of declining interest rates is not new, and low interest rates are likely to persist for a decade or more. While the COVID-19 pandemic has reversed the negative yield trend on long-term rates, the economic environment that has produced ultra-low interest rates is still present. Rising income and wealth inequalities, slow jobless recoveries, low inflation, and long-term

[1] For example, see Agustino Fontevecchia "PIMCO's Bill Gross Shorts Treasuries As Experts Eye Inflation" *Forbes.com* (April 11, 2011). Bill Gross's position has not changed 10 years later, see Emily Graffeo "Bill Gross is shorting US Treasurys and says inflation will be as high as 4% in coming months" *Business Insider* (May 17, 2021).

[2] See John Ainger "Bond World Is Backing Away From All That Negativity as 2019 Ends" *Bloomberg* (December 23, 2019); Eric Lascelles "Adapting Investment Strategy to the Negative Yield Environment," *RBC Wealth Management* (November 20, 2019); Dhara Ranasinghe "Almost 70% of Euro Zone Bond Yields Have Sub-Zero Yields—Tradeweb," *Reuters* (October 3, 2019). Laura Benitez and Tasos Vossos "Sub-Zero Yields Start Taking Hold in Europe's Junk-Bond Market," *Bloomberg* (July 9, 2019).

Handbook of Economic Stagnation
ISBN: 978-0-12-815898-2
https://doi.org/10.1016/B978-0-12-815898-2.00010-0

trends toward a shrinking population in developed economies point toward the persistence of a low-growth, low-interest-rates economic environment. Unless economic policies are put in place to reverse the stagnationist trends, central banks will have limited willingness and ability to raise their policy rates in any significant way and so other interest rates will tend to stay low. This has important implications for the financial stability of Money Manager Capitalism because a low-interest-rate environment is prone to promote the reliance on leverage and capital gains, aka Ponzi finance, to reach targeted rates of return. Economic stagnation also brings forward the central role governments can play to put an economy on a more sustainable and equitable growth path.

The first part of the chapter reviews the trend in interest rates over the past century and argues that monetary policy is the overwhelming determinant of this trend. Fiscal policy and credit risk are at best secondary determinants and inflation plays a role mostly through its impact on monetary policy. As such, to gain an understanding of what the future trend of interest rates will be, one must gain some insights into the underlying factors that could influence the decisions of the Federal Open Market Committee (FOMC). The second part of the paper argues that the fundamental economic trends in the economy point to a limited ability and willingness of the FOMC to raise interest rates. The third part of the paper argues that a protracted period of low interest rates and low economic growth has major negative impacts for the dynamics of Money Manager Capitalism and that the government has an important role to play to overcome such dynamics.

Interest rates over the past century

Before making any prediction about the future, it is instructive to study what the past century tells us about the dynamics of interest rates. Several things are worth noticing from Fig. 16.1. First, the downward trend in interest rates is not new. Over the past 40 years, the average rate on long-term safe debts has come down from 15% in 1981 to less than 2% in 2020. Second, interest rates on long-term safe debts are exceptionally low today; even during World War Two, such interest rates did not go below 2% on average. The last, and most important, observation is that a key driver of interest rates in the United States is monetary policy. This is actually the case in any country where the government issues its own currency and issues securities denominated in its own currency (Akram and Li, 2020; Borio et al., 2017; Biefang-Frisancho Mariscal and Howells 2002;

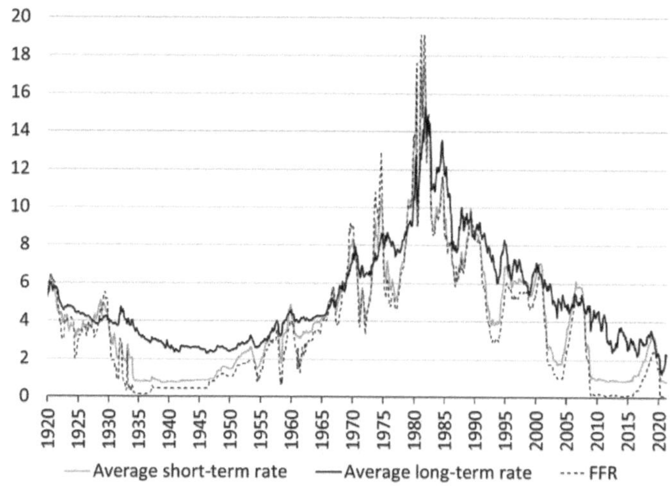

Figure 16.1 A century of interest rates on safe debts in the United States, percent. Note: The average short-term rate is composed of the rate on three-month United States Treasury securities (USTs), 1-year UST, 3-month AA commercial paper and short-term prime bank loan. The average long-term rate is composed of the rate on 10-year UST, 20-year UST, and AAA corporate bond. *Sources: Board of Governors of the Federal Reserve System (series H.15), Freddie Mac, National Bureau of Economic Research.*

Cook and Hahn, 1989; Atesoglu, 2003, 2005; Roley and Sellon, 1995). While operating procedures have changed overtime, monetary policy consists in providing an elastic currency, which in practice means managing at least one interest rate—currently the federal funds rate (FFR) in the United States. One has to go back to the Great Depression to find a near-zero FFR. World War Two led the Fed to expand its interest-rate targeting to the entire yield curve with the rate on T-bills set at 3/8 of 1% and T-bonds purchased by the Fed at a quantity and a price consistent with the maintenance of a 2.5% yield. Following the end of the war and the 1951 Accords,[3] monetary policy tightened and other rates followed until the early 1980s, when the FFR started its long decline to the present level. Over the past century,

[3] In 1942, the Federal Reserve and the U.S. Treasury agreed on a monetary policy framework that consisted in targeting the yield curve and that required the preapproval of the Treasury to change any interest rate targets. The Treasury-Federal Reserve Accord allowed the Federal Reserve to pursue a more independent and active monetary policy focused on stabilizing money-market conditions. Open market operations developed in the 1950s and the Fed monitored the T-bill rate without explicitly targeting it. The FFR became an operating tool of monetary policy in the 1970s as the overnight interbank market developed in the 1960s (Meulendyke, 1998, 35—45).

the relation between the FFR (taken as a proxy of US monetary policy tool for the entire period) and all other interest rates is extremely strong regardless of the term to maturity and holds through time (Fig. 16.2).

While monetary policy plays a central role in setting the trend of interest rates, two other variables are usually emphasized when making interest-rate forecasts. The first one is the fiscal balance. The common view is that fiscal deficits push up interest rates, which crowds out private investment. A causal look at the data shows that there is no relationship between interest rates and the fiscal position of the US government. Recent theoretical and empirical work emphasize the key role played by monetary sovereignty in influencing that relation, with the relation being weak when governments are monetarily sovereign. The fiscal and monetary branches of government coordinate their operations to limit the impact of government financial operations on the payment system (Sharpe, 2013; Tymoigne, 2020).

Besides the fiscal balance, another often-cited variable that is supposed to influence interest rates is inflation. The relation is explained by the influential work of Irving Fisher (1930). Many empirical studies, including Fisher's, have shown that the Fisher effect does not hold. Cooray (2002) provides a review of the empirical literature and additional references can be found in Ghazali and Ramlee (2003), Koustas and Serletis (1999), Sargent (1976), and Haliassos and Tobin (1990). Fig.16.3 shows that, in the US, there is no relation between inflation measured by the CPI and interest rates, whatever the

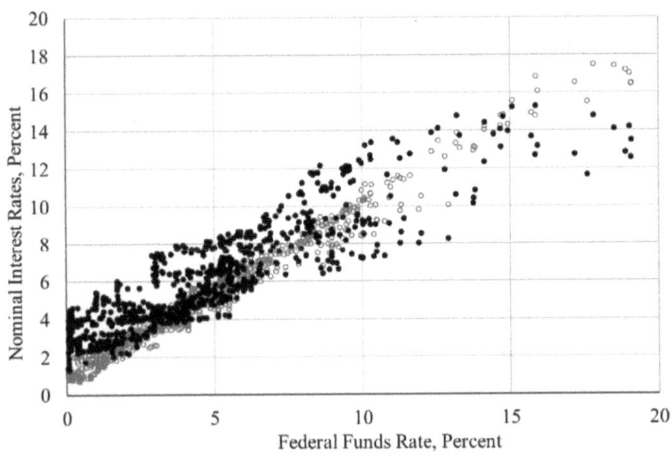

Figure 16.2 Monetary policy and nominal interest rates, January 1919 to June 2021. *Sources: National Bureau of Economic Research (Macrohistory Database), FRED.*

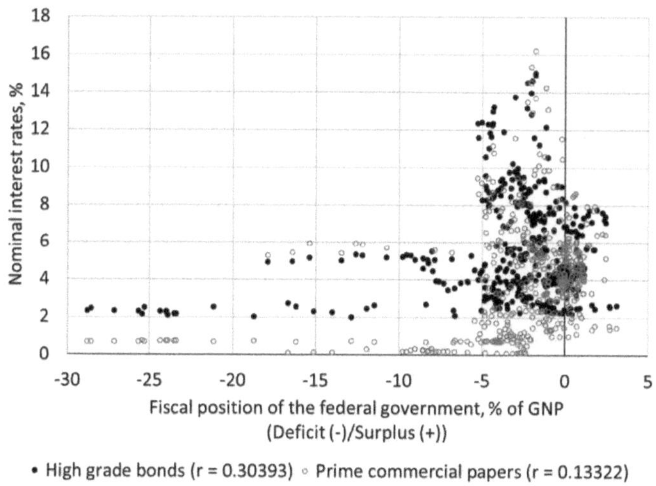

Figure 16.3 Fiscal balance and interest rates, 1900 to 2021. National Bureau of Economic research (Macrohistory Database, Tables from "the American business Cycle"), Treasury Bulletin (via FRASER), FRED, Bureau of fiscal service (*Monthly Receipts, Outlays, and Deficit or Surplus, Fiscal Years, 1981—2021*).

maturity, until the mid-1950s. After that period, interest rates are more closely related to inflation. Friedman and Schwartz (1976) and Summers (1983) argue that, perhaps, financial-market participants have "learned their Fisher." Tymoigne (2006) provides a different explanation of the break in the relationship between interest rates and inflation. The break in the date can be explained by the change in monetary policy following the Treasury Accord of 1951 (Fig. 16.4). By 1953, the Fed had freed itself completely from any commitment to ensure the perfect liquidity of Treasuries (Beard, 1964). Following this operational change, and given the growing concerns

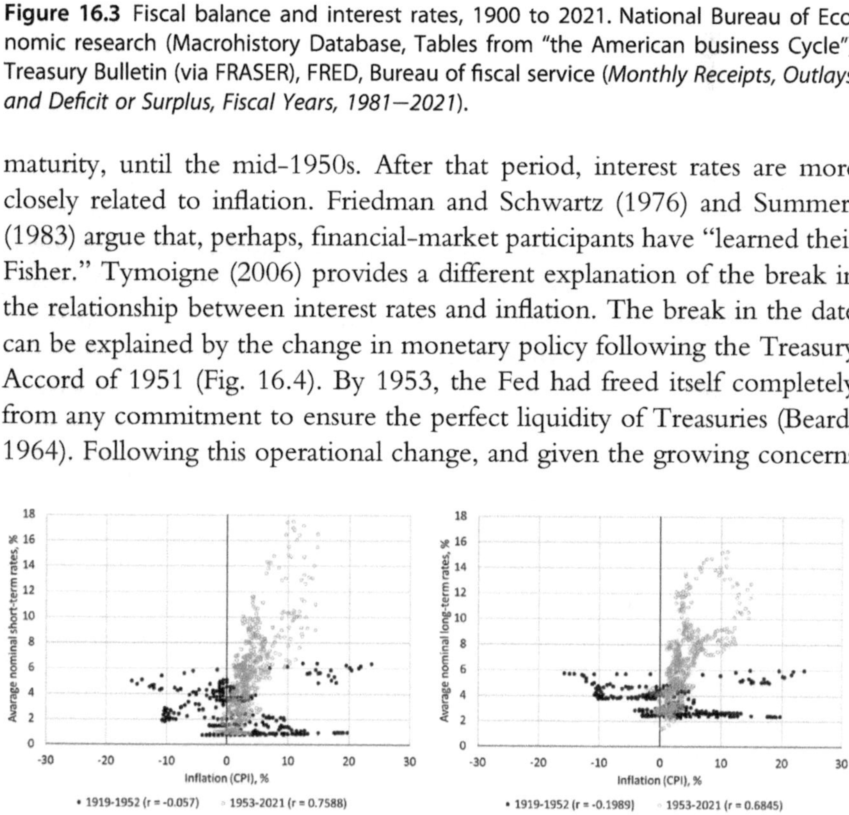

Figure 16.4 Inflation and interest rates, 1919 to 2021. *Sources: Board of Governors of the Federal Reserve System (Series H.15), National Bureau of Economic Research (Macrohistory Database), Bureau of Labor Statistics.*

about inflation and the spread of Monetarism in policy circles, the Fed oriented its policy toward managing inflation. As a consequence, the policy rate became correlated with the growth rate of the consumer-price index and so did other rates. The higher coefficient of correlations after 1953 do not reflect the fact that financial market participants suddenly became more preoccupied with inflation; rather, they reflect the continuity of interest-rate dynamics based on the dominance of monetary-policy decisions.

Credit risk and other spread-influencing factors create variations around the trend of interest rates but are not key determinant of the trend. An important distinction to make to understand the role of credit ratings in influencing rates is between government securities and nongovernment securities. With monetary sovereignty, there is no difficulty to service the public debt denominated in the domestic currency, and default is a remote possibility in normal times. Cantor and Parker (1995) provide some examples of such defaults and note that "domestic currency defaults have usually been the result of an overthrow of an old political order—as in Russia and Vietnam—or the byproduct of dramatic economic adjustment programs aimed at curbing hyperinflation—as in Argentina and Brazil" (Cantor and Parker, 1995). Involuntary defaults have occurred also for technical reasons. For example, Venezuela is counted as having defaulted because "the person who was supposed to sign the checks was unavailable at the time" (Cantor et al., 2008, 17). The U.S. also defaulted in 1979 due to "unanticipated failure of word processing equipment used to prepare check schedules" (Zivney and Marcus, 1989). Thus, while there have been a few cases of default on the domestic-denominated public debt by monetary sovereign governments, in normal times they are benign. For analytical purposes, one can assume that the probability of default on such government securities is zero; a credit rating is irrelevant. If such a rating exists, it has no predictive power and has no influence on the interest rates of domestic-currency-denominated public debt when monetary sovereignty prevails. Thus, credit ratings have a role only in so far as they influence the interest rates on debts issued by entities that are nonmonetarily sovereign, or on foreign debts issued by monetarily-sovereign governments, but such influence is secondary relative to the role of monetary policy.

Finally, contrary to credit rating agencies (CRAs) (e.g., Standard and Poor's, 2007), such default risk must be clearly differentiated from inflation risk for three reasons. First, a government usually does not promise a constant purchasing power on upcoming public debt service payments so it is not defaulting if the currency's purchasing power falls. Equally, government security holders are not required to compensate a government for any windfall loss of purchasing power due to deflation. Nominalism applies in the law so governments are under no obligation to provide a hedge against inflation; bondholders take upon themselves the inflation risk. Governments may promise to do so via inflation-indexed securities—in which case failure to maintain purchasing power is a default event—but they do not have to do it and usually do not. Second, CRAs see tax revenues as the sound means to service the public debt but inflation raises tax revenues and so raises the ability to service the debt, which lowers the default risk. Third, the CRA view of default risk implicitly assumes that the government is responsible for inflation. Not only is there no clear link between fiscal deficits and inflation (Fig. 16.5), but also all forms of spending can be inflationary and there are other sources of inflation than spending (such as energy cost, medical cost, overhead corporate cost structure, among others).

Given the tremendous influence of current and expected monetary policy on interest rates, any opinion about the future direction of interest rates must be made with a view of future monetary policy. One must study what could lead the FOMC to raise its FFR target. The mandate of the Fed is to promote price stability (defined as inflation around 2%) and maximum employment (defined as employment consistent with price stability). The FOMC informs its decisions by looking at a wide range of indicators including labor market conditions, inflation, and inflation expectations.

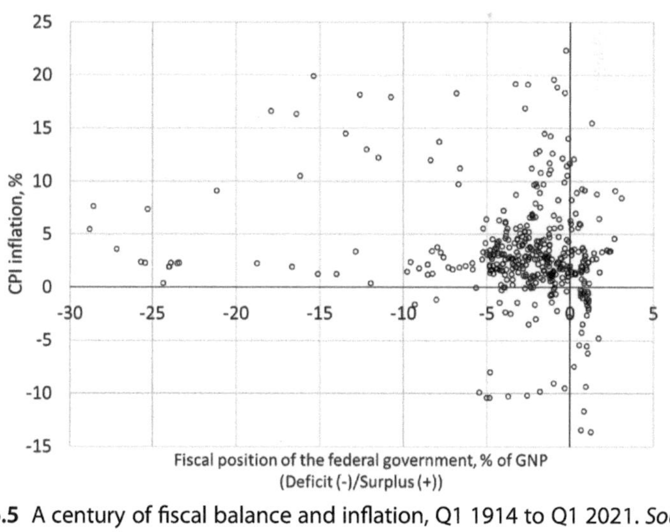

Figure 16.5 A century of fiscal balance and inflation, Q1 1914 to Q1 2021. *Sources: See Fig. 3 and Bureau of Labor Statistics.*

Short-term and long-term outlooks for these factors are pointing to interest rates that will stay low for an extended time. While the FOMC may decide to raise its FFR temporarily, the long-term trend is for the FFR and other rates to remain very low for a very long time.

The following section argues that short-term and long-term economic forces indicate that the FOMC will have limited ability and willingness to raise rates in any significant fashion.

Secular stagnation and interest rates

In 2020, loss of consumer confidence and lockdowns depressed economic activity throughout the world. While the economy has been recovering in some parts of the world, the global economy is still in recovery mode. Table 16.1 shows that real gross domestic product (GDP) in the United States fell by 9% in the second quarter of 2020 compared to the same quarter in 2019. Labor market conditions worsened significantly in the second quarter 2020 when the official unemployment rose steeply to 13.1%, and the employment-population ratio fell in April to its lowest level ever recorded, 51.3% of the civilian population available for work actually employed. Similarly, the capacity utilization rate fell to 65.6%, its lowest level ever recorded since data became available. The sharp drop in economic activity, driven by a large decline in private domestic consumption, led to a sharp decline in core inflation, well below the implicit 2% inflation target of the Fed. While the economy has recovered somewhat since the middle of

Table 16.1 Short-term economic outlook: A depressed economy.

	2019				2020				2021
(Percent)	**Q1**	**Q2**	**Q3**	**Q4**	**Q1**	**Q2**	**Q3**	**Q4**	**Q1**
Annual real GDP growth	2.3	2	2.1	2.3	0.3	−9.0	−2.8	−2.4	0.4
Core CPI inflation	2.1	2.1	2.3	2.3	2.3	1.3	1.7	1.6	1.4
5-year inflation expectation	1.8	1.7	1.5	1.6	1.4	0.9	1.2	1.2	1.3
Unemployment rate	3.9	3.6	3.6	3.5	3.8	13.1	8.8	6.8	6.2
Employment–population ratio	60.7	60.6	60.8	61.0	60.7	52.9	56.1	57.4	57.6
Capacity utilization	78.3	77.5	77.2	76.6	75.3	65.6	71.9	73.4	73.9

Source: Bureau of Labor Statistics, Bureau of Economic Analysis, Federal Reserve Bank of Cleveland, Board of Governors of the Federal Reserve System.

2020, millions of jobs lost to the pandemic have yet to be recovered. Given the worsening economic situation and the slow recovery, it is easy to understand why the FFR has fallen sharply and has stayed low, with short-term rates matching the same trend. However, long-term rates also fell sharply, reflecting expectations among market participants that the FFR will stay low in the upcoming years.

While Covid-19-related economic events explain the short- to medium-term interest rate dynamics, Fig. 16.1 points to a long-term downward trend. This trend is explained by structural changes that have led to a slower and more unstable U.S. economy. Decline in the tax burden on the wealthier households, deregulation and lax enforcement, financialization, and globalization of the economy and the decline in labor protections have destroyed shared prosperity. They have also led to jobless recoveries, lowered inflationary pressures, and limited capital investment in the economy. As a consequence, a growing majority of households is not enjoying the fruits of an economic prosperity that has weakened overtime. Given this stagnationist trend, one may expect interest rates to stay low over the upcoming decade and beyond (Table 16.2).

Table 16.2 Long-term economic outlook: Toward Secular Stagnation.

Beginning of expansion	1954	1958	1961	1970	1975	1982	1991	2001	2009
Average real GNP per capita growth rate (%)	1.6	1.8	3.5	3.1	3.0	4.0	1.3	2.0	1.6
Gini index	N/A	N/A	N/A	0.394	0.397	0.412	0.428	0.462	0.468
Percent of income gain going to top 10%	27.8	32.3	32.9	43.0	45.0	80.0	73.0	98.3	76.9[a]
Time to recover jobs lost (months)	23	18	20	18	19	28	32	47	76
Job quality index	N/A	N/A	N/A	N/A	N/A	N/A	89	87.8	81.4

[a]Updated to 2018.

Sources: Census Bureau, Bureau of Labor Statistics, Bureau of Economic Analysis, JQI IP Holdings LLC, and Pavlina R. Tcherneva "Reorienting Fiscal Policy: a bottom-up approach," *Journal of Post Keynesian Economics* (December 2014).

The annual growth rate of real gross national product per capita has slowed to 2% percent or less since the 1990s. At the same time, income and wealth inequalities have soared with the top 1% of the population recording a large increase in their share of income and wealth to the detriment of the rest of the population. In terms of income, the top 1% share grew from about 12% of national income in the late 1960s to about 20% of national income in the 2010s. This gain came almost entirely from a loss of income share of the bottom 50% of the U.S. income earners (Fig. 16.6). While the benefits of economic expansion used to be relatively broadly shared, since the 1980s, national income gains have gone almost entirely to the top 10%. During the last economic expansion (June 2009 to February 2020), 76.9% of the national income gain went to the top 10% of income earners. In terms of wealth share, given that the bottom 50% of the U.S. population has little to no wealth, all the transfer of wealth share to the top 1% came from the 49% of the population below them. The top 1% share of wealth almost doubled from 21% in the mid-1970s to 37% of national wealth in 2016 according to the World Inequality Database.

The main effect of such a lack of shared prosperity has been the disappearance of a middle class that can earn sufficient income to sustain its consumption and home purchases, both of which are key drivers of U.S. economic growth. More broadly, low and middle class households have used debts and their savings, if any, to sustain their housing, education, casual consumption, and health needs, among others. This has led to a very rapid

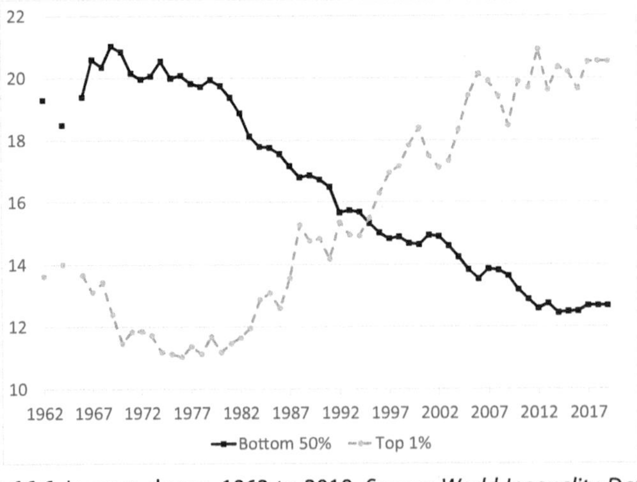

Figure 16.6 Income shares, 1962 to 2019. *Source: World Inequality Database.*

increase in the debt-to-income ratio of the bottom 50% and middle 40% of income earners (Batsher et al., 2020). Instead of income growth, debt growth and asset-price growth have become key means to sustain economic activity, which has promoted financial instability over the past half-century (Tymoigne and Wray, 2014).

Related to growing inequalities, another factor that has led to stagnation is the growing joblessness of economic expansions over the past 40 years. Prior to the 1980s, it took less than 2 years to recover the jobs lost during a recession, but the past four expansions required more than 2 years. The jobs lost during the minor 2001 recession were regained after 4 years. The job losses of the Great Recession took 6 years to be eliminated. One has to go back to the Great Depression to see a longer period of recovery. Not only has it taken more time to recover from recessions, but also job precariousness has grown with job quality falling constantly since data became available in 1991. Jobs have become more insecure, more intermittent and have not provided the same salary and benefits as they used to.

Finally, there has been a marked decline in the growth rate of investment. This is true not only for business investment but also for public infrastructure investment. On the business investment side, profits have grown rapidly but investment growth has slowed, and a growing proportion of profit has come from financial income (Tori and Onaran, 2017). On the infrastructure side, public investment has not kept up with the needs of the economy, and maintenance has been poor, leading to low quality infrastructure in the United States. The *Infrastructure Report Card* published by the American Society of Civil Engineers has consistently graded U.S. infrastructure around "D" for the past 3 decades, which has generated millions of job losses and thousands of dollars of income loss for U.S. households (American Society of Civil Engineers, 2016).

Unless major changes in economic policy or economic enviromnent occur to counter the previous trends, the economy will continue to record low growth, low-inflation, growing inequalities and growing precariousness of employment for the upcoming decades. All these elements give less of an incentive to the FOMC to raise significantly its policy rate quickly. They also point toward a more unstable economy, which gives less ability to the FOMC to raise interest rates quickly without generating financial instability. While the FOMC may start raising its FFR target, it will not be able to do it quickly and permanently without generating major instability. Thus, unless there is a dramatic shift in the way the U.S. economy is managed, the default expectation of market participants should be that interest rates continue to stay low for the upcoming decade and more. A low-growth highly leveraged economy can only accommodate so much in terms of interest rate hikes.

Implications

Secular stagnation and its impact on interest rates have important implications for the sustainability of our current form of capitalism—one that is heavily reliant on finance and money managers—and for the role of government in such an economic environment. Declining and low interest rates promote financial instability by forcing money managers to rely on, and spread the use of, Ponzi finance. Secular stagnation restores the importance of government in taking a lead to solve our pressing socioeconomic problems and sustaining and raising economic growth.

While a low-interest-rate environment makes debt servicing easier, it creates challenges for money managers (pension funds, mutual funds, and others) to meet their target rate of return on equity (ROE) target. The rate of ROE can be split into two components, the rate of return on asset (ROA) and the leverage ratio:

$$\text{Net Income/Equity} = \text{Net Income/Assets} * \text{Asset/Equity}$$

In a world with low interest rates, ROA on financial assets is depressed for any given level of risk on assets. To offset that, money managers can buy securities that pay a higher interest rate, which means buying riskier financial assets. As the 2008 financial crisis showed, the riskiness may not be captured properly by credit ratings. Pension funds bought exotic investment-grade securities that promised higher ROA than traditional corporate bonds with similar ratings. They were able and willing to do because the rating did not account for the embedded leverage and poor quality of the assets underlying the securitization process upon with the exotic securities were based. The demand for such exotic securities in turn fueled the mortgage and securitization boom of the first part of the 2000s, with bankers pushing existing homeowners to refinance into exotic mortgages and pushing people with no income, no job, and no assets to buy a home. The entire scheme could only be sustained by capital gains from home foreclosures, a giant Ponzi scheme predicated on the failure of homeowners to make their mortgage payments (Tymoigne and Wray, 2014). The other way to boost ROE is to use more leverage in the financing of the acquisition of assets and, as shown in

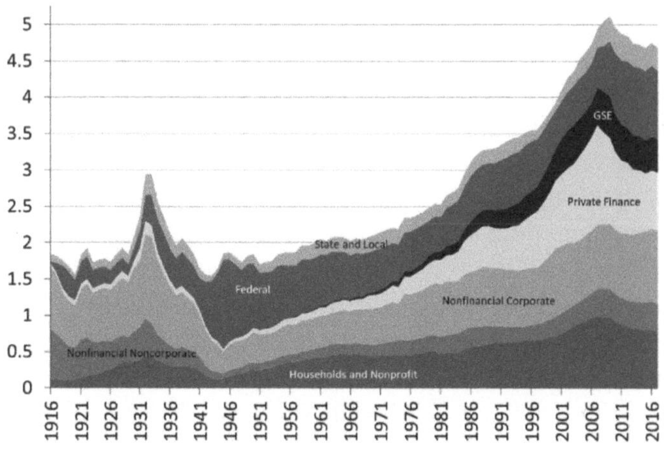

Figure 16.7 Liabilities to GDP in the United States, 1916—2017. Note: The government sector excludes all financial activities of the government (retirement funds, GNMA, etc.). GSE sector includes government-sponsored enterprises and agency- and GSE-backed mortgage pools (includes, among others, GNMA and FHA pools). "Financial" excludes the GSE sector and monetary authorities (which are both part of the financial sector in the Flow of Funds accounts). Before 1945, data for financial institutions are computed from data of the Census Bureau by taking all the liabilities (excluding equity) of commercial banks, credit unions, savings institutions, life insurance stock companies, and property and life insurance companies, and by removing private banks notes, all deposits, and life insurance reserves. From 1945, the total liabilities of the financial sector excludes, net interbank liabilities of commercial banks, liabilities of monetary authorities, private and public pension fund liabilities, money market mutual funds shares, mutual funds shares and the items previously cited. The liabilities of monetary authorities are not included anywhere. *Sources:* Historical Statistics of the United States: Millennium Edition *(Tables Ca9-19, Ce42-68, Cj265-272, Cj362-374, Cj389-397, Cj437-447, Cj748-750, Cj751-765, Cj787-796, and Cj870-889),* Historical Statistics of the United States: Colonial Times to 1970 *(Series X 689—697), NIPA, Flow of Funds (from 1945).*

Fig. 16.7, a very sharp increase in the use of debt within the financial sector. However, a large part of this leverage is hidden through the use of derivative and special purpose entities that promote the layering of debts.

By focusing on riskier segments of the credit market and/or using more leverage in their financial strategies, money managers have promoted the use of leverage in the rest of the economy, increased systemic financial fragility, and ultimately generated financial instability. As such, it seems doubtful that a private-based retirement system, a core component of money manager capitalism, is a sustainable means to achieve financial safety for retirees while at the same time promoting financial stability for the overall economy. This is all the more so that financial investment opportunities based on long-term income growth are far fewer than the funds available to portfolio managers. A stable, low-key and reliable financial means to buy the basic retirement necessities (food, shelter, and health care) can be achieved through a public retirement system. This, however, only deals with one part of the problem of an aging society, the other part is to make sure that the economic system provisions itself while the population is aging. Fortunately, the economic adjustments required on the production side are manageable (Wray, 2006).

Government can also play a major role in countering the destabilizing and stagnationist impact of investment-led growth. Domar (1946) extends Keynes's static approach to the problem of economic growth and shows that investment-led growth is unsustainable because the level of net investment grows productive capacity while aggregate demand only grows by a multiple of the change in investment. Minsky complements Domar by showing that the achievement of financially sustainable long-term full employment and price stability cannot be based on promoting the growth of private investment (through tax breaks, subsidies to private business, among others). Minsky also notes that the emphasis on investment creates inflationary pressures and income inequality (Minsky, 1973, 1981, 1986). Steindl (1979), Walker and Vatter (1989) and Vatter et al. (1995) build on Harrod's, Domar's and Minsky's analysis by showing that the main constraint on economic growth has been too low growth in aggregate demand not a too low growth in aggregate supply (Wray, 2008). They conclude that the government has a crucial role government to play, not only in stabilizing the economy, but also in putting it onto a higher growth path.

> *The mistaken emphasis upon physical capital· accumulation reveals [...] a defect in the ruling growth models to which we have called attention: they are essentially laissez faire constructs. Acknowledgment of the long-established presence of big government is considered ancillary to long-run growth analysis. Government is allowed to intrude mainly and merely into such matters as subsidization of sectors, regulation, research, and education of the labor force. Big government as the decisive, dynamic, autonomous source of demand growth, historically coming to replace private fixed investment is, like the demand side in general, omitted from the usual model.*
>
> ***(Walker and Vatter, 1989, 344–345).***

Contrary to the loanable funds approach (in which government competes for resources with private investors) and the efficient market framework (in which government intervention leads to misallocations and stifle innovations), government spending has been a necessary complementary component to economic growth and innovation. A big government and a big bank are complementary elements, not the antithesis, of a market economy (Minsky, 1993).

In terms of stabilizing the economy, there has been a sharp change in the behavior of developed capitalist economies in the 20th century. The larger involvement of national governments in the economy has considerably reduced the volatility of economic growth (Taylor et al., 2012; Hein, 2018; Tymoigne, 2009). In the United States, following the 1930s, the economy has recorded fewer contractions; contractions have been much milder, much less lengthy, and less frequent. This is explained by the beneficial income, cash flow, and portfolio effects of fiscal deficits (Minsky, 1986). Fiscal deficits sustain private incomes by injecting more money in the economy than they remove through taxes, which in turn stabilizes private investment by stabilizing aggregate demand. Expected sales, not interest rates, are the main driver of business investment and fiscal deficits stabilize sales while having a negligible impact on the cost of credit. Fiscal deficits also lead to the injection of safe financial assets in private balance sheets, which improves their liquidity and solvency. In terms of the trend of economic growth, the US economy has been growing below potential since 1910 and, throughout the 20th century, it would have been possible to sustain a 4% growth rate by relying on growing government spending instead of trying to stimulate private domestic investment back to its pre-1910 growth rate (Vatter et al., 1995).

Overall, economic growth and economic development is demand-led (Lavoie, 2014) with government playing a big role in sustaining growth. This does not mean that government spending can grow by an unlimited percentage but rather that productive capacities, especially labor, are usually flexible enough to respond quickly, and ultimately adapt, to the requirement of growing expenditures. While this has been well understood in the Keynesian literature, both heterodox and mainstream (hysteresis effect), it rarely enters policymaking discussions except when facts stubbornly show that the economy can operate far beyond what is at the time considered full employment. For example, Greenspan noted in 1999, after years when the unemployment rate fell below the NAIRU and inflation did not accelerate much to the dismay of other FOMC members (prompting estimates of NAIRU to be revised down), that:

> *Let me just say very simply — this is really a repetition of what I've been saying in the past — that we have all been brought up to a greater or lesser extent on the*

> *presumption that the supply side is a very stable force. [...] In my judgment our models fail to account appropriately for the interaction between the supply side and the demand side largely because historically it has not been necessary for them to do so.*
>
> ***(Federal Open Market Committee, 1999, 46–47).***

The inability, or unwillingness, of policymakers to recognize the positive feedback between aggregate demand and productive capacity leads them to be too cautious, by raising interest rates prematurily and/or by conceptualizing government spending merely as a quick temporary recession fighting tool, with the result of lowering the growth path of the economy. Instead of tightening immediately as inflation rises (or even in anticipation of expected inflation), policymakers should give time to productive capacities to adapt to the growth of demand (Fontana and Palacio-Vera, 2007).

There is today ample role for governments to tackle several major challenges of developed economies; their population is aging, trillions of dollars of infrastructure upgrade and expansion are needed (American Society of Civil Engineers, 2021) and climate change is the major socioeconomic threat. Climate change requires—in addition to a major environmental policy oriented toward restoration and conservation—an aggressive, radical, and thorough transformation of our energy system centered on keeping fossil fuels in the ground starting today (Fig. 16.8):

> *If we are to have a fighting chance of reaching net zero by 2050 and limiting the rise in global temperatures to 1.5°C [...] our Roadmap shows that there are still pathways to reach net zero by 2050. The [...] most technically feasible, cost-effective and socially acceptable [pathway] [...] requires vast amounts of investment, innovation, skilful policy design and implementation, technology deployment, infrastructure building, international co-operation and efforts across many other areas [...] The energy sector is the source of around three-quarters of greenhouse gas emissions today and holds the key to averting the worst effects of climate change, perhaps the greatest challenge humankind has faced. [...] This calls for nothing less than a complete transformation of how we produce, transport and consume energy. [...] The global pathway to net-zero emissions by 2050 [...] requires all governments to significantly strengthen and then successfully implement their energy and climate policies. [...]. Major innovation efforts must occur over this decade in order to bring these new technologies to market in time. [...] Clean energy innovation must accelerate rapidly, with governments putting R&D, demonstration and deployment at the core of energy and climate policy. Government R&D spending needs to be increased and reprioritised. [...] There is no need for investment in new fossil fuel supply in our net zero pathway. Beyond projects already committed as of 2021, there are no new oil and gas fields approved for development in our pathway, and no new coal mines or mine extensions are required.*
>
> ***International Energy Agency (2021).***

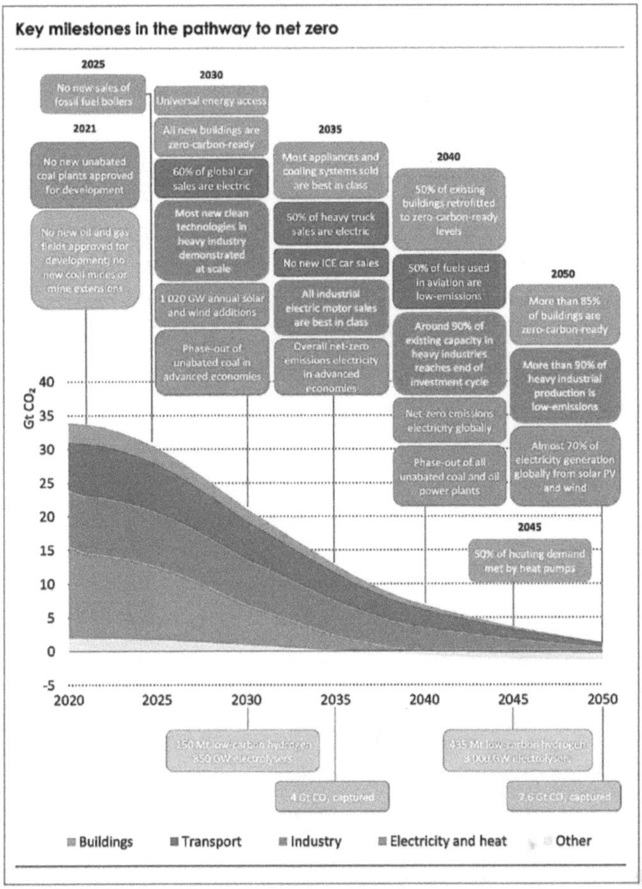

Figure 16.8 Roadmap to Net Zero Emission by 2050 (consistent with a +1.5c warming of the planet). *Reproduced from International Energy Agency (2021).*

This sort of drastic shift in economic structure, similar to what happened during World War Two, is manageable but can only be done under the stewardship of governments. Governments, throughout the developed world especially, need to mobilize their domestic resources if a rapid transition to clean energy is to occur. Governments will be needed to meet these challenges at all levels of the economy, from research and development, to the transition from invention to innovation, to the spread of new technology in the economy by creating and promoting markets, which is something governments have done on a routine basis for many decades (Mazzucato, 2013). Through such a policy, governments will help create many jobs, retrain the labor force, and put economies on a more ecologically sustainable growth path.

These increases in government spending may lead to higher fiscal deficits relative to the size of the U.S. economy. The tendency toward higher deficits, however, will be mitigated by the boost to economy growth that will raise tax revenues. In any case, a rapid increase in the domestic-currency public debt will not only promote financial stability but also be sustainable as long as interest rates on the public debt stay low relative to the growth rate of the economy. Some market participants may wonder about the impact of a higher public debt on interest rates. As explained above, for economies that are monetarily sovereign such as Japan, the United Kingdom, and the United States, there's no significant relation between the size of government deficits (or public debt) and interest rates. As usual, central banks, not bond vigilantes, will play a major role in accommodating fiscal needs by keeping interest rates low enough to make the public debt sustainable (Fullwiler, 2020; Tymoigne, 2020).

References

Akram, T., Li, H., 2020. An inquiry concerning long-term U.S. interest rates using monthly data. Applied Economics 52 (24), 2594–2621.

American Society of Civil Engineers, 2016. Failure to Act: Closing the Infrastructure Investment Gap for America's Economic Future. Economic Development Research Group, Boston.

American Society of Civil Engineers, 2021. 2021 Infrastructure Report Card. American Society of Civil Engineers, Reston, VA.

Atesoglu, H.S., 2003. Monetary transmission—federal funds rate and prime rate. Journal of Post Keynesian Economics 26 (2), 357–362.

Atesoglu, H.S., 2005. Monetary policy and long-term interest rates. Journal of Post Keynesian Economics 27 (3), 533–539.

Batsher, A.K., Kuhn, K., Schularick, M., Steins, U.I., 2020. Modigliani Meets Minsky: Inequality, Debt, and Financial Fragility in America, 1950–2016. New York Federal Reserve Bank. Staff Report No. 924.

Beard, T.R., September 1964. Debt management: its relationship to monetary policy, 1951–1962. National Banking Review 2, 61–76. Reprinted in H.A. Wolf and R.C. Doenges (eds) (1968) Readings in Money and Banking, 367–384, New York: Appleton-Century-Croft.

Biefang-Frisancho Mariscal, I., Howells, P., 2002. Central banks and market interest rates. Journal of Post Keynesian Economics 24 (4), 569–585.

Borio, C., Disyatat, P., Juselius, M.I., Rungcharoenkitkul, P., 2017. Why So Low for So Long? A Long-Term View of Real Interest Rates. BIS Working Paper, No. 685. Available at: https://www.bis.org/publ/work685.pdf.

Cantor, R., Parker, F., 1995. Sovereign credit ratings. Federal Reserve Bank of New York Current Issues in Economics and Finance 1 (3), 1–6.

Cantor, R., Emery, K., Duggar, E., Cailleteau, P., March 2008. Sovereign Default and Recovery Rates, 1983-2007. Moody's Global Credit Research.

Cook, T., Hahn, T., 1989. The effect of changes in the federal funds rate target on market interest rates in the 1970s. Journal of Monetary Economics 24 (3), 331–351.

Cooray, A., 2002. The Fisher Effect: A Review of the Literature. Macquarie University-Sidney, Department of Economics. Research Paper No. 6/2002.

Domar, E., 1946. Capital expansion, rate of growth, and unemployment. Econometrica 14 (2), 137–147.

Federal Open Market Committee, 1999. Transcript of the October 5th meeting. Website of the Board of Governors of the Federal Reserve System. Accessed November 18, 2021 at https://www.federalreserve.gov/monetarypolicy/files/FOMC19991005meeting.pdf.

Fisher, I., 1930. The Theory of Interest. Macmillan, New York.

Fontana, G., Palacio-Vera, A., 2007. Are long-run price stability and short-run output stabilization all that monetary policy can aim for? Metroeconomica 58 (2), 269–298.

Friedman, M., Schwartz, A.J., 1976. From gibson to Fisher. Exploration in Economics 3 (2), 288–291.

Fullwiler, S.T., 2020. When the interest rate on the national debt is a policy variable (and 'printing money' does not apply). Public Budgeting and Finance 40 (3), 72–94.

Ghazali, N.A., Ramlee, S., 2003. A long memory test of the long-run Fisher effect in the G7 countries. Applied Financial Economics 13 (10), 763–769.

Haliassos, M., Tobin, J., 1990. The macroeconomics of government finance. In: Friedman, B.M., Hahn, F.H. (Eds.), Handbook of Monetary Economics, vol. 2. North-Holland, Amsterdam, pp. 889–959.

Hein, E., 2018. Autonomous government expenditure growth, deficits, debt, and distribution in a neo-Kaleckian growth model. Journal of Post Keynesian Economics 41 (2), 316–338.

International Energy Agency, 2021. Net Zero by 2050: A Roadmap for the Global Energy Sector. International Energy Agency, Paris.

Koustas, Z., Serletis, A., 1999. On the Fisher effect. Journal of Monetary Economics 44 (1), 105–130.

Lavoie, M., 2014. Post Keynesian Economics: New Foundations. Edward Elgar, Northampton.

Mazzucato, M., 2013. The Entrepreneurial State: Debunking Public vs. Private Sector Myths. PublicAffairs, New York.

Meulendyke, A.-M., 1998. U.S. Monetary Policy and Financial Markets. Federal Reserve Bank of New York, New York.

Minsky, H.P., 1973. The strategy of economic policy and income distribution. In: Weintraub, S., Special (Eds.), The Annals: Income Inequality, 92-101. American Academy of Political and Social Science, Philadelphia.

Minsky, H.P., 1981. The breakdown of the 1960s policy synthesis. Telos 50 (Winter), 49–58.

Minsky, H.P., 1986. Stabilizing an Unstable Economy. Yale University Press, New Heaven.

Minsky, H.P., 1993. On the non-neutrality of money. Federal Reserve Bank of New York Quarterly Review 18 (1), 77–82.

Roley, V.V., Sellon Jr., G.H., 1995. Monetary Policy Actions and Long-Term Interest Rates. Federal Reserve Bank of Kansas City Economic Review, pp. 73–89, 4th quarter.

Sargent, T.J., 1976. Interest rate and expected inflation: a selective summary of recent research. Explorations in Economic Research 3 (3), 303–325.

Sharpe, T.P., 2013. A modern money perspective on financial crowding-out. Review of Political Economy 25 (4), 586–606.

Standard and Poor's, 2007. Sovereign Credit Ratings: A Primer. Standard and Poor's, New York.

Steindl, J., 1979. Stagnation theory and stagnation policy. Cambridge Journal of Economics 3 (1), 1–14.

Summers, L.H., 1983. The non adjustment of nominal interest rates: a study of the Fisher effect. In: Tobin, J. (Ed.), Macroeconomics, Prices, and Quantities. The Brooking Institution, Washington, DC, pp. 201–244.

Taylor, L., Proaño Laura de Carvalho, C.R., Barbosa, N., 2012. Fiscal deficits, economic growth and government debt in the USA. Cambridge Journal of Economics 36 (1), 189–204.

Tori, D., Onaran, Ö., 2017. The Effects of Financialisation and Financial Development on Investment: Evidence from Firm-Level Data in Europe. Greenwich Political Economy Research Center. Working Paper 44.

Tymoigne, E., 2006. Central Banking, Asset Prices and Financial Fragility. Routledge, New York.

Tymoigne, E., 2009. Minsky and economic policy: 'keynesianism' all over again? In: Papadimitriou, D., Wray, L.R. (Eds.), The Elgar Companion to Hyman P. Minsky. Edward Elgar, Northampton, pp. 47–83.

Tymoigne, E., 2020. Monetary sovereignty: nature, implementation, implications. Public Budgeting and Finance 40 (3), 49–71.

Tymoigne, E., Wray, L.R., 2014. The Rise and Fall of Money Manager Capitalism: Minsky Half-Century from World War Two to the Great Recession. Routledge, New York.

Vatter, H., Walker, J., Alperovitz, G., 1995. The onset and persistence of secular stagnation in the U.S. Economy: 1910–1990. Journal of Economic Issues 29 (2), 591–600.

Walker, J.F., Vatter, H.G., 1989. Why has the United States operated below potential since world war II? Journal of Post Keynesian Economics 11 (3), 327–346.

Wray, L.R., 2006. Social Security in an aging society. Review of Political Economy 18 (3), 391–412.

Wray, L.R., 2008. Demand constraints and big government. Journal of Economic Issues 42 (1), 153–173.

Zivney, T.L., Marcus, R.D., 1989. The day the United States defaulted on treasury bills. Financial Review 24 (3), 475–489.

CHAPTER SEVENTEEN

Monetary policy after the subprime crisis: a Post-Keynesian critique

Olivia Bullio Mattos
St. Francis College, Brooklyn, NY, United States

Introduction

After more than 10 years since the Great Recession, Central Banks (CBs) are still fighting its effects. Financial markets are still volatile, inflation is still low, and recovery in economic growth has not been strong, despite the aggressive unconventional monetary policy that was put in place. Due to its proportion, the crisis sparked a debate on the role of CBs, monetary policy, and financial systems. This chapter aims to contribute to this discussion

The 2008 crisis was not an unexpected event for economists following J. M. Keynes's and Hyman Minsky's lessons. Uncertainty, liquidity preference, excess leverage, Ponzi finance, underestimation of risks: all elements that are intrinsic to the functioning of a capitalism economy and were present before (and after) the crisis. Nonetheless, armed with unshaken and unrealistic models, the prevailing economic thinking both in academia and in CBs accepted the view that markets are perfect and complete, that agents are rational, and that deregulation was the best strategy to achieve equilibrium. Before the crisis, the so-called New Monetary Consensus argued that banks serve only as intermediaries between savings and investment, and that monetary policy should focus only on the short-term interest rate. After the crisis, these mainstream ideas were proven wrong and outdated, causing some mainstream economists to "rethink" macroeconomic theory and policy. However, this rethinking falls short in understanding the nature of monetary, capitalist economies. It is pressing to expand the scope in which we understand CBs as institutions that manage money and credit at the same time

Handbook of Economic Stagnation
ISBN: 978-0-12-815898-2
https://doi.org/10.1016/B978-0-12-815898-2.00006-9

that they guarantee financial stability. To aid the CB in this task as the "Big Bank," economies need "Big Governments" as well, doing permanent fiscal policy and coordinating crucial private decisions that generate income and jobs.

The discussion in this chapter is as follows. First, the unconventional monetary policy put forth during and after the crisis is briefly discussed, focusing on three important CBs: the Federal Reserve (Fed), the European Central Bank (ECB), and the Bank of Japan (BoJ). Second, we examine the evolution of macroeconomic (and especially monetary) theory and policy in the last decades, and how the mainstream is currently reconsidering those in their analyses. Third, we propose an alternative view of CBs and their functions, arguing for a Post-Keynesian framework to truly rethink monetary policy in coordination with other policies. The final section is dedicated to some concluding remarks.

Unconventional monetary policy after the crisis

For the past 40 years, monetary policy has been "the only game in town," as famously characterized by El-Erian (2016). Central bankers have had the task to be the sole managers of aggregate demand, once governments, especially in developed countries, have become increasingly worried about higher fiscal deficits.[1] So, when the Global Financial Crisis (GFC) hit the global economy in 2008 with the failure of the investment bank Lehman Brothers, monetary authorities were fast to tackle the most immediate consequences in financial markets.

The Fed, the ECB, and the BoJ,[2] have made extraordinary and unconventional monetary interventions to rescue whole markets, put the wheels of finance back on track, and stimulate economic growth. Among those measures, the most important were the creation of new loan and rescue facilities for banks and other financial institutions, large-scale asset purchases, also known as Quantitative Easing (QE) programs, forward guidance, very-low and zero interest rate policy (Zero Lower Bound—ZLB) and in some cases negative nominal interest rates (NNIR), and yield curve control. Table 17.1 presents those measures and the CB that has adopted them.

[1] Albeit with a short-lived resurgence of Keynesian expansionary fiscal policy in 2009.

[2] It is important to mention that the Bank of England (BoE) was also taking unconventional monetary policy measures during and after the crisis. This chapter discusses only the Fed, ECB, and BoJ.

Table 17.1 Unconventional monetary policy after the crisis.

	Adopted by		
Unconventional policies	**US**	**Japan**	**EU**
LSAP/QE	√	√	√
Ultra-low/zero interest rate (ZLB)	√	√	√
Negative interest rates		√	√
Loans through new facilities	√	√	√
Forward guidance	√	√	√
Yield curve control		√	

Adapted from Bullio Mattos et al. (2019).

In normal times, the "conventional" policy that CBs use to influence the economy is periodically adjusting the short-term nominal interest rate, that is, the price at which banks finance themselves in the market, with the primary goal of keeping low and stable inflation rates. Markets should determine longer-term interest rates, and monetary policy would then be "transmitted" to the rest of the economy through traditional channels—asset prices, credit, exchange rates, and expectations. In the absence of external supply shocks and with an independent CB, there would be no reason to expect these four channels would not work the way they should; therefore, the CB would have an easy job. If there is ever a banking crisis, the monetary authority will act as a "fireman" putting in place its lender of last resort function (Dymski, 2013).

When the GFC started, the initial reaction from the Fed—the first CB to act—was to use its conventional monetary policy instruments: decreasing the short-term interest rate and lowering the discount rate. However, it soon became apparent that these actions would not be sufficient, since those tools were created to deal with a system dominated by traditional banks. In the decades leading to the GFC, financial markets in developed countries had gone through significant transformations: they became even deeper and more complex. Traditional banking activity lost importance to institutions in the so-called shadow banking system,[3] which was connected to banks in wholesale money markets, with no access to official CB liquidity and dependent on refinancing positions daily with overnight collateralized

[3] For an in-depth discussion on the shadow banking system, see Mehrling et al. (2013).

operations (like repurchase agreements—repos). Those markets were so vulnerable to a sudden crash that when the crisis hit, the capacity of such shadow banks to find liquidity in the market was quickly compromised.

Due to the nature of this "new" system, it was necessary to take unconventional measures to guarantee that markets would continue to function and to avoid generalized bankruptcy from financial institutions due to asset prices falling. First, The Fed created several lending facilities to rescue both banks and nonbanks. In December 2008, when the short-term interest rate (federal funds rate) reached the 0%—0.25% per year range (and the ZLB), the Fed started to inject massive amounts of liquidity in the form of bank reserves with QE programs, greatly expanding its balance sheet. These measures aimed to: (1) put a floor in the price of financial assets, (2) stimulate banks to start lending again, thus boosting demand through credit, and (3) influence future economic conditions by proving "forward guidance." With three rounds of QE, buying government securities, agency debt securities, and mortgage-backed securities, the Fed expanded its balance sheet from about USD 800 billion to around USD 4.5 trillion in 2015, when it discontinued the asset purchasing program and committed to a "normalization" of monetary policy.[4]

The ECB was late in creating new instruments to deal with the immediate financial impacts of the crisis and with the sluggish demand that ensued. In 2010, the ECB launched the "Securities Market Program" aimed to purchase government securities from Eurozone countries suffering from sovereign debt crises, guaranteeing that markets would continue to trade those instruments without much impact on the price. However, those purchases were sterilized, with no significant effect on the ECB's balance sheet size. In 2012, they replaced this program with Outright Monetary Transactions (OMTs) to continue buying bonds (albeit also sterilized) and further calm financial markets.[5] According to Mario Draghi, then president of the ECB, he would do "whatever it took" to save the euro. Besides, the ECB started to lower its policy rates (the marginal lending facility, the deposit facility, and main refinancing operations[6]) in October of 2008, reaching

[4] In September 2019, however, amidst issues in the private repo market, the Fed started again intervening in markets by buying assets and supplying liquidity.

[5] For more on the OMTs program, see http://markets.ft.com/research/Lexicon/Term?term=outright-monetary-transactions-OMT.

[6] Respectively, the price that banks pay when borrowing from the ECB overnight, what banks earn for leaving their reserves deposited at the ECB overnight, and what they pay when borrowing from the ECB for 1 week.

the ZLB for the deposit rate in mid-2012 and for the main refinancing operations in March of 2016. Facing low inflations rates, the ECB decided to decrease the deposit rate even further, sinking into negative rates and effectively charging banks for keeping their reserves deposited at the ECB. The ECB started its QE in 2015 ("expanded asset purchases") to advance the monetary stimulus for the Eurozone economy by buying bonds without sterilization. In December of 2018, the program was phased out, but in September of 2019 Draghi, in one of his last meetings as ECB president before being replaced by Christine Lagarde, announced that the net asset purchases would restart. From 2015 to 2018, the ECB bought around 2.6 trillion euros in assets (mainly government securities, corporate bonds, and asset-backed securities). The ECB's balance sheet expanded from approximately 2.2 trillion euros in early 2015 to more than 4.6 trillion euros in 2018.

As for the BoJ, it has been taking unconventional monetary policy measures since the late 1990s to deal with deflation and low growth. In addition to the zero interest rate policy in 1999, the BoJ adopted QE from 2001 to 2006, serving as a "model" to the Fed's QE programs after the GFC. Facing the contagion effects from the GFC, the BOJ has to resume asset purchases in 2008, in addition to using traditional instruments like lowering the short-term policy rate. Although with some differences from the QE programs in the US and Europe,[7] unconventional measures in Japan also involved massive purchases of government and corporate bonds and other financial assets, expanding its monetary base by almost four times from 2012 to 2019. Failing to achieve higher economic growth and inflation, the BoJ announced in 2016 that it would pursue a "quantitative and qualitative monetary easing with a NNIR" and a stricter control of the yield curve and longer rates. BoJ's balance sheet more than tripled its size from 2008 to 2019.

However, even with all these extraordinary measures, "twin evils" still threaten advanced economies: low, stagnant demand and persistent, low inflation (Aglietta and Valla, 2016). Markets continue to be extremely volatile, asset prices have been historically high, and there is no sign of a steady increase in investment. In light of this situation, some important economists belonging to mainstream Macroeconomics started to review their analyses

[7] The BoJ replaced its QE program for "QQE" (Quantitative and Qualitative easing) in 2013 and did a second round of QQE in 2014.

and proposals for macroeconomic policy. They did not have any clear prescription as to how monetary policy should react to a crisis beyond decreasing the short-term interest rate.[8] The next section discusses this debate within the mainstream after the GFC.

Mainstream theory reconsideration of monetary policy after the GFC

If the field of Macroeconomics was "born" in the 1930s with Keynes's General Theory (GT) of Employment, Interest, and Money (Keynes, 1936), it was only during WWII and the 2 decades that followed that macroeconomic policy and especially fiscal policy truly became central tools to manage aggregate demand. Finance was strictly regulated, due in great part to the reforms put in place after the Great Depression. Keynesian policies were seen as being responsible for the great US and UK economic performances in the postwar period, when unemployment and rebuilding economies were the main problems to be tackled. However, from the late 1960s on, those same policies started to be seen as "guilty" for the stagflation of that time. Inflation then became the main concern for policymakers, with theoretical developments in the Economics discipline focusing on the inability of macroeconomic policy to stimulate output growth in the long run.

The impact that Monetarism—the school that started this change in Macroeconomic thinking—had on policymakers was tremendous. In the beginning of the 1980s, then chairman of the Fed, Paul Volcker, unilaterally raised the short-term interest rate with a declared goal of controlling the accelerating inflation facing the US since the 1960s. The *defacto* effect was to reaffirm the US dollar supremacy in the global economy (Belluzzo, 2012). From October of 1979 to October of 1982, the US CB put in place a policy to control the quantity of bank reserves, following Monetarist ideas.[9] In 1982, the Fed abandoned this plan and returned its focus to the rate on reserves instead of the quantity of reserves. Although it did not succeed as a policy, the Monetarist thinking left an important legacy: the

[8] Some exceptions include Krugman et al. (1998) that discussed the possibility of *liquidity trap* in the Japanese economy in the 1990s. For them, a liquidity trap would occur when, in a crisis, the neutral rate falls below zero.

[9] Wray and Papadimitriou (2010) call this "the Great Monetarist Experiment."

primacy of price stability as the main goal for monetary policy. The target instrument became the short-term interest rate, with the quantity of reserves adjusting to its level.

The 1980s saw the beginning of the "neoliberal era." The idea of "Small Government"' makes its return to political rhetoric and actions, especially in the US and the UK. From 1984 to 2004, a period when inflation was low without severe output fluctuations, became known as the "Great Moderation" with monetary policy being seen as the main tool and Alan Greenspan, the chairman of the Fed from 1987 to 2006, hailed as the "maestro." In reality, in the words of Aglietta (2013: 25), this period was "the Great Financial Divergence," since the fragility of the system was increasing with shadow banking system operations that ultimately led to the GFC.

Behind this development in policymaking was the "New Macroeconomic Consensus" (NMC)—a merger of New Classical (the direct successor of Monetarism) and New Keynesian ideas that have been a major influence in CBs around the world. The recommendations coming from these two mainstream schools—albeit with some theoretical differences between them—was the same: (1) monetary policy should be kept in the hands of independent, technical CBs that would have only one main target—price stability—following explicit rules; (2) the CB should not, under any circumstances, issue money to finance public spending, since this would be inflationary; (3) the CB should try to target only "monetary" variables, since real variables respond to real economic processes and if the CB tries to influence them its reputation and credibility will be undermined as the "keeper" of price stability; (4) the best tool available for the CB to influence price levels is the short-term interest rate. Other relevant prices, such as long-term interest rates and exchange rates, should be determined by the market.

According to Mehrling (2011), this school is strongly influenced by Knut Wicksell, to whom there is a "natural rate of interest"[10]—the one that equates savings and investment. This rate is not observable, but the monetary authority can, through price movements, know if the current rate is below or above the natural rate. If prices are going up, it is a sign that consumption and investment are increasing in response to more bank credit, signaling that the market rate is lower than the natural rate. Hence, the CB can adjust

[10] Also called the "neutral rate of interest," r-star, or r^*.

the short-term market rate by following a clear rule, such as the Taylor Rule (Taylor, 1993):

$$i_t = r^* + \Pi_t + a(\Pi_t - \Pi^*) + b(y_t - y^*)$$

This equation shows that the short-term nominal interest rate (i_t) should be equal to the equilibrium real rate of interest (r^*)—which is the natural rate of interest proposed by Wicksell, plus the current inflation rate (Π_t) and two parts that take into consideration how monetary policy should respond to, respectively, the deviation of the current inflation rate (Π_t) from the target (Π^*) and the deviation of the current output (y_t) from the potential output (y^*). Before the crisis, major CBs—especially the Fed—tended to strictly follow this formula in its decisions (Guttmann, 2012). It is important to highlight that, in this formula, there is no place for asset prices since they represent fundamentals that are widely known to the market but not to the CB. If the CB tries to influence the price of a certain asset by using the short-term interest rate, there could be perverse effects in other markets. Hence, the recommendation from the NMC is to "benign neglect"—do not try to pop asset bubbles, as financial stability would be guaranteed with macroeconomic policies focused on low inflation rates. The rest of the economy would be impacted through well-defined transmission channels—interest rates, exchange rates, asset prices, and credit.

Central bankers influenced by NMC, combined with "the Great Moderation," brought the feeling that macroeconomic models were in fact working. As Robert Lucas, one of the founders of the New Classical School, said in 2003: "My thesis in this lecture is that macroeconomics in this original sense has succeeded: its central problem of depression prevention has been solved, for all practical purposes, and has in fact been solved for many decades" (Lucas, 2013: 1). The risks were, in fact, hidden, as it was suddenly discovered in 2007: "This is how asset markets work: poor risk assessment becomes endemic, especially when long periods of low volatility and well-behaved inflation prevail" (Belluzzo, 2012: 148, own translation).

When the crisis hit, no economist within the NMC tradition had anticipated it. So, there was no guidebook as to how CBs should react. In 2010, Olivier Blanchard, then the IMF's Chief Economist, published a paper titled "Rethinking Macroeconomic Policy," one of the first to recognize the need to reframe mainstream macroeconomic framework including more goals and tools, highlighting the importance of countercyclical fiscal policy, and advocating for more regulatory policies. In 2019, the same Olivier Blanchard and Lawrence Summers, another important economist within the NMC tradition, published a book titled "Evolution or Revolution: Rethinking Macroeconomic Policy after the Great Recession," a collection of articles from mostly mainstream economists discussing monetary policy, fiscal policy, financial policy, inequality and political economy, and international economy issues. The book can be viewed as a summary of the current mainstream's main proposals. In the introduction, Blanchard and Summers set the tone for the book, stating that "the crisis has forced macroeconomists to (re)discover the role and the complexity of the financial sector and the importance of financial developments, including financial crises, in affecting economic activity. But the lessons go beyond these observations and *force us to question a number of cherished beliefs*" (Blanchard and Summers, 2019: xi, emphasis added). The authors point to three main lessons learned.

The first one is what they call "the centrality of finance." Here, Blanchard and Summers cite Hyman Minsky and the fact that he had for decades pointed out the disastrous consequences of financial fragility. However, this is the farthest they go in acknowledging Minsky's contribution, stating that "our understanding of the financial system has improved, but it remains limited" (Blanchard and Summers, 2019: xix).

The second lesson is "the nature of fluctuations." For the NMC tradition, short-term economic fluctuations were seen before the GFC as a result of external shocks, with the economy returning to its equilibrium state in the long run. This was also the view inside CBs, with most of their staff coming from mainstream universities. If the monetary authority followed a reaction rule, like the Taylor Rule, it would be sufficient to avoid extreme fluctuations in inflation and output. Fiscal policy was not even considered: "Fiscal policy was ignored as a stabilization tool" (Blanchard and Summers, 2019: xx). However, the GFC has showed that financial crises are not unexplained shocks, but events that appear to build up slowly, in the form of either asset prices bubbles or credit booms, until perceptions change, prices crash, and the financial system is impaired (Blanchard and Summers, 2019: xx); and that financial crises are followed to prolonged periods of low output growth. They do not go as far as accepting that crises are an endogenous process, and that financial fragility arises from normal operations in capitalist economies, as discussed by Minsky (1986).

The third lesson for them is the very low interest rate (especially long-term rates) environment that developed economies have been currently facing. In a speech at the IMF 14th Annual Research Conference in 2013,[11] Summers has characterized this as "secular stagnation," recovering Hansen's (1939) argument: since the 1980s, the "natural rate of interest"—where savings and investment are in equilibrium at the level of full employment—has become negative, leading to stagnation, in a Japanese-style permanent state of depressed demand. According to him, economies could only grow under this condition through asset bubbles (and subsequent "popping"). This stagnation scenario is explained by two main causes: a higher rate of savings and a lower rate of investment in recent decades, and higher demand and lower supply of safe assets. The result is that monetary policy is impaired, obligating CBs to use alternative tools with an added need for other strategies, like a more active use of fiscal policy as a stabilization tool. Blanchard and Summers (2019) view secular stagnation as the result of real forces, and it is only because of those forces that monetary policy is not any longer an effective instrument to manage aggregate demand. As we will discuss in the next session, this is very far from Keynes's and Minsky's perceptions on the role of macroeconomic policies to deal with the unstable nature of capitalist economies.

However, Blanchard and Summers (2019) conclusion can give us a little bit of hope. In their words, and in a stark contrast with the mainstream view before the GFC: "as the crisis fades in the rear-view mirror, we perceive a risk that macroeconomic policy returns to business as usual, that central banks return to the inflation targeting of the past, that little progress is made on the use of fiscal policy, and that there is a successful pushback on the part of financial institutions against what they argue as excessive capital and liquidity requirements" (xxxviii).

A Post-Keynesian alternative on the role of the Central Bank

Although some mainstream, NMC economists are reconsidering their views on what roles monetary policy should have, current actions by CBs reassert that a belief in traditional, mainstream monetary transmission channels is still prevalent. The money multiplier and exogenous money models remain in place, since CBs are still expecting the supply of credit will recover and economic conditions will improve through monetary easing.

[11] See http://larrysummers.com/imf-fourteenth-annual-research-conference-in-honor-of-stanley-fischer/.

Kesarios (2012) transcribes a 2012 interview of Ben Bernanke, then chairman of the Fed, by Reuters' Pedro da Costa. Questioned about QE programs and their weak effects in the real economy, Bernanke said that the goals were to boost asset prices and cause a "wealth effect," which would make families consume more, consequently increasing productive investment with perspectives of increasing demand:

> *One of the main concerns that firms have is there's not enough demand. There are not enough people coming and demanding their products. And if people feel that their financial situation is better because their 401(k) looks better or for whatever reason – their house is worth more – they're more willing to go out and spend, and that's going to provide the demand that firms need in order to be willing to hire and to invest.*[12]

However, the slowest recovery in the postwar period (Papadimitriou et al., 2015) and low inflation rate since 2007 in the US, Europe, and Japan, reveal how wrong the NMC economic thinking was as to how a CB influences the economy, and the extent of this influence. In a crisis, preference for liquidity can become very strong: nonfinancial companies hoard liquid assets, families increase their holding of demand deposits and cash, and banks hold more reserves in the CB. Those liquid assets are held for (1) *precaution*, as discussed by Keynes (1936: 196): "To provide for contingencies requiring sudden expenditure and for unforeseen opportunities of advantageous purchases [...]" (in the case of families and nonfinancial corporations); (2) *speculation* with financial assets (in the case of banks and large nonfinancial corporations); and (3) uncertainty regarding future demand (in the case of nonfinancial corporations).

Despite the impressive amount of liquidity that CBs have created in the form of reserves, one can see in Fig. 17.1, using the US as a case, that private money creation (bank credit and M2) has not experienced a similar vigorous increase.

The lack of response in bank credit combined with the massive creation of reserves made the official M1 money multiplier (relation between monetary base and M1) (Fig. 17.2) drop below one from 2008 to 2018, a situation that was not even considered possible by traditional mainstream, NMC authors as Mishkin (2011). It further proves how mainstream theory got it wrong: "QE represents an inapplicable view of banking and credit based

[12] http://seekingalpha.com/article/867351-are-elevated-asset-prices-enough-to-revive-the-economy.

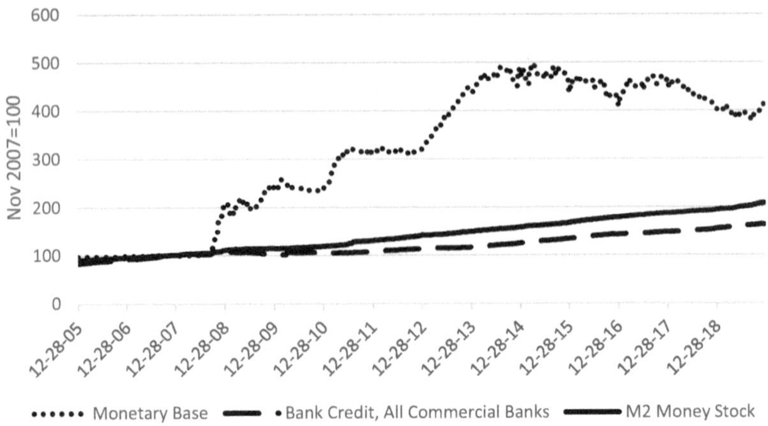

Figure 17.1 Monetary base, M2 and bank credit US, 2006–19. *Source: Federal Reserve Bank of St. Louis.*

Figure 17.2 M1 money multiplier US, 2007–19. *Source: Federal Reserve Bank of St. Louis.*

upon the money multiplier model." (Fullwiler, 2013: 186). If there were any stable relation between M1 and reserves, the money multiplier should have "exploded" after the crisis, as should have inflation.

Mehrling et al. (2013) and Bayoumi et al. (2014) argue that CBs, and especially the Fed, were nothing more than "lenders of last resort" in new clothes. And this would be the "new normal" for monetary policy: bailing out whole markets when there is a liquidity crisis by creating reserves. However, this "new normal" argument is extremely harmful if we want a real change in monetary thinking. The Fed and other CBs responded as necessary at the time to avoid a bigger collapse of the financial system as we knew it before the crisis. Monetary policy was able to make markets function again, but the reliance on short-term liquidity and the tendency to increase leverage based on asset prices and speculation continue. CBs are, as discussed by Belluzzo (2012), "condemned" to stop a financial crash and deal with the arising imbalances caused by asset devaluation and the fixity of liabilities in nominal terms.

The NMC prescribed only one instrument for the CB—the short-term interest rate. If the monetary authority based its decision in a rule like the Taylor one, there was no reason to expect that the trajectory for the real economy would be unpredictable. However, the future is always uncertain, and monetary policy cannot be thought as a golden rule that is applicable everywhere and every time. In the words of Aglietta (2004, 95 and 99, own translation): "Although monetary policy often implies dogmatic measures, the responsibilities that it involves do not match well with intellectual inflexibility. [...] It is impossible for monetary policy not to be discretionary." An update of monetary thinking, one that stems from the reality of financial systems, is pressing.

Nonetheless, reforms after the crisis do not go in this direction. As Kregel (2009) discusses, after the 1929 crisis there was a prompt identification of causes for the collapse and, a few years after, a whole new financial structure was in place. Today, however, the approach by the Fed and other CBs is to buy assets and lower short-term interest rate until the system returns to normal, just like "*business as usual.*" The reform proposals by NMC economists discussed in the previous section only suggest that the CB should take into consideration the "centrality of finance," without actually discussing how this should be pursued (Palley, 2011). Arguments that the GFC resulted from external shocks and fraudulent behavior, and that banks respond automatically to CB's policies are still present; there is still no admission on the unstable nature of banking. In the words of Minsky (1986: 252): "The narrow view that banking affects the economy only through the money supply led economists and policy makers to virtually ignore the composition of bank portfolios." By ignoring the unstable nature of financial systems until there is a crisis, the CB ends up encouraging the very operations of the euphoria phase and thus laying the groundwork for the next expansion and crash:

> *Over an expansion, new financial instruments and new ways of financing activity develop. Typically, defects of the new ways and the new institutions are revealed*

when the crunch comes. The authorities intervene to prevent localized weakness from leading to a broad decline in asset values; this intervention takes the form of the Fed accepting new types of instruments into its portfolio or acquiescing in refinancing arrangements for new institutions and markets. Since the intervention by the authorities tends to validate the new ways, the CB sets the stage for a broader acceptance and use of the new financial instruments in subsequent expansions (Minsky, 1986: 281).

Although the NMC is now admitting that monetary policy has a limited ability to affect the real economy, this has been long recognized by Post-Keynesians, but for different reasons that are not related to "secular stagnation." In Keynes's GT, in 1936, the limitations of monetary policy were already laid out:

If, however, we are tempted to assert that money is the drink which stimulates the system to activity, we must remind ourselves that there may be several slips between the cup and the lip. For while an increase in the quantity of money may be expected, cet. par., to reduce the rate of interest, this will not happen if the liquidity-preferences of the public are increasing more than the quantity of money; and while a decline in the rate of interest may be expected, cet. par., to increase the volume of investment, this will not happen if the schedule of the marginal efficiency of capital is falling more rapidly than the rate of interest; and while an increase in the volume of investment may be expected, cet. par., to increase employment, this may not happen if the propensity to consume is falling off (Keynes, 1936: 173).

In this important passage, Keynes teaches us that monetary policy alone is not able to stimulate aggregate demand especially when liquidity preference is high—even with monetary injections, economic variables will not respond in the way that the monetary authority desires. Even with interest rate decreasing: (1) the public may increase their cash hoardings, (2) capitalists may not invest if the marginal efficiency of capital (the relation between the prospective yields of a certain investment discounted using the interest rate and the replacement cost of capital assets) is not high enough and if there is not enough projected demand for the future, even with a low borrowing cost, (3) the public may increase their propensity to save, cutting consumption for consumer goods thus reducing employment in this sector. Of all those factors, none is actually in the hands of the CB.

To this idea, Minsky (1986) adds the inherent and endogenous instability of capitalist economies due to the nature of debt contracts. Economic units, when acquiring assets (real and financial) and going into debt to finance the purchase, tend to take risky positions. Their margins of safety are reduced, increasing leverage and thus financial fragility. How much assets will yield is always uncertain, but debt payment is a commitment. Thus, if expectations regarding future cash flows are not confirmed, units will not be able to fulfill those obligations. If credit lines are not renewed or interest rate increases, agents will have trouble refinancing and will be insolvent, provoking assets fire sales. The economy then faces a "debt deflation" process, with lower asset prices but unaltered payment commitments from the stock of old debts. For Minsky, this process is "natural" for capitalist economies. Financial fragility is not the result of external shocks but stems from normal operations. When fragility turns into instability, only the *Big Bank*, acting as lender of last resort, and the *Big Government,* with anticyclical fiscal policy, are able to stop the deflationary spiral of asset prices.

For both Keynes and Minsky, money, banks, and credit are at the center of any capitalist economy. First, Banking is innovative, as banks are always creating new financial instruments to increase profits and escape regulation. Second, banks are pro-cyclical, expanding their leverage during a *boom* but quickly contracting activities and deleveraging at a smallest sign of turbulence. This view contrasts with the one still prevalent in mainstream analyses (that Minsky calls "the village fair paradigm") that still consider banks as passive intermediaries between savings and investment. NMC views banks as "isolated" firms, and not part of a banking *system* capable of creating money *ex-nihilo* to mobilize capital and finance economic growth, while also generating instability.

Minsky's "Wall Street paradigm," in contrast to the village fair paradigm, paints a close connection between the financial structure of an economy and its macroeconomic stability (Argitis, 2015). More than acting as lender of last resort in periods of crises, a CB needs to have tools in place to manage banks' leverage ratios and balance sheets, so the instability arising from banks and other financial agents' operations is at least reduced, and the systemic risk is controlled. This involves much more than just using the short-term interest rate. In the words of Aglietta (2013: 31), emphasis added: "Therefore a new framework of monetary policy aiming at preventing systemic risk at the turning point in the financial cycle, must control credit expansion strongly enough to mitigate the momentum in asset markets. *It cannot be done with the policy rate alone.*"

For Minsky, a CB needs to have two main roles: to stabilize the financial and monetary systems, and to regulate financial practices, avoiding Ponzi finance (Argitis, 2015). The first involves guaranteeing that markets are functioning properly, serving as a lender of last resort not only in crises, but in any moment. Minsky proposes that the normal functioning of the banking system demand that banks take reserves in the discount window, not in open market operations, with stable and low interest rates. This would facilitate refinancing, by avoiding liquidity risk and stimulating hedge finance. The discount window could even be used as an instrument to direct credit, depending on what the CB accepts as collateral. The second role, the monitoring and regulation of financial practices, would also be an easier task if banks and other financial institutions are using the discount window. "*As long as bank reserves are mainly the result of open Market purchases of government securities, the giant banks are virtually immune to Federal Reserve pressures*" (Minsky, 1986: 282). In other words, financial institutions would then not have to "make position by selling out position," since refinancing through the CB would be always possible. As Kregel puts it (2013), *QE* has to be replaced for a *Qualitative Easing,* with controls over all financial agents' balance sheets.

The Fed and other CBs acted unconventionally during and after the crisis because they did not take into consideration in the years preceding the crash: (1) the relation between different markets and the risk of contagion if a fire sale happened in one of them; (2) underestimation of risks from financial agents; (3) new and unpredictable monetary policy transmission channels; (4) the massive leverage from nonbanking institutions that operated with banks, putting the whole system at risk. The regulatory framework has to be adequate and frequently reviewed; the CB needs to be more alert to changes in markets, since regulation itself ends up stimulating new financial practices that erode the set of policies that were in place (Tymoigne and Wray, 2014). Banks and other financial institutions should be smaller, as should their interconnections and complexity.

Regulation needs to simplify the financial system, not contribute to its complexity. In this sense, regulation should be more focused on the role a particular institution is playing within the system, constantly monitoring new financial products and practices. However, those goals are not easily achieved, especially in the modern financial system:

> *To control the disruptive influence that emanates from banking, it is necessary to set limits upon permissible leverage ratios and to constrain the growth of bank equity to a rate that is compatible with noninflationary economic growth. This principle should guide policy, but in an economy which new financial usages and institutions appear in response to profit opportunities, it is a principle that is* ***much easier to state than to translate into practice*** *(Minsky, 1986: 272, emphasis added).*

Lastly, a Minskyan "Big Bank" cannot work without a "Big Government." Macroeconomic policy has to include a broader coordination between monetary policy, financial regulation, and fiscal policy. The State issues public bonds that are used both by the CB in short-term liquidity management operations and by financial institutions as collateral in short-term markets. After the GFC, the Fed and other CBs bought great amounts of public and private bonds, but those purchases happened mostly in the secondary market, and reserves that were created are still "parked" in CBs. This new money did not enter the industrial circuit. If those reserves had been used to monetize public debt in the primary market, the impacts could have been greater and faster (Farhi, 2014).

The same way that a Big Bank has to be an ever-present institution, not only in times of crises, Big Government's fiscal policy also needs to be an ongoing task in order to curb the instability of a capitalist economy. It is worth recovering Keynes (1936) argument in Chapter 24 of the GT: stability, full employment, and social justice would only be achieved with a more active state coordination in productive investment, with what he calls "comprehensive socialization of investment" (378). Only the "Big Government" is able to mitigate the uncertainty that surrounds private investment decisions and, thus, the creation of jobs, income, and wealth.

Concluding remarks

Transformations in the decades leading to the GFC changed how a CB affects the economy. New financial institutions, new operations, new instruments, and more leverage and thus higher volatility undermined traditional monetary policy instruments and transmission channels. The way monetary authorities responded to the crisis is a clear reflection of those transformations. The current operation of the system is not and should not be considered just as "the new normal"; it is the "new reality." It is possible and necessary to contemplate a change in this reality with macroeconomic policies that take into consideration the true nature of money and banks in a capitalist economy. So far, this has not happened.

When the system collapsed all but in 2008, CBs had to be creative since they were still caught in the traps of the Great Moderation and NMC ideas. More than 10 years since the crash, the ultra-low, sometimes negative interest rates and QE programs proved not sufficient to produce robust and lasting economic growth. Nevertheless, we can see other effects: financial asset prices are extremely high, and markets have become addicted to CB liquidity. Responsibilities for dealing with financial imbalances and economic instability are still in the hands of CBs, without a significant change in the dysfunctional financial structure after the crisis (Deos, 2015). The system no longer functions without a Big Bank.

Solutions must involve rethinking the role of a CB in Keynesian and Minskyan terms. For both, monetary policy alone is never sufficient to deal with the intrinsic instability of capitalist economies. Keynes, focusing on the volatility of productive investment, proposes the socialization of investment, with the State guaranteeing that private decisions that create jobs will be less uncertain: "[...] a somewhat comprehensive socialization of investment will prove the only means of securing an approximation to full employment; though this need does not exclude all manner of compromises and of devices by which public authority will co-operate will private initiative." (Keynes, 1936: 378). For Minsky, Big Government, more than just doing anticyclical and one-off fiscal interventions when there is a crisis, must have tools to guarantee that economic instability caused by financial fragility and the lack of aggregate demand will not hurt employment. One of his most famous proposals is the State assuming the role of "Employer of Last Resort" (Wray, 2016), a bold and timely idea in today's world.

References

Aglietta, M., 2013. The Zero Lower Bound and the Financial Instability Hypothesis: An Inquiry into the Arcane of Monetary Policy. http://www.univ-paris13.fr/cepn/img/pdf/texte_cepn_150313.pdf.

Aglietta, M., 2004. Macroeconomia Financeira: crises financeiras e regulação monetária, vol. 2. Loyola, São Laulo.

Aglietta, M., Valla, n., 2016. Taux d'intérêt négatifs et stagnation séculaire: politique monétaire ou choix sociétal? Panorama du cepii n. 2016-01.

Argitis, G., 2015. Alternative Monetary Policy and Central Banking. FESSUD Working Paper Series n. 90.

Bayoumi, T., et al., 2014. Monetary Policy in the New Normal. IMF staff discussion note 14/3.

Belluzzo, L.G.M., 2012. O Capital e Suas Metamorfoses. Editora Unesp, São Paulo.

Blanchard, O., Summers, L.H. (Eds.), 2019. Evolution or Revolution? Rethinking Macroeconomic Policy after the Great Depression. The MIT Press, Cambridge, MA.

Bullio Mattos, O., et al., 2019. Unconventional monetary policy and negative interest rates: a post-Keynesian perspective on the liquidity trap and euthanasia of the rentier. Review of Keynesian Economics 7 (2), 185–200 summer.

Deos, S., 2015. Tranformações no sistema bancário norte-americano e o papel da regulação. Revista Política Social e Desenvolvimento 23 dimensões estratégicas do desenvolvimento brasileiro: desafios da dinâmica internacional. http://plataformapoliticasocial.com.br/wp-content/uploads/2015/10/revista_23.pdf.

Dymski, G., 2013. Can the US economy escape the law of gravity? A Minsky-Kalecki approach to the crisis of neoliberalism. In: Yagi, K., et al. (Eds.), Crisis of Global Economies and the Future of Capitalism: Reviving Marxian Crisis Theory. Routledge Studies in the Modern World Economy, New York.

El-Erian, M.A., 2016. The Only Game in Town: Central Banks, Instability, and Avoiding the Next Collapse. Yale University Press, New Haven.

Farhi, M., 2014. Revelações da crise: moeda fiduciária e as relações tesouro/banco central. Revista de Economia Política 34 (3 (136)), 396–412.

Fullwiler, S.T., 2013. An endogenous money perspective on the post-crisis monetary policy debate. Review of Keynesian Economics 1 (2), 171–194.

Guttmann, R., 2012. Central banking in a systemic crisis: the federal reserve's "credit easing". In: Rochon, L.P., Olawoye, S.Y. (Eds.), Monetary Policy and Central Banking: New Directions in Post-Keynesian Theory. Edward Elgar, Northhampton.

Hansen, A., 1939. Economic progress and declining population growth. American Economic Review 29 (1), 1–15.

Kesarios, G., 2012. Are elevated asset prices enough to revive the economy? Seeking Alpha. http://seekingalpha.com/article/867351-are-elevated-asset-prices-enough-to-revive-the-economy.

Keynes, J.M., 1936. The General Theory of Employment, Interest and Money. Harcourt, Brace & World, Inc, New York.

Kregel, J., 2009. It's that 'vision' Thing: Why the Bailouts Aren't Working, and Why a New Financial System Is Needed. The Levy Economics Institute of Bard College Public Policy Brief, Annandale-on-Hudson n. 100.

Kregel, J., 2013. We need a new Q: replace quantitative with qualitative monetary policy. In: 22nd Annual Hyman P. Minsky Conference on the State of the US and World Economies: Building a Financial Structure for a More Stable and Equitable Economy.

Krugman, P., Dominquez, K., Rogoff, K., 1998. It's baaack: Japan's slump and the return of the liquidity trap. Brookings Papers on Economic Activity 137–205.

Lucas Jr., R.E., 2013. Macroeconomic priorities. In: Presidential Address, One-hundred Fifteenth Meeting of the American Economic Association. Washington, DC.

Mehrling, P., 2011. The New Lombard Street: How the Fed Became the Dealer of Last Resort. Princeton University Press, Princeton.

Mehrling, P., et al., 2013. Bagehot Was a Shadow Banker: Shadow Banking, Central Banking, and the Future of Global Finance. http://papers.ssrn.com/sol3/papers.cfm?abstract_id=2232016.

Minsky, H., 1986. Stabilizing an Unstable Economy. Yale University Press, New Haven.

Mishkin, F.S., 2011. The Economics of Money, Banking, and Financial Markets. 15th. Pearson Addison Wesley.

Palley, T., 2011. Monetary Policy and Central Banking after the Crisis: The Implications of Rethinking Macroeconomic Policy. IMK working paper: 8.

Papadimitriou, D., et al., 2015. Fiscal Austerity, Dollar Appreciation, and Maldistribution Will Derail the US Economy. Levy Economics Institute of Bard College Strategic Analysis.

Taylor, J.B., 1993. Discretion versus policy rules in practice. In: Carnegie-Rochester Conference Series on Public Policy, vol. 39.

Tymoigne, e., Wray, L.R., 2014. The Rise and Fall of Money Manager Capitalism: Minsky's Half Century from World War Two to the Great Recession. Routledge, New York.

Wray, R., 2016. Why Minsky Matters: An Introduction to the Work of a Maverick Economist. Princeton University Press, Princeton.

Wray, L.R., Papadimitriou, D.B., 2010. Introduction: Minsky on money, banking and finance. In: The Elgar Companion to Hyman Minsky. Edward Elgar Publishing.

CHAPTER EIGHTEEN

Biden's build back better proposal and the future of secular stagnation*

Yeva Nersisyan[1], **L. Randall Wray**[2]
[1]Franklin and Marshall College, Lancaster, PA, United States
[2]Economics, Levy Economics Institute and Bard College, Annandale-on-Hudson, NY, United States

Introduction

The global COVID pandemic ended the long and slow recovery from the Global Financial Crisis. Economies quickly crashed into a very unusual recession as the supply side was constrained by shut-downs for safety reasons. That morphed into insufficient aggregate demand as people lost income because they could not go to work. Within less than a year, Congress appropriated a total of nearly $5 trillion for economic relief through the CARES act (March 2020, $2.2 trillion), the Consolidated Appropriations Act (December 2020, $900 billion) and the American Rescue Plan Act (March 2021, $1.9 trillion).

This was a good start that signaled the return of fiscal policy and the end of America's disastrous half-century long experiment with "small government" neoliberalism. The COVID crisis clearly demonstrated that government can be the solution rather than the problem. Congressional action put much-needed money in the pockets of American households and businesses, while federal funding provided to pharmaceutical companies fast tracked the development of vaccines. The administration was right to capitalize on this sentiment to push for its climate and infrastructure agenda.

It seems there is one lesson we should (but did not) learn from the response to the COVID crisis: that government spending does not need to be "paid for" in the same sense that private spending does. The usual worry about "how will we pay for it" was put on the back burner because this was seen as an emergency response. However, with President Biden's

* A version of this paper was first published as a Levy Economics Institute Policy Brief.

Handbook of Economic Stagnation
ISBN: 978-0-12-815898-2
https://doi.org/10.1016/B978-0-12-815898-2.00017-3

two new proposals, the American Jobs Plan and the American Families Plan, which total less than the COVID relief spending, the "pay for" logic returned. The administration proposed to "finance" infrastructure spending by raising the corporate tax rate from 21% to 28%, and the other rounds of spending would be "paid for" with taxes on high-earners and the wealthy (Tankersley and Cochrane, 2021). They viewed this as fulfilling a campaign promise since the president "had pledged that his long-term economic agenda would not add further to the growing national debt." (Tankersley and Cochrane, 2021) According to the White House, with Biden's tax plan, the spending "will be fully paid for within the next 15 years and *reduce deficits in the years after.*" (The White House 2021a).

Unsurprisingly, conservatives opposed tax increases. Business groups weighed in against them as well, while generally supporting the spending side of the program. Liberals seemed to be the ones most enamored with the idea of tying the spending bill to tax increases. They see it as killing two birds with one stone—getting the much-needed boost to the public sector and taxing the rich as well as the corporations that have long pushed the agenda of neoliberalism.

Ironically, linking spending to taxes hurts both objectives the administration wanted to accomplish: spending on progressive policy is limited to what can be raised through taxes, and tax revenues should match spending. This shortchanges both objectives. The belief that spending needs to be paid for figured into the amount of spending the administration has proposed.[1] At the same time, even if the new taxes proposed were to become law, they would do little to accomplish the objective of reducing the obscene level of income and wealth inequality in the country—as they were constrained to match spending.

A better approach to public policy would be to focus on goals instead. On the spending side, we need to address two questions: (1) how much is needed to accomplish the public purpose (to transition to green energy and improve our crumbling infrastructure, for instance) and (2) can the economy absorb that amount of spending without price pressures. If the amount we want to spend exceeds what the economy can absorb without inflation, then we need to think about not only raising taxes, but also

[1] AOC joined with environmentalists in arguing that the commitment to the environment, alone, should be more like $10 trillion if we are going to stop climate change.

pursuing other policies that have been successfully used in the past to prevent inflation.

Note that we are not arguing against increasing taxes, but any tax hikes should be formulated to achieve well-stated objectives such as reducing inequality, punishing polluters, reducing high speed trading, or improving the fairness of the tax system. Finally, it is possible that general tax hikes might be needed to prevent spending programs from fueling inflation pressures, but we argue that the taxes typically proposed have not been formulated to achieve such objectives because the focus has been on raising revenue to match spending.

The rest of the paper is organized as follows. Section Building back better: the plan(s) discusses the two Biden spending plans and how the administration proposes to pay for them. Section Should we raise taxes to pay for spending? An alternative view of taxation introduces an alternative view of taxation, arguing that taxes need not be raised just because spending is going to increase. Section Will the spending be inflationary if not paid for? addresses the issue of whether inflation may result from increased government spending. We argue that in real terms infrastructure spending pays for itself. Section Conclusion concludes.

Building back better: the plan(s)

The "American Jobs Plan" is ambitious: to transition the U.S. to "100% carbon pollution-free electricity" by 2035 (Rappeport and Tankersley, 2021).[2] At a price tag of $2.3 trillion over 8 years, it "includes a wide range of investments in highways, transit and electric vehicle charging systems and upgrades to water pipes, the electric grid and veterans' hospitals." (Tankersley and Cochrane, 2021) It proposes $621 billion spending on transportation infrastructure for roads and bridges, spending on electric vehicles (and related infrastructure), modernizing transit systems, and repairing and expanding Amtrak. The plan would spend $213 billion on building and retrofitting affordable housing, $100 billion for improving infrastructure at public schools, $100 billion to build high-speed broadband, and $400 billion on creating affordable care for the elderly and people with disabilities. Around $300 billion would be invested in manufacturing, and $180 billion on new research and

[2] More recently, it was reported that Biden will announce a plan to "cut planet-warming emissions nearly in half by the end of the decade, a target that would require Americans to transform the way they drive, heat their homes and manufacture goods." (Friedman and Davenport 2021).

development on climate change related research (Zarracina et al., 2021). These proposals would fundamentally transform the American economy—not only by boosting growth over the next decade but also by increasing productive capacity in an environmentally sustainable manner.

According to the *New York Times*, the President's tax plan to "pay for" his spending proposal includes raising the corporate tax rate to 28% from 21%, imposing a minimum tax on global profits and cracking down on companies that try to move profits offshore. It would also impose a 15% tax on the profits big corporations report to investors—whether they owe taxes or not. The Biden administration calculates this would affect about 45 corporations that have avoided tax liabilities even while earning $2 billion or more per year. In addition, the plan would double the global intangible low-taxed income tax to 21%, "which would narrow the gap between what companies pay on overseas profits and what they pay on earned income in the U.S." A provision called SHIELD (Stopping Harmful Inversions and Ending Low-tax Developments) targets domestic firms that move their headquarters abroad for tax purposes—what are called "inversions." The proposal would also prevent companies from lowering their US income tax bill by sending their profits as payments to their headquarters (Rappeport and Tankersley, 2021).

The "American Families Plan" is investment in human infrastructure. According to the White House, it adds 4 years of free education to the existing system by providing universal free access to 2 years of preschool and 2 years of community college education. It provides direct support to children and families, including childcare assistance to some families (based on income), extending the tax credits from the American Rescue Plan till 2025 and expanding Obamacare (ACA) subsidies. The package also includes financing for a federal paid leave program to eventually guarantee 12 weeks of paid parental, family, and personal illness leave. "In all, the American Families Plan includes $1.8 trillion in investments and tax credits for American families and children over 10 years. It consists of about $1 trillion in investments and $800 billion in tax cuts for American families and workers." (The White House, 2021b) The plan would also "invest $9 billion in American teachers, addressing shortages, improving training and supports for teachers, and boosting teacher diversity" (The White House, 2021b). Again, this would transform the American economy, reducing inequality and increasing productivity over coming decades through expanded access to education, health care, and childcare.

To "finance" this spending, the administration proposes to raise the top marginal tax rate from 37% to 39.6%, restoring it to its pre-2017 level, and end capital income tax breaks and other loopholes for the very top. It plans to close the carried interest loophole, eliminate the cap on income subject to the Medicare tax and raise the capital gains tax so that "households making over $1 million—the top 0.3% of all households—will pay the same 39.6% rate on all their income, equalizing the rate paid on investment returns and wages." (The White House 2021b).

Note that the spending takes place over 8 years, while the taxes to "pay for it" are planned for a 15-year period, that is, it's not "paid for" in the traditional sense. As reported, "[t]he unusual 15-year window for a tax increase to offset spending could help Democrats if they choose to attempt to push Mr. Biden's plan via budget reconciliation, a parliamentary process that would allow them to bypass the 60-vote requirement imposed by the Senate filibuster and pass the plan with only Democratic votes." (Tankersley and Cochrane 2021) In other words, this appears to be a maneuver to get around a political constraint rather than for economic reasons—Republicans would filibuster, and the Democrats are highly unlikely to obtain the 60 votes they would need to move forward.

Of course, this raises the question: if an 8-year program can be "paid for" over a 15-year period, could we extend the payments to 25 years? Some indefinite future? What does "pay for" mean? We return to this issue in Should we raise taxes to pay for spending? An alternative view of taxation section.

Should we raise taxes to pay for spending? An alternative view of taxation

While raising taxes to "pay for" spending might seem intuitive, there is no economic reason to do so. Taxes can serve several important functions in the economy, but "paying for" the national government's spending is not one of them. The federal government always pays for its spending by crediting bank accounts, whether the amount of spending is offset by taxes or not. It is able to do so by virtue of being the monopoly issuer of the national currency. Any spending that takes place has already been "paid for".[3] This

[3] Technically, when treasury spends (either electronically or by issuing a check), the Fed credits a bank's reserves and that bank credits the demand deposit of the recipient of the spending. This is always true, whether the federal government's budget over the course of the year turns out to be in balance, in deficit, or in surplus (see Wray, 2015).

should be obvious from the Biden administration's plan to continue to "pay for" spending for 7 years beyond the end of the proposed spending.

This was recognized by Chairman of the Federal Reserve Bank of New York (also a New Dealer and the "father" of income tax withholding) Beardsley Ruml who rightly argued that taxes are "obsolete" as a source of revenue (Ruml, 1946). Instead, taxes serve to:

(a) remove private demand in order to free up resources to be used for government programs;
(b) reduce inequality of income and wealth;
(c) distribute costs on the beneficiaries of the government program (not to "pay for" the program but rather for equity purposes and to reduce command over resources by the program's beneficiaries);
(d) punish "bad behavior" or encourage "good behavior".[4]

Coming out of WWII, Ruml (1946) argued that

> *"[t]he war has taught the government, and the government has taught the people, that federal taxation has much to do with inflation and deflation ... If federal taxes are insufficient or of the wrong kind, the purchasing power in the hands of the public is likely to be greater than the output of goods and services with which this purchasing demand can be satisfied. If the demand becomes too great, the result will be a rise in prices, and there will be no proportionate increase in the quantity of things for sale ... The dollars the government takes by taxes cannot be spent by the people, and therefore, these dollars can no longer be used to acquire the things which are available for sale". (Ruml, 1946)*

In Ruml's view, taxes are not imposed to raise revenue, but to accomplish specified goals from controlling inflation to discouraging undesirable behavior. Point (a) above, for instance, addresses inflation pressure—taxes remove private income (or wealth) to reduce private spending and hence free up real resources. By pairing taxes with spending (as the "pay for" approach suggests) we imply that every increased dollar of spending by the government should be offset with a tax hike that will withdraw a dollar of spending from the economy. There are times when this might be

[4] Ruml's list of legitimate purposes of taxes follows in general terms what the Musgraves had incorporated into perhaps the most import public finance textbook (Musgrave and Musgrave, 1984). We are not going to provide a detailed summary, but would include it as among the most important to the current discussion (see also Lane and Wray, 2020).

desirable (e.g., if the economy is already at full employment and the government still wants/needs to spend on more), but that is not the usual situation. Whether we want to inject spending or withdraw it depends on conditions in the economy.

Ruml's functional approach to taxes implies that they need to be well-targeted to efficiently accomplish their purpose. If the goal is to control inflation, which is what matters from a macroeconomic perspective, matching spending with taxes without care for the kind of spending and the kind of taxes will not be very effective because not all taxes have the same impact on private spending. A dollar tax on high income, or on financial transactions, is not likely to reduce spending on output as much as a dollar of tax on low wage workers. If we really need to reduce private spending by one dollar, we might need a tax of $100 on a high-income household.[5] If we wish to reduce spending on a wide range of consumer goods and services (freeing up the resources used to produce them), we would want a broad-based tax on income or perhaps on consumption.

In other words, we should not pursue "balance" in terms of spending and tax revenue, but rather "balance" in terms of matching the increased government demand on resources relative to the resources released by the tax imposed. While it would be impossible to ensure a perfect match in terms of impact on resource use, there is no reason to believe that the "pay for" approach comes closest to achieving the ideal, especially because it does not even operate with a view to achieving the ideal. Pursuing taxes for revenue purposes is not fit for the purpose of releasing real resources and may well be in conflict with that purpose. A case in point is the Biden tax plan that aims to inject spending over 8 years, but to withdraw it (through taxes) over 15 years. Clearly, if the goal is to fight inflation, it makes no sense to continue to withdraw demand for 7 years beyond the end of program spending—when the economy might face disinflation or even deflation because of the reduction of spending (see the chapter by Wray in this volume).

Even as we must drop the notion that the projected tax revenue should match the proposed spending dollar-for-dollar, we must still consider equity

[5] Note that a one dollar tax on a very low-income household might not reduce its spending, either, if it is already living on the edge of subsistence. Instead, they would have to maintain spending by running down saving or charitable giving.

issues as we examine alternative taxes that might free-up resource space. For example, is it better to impose the burden on low wage workers or on high-income individuals? From an equity perspective, it is better to aim taxes at excessive, luxurious, and destructive (socially and environmentally) consumption of the nation's resources rather than at income that promotes adequate living standards for lower income households. We would not want to reduce consumption below socially accepted subsistence levels (generously defined). Sales taxes on consumption often exempt food and other necessities precisely for that reason, but an income tax with a generous exclusion for low-income households is probably better.

Even better is a progressive and high marginal income tax rate above an exemption level to significantly reduce the nonessential consumption of resources by well-off households. If we are implementing a time-limited spending program (such as to fight a war, or to implement a Green New Deal), then it would be better still to postpone consumption (especially by the general population) rather than to permanently reduce it. This is the approach we have previously taken in our Green New Deal proposal that would impose a temporary surcharge on payroll taxes for a decade, with a hike to Social Security payments to return income later as postponed consumption during retirement years (Nersisyan and Wray, 2021).

Alternatively, high marginal tax rates on high income, together with steep taxes on high wealth and large inheritances can further the effort to free up resources even as they reduce income and wealth inequality. Many "progressive" proposals advocate small rate hikes (a few percentage points) on billionaires and millionaires (and corporations) to "pay for" the spending proposals. We believe this is wrong-headed. To fight inflation and inequality, the higher the rate hikes on high income and high wealth, the better.[6] There is no reason to limit the rate increases to what is believed to raise sufficient revenue to match the spending proposed, and, indeed, that would almost certainly be counterproductive as it would not reduce consumption by the rich sufficiently to free up the resources needed for the

[6] To further prove our point, Saez and Zucman (2019) demonstrate that setting a lower wealth tax rate leads to little deconcentration of wealth, although it raises "revenue" forever, while higher tax rates rapidly lower the concentration of wealth, but do not raise revenue for long. If the objective of taxation, therefore, is to reduce wealth inequality, as we maintain it should be since the state is not revenue constrained, then a higher wealth tax rate is what's desirable.

projects, nor would it make much of a dent in inequality.[7] From our perspective, such proposals fail to promote either of the important goals (releasing resources and reducing inequality).[8] Moreover, if the goal is to reduce income inequality, taxation policy should be combined with other measures, such as raising the minimum wage, Job Guarantee programs, and other measures, for creating a robust labor market (see the chapter by Dantas and Wray in this volume).

Taxes can also serve a useful role in discouraging "bad" behavior and encouraging "good behavior" (point (d) above). Taxes might be placed on polluters (e.g., carbon taxes) with tax incentives provided to those who adopt environmentally-friendly solutions (e.g., roof-top solar panels) to achieve environmental objectives. Such practices are widely discussed, and we believe that they can play some role in furthering the effort to slow and ultimately reverse climate catastrophe. We do not have anything important to add to the discussion except to insist that taxes and tax incentives should be imposed where they can be effective in achieving program goals and not with regard to how much revenue can be raised (or lost) by taxes and incentives.

Biden's tax plan does contain certain provisions that correspond to this logic: it includes tax incentives for electrical transmission lines and for electricity storage projects, as well as various clean energy tax credits. Further, it plans to eliminate tax preference for the fossil fuel industry (The White House, 2021a). While the Treasury Department has estimated that eliminating fossil fuel subsidies would increase tax revenue by $35 billion over the coming decade, that is beside the point. What matters is whether these tax changes can help accomplish the goal of transitioning to green energy.

The pay-for approach to federal budgeting, in addition to not accomplishing the goal of deconcentrating income and wealth inequality, is also inconsistent with the objectives policymakers are trying to accomplish on the spending side. While the infrastructure plan is ambitious by today's

[7] Indeed, the Biden plan merely restores the highest marginal tax rate to its pre-Trump level. But if that level of taxation was sufficient to achieve a more equal distribution of income, we would not observe the obscene income inequality that exists in the U.S.

[8] Further, the American Families Plan includes cost-sharing with state governments, which have to rely on often regressive taxes to finance their spending. This in turn exacerbates the problem of income inequality which the administration is attempting to solve. Again, this is an example of how formulating policy based on the inaccurate thinking that the federal government is financially constrained leads to the opposite of what the policy is trying to accomplish.

standards, it might fall short of what we need to fully transition to a green economy.[9] In Nersisyan and Wray (2020) we looked at different estimates of "greening" the economy, most of which exceed $1 trillion per year for 10 years (Senator Bernie Sanders's plan comes in at $1.6 trillion/year). This amounts to around 5% of US GDP per year. By contrast, the administration's proposal is just 1% of GDP per year, and only a portion of that is geared toward greening the economy. Although it is not clear how the administration has come up with its spending numbers, it is likely that striving to match the spending with the tax revenue that can be raised has played a role. If we delink spending from the revenue that can be raised from what are probably viewed as the limits of politically viable tax hikes, we can pursue a proposal that is big enough to accomplish the necessary transition.

In conclusion, there is no economic reason why spending programs need to be matched with tax proposals with respect to revenue generated. The two sides of the government's budget accomplish different goals and should be judged based upon their effectiveness in accomplishing those goals. The merits of the tax plan should be debated not with the goal of raising revenue, but based on accomplishing the public purpose. The Trump and Biden relief programs proved not only how popular spending delinked from tax hikes can be, but also that none of the supposed consequences of larger deficits and debts materialized—such as higher interest rates, more inflation, currency depreciation, or attacks by bond vigilantes and government default.

Some might argue that our functional approach makes it less likely for higher taxes to ever become a reality. But framing the issue as if we are taking the money from the wealthy to pay for services for the poor is not a winning argument in the U.S. It creates resistance because it gives the impression that the rich are paying for "goodies" for everyone else. In reality, we are paying for public services with public money, by utilizing the state's own monetary system. What we accomplish by taxing the affluent is not raising funds to pay for spending but preventing the rich from

[9] We not only need to build infrastructure to promote greening of the economy, we need to shut down operations that are creating the climate catastrophe. John Kerry is working in the Biden Administration, trying to get Wall Street on board to finance greening investments but is not applying enough pressure to defund fossil fuels. We cannot have it both ways, and defunding destructive activities is the quickest and technically easiest move the administration could pursue (McKibben, 2021). The administration should push to remove all government support for fossil fuels and as well pressure private finance to remove its support of environmentally and economically unsound investment. This is not to preserve "revenues" to spend but to reduce resources used and environmental damage done by the fossil fuel sector.

devouring an oversized share of society's resources. Still, we cannot let the survival of human civilization be conditional on our ability to overcome rich people's resistance to paying taxes.

Will the spending be inflationary if not paid for? Scattered rise in prices, but no true inflation

Some were worried about inflation even before Congress considered Biden's proposals as spring 2021 inflation data indicated a sharp rise in the CPI. In addition, market jitters that bumped up interest rates on longer term bonds were supposedly due to investors expecting higher inflation (and wanting to protect inflation-adjusted returns). Because conventional theory now believes that inflation is largely driven by expectations, market expectations of inflation will be self-fulfilling according to many pundits.

We believe that because the plan will add only about 2% of GDP worth of new spending into the economy each year (with much of that time-limited), it is unlikely to be inflationary.[10] There could be bottlenecks and price pressures in different industries, but not true inflation—which would occur only if the economy were pushed beyond full employment of its labor and capital resources. These could be dealt with by careful planning that releases spending gradually and allocates it in a way to avoid inflation.

In fact, inflation has not really been a problem for the US economy for a few decades, as shown in Table 18.1. Further, there is no clear inverse relationship between economic growth and inflation which means that even if spending programs raise the rate of growth, they need not cause inflation. The average inflation rate since the 1990s has been 2.4%, just slightly above the Fed's target. In this period, we have had two of the longest recoveries on record, neither of which were able to push the economy into out-of-control inflation territory. We will not go into detail, but we believe that global structural transformation has played a big role in reducing the inflationary potential of domestic growth. Global supply chains and competition with low-wage suppliers have reduced production costs and prices. While there

[10] This is approximately in-line with our earlier estimate of the net impact on GDP of a full-scale AOC-type of a Green New Deal proposal, which would have been phased-in over a 10-year period. See Nersisyan and Wray (2020). Unlike Biden's proposal, the GND proposal would have included programs that would have resulted in a net reduction of resource use (such as Medicare-for-all) and, as discussed, the "greening" programs were more ambitious. On the other hand, the Biden proposal has more spending on social welfare programs.

Table 18.1 Average inflation and growth rates in the U.S.

Decade	Inflation rate	Growth rate
1950–59	2.1	4.24
1960–69	2.4	4.53
1970–79	7.1	3.24
1980–89	5.6	3.13
1990–99	3.0	3.23
2000–09	2.6	1.92
2010–19	1.8	2.3

Source: BLS for Inflation and BEA for Growth.

have been disruptions due to COVID, recovery of production will keep costs in check.

To be sure, some output prices are (or will be) rising significantly—partly due to relief already distributed and partly due to effects of the pandemic on the economy. Many households have not experienced a reduction of their market-derived income but have received relief checks. Much of that relief has been saved or used to pay bills, although some has been spent on home renovation, new homes, outfitting home offices, purchasing recreational vehicles, and—soon—will be spent on postponed vacations. Production of some of the goods and services they desire has been hampered by the pandemic, meaning supplies are still short. Global supply chains were disrupted (auto manufacturers are short of the electronics they need). All of this means that we should expect, and not be overly concerned about, scattered but significant price hikes.

On the other hand, global production will return (and in the case of China, recovery was well underway by spring 2021). Foreign exporters still want to sell output for US dollars; low wages and prices abroad will hold down inflation in the US. Higher domestic prices will provide the incentive needed to induce suppliers to produce more. That is how markets are supposed to operate.

While capacity utilization has recovered significantly from the bottom of the COVID crisis, it remained below the pre-COVID levels as of spring 2021. Further, Fig. 18.1 shows the downward trend in capacity utilization in the post-WWII period. This indicates that even recoveries have not strained productive capacity—which is part of the explanation for the long-term trend to lower inflation rates, and as well for the secular stagnation that is the subject of this volume. The economy has persistently operated well below capacity, which has constrained demand by reducing the

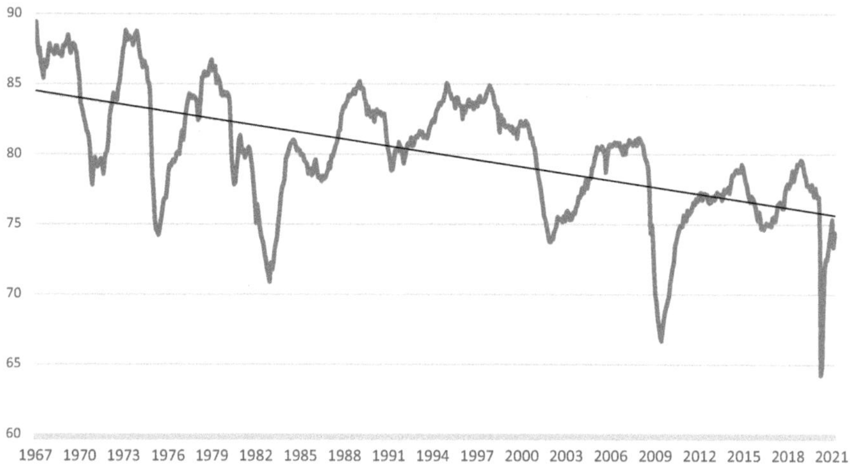

Figure 18.1 Capacity utilization index (% of capacity) January 1967–March 2021. *Source: Board of Governors of the Federal Reserve System, retrieved from FRED.*

incentive to invest. Government's investment in infrastructure has lagged considerably behind our needs for the last half-century. We are now "paying the piper" with the multiple pandemics we face: COVID, crumbling public infrastructure, "forever fires" in the west, damage from flooding, hurricanes, and tornados, rising homelessness, and inadequate public resources to accommodate climate refugees.

Infrastructure spending "pays for itself"

Probably the most popular part of Biden's plan is the proposal to ramp up spending on infrastructure. Not only would it promote transitioning to a more sustainable economy but it would also generate well-paying jobs. Further, parts of his plan have been favorably compared to Franklin Delano Roosevelt's WPA and other programs that essentially developed America and created the nation's twentieth century economy. Before the New Deal, the US was largely an underdeveloped country unfit to compete. Unfortunately, that description is uneasily too apt for today's America, which is rapidly being left behind by China. FDR's words ring too true with respect to our current position: "I see one-third of a nation ill-housed, ill-clad, ill-nourished … The test of our progress is not whether we add more to the abundance of those who have much; it is whether we provide enough for those who have too little." (FDR, 1937) As John Steinbeck said at the memorial service for Harry Hopkins—who ran

FDR's New Deal employment programs–"Human welfare is the first and final task of government. There is no other." (Hopkins, 2021) President Biden might be the president to resurrect this long-dormant notion.

It is interesting to look at another infrastructure project that preceded FDR's New Deal, not only for its accomplishment, but also for the argument made to justify its finance. In 1921 H Ford proposed a major energy infrastructure project (at Muscle Shoals) to be funded by government through issue of currency. As reported in a New York Times (1921) interview[11]:

> *"But would not Mr. Ford's suggestion that Muscle Shoals be financed by a currency issue raise some objections?" Mr. Edison was asked.*
>
> *"Certainly. There is a complete set of misleading slogans kept on hand for just such outbreaks of common sense among people. The people are so ignorant of what they think are the intricacies of the money system that they are easily impressed by big words. There would be new shrieks of 'fiat money,' and 'paper money' and 'green-backism,' and all the rest of it — the same old cries with which the people have been shouted down from the beginning."*[12]

He explained that so long as the money created to finance government spending increases productive capacity, it will remain sound:

> *Now, here is Ford proposing to finance Muscle Shoals by an issue of currency. Very well, let us suppose for a moment that Congress follows his proposal. Personally, I don't think Congress has imagination enough to do it, but let us suppose that it does. The required sum is authorized — say 30 million dollars. The bills are issued directly by the Government, as all money ought to be. When the workmen are paid off, they receive these United States bills. When the material is bought it is paid in these United States bills .... They will be based on the public wealth already in Muscle Shoals, and their circulation will increase that public wealth, not only the public money but the public wealth — real wealth.*
>
> ***New York Times (1921).***

[11] Note that Ford's offer was held up in the Senate by those who supported public over private ownership and never approved; the project was eventually completed by FDR's Tennessee Valley Authority (n.d.).

[12] Edison went on with a view that is particularly apt as a description of the political quagmire Biden faces: "But maybe we have passed beyond the time when the thoughtful 2%—you know, I gather from my questionnaire that only 2% of the people think," and Mr. Edison smiled broadly. "Maybe they can't shout down American thinkers any longer. The only dynamite that works in this country is the dynamite of a sound idea. I think we are getting a sound idea of the money question. The people have an instinct which tells them that something is wrong, and that the wrong somehow centers in money. They have an instinct also, which tells them when a proposal is made in their interests or against them."

When these bills have answered the purpose of building and completing Muscle Shoals, they will be retired by the earnings of the power dam. That is, the people of the United States will have all that they put into Muscle Shoals and all that they can take out for centuries — the endless wealth-making water power of that great Tennessee River — with no tax and no increase of the national debt.

New York Times (1921).

What is interesting about this interview is that Edison recognized the inflation danger of government spending, but argued that the spending would be producing real wealth and productive capacity. Purchasing the electricity derived from the project would absorb income and return currency to the government—what Modern Money Theory (see Wray, 2015) calls "redemption," the notion that the purpose of taxes is to "redeem" currency issued by government, taking it out of circulation rather than "to pay for" the spending (that had already occurred). No taxes would be needed to "pay off" debt (or interest). And long after all the currency had been redeemed, the project would continue to provide electricity to drive further production.

In truth, the long run impact of the project could be disinflationary, not inflationary—once the major construction was finished, the project would absorb income (purchasing energy), not create more income (except what was needed to keep producing electricity). By increasing productive capacity (through the increased supply of energy) the long run impact would be disinflationary—which should be the long run impact of public infrastructure investment more generally.[13] Indeed, when the US emerged from WWII and returned its productive capacity to civilian use, it enjoyed a period of unprecedented prosperity with low inflation. While it had been feared that the nation would slip back into depression at war's end, the pent-up demand—fed in part by substantial "patriotic savings" that included government debt accumulation equal to 100% of GDP—kept consumption high enough to utilize the capacity.[14]

[13] Schumpeter distinguished between the short run inflation from innovators withdrawing resources from other uses, versus the long run deflationary impact of the innovations that increased output. Greening the economy should be expected to temporarily move resources to solar panel production, etc., but will eventually increase capacity while improving the environment (which will free-up resources that now must be used to clean up after environmentally destructive activities).

[14] Inflation did come later, at the end of the 1960s and especially in the 1970s. This might be attributed at least in part to the Vietnam war (which drained the nation's resources without an accompanying strategy to reduce domestic civilian spending; this often results in inflation during war-time) and, later, to OPEC oil price hikes.

The economy's potential is not set in stone but can be expanded by maintaining sufficient aggregate demand. As an example, the CBO revised estimates of potential nominal GDP sharply down in July 2020 (compared to January 2020), only to then revise them upward in February of 2021 (see Fig. 18.2). Fiscal policy actions, such as the CARES act, changed the trajectory of the economy and thus the trajectory of its potential by maintaining aggregate demand (similarly, in the post-GFC period the estimates for potential GDP were consistently lowered as the real world collapse of GDP forced a reappraisal of the growth of potential output going forward).

To some degree, one could criticize the "moving target" approach to calculating potential—as if the forecasters are embarrassed that actual economic performance would move ever-further away from what had been thought to be potential, so potential is readjusted downward. On the other hand, current performance impacts future performance. If government programs keep spending in the economy up, this leads to more investment in both physical and human capital, thus increasing GDP now, as well as affecting productivity and the economy's potential. In other words, government adds to aggregate demand, but also to aggregate supply as investments expand capacity (see the chapter by Wray, this volume). Further, any well-planned infrastructure spending is going to raise the country's potential output significantly—which would produce disinflationary pressures and keep inflation at bay even as growth improves.

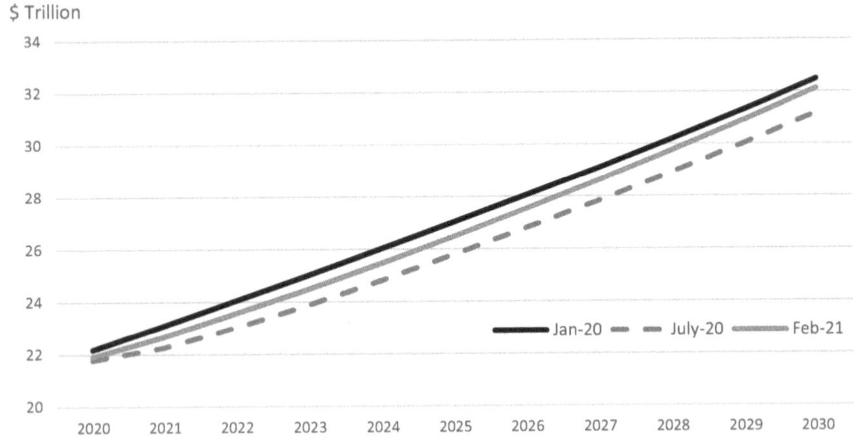

Figure 18.2 Nominal potential GDP estimates, 2020–30. *Source: CBO.*

Given these two points—that potential is neither "natural" nor known with certainty, and that increasing spending not only can move the economy closer to today's potential but actually increase tomorrow's potential—we should not be overly concerned about adding 2% of GDP worth of spending to aggregate demand. To the degree that spending provides both physical capital and human capital, it is likely that the supply side of the economy could grow as fast as, or faster than, the demand side—as Vatter and Walker claimed (see the chapter by Wray, this volume). And if that is the case, the notion that we need tax revenue (which can reduce demand) to keep pace with government spending (that generally boosts demand) is wrong-headed.

As we have argued above, however, even if growth of demand outpaces growth of supply the proper set of taxes would not be one that keeps revenue growth even with growth of government spending. Rather, the proper tax structure would release real resources to be mobilized for the growth of government programs. And, indeed, that mobilization would be designed to only temporarily remove resources from alternative uses—that is, during the development phase of the physical and human capital. After that, policy would need to stop subtracting private demand and instead promote more demand so that the infrastructure could be fully utilized. This was the principle that J.M. Keynes stressed in his 1940 pamphlet (*How to Pay for the War*), and why he proposed "deferred consumption" over taxes that would permanently reduce income. And that is what was done after WWII as consumption was unleashed and supported by wealth (financial and real) accumulated during the war. For the Green New Deal, we have suggested use of a temporary surcharge on a broad-based income source (such as wages, salaries, and selfemployment income), with a boost to consumption later (such as more generous Social Security payments) (Nersisyan and Wray, 2021).

Conclusion

The Biden administration's spending proposals are a welcome change from the austere approach to government spending that has dominated policymaking for decades and contributed to secular stagnation. However, as we argued in this paper, the insistence that the programs be paid for with tax hikes threatens to undermine both the likelihood of their passage in Congress and their success in accomplishing the set goals. In particular, limiting spending to tax revenue that can be raised undermines the goal of fighting climate change. Similarly, minor tax hikes are insufficient to fight income and wealth inequality; we need much more drastic measures to deconcentrate wealth and incomes.

We have proposed to abandon this "pay for" approach to spending and taxation in favor of a functional approach. There is a legitimate use for taxation in our approach, which is to remove purchasing power and hence free up resources to accomplish the public purpose without causing inflation. Whether or not policy is feasible depends on our ability to mobilize the needed real resources, not on raising tax revenue. This and not finding money should be the concern of policymakers.

We do not believe the Biden plans, even if enacted without offsetting tax increases, will cause true inflation. Spread over 8 years, they merely amount to a 2% of GDP spending injection per year. The economy will likely be able to accommodate this spending without a general price inflation. Further, the economy's potential is not fixed. Investments in infrastructure and education will enhance our productive capacity thus containing long-term inflation.

References

FDR, January 20, 1937. FDR's Second Inaugural Address. Available at: https://www.npr.org/templates/story/story.php?storyId=4457244.

Friedman, L., Davenport, C., April 20, 2021. Biden Will Pledge to Cut Greenhouse Gas Emissions Nearly in Half. The New York Times. Available at: https://www.nytimes.com/2021/04/20/climate/biden-climate-change.html?campaign_id=56&emc=edit_cn_20210421&instance_id=29523&nl=on-politics-with-lisa-lerer&regi_id=77048444&segment_id=56056&te=1&user_id=72804634038165706666b094c605ab240.

Hopkins, J., April 30, 2021. Harry Hopkins, the First and Final Task of Government. The Living New Deal. Available at: https://livingnewdeal.org/harry-hopkins-the-first-and-final-task-of-government/.

Keynes, J.M., 1940. How to Pay for the War: A Radical Plan for the Chancellor of the Exchequer. Macmillan, London.

Lane, E., Randall Wray, L., November 2020. Is it time to eliminate federal corporate income taxes?. In: Levy Economics Institute Working Paper No. 979.

McKibben, B., April 7, 2021. Finally, Green Infrastructure Spending in an Amount that Starts with a "T": But Is it Enough? and How Would We Know if it Were? Available at: https://www.newyorker.com/news/annals-of-a-warming-planet/finally-green-infrastructure-spending-in-an-amount-that-starts-with-a-t.

Musgrave, R.A., Musgrave, P.B., 1984. Public Finance in Theory and Practice, fourth ed. McGraw-Hill, New York.

Nersisyan, Y., Wray, L.R., 2020. Can we afford the green new deal?. In: Levy Economics Institute Public Policy Brief No. 148.

Nersisyan, Y., Wray, L.R., 2021. Can we afford the green new deal? Journal of Post Keynesian Economics 44 (1).

New York Times, December 6 1921. Ford Sees Wealth in Muscle Shoals. Available at: https://timesmachine.nytimes.com/timesmachine/1921/12/06/98768710.html?pageNumber=6.

Rappeport, A., Tankersley, J., April 7, 2021. What's in Biden's Tax Plan? The New York Times. Available at: https://www.nytimes.com/2021/04/07/business/economy/tax-plan-biden.html.

Ruml, B., 1946. Taxes for revenue are obsolete. American Affairs 8 (1), 35–39.

Saez, E., Zucman, G., 2019. Progressive wealth taxation. Brookings Papers on Economic Activity 2019 (2), 437–533.

Tankersley, J., Cochrane, E., April 22, 2021. Biden Wants to Pay for Infrastructure Plan with 15 Years of Corporate Taxes. The New York Times. Available at: https://www.nytimes.com/2021/03/30/business/economy/biden-infrastructure-taxes.html.

Tennessee Valley Authority, n.d. A Dam for the People. Available at: https://www.tva.com/about-tva/our-history/built-for-the-people/a-dam-for-the-people.

The White House, March 31, 2021a. Fact Sheet: The American Jobs Plan. Available at: https://www.whitehouse.gov/briefing-room/statements-releases/2021/03/31/fact-sheet-the-american-jobs-plan/.

The White House, April 28, 2021a. Fact Sheet: The American Families Plan. Available at: https://www.whitehouse.gov/briefing-room/statements-releases/2021/04/28/fact-sheet-the-american-families-plan/.

Wray, L.R., 2015. Modern Money Theory: A Primer on Macroeconomics for Sovereign Monetary Systems. Palgrave Macmillan, New York, 2012.

Zarracina, J., Garrison, J., George, P., April 1, 2021. Joe Biden wants to spend $2 trillion on infrastructure and jobs. These 4 charts show where the money would go. USA Today. https://www.usatoday.com/in-depth/news/politics/2021/04/01/2-trillion-infrastructure-bill-charts-detail-bidens-plan/4820227001/.

Index

Page numbers followed by "f" indicate figures, "t" indicate tables, and "b" indicate boxes

FSC
www.fsc.org
MIX
Papier | Fördert
gute Waldnutzung
FSC® C083411

Kolibri 360 GmbH
Ferdinand-Jühlke-Straße 7
99095 Erfurt, Deutschland
produktsicherheit@kolibri360.de